OTHER BOOKS BY H.W. BRANDS

T.R.: The Last Romantic

The Reckless Decade: America in the 1890s

MASTERS *of* ENTERPRISE

GIANTS OF AMERICAN BUSINESS

from

JOHN JACOB ASTOR

and

J.P. MORGAN

to

BILL GATES

and

OPRAH WINFREY

H. W. BRANDS

The Free Press

*f*P

THE FREE PRESS
A Division of Simon & Schuster Inc.
1230 Avenue of the Americas
New York, NY 10020

THE FREE PRESS and colophon are trademarks
of Simon & Schuster Inc.

Designed by Carla Bolte

Manufactured in the United States of America

10 9 8 7 6 5 4 3 2 1

Library of Congress Cataloging-in-Publication Data

Brands, H. W.
    Masters of enterprise : giants of American business from John Jacob
Astor and J. P. Morgan to Bill Gates and Oprah Winfrey / H. W. Brands.
        p. cm.
    Includes bibliographical references and index.
    ISBN 0-684-85473-2
    1. Businesspeople—United States—Biography.   2. Industrialists
—United States—Biography.   I. Title.
HF3023.A2B68   1999
338.092′273—dc21
    [b]   98-51054
                                                       CIP

CONTENTS

PROSPECTUS

When Thomas Jefferson declared in favor of life, liberty and the pursuit of happiness in 1776, the first two items on his list were more or less self-explanatory; the third he left to readers' own inclinations—which, of course, was precisely the point. Another manifesto published the same year, by Adam Smith, lacked Jefferson's succinctness but suggested how happiness might be pursued. Smith, a professor of moral philosophy in Glasgow before becoming a founding father of free-market capitalism, didn't equate happiness with material well-being, but he appreciated that for most people the latter significantly facilitated the former.

Much of American history can be understood as an elaboration of the ideas of Jefferson and Smith; yet in actual history, as opposed to abstract political or economic theory, ideas invariably come clothed in human form. The humans most responsible for putting Jefferson's ideas into practice are well known; they are the great figures of American politics. The heroes of Smith's marketplace are less famous. To be sure, the names of Carnegie, Rockefeller, Ford and a few others conjure images of power and wealth; but beyond general outlines these images are typically hazy and blurred. As for the score or so of others whose achievements fall only slightly shy of this acme of accomplishment, comprehension—recognition even—is more elusive still.

The book at hand attempts to fill this knowledge gap. The twenty-five individuals profiled here were all brilliantly successful in commerce, manufacturing or finance. Most became very wealthy, some fabulously so; more to the present purpose, all contributed creatively to the practice of American business. Several established industries that provided livelihoods for millions of workers, and goods and services for millions more of customers. Some supplied innovative solutions to problems endemic to a modernizing economy. Some adapted novel technologies to unrelieved needs. Some expanded market niches into substantial sectors. Some exploited synergies among previously unrelated businesses.

Twenty-five is no magic number. Fifteen individuals might have been selected; conceivably the list could have stretched to fifty. But fifteen would have failed to do justice to the diversity of business accomplishment in American history, whereas fifty would have taxed the reader's patience—or short-shrifted those profiled.

The chapters below are self-contained, and needn't be read in strict order. Fans of J. P. Morgan can get their financial fix first; readers hungry to know how McDonald's sold a billion burgers can belly right up to Ray Kroc in chapter 16. This said, there is a historical logic in the evolution of the American economy, a logic readers who take the chapters in order will be better able to appreciate. There are definite progressions here, from a preindustrial age to industrial and postindustrial ones; from mercantile capitalism to industrial capitalism to financial capitalism to venture capitalism; from waterways to railways to highways to airways; from Pony Express to telegraph to radio to television to the Internet; from goods to services to information; from the primacy of producers to the ascendancy of consumers; from "robber barons" to "malefactors of great wealth" to "masters of the universe"; from fights over Manhattan house lots to struggles for space on satellites; from the boardroom as an all-male, all-white preserve to a place where women and people of color also get their turns.

Plutarch, who created and really still owns the art of capturing a life in brief, said that "the most glorious exploits do not always furnish us with the clearest discoveries of virtue or vice in men; sometimes a matter of less moment, an expression or a jest, informs us better of their characters and inclinations than the most famous sieges, the greatest armaments or the bloodiest battles." Without slighting famous sieges or bloody battles—what would the tale of the past be without its stirring victories and grand failures?—the profiles here are written in Plutarch's spirit. Each is a sketch rather than a fully executed portrait; the goal is not to elaborate a life but to distill it, to explain what difference this life made. Plutarch sought lessons of political leadership; the lessons here involve business leadership.

If the primary purpose of this book were to render readers as rich as the men and women depicted, the title would certainly say so (with the obvious hope of siphoning some of those riches to the account of the author). The actual aim is more modest—but not necessarily less worthy. The twenty-five portrayed here cover fairly well the history of American enterprise; to understand them is to go far toward understanding what makes the American economy at the end of the second millennium the world wonder it is. Knowledge apart, the twenty-five stories here can be read simply for their entertainment value. American history contains few characters more combative than Cornelius Vanderbilt, more manipulative and unscrupulous than Jay Gould, more willful than J. P. Morgan, more eccentric than Henry Ford, more inclined to bare her soul in public than Oprah Winfrey, more outrageous than Ted Turner. This is hardly a phalanx of gray-flannel suits; it comprises some of the most colorful figures in two-and-a-quarter centuries of American national life.

Such disclaimers notwithstanding, it would be disingenuous to deny all desire to increase the gross domestic product. History teaches, and if it teaches the present—including the present readership—a few of the wealth-creating tricks of the past, then all the better for history, and all the better for its students.

1

GROWING UP WITH
THE COUNTRY

John Jacob Astor

. . .

I N JANUARY 1789, IN ACCORD WITH THEIR FRESHLY RATIFIED CONSTI-
tion, Americans began electing members of their new federal government, which would shortly take up business in New York City. In that
same month, in the same city, a local newspaper carried a notice:

> *John Jacob Astor*
> *At No. 81 Queen Street,*
> *Next Door but one to the Friends' Meeting House,*
> *Has for sale an assortment of*
> *Piano Fortes of the Newest Construction,*
> *made by the best makers in London, which*
> *he will sell at reasonable terms.*
> *He gives cash for all kinds of Furs*
> *And has for sale a quantity of Canada*
> *Beavers and Beavering Coating, Raccoon Skins,*
> *and Raccoon Blankets, Muskrat Skins, etc., etc.*

Music soon became a sideline for Astor, but otherwise his commercial
activities thrived. As the new country grew, spreading its boundaries across
North America, so did Astor's mercantile empire. His agents ranged north
into Canada and west to the Pacific. His ships traveled still farther—to the
Orient and around the world.

Yet the core of what became, by his death in 1848, America's greatest fortune lay much closer to his Manhattan home. Sooner than most of his contemporaries, Astor understood that long-term real-estate values in a growing country like the United States could only go up. He acted on that understanding, riding out the short-term bumps that discouraged some of his less resolute contemporaries and profiting enormously from his insight and perseverance.

By heritage and training, Astor should have been a butcher rather than a merchant or a real-estate investor. But his father, Jacob Astor, a butcher in the German town of Waldorf, had never made much of meat, and John Jacob didn't see how he could either. Evidently the feeling was common among the Astor boys, who had already begun to scatter. George lived in London; John Henry had gotten as far as New York, perhaps as one of the Hessian mercenaries employed by the British during the American Revolutionary War. In any event, when George invited John Jacob to join him in England, the boy accepted with alacrity. He left Waldorf with a bundle slung over his shoulder; later legend had him stopping at the edge of the village, looking back and pledging, as if to the dear mother who had died before his fifth birthday, to be honest and industrious and never to gamble. In his business dealings he would adhere to the first two of these three pledges; in his personal affairs to the last two.

John Jacob spent four years in London learning English and saving his shillings for passage to America, which seemed to him the obvious destination for an ambitious young man. He probably would have left before 1783 but the Revolutionary War still raged; as it was, no sooner had word arrived from Paris of the peace treaty with the now-former colonies than he booked a berth west. He sailed in the autumn of 1783 with five guineas in his pocket and seven flutes under his arm; the former constituted his life savings while the latter, purchased from his brother, a manufacturer of musical instruments, were the entire stock-in-trade of a twenty-year-old who hoped to make a career as a merchant.

The ship left late in the sailing season and consequently arrived in the Chesapeake Bay after ice had already begun to form. Ill winds stalled the vessel a day south of Baltimore; cold days and colder nights locked the craft in the ice. A few of the more intrepid and impatient passengers struck out on foot; Astor, knowing no one in Baltimore and having paid for food and lodging until the ship reached its destination, sat tight. Part of the attraction of doing so derived from the knowledge he was gleaning from fellow passengers regarding what they characterized as the most promising part of the peddling business for a hardy fellow: furs. Accounts vary as to who these informants were—English merchants in the Canada trade, in one version; a German immigrant with personal experience in the woods, in another. But whoever they were, they fired Astor's imagination about the possibilities that lay ahead. Although the heat thus produced didn't melt the ice still gripping the vessel, it drove him over the side, across the frozen bay and on to Baltimore.

There he tarried briefly before continuing to New York. The latter city had several advantages over Baltimore, not all of which a newcomer could have known. Of those that would prove most important to Astor, the first was its unmatched position as port and entrepôt. New York's harbor was the finest on the Atlantic seaboard; commanding the Hudson Valley, it afforded access to the fur-bearing regions of upstate New York and Canada. The second advantage was the circumstance that New York's economy had been ravaged by the Revolutionary War. During the course of the fighting the city had been nearly depopulated; now that the war was over, it was on the rebound, which provided all manner of commercial opportunities.

Astor caught the bounce and soon set himself up in business. He peddled his flutes and other musical instruments but quickly broadened out into other items, notably furs. As he soon discovered, if he hadn't already been told, the fur business was not for the faint-hearted or discomfort-averse. With the spring he headed up the Hudson to meet the Indian, Canadian and American trappers who actually procured the pelts. One contemporary left a picture of the merchant about his business:

> John Jacob Astor, with a pack of Indian goods upon his back, wandered from the Indian trail, got lost in the low grounds at the foot of Seneca Lake in an inclement night, wandered amid the howl and the rustling of wild beasts, until almost morning, when he was attracted by the light of an Indian cabin, near the old castle, and following it, obtained shelter and warmth.

Like many another business traveler, Astor missed his hearth and home. In his case these had both personal and commercial significance. Astor married Sarah Todd in the autumn of 1785; the union brought not only companionship but a $300 dowry and a second set of eyes shrewd for value. Astor didn't dispute reports that soon began circulating that Sarah was a better judge of furs than he; it was later said, after the family business prospered beyond any but the idlest early dreams of either, that she half-jokingly insisted that he pay her $500 an hour for her skills in inventory appraisal and strategic planning, and that he unhesitatingly agreed. (Any conversion to 1990s dollars is problematic, but suffice it to say that Sarah would have been getting well over $5000 an hour in 1998.)

Other family members took to the business less cheerfully. A market panic in the early 1790s left Astor momentarily illiquid; he approached his brother Henry for a $200 loan or, failing that, Henry's signature on a note. Henry adhered to the conservative philosophy about being neither borrower nor lender; he refused his brother's request but made a counteroffer. "John," he said, "I will *give* you $100 if you will agree never to ask me to loan any money, endorse a note, or sign a bond for you, or be obligated for you in any manner whatsoever." Astor thought this over, decided he needed the $100 and probably wouldn't get anything else from Henry anyway, and took it.

The business survived this and various other early trials until by 1800 Astor was one of the leading figures in New York commerce and the first factor (as fur traders were called) in the pelt-and-skin business. At that time he decided to expand his business, taking advantage of what a later generation of business analysts would call synergy. In the 1780s and 1790s American merchants began tentatively exploring the Chinese market, sending vessels from Boston and New York to trade for tea, silk and other high-value items that had formed the core of commerce with the East for centuries. But what to sell the Chinese in return had always been a problem. The Chinese government took the position that it required nothing the West had to offer. China had not "the slightest need of your country's manufactures," the emperor informed King George III in 1793. Eventually the British, the world leaders in the China trade, would hit on opium as a product Chinese consumers couldn't refuse; when the Chinese government launched one of the first offensives in the war on drugs by banning opium, the British forcibly resisted, thereby triggering the so-called Opium War of 1839–1842.

From the macroeconomic perspective of the mercantilist-minded governments of the late eighteenth and early nineteenth centuries, the quest for goods to sell to China represented an effort to correct an adverse trade balance; for individual merchants it was an effort to fill their trading ships in both directions and make money going out as well as coming home. Luckily for Astor, some early merchant, probably from Russia, discovered that the Chinese loved furs, especially those of the Pacific sea otter, which the Russians called "soft gold." Selling furs to the Chinese seemed a likely and lucrative way for Astor to expand his commercial activities.

Astor learned about the China trade in some detail from certain of Sarah's relatives who were actively involved. He tested the market during the 1790s before taking a major position in 1800 when he purchased an interest in the *Severn*, a ship commanded by the husband of one of Sarah's nieces and carrying more than 30,000 skins from New York to Canton. The experiment went well; the skins and some other goods were exchanged for tea, silk, satin, chinaware and assorted other items, which arrived back in New York in the spring of 1801 after a round trip of thirteen months.

Precisely how much profit Astor cleared on this voyage and subsequent voyages is unclear, but it was sufficient to persuade him to purchase the *Severn* outright and afterward to commission the construction of other ships, including the *Magdalen*, named for his and Sarah's daughter, and the *Beaver*, named for the backbone of his North American business. By 1809 five vessels carried Astor's cargoes from New York to Canton and back.

By then he had conceived an ambitious—indeed audacious—plan for expanding both the fur trade and the China trade and for connecting the two even more intimately than before. Heretofore Astor had purchased the bulk of his furs in Montreal from two Canadian companies, of which the larger and more powerful was the North West Company. The Canadian firms naturally took advantage of their favored position to raise prices above what Astor would have liked to pay; more annoying to the patriotic sense of an adopted American, most of those furs came from territory within the boundaries of the United States, in particular the upper Mississippi and Missouri valleys. To pay cartel prices to Canadians for Canadian goods was one thing; to pay such rates for American goods was something else.

In 1804 the American explorers Lewis and Clark set out to survey the Missouri valley and the territory west to the Pacific; on their return in 1806 Astor developed a plan for breaking the Canadian grip on the American fur trade, for lowering his own costs and for expanding his share of the China market. The Canadians' control of the trade rested on their relationships with Indian tribes and individual trappers between St. Louis and the crest of the Rocky Mountains; Astor proposed an assault from the rear. He would establish a trading network on the far side of the Rockies, in the basin of the Columbia River. Its headquarters would be at the Columbia's mouth, near the place where Lewis and Clark had wintered; with luck this post would command the commerce of the entire basin. In addition it would give Astor a head start to China, for the furs collected from the ten thousand streams and hundreds of thousands of square miles of forest of the Oregon country (as the Columbia region generally was called) would be sent directly across the Pacific.

It was a grand scheme, which Astor set in motion in 1810. He dispatched an expedition to travel overland to Oregon, scouting the land and its prospects along the way; at the Pacific this group would be met by a supply ship sent around South America's Cape Horn. Together the two parties would establish a fort and commence business.

The ship arrived first, and in the spring of 1811 its officers and men began construction of the fort that would be the centerpiece of a town called Astoria. But shortly thereafter tragedy struck. The ship was commanded by a martinet who was as contemptuous of the Indians as he was of his own men. He was also careless, allowing armed Indians to come aboard his vessel; one day the Indians overpowered the crew in bloody fighting. Somehow in the confusion of the melee a spark reached the ship's magazine, blowing the vessel and both its attackers and defenders halfway to Hawaii.

This was a sharp setback to Astor's plan—but it was merely the first. The overland party ran into various difficulties, straggling into Astoria only at the beginning of 1812. Shortly thereafter the United States and Britain went to war. The European conflicts that triggered the war had vexed American trade with the Continent for years; Astor's business had suffered along with the rest. Now the war with Britain destroyed his hopes of a fur-trading empire in Oregon. The British had next to no navy in the Pacific, but the United States had none at all, and when a British warship approached Astoria in 1813, Astor's agent there realized the post was indefensible. He sold the operation to a representative of the British-backed North West Company conveniently and uncoincidentally on the scene. Not surprisingly the buyer got a bargain.

Having lost a sizable investment through the actions of his government (in declaring and waging war against Britain), Astor felt justified in applying for government assistance to recoup that investment—and more. After the end of the War of 1812 he lobbied for legislation to bar foreigners from trading with Indians on American soil. When Congress approved the measure in 1816 Astor's Canadian competitors were effectively excluded from the American fur trade. Congress conferred another boon when it closed trading posts that had been operated by the government since the end of the eighteenth century.

Astor wasn't the only one to benefit from the exclusion of foreigners and the privatization of the fur trade; the 1820s witnessed lively (and, given the rough-hewn nature of the fur trade, occasionally deadly) competition between Astor's American Fur Company and smaller firms operated by his rival compatriots. Some of his competitors eventually accepted his offers to join forces with him; others, in particular the Rocky Mountain Fur Company, fought stubbornly on.

But the business was no longer what it had been. The fur regions were being depleted, which made competition that much more bitter and profit margins that much thinner. Worse, fur had always been a fashion item, and fashions change. Beaver hats—hats made of felt pounded from the soft inner fur of beavers—went out of style in Europe and America, seriously eroding the market for Astor's staple product. Deciding to leave the business to younger men, Astor in 1834 sold his fur interests.

By then his wealth had another basis. As early as the 1790s Astor had begun speculating in real estate. Like many another investor in that preindustrial era he looked to land as the obvious place to put money he didn't have any current use for. Again like others then, and later, he had the idea of purchasing land that was essentially wilderness, of surveying and subdividing it, of building roads to make it accessible, of marketing it to smaller purchasers, and of watching his investment multiply in the process. To some extent the return he would realize would result from the services and infrastructure he provided; to some extent it would simply reflect the increasing scarcity of land, of which there was (and always is) a fixed supply, relative to population, which in America in those days (and for many generations after) was growing rapidly.

Astor took fliers in undeveloped properties in Canada just across the border and in the Mohawk valley of upstate New York. The investments turned out not to be particularly profitable, entangling Astor in squabbles regarding titles, management services and fees. But he learned a valuable lesson: It wasn't necessarily any easier to earn money in real estate than in trade. In each case investments had to be selected judiciously and tended carefully. Money didn't grow on trees in the New York backcountry any more than furs brought themselves to market or ships sailed themselves to China.

Astor had better luck in real estate in Manhattan. In his home city he had the advantage of proximity; he knew the properties from personal experience and daily observation, and the market from constant exposure. More important, he had a feel for the growth of the city—for the patterns of population, the direction of development, the evolution of the economy.

Astor first entered the Manhattan property market in the late eighteenth century, but not until the beginning of the nineteenth did he make a serious effort in real estate there. Two considerations influenced his timing. One was the uncertainty surrounding overseas trade during the Napoleonic era. With Britain and France seizing American vessels, and the U.S. government fitfully embargoing commerce with those belligerents, merchants had to think twice about plowing their profits back into the overseas trade.

The second consideration was the phenomenal growth of population and business activity in New York. The federal constitution specified a decennial census; that ten-year tally revealed that the population of New York City nearly doubled between 1790 and 1800, from 33,000 to 60,000. It more than doubled again by 1820, and much more than doubled between 1820 and 1840. Such breathtaking expansion called out for investment; Astor heard the call and heeded it.

He made his initial plunge with the profits from his first China ship, the *Severn*. In 1803 he put $180,000 into various lots and buildings; in 1804 $80,000; in 1805 $80,000; in 1806 $125,000. His purchases lagged during the period when he was preparing and executing his Astoria adventure; they also fluctuated according to the returns from particular voyages to China. But by 1820 he had invested well over half a million dollars in New York real estate and was, if not the largest property-holder in the city, certainly one of the largest.

An associate described Astor's approach to property purchases:

When he had first trod the streets of New-York, in 1784, the city was a snug, leafy place of twenty-five thousand inhabitants, situated at the extremity of the island, mostly below Cortlandt street. In 1800, when he began to have money to invest, the city had more than doubled in population, and had advanced nearly a mile up the island. Now, Astor was a shrewd calculator of the future. No reason appeared why New-York should not repeat this doubling game and this mile of extension every fifteen years. He acted upon the supposition, and fell into the habit of buying land and lots just beyond the verge of the city.

One little anecdote will show the wisdom of this proceeding. He sold a lot in the vicinity of Wall street [purchased around 1802], about the year 1810, for eight thousand dollars, which was supposed to be somewhat under its value. The purchaser, after the papers were signed, seemed disposed to chuckle over his bargain .

"Why, Mr. Astor," said he, "in a few years this lot will be worth twelve thousand dollars."

"Very true," replied Astor; "but now you shall see what I will do with this money. With eight thousand dollars I buy eighty lots above Canal street. By the time your lot is worth twelve thousand dollars, my eighty lots will be worth eighty thousand dollars," which proved to be the fact.

Even when allowance is made here for exaggeration, Astor's success in anticipating appreciation of property values was striking. He quadrupled his money on one water-lot (a piece of property submerged at high tide but potentially reclaimable for development) in twelve years. On another piece, of dry land this time, he doubled his money in three years.

Astor initially specialized in developing unimproved property. He purchased country estates outside the built-up area of the city, then subdivided them and sold off the smaller units. In 1805, for example, he purchased half of the Greenwich Village estate of George Clinton (who had just been elected vice president of the United States) for $75,000. He divided his purchase into 243 lots; he sold some thirty of these during the next several years at an average markup of 250 percent. The rest he held onto, watching their value continue to grow.

In this case, as in many others as the years went by, Astor added the role of landlord to that of developer. With rents rising in the downtown area and nearby neighborhoods, he increasingly chose to take his returns as lease payments rather than as sale prices. By 1826 he was reaping some $27,000 annually from 174 properties. Where once his surpluses from the fur trade financed his real-estate purchases, increasingly the real-estate side of his ledgers financed themselves.

After he withdrew from the fur trade, real estate was his primary occupation and source of income. Between 1835 and 1848 Astor invested $830,000 in Manhattan real estate. His pockets were capacious enough that he could increase his play precisely when everyone else was retrenching, as they did following the financial panic of 1837. Philip Hone, a New York businessman whose eventual claim to historical fame was the detailed and opinionated diary he kept from 1828 to 1851, lamented that the panic had ruined New York.

> Trade is stagnant. Local stocks are lower than ever; real estate is unsalable at any price; rents have fallen and are not punctually paid, and taxes have increased most ruinously. The pressure is severe enough upon the owners of houses and stores who are out of debt, but if the property is mortgaged and the seven per cent interest must be regularly paid, God help the owners!

Not surprisingly landlords and mortgage-holders came in for criticism as battening on the misfortunes of the masses; Astor, as the largest landlord in the city and a not-insignificant holder of mortgages, received his share of criticism. But there is little evidence that he was more ruthless than any number of others in this regard. For the most part the panic simply afforded an opportunity to purchase more property, when the market was low. In 1838 alone he sank another $224,000 into real estate.

Most of his properties were nondescript and anonymous, but a few became landmarks of the city. According to the semi-official chronicler of Astor's accomplishments, Washington Irving, Astor had from his earliest days in New York planned to construct the most magnificent dwelling in the city.

> Almost a stranger in the city, and in very narrow circumstances, he passed by where a row of houses had just been erected in Broadway, and which, from the superior style of their architecture, were the talk and boast of the city. "I'll build, one day or other, a greater house than any of these, in this very street," he said to himself.

Plans changed slightly over the intervening half-century; by the time Astor actually began building the grand structure of his dreams it had evolved into a hotel—characteristically a money-making venture rather than a monument to personal excess. The Park Hotel—soon renamed the Astor House—at its opening in 1836 became the most fashionable home-away-from-home in the country. Its granite walls rose five stories above Broadway, surrounding a private court and enclosing three hundred guest rooms fitted out in black walnut. Ponderous Doric columns flanked the front door, through which visitors entered an ornate lobby with inlaid marble floors. Each floor featured several bathrooms, unusual for the time, and a steam-driven pump pushed water to a tank on the roof, whence it flowed by gravity to the faucets and lavatories below. The staff of hundreds provided service renowned for its quality, the philosophy of which was summarized by the manager-candidate who won the job by declaring that he was "a hotel keeper, not a tavern keeper." Pressed to define a hotel-keeper, he continued, "A hotel-keeper is a gentleman who stands on a level with his guests."

The second edifice that bore Astor's name wasn't completed until after his death. In the 1830s he began planning a splendid library, a building that would simultaneously elevate the human spirit by its appearance and inform the human intellect by the books and manuscripts it contained.

Compilation of the collection began at once; construction of the building awaited the $400,000 Astor left in his will for the library. The library opened in 1854, six years after he died.

The books in the Astor Libary contained the wisdom of the ages; a lesser pearl, yet one that made the library possible, was contained in a comment Astor made shortly before his death. By now his sight was beginning to dim, but not the vision that had allowed him to see better than others of his era that a person would never go wrong betting on the long-term future of America. Asked whether he would have done anything in his life differently, Astor replied, "Could I begin life again, knowing what I now know, and had money to invest, I would buy every foot of land on the Island of Manhattan."

2

THE WARRIOR

Cornelius Vanderbilt

. . .

THE METAPHORS OF BUSINESS FREQUENTLY LIKEN CAPITALIST COM-
petition to physical combat. Salesmen battle for accounts; upstart
firms seize market share; managers beat back takeover bids. In the genteel
days of the late twentieth century these images remain mostly metaphors;
rarely do business competitors trade blows outside the salesroom, the
boardroom, the courtroom. But six generations ago the metaphorical
often merged with the actual. Businessmen captured market share by
force; they defended their territory by physically fending off their rivals. A
good head has never been bad for business, but at the dawn of the industrial era a stout pair of arms and two iron fists didn't hurt either.

Cornelius Vanderbilt had a good head, but without his arms and fists
he never would have won the success he did. He was a big kid from birth
in 1794, and he took to strenuous activity like a duck to water—or like
himself to water. He learned to swim almost as soon as he could walk;
while the other children contented themselves splashing along the shore
near the family's Staten Island farm, Corneel (as his parents called him)
would swim out through the surf and far beyond the breakers. In his row-
boat he would go even farther. Careless of his own safety and fearless of the
weather, he would row south to Sandy Hook or east across the Hudson estuary to Long Island.

But it was when he learned to sail that his horizons really began to
open. He hated school almost as much as he hated hoeing the stony soil on

the farm; a sailboat was his escape from both. At fifteen he threatened to run away from home and ship before the mast of some merchantman; his mother, the only person who could control the headstrong lad, and then only intermittently and by persuasion, offered a counterproposal. If Corneel would work another month until his sixteenth birthday, she and his father would lend him $100 to purchase a boat he had had his eye on. He could start a ferry business between Staten Island and New York City. This would keep him close to home but would give him an income and just about all the freedom any young man could require.

Vanderbilt accepted the offer, and in a short time was master of his own craft—and, it seemed, his own destiny. As an old man he remembered the day of his emancipation as though it had just happened: "I didn't feel as much real satisfaction when I made two million in that Harlem corner as I did on that bright May morning sixty years before when I stepped into my own periauger"—a flat-bottomed boat with two masts—"hoisted my own sail and put my hand on my own tiller."

The carrying trade the teenager entered was thick with men who were every bit as determined as he. They weren't happy to witness another competitor enter their already cutthroat business, and some of them weren't above sabotage and other physical forms of dissuasion. But Vanderbilt, by now a young bull of a man with blond hair that stood out straight behind him in a gale and blue eyes that flashed like the lightning he laughed at, gave as good as he got. On one occasion during the War of 1812, when he was ferrying a load of soldiers from a fort at the Narrows upriver to Manhattan, he was accosted by an officer in another boat. This gentleman insisted that Vanderbilt transfer his passengers onto the officer's boat for inspection. Vanderbilt might have done so had he not recognized the officer's boat as belonging to one of Vanderbilt's competitors on the river. Vanderbilt hadn't yet been paid for his cargo, and he guessed that he wouldn't once the soldiers were spirited away in the other boat. So he declared—employing the curt directness for which he was becoming known on the water—that the soldiers would stay right where they were. The officer grew outraged at this effrontery and, drawing his sword, leaped into Vanderbilt's vessel to chasten this young buck. Vanderbilt was ready for the assault. He dodged the sword and with one blow flattened the officer, laying him out in the bottom of the boat. Then, grabbing him by the breeches, he hurled him into the other boat, and proceeded up the river to his destination.

Had Vanderbilt relied solely on muscle and courage he might have provoked still more resentment than he did. But even his most bitter rivals recognized that he owed his success primarily to his capacity for hard work and his utter indifference to fatigue, hunger, fear and the other afflictions of ordinary mortals. From dawn until long after dark he would ferry passengers from Stapleton on Staten Island to Whitehall Landing at the southern tip of Manhattan. The fare was eighteen cents one way, a quarter for the round trip. The bulk of the traffic consisted of regular commuters, especially farmers taking their vegetables and other truck crops into the city in the morning and returning in the afternoon. Vanderbilt soon won a reputation for punctuality—no small thing in an era of sail when an adverse breeze could throw schedules almost literally to the wind. More skilled at the sailor's art than most ferrymen, and willing and able, on necessity, to propel his craft by oar and pole, he almost invariably picked up his passengers when he said he would and deposited them on or before the pledged moment.

Nor did he let bad weather cancel a passage. Passengers sometimes were treated to wild rides, but if they were game so was he. In one instance, again during the War of 1812, an officer asked him if he could get a contingent of troops through a terrible storm to Whitehall Landing. "Yes," he said, "but I shall have to carry them under water part of the way." He lived up to both parts of his promise; on arrival one of the soldiers declared that he hadn't managed a full breath of air the entire journey.

Where most of his competitors went home at the end of a twelve- or fourteen-hour day, Vanderbilt hired out his boat for moonlight jobs. He hauled cargoes of freight about the Hudson estuary; he took tourists and partygoers for cruises around Manhattan. No one could tell if he ever slept or had a home beyond his boat; such meals as he consumed were snatched at the tiller or while passengers boarded or exited the craft.

Not surprisingly his business prospered. He quickly repaid his parents' $100 loan and contributed several times that amount to the general family fund. But he kept enough for himself to purchase a minority interest in two other vessels.

Although the War of 1812, with its British naval blockade, cut seriously into the business of overseas traders like John Jacob Astor and of long-distance coastal carriers, it created a new niche for short-haulers such as Vanderbilt. Instead of contracting for a single voyage from Baltimore to Boston, for example, merchants would break the journey into shorter legs that were harder for the British blockaders to interdict. There were hazards, to be sure; small vessels like Vanderbilt's were defenseless against the British men-of-war if caught out in the open. But the rewards to daring and skill more than offset the dangers. At least they did in the thinking of Vanderbilt, who employed every opportunity to serve both country and self.

Besides confirming his fearlessness, the war reinforced Vanderbilt's reputation for reliability. In 1814, during the darkest hours of the conflict, New Yorkers braced for a direct assault on the city by the Royal Navy and the troops the British ships carried. The commanding general of the defending American forces ordered his quartermaster to take whatever measures were necessary to ensure the adequate provisioning of the forts and batteries in the area. The quartermaster entertained bids from scores of boatmen, many of whom consciously bid well below cost—not out of patriotism per se but from a desire to exercise the successful bidder's right to exemption from militia duty.

Vanderbilt initially declined to enter the bidding contest—again not from any excess of patriotism but from a recognition that any competitive bid wouldn't come close to covering costs, let alone providing a profit. But his father urged him to submit a bid nonetheless—a reasonable bid that would do justice to the bidder as well as to the job. So he did, with no expectation of any positive result. To his astonishment he won the contract; on his inquiring why, the quartermaster explained, "Because we want the work done and we know you will do it."

The work indeed was done, and New York was spared, although for reasons that had nothing to do with Vanderbilt's efforts (the British attacked and burned Washington instead). Yet the success of those efforts brought him more business than he could handle, and when the hostilities had ended he set about expanding operations. His plan was to commence coasting north and south from New York, providing the kind of long-distance delivery service that once more became available. A first step was to purchase a schooner from the government, a flat-bottomed craft heretofore used mostly for harbor work but that could be converted to the coasting trade by the addition of a centerboard.

No sooner had he taken possession, however, than word arrived from the Chesapeake Bay that the shrimp harvest was about to begin. As was customary a whole fleet embarked from New York to meet the shrimpers and return with the crustaceans for the dinner tables of Manhattan. Time was of the essence, for the first boat back would carry the freshest cargo and fetch the highest price.

Vanderbilt hired a pilot who knew more about the coast to the south of Sandy Hook than he did, and set out. Initially his flat-bottomed vessel, which couldn't hold a tack, fell far behind the other boats, but overnight the wind shifted to the north and he caught and passed them. On arrival at the oyster grounds he took on an enormous cargo, nearly swamping the boat, to the alarm of his crew. Their alarm increased when, on the return voyage, heavy weather and high seas prompted the pilot to advise heading for the nearest port. Vanderbilt ignored the advice, assuring all hands that he knew what he was doing. Perhaps he did; perhaps he just got lucky. But in either case they arrived back at New York in near-record time. Their pink cargo turned to gold at the dock, and Vanderbilt paid for the boat with the profits from this single voyage.

He quickly expanded his fleet to several craft, some built to his order and specifications. On the whole his knowledge and feel for wind and water served him well in directing the shipwrights, but on one embarrassing occasion a top-heavy vessel of his design capsized off Whitehall Landing in full view of his competitors and the public. He salvaged and rerigged the ship; salvaging his pride took rather longer. Yet by the end of 1817 Vanderbilt's fleet ranged the coast from Boston to Charleston and up the Hudson and other principal rivers. Although his primary business was transporting goods for paying customers, he continued to trade on his own account: in shad when those fish attempted to spawn, only to be intercepted by the nets of waiting fishermen; in melons when the crop ripened to the south of New York and set mouths watering in the city.

Then, to the amazement of friends and rivals both, he sold all his sailing boats and signed on as captain of a ferry owned by Thomas Gibbons, which operated between New Brunswick, at the head of the estuary of New Jersey's Raritan River, and New York. This decision demonstrated neither weariness with the competition of the waterfront nor a desire to spend more time with his wife and growing family (Sophia would bear him thirteen children in all); rather it reflected an appreciation that the carrying trade had turned a technological corner and entered a new era. The boat he captained was a steam vessel, a far more complicated and expensive craft than the sloops and schooners he was accustomed to. Working for Gibbons was Vanderbilt's way of mastering the novel technology on someone else's nickel.

Indeed, far from marking a retreat from the combat of competition, Vanderbilt's alliance with Gibbons threw him smack into the middle of one of the most contentious—and ultimately portentous—commercial rivalries in American history. Several years earlier the New York legislature had been so impressed by the feat of Robert Fulton's *Clermont* in ascending the Hudson under steam power that it granted Fulton and his partner

Robert Livingston an exclusive concession to operate steam craft in New York waters. This monopoly was challenged by Aaron Ogden of New Jersey, who saw no reason why the New Yorkers ought to gain all the benefit of the new means of locomotion; Fulton and Livingston responded by licensing Ogden to operate a ferry between New Jersey and New York.

It was this coalition that Gibbons enlisted Vanderbilt to break. The challenge had numerous nasty overtones that had nothing to do with steam ferries; among these was the galling (for Gibbons) circumstance that his wife had enlisted the legal advice of Ogden against her own husband in a dispute involving the alleged seduction of Gibbons' only daughter. Gibbons, determined that not even death should deprive him of (perhaps posthumous) satisfaction, rewrote his will to include a war chest for carrying on the battle after he was gone. Vanderbilt was not apprised of all the ugly details of the vendetta, but he had no trouble perceiving that Gibbons was determined to ruin Ogden.

Having generally been an underdog himself, Vanderbilt was happy to join any fight against what he conceived to be entrenched privilege. At about this time he castigated John Jacob Astor as a dangerous monopolist and insisted that "no man ever ought to be worth more than $20,000." (Success would cause him to revise his ceiling sharply upward.) In the ferryboat monopoly case he urged Gibbons to ignore a New York court's injunction against landing in Manhattan; on receiving his employer's approval he hoisted a flag proclaiming "New Jersey Must Be Free!" and steamed ahead.

The New York authorities repeatedly attempted to arrest him; repeatedly he foiled their efforts. Sometimes he would simply hide as the constables drew near, mingling with the dockside crowd until the moment of casting off, when he would leap aboard and direct the escape. Occasionally he would start to pull away from the pier with a law officer still aboard; the officer, knowing the lack of sympathy he could expect in New Jersey, where the New York law, which naturally (or unnaturally) raised ferry prices, was exceedingly unpopular, would himself leap the widening chasm, back to safety.

So clever was Vanderbilt at evading the New York law that Gibbons raised his salary to the princely sum of $2,000, whereupon the New York monopolists offered him $5,000 to defect. "I shall stick to Gibbons," Vanderbilt replied. "He has always treated me square, and been as good as his word. Besides, I don't care half so much about making money as I do about making my point, and coming out ahead."

Vanderbilt's point was that monopoly had no place on the water; he calculated that he would come out ahead if the courts accepted this view. Eventually they did. In the celebrated 1824 case of *Gibbons v. Ogden*, the U.S. Supreme Court defended the commerce clause of the federal constitution against such interstate encroachments as that by the New York legislature.

Vanderbilt remained in Gibbons's employ long enough to savor the victory, to see how shipping sorted out in conditions of open competition and to husband sufficient resources to enter the steamboat business on his own. In 1829 he purchased three vessels and, in alliance with some stage drivers who handled the overland leg from New Brunswick to Trenton, he commenced service between New York and Philadelphia. This placed him in competition with an established line operated by the Stevens family; to win passengers he set his prices below the Stevenses'. When the Stevenses countered with a price cut of their own, Vanderbilt slashed again. Eventually he drove fares down to one dollar between New York and Philadelphia. The Stevenses, unwilling to continue losing money indefinitely, offered to buy him out for an undisclosed but evidently ample sum. He accepted, gaining not merely money but additional stature. One veteran of the water wars, employing the nickname by which Vanderbilt was coming to be known, remarked, "The Commodore stuck to the Stevenses and fought them so hard that he left here with a reputation that scared people."

As part of the buy-out agreement Vanderbilt swore off returning to competition on the southern route; instead he devoted his energies to the Hudson River. Because the Supreme Court decision in *Gibbons v. Ogden* applied only to interstate commerce, freeing traffic within New York required a decision by New York courts. But deregulation was in the air—or on the water, at any rate—and the state Court of Errors duly annulled the old monopoly against which Vanderbilt had previously battled. He began operating between New York and Peekskill, a route that proved quite profitable.

His profits attracted competition, in the person of Daniel Drew. A shady dealer in an age of shady dealers, Drew was reputed to have pioneered the technique of "watering stock." The early version involved real (live)stock; while working as a drover, Drew would feed the animals salt so they would drink large amounts of water and put on weight just prior to sale. Whether or not Drew actually invented the ruse, he became a virtuoso at its application to corporate stocks after leaving the cattle pens for the trading pit of Wall Street.

In the early 1830s he took on Vanderbilt on the Hudson. Shortly the two were battering each other with price reductions, to the delight of customers who watched fares fall to twelve-and-a-half cents between New York and Peekskill. This time it was Vanderbilt who bought out his competitor; Drew, without consulting his minority partners, retired from the Hudson. (Those partners subsequently vowed violence if they ever caught up with him.)

Vanderbilt thereupon extended his service north to Albany, placing a new boat he built for the purpose squarely athwart the vessels of an established association of steamboat operators. As before, Vanderbilt attacked on price; as expected, the association attacked back. Reduction chased reduction until the fare fell to ten cents, then to zero. This didn't wipe out revenues entirely because Vanderbilt and the association still made money selling food and drink to passengers. The passengers needed strong drink to fortify themselves against a time-saving tactic known as "landing on the fly." To avoid having to stop and start at wharves along the river, a steamboat would pile disembarking passengers into a skiff towed alongside; this would be steered toward the wharf by a crew member. As the wharf drew within reach the passengers would jump or be pushed before the tow line snapped the skiff out from under their feet. The procedure was thrilling when it worked, dousing when it didn't.

The fun lasted just long enough for the association to determine that it couldn't beat Vanderbilt and to decide it had better buy him off. It paid him $100,000 up front and $5,000 annually for ten years to quit the river that long.

Barred—albeit handsomely—from doing business south and north of New York, Vanderbilt now ventured east. He commissioned and christened a new boat, the *Lexington*, which, after completing an early record run through Long Island Sound to Providence, earned the title "fastest boat in the world." During the next several years Vanderbilt augmented his fleet, until by the 1840s he owned and operated more, and more luxurious, steam vessels than anyone else in the country. The *Cornelius Vanderbilt* was the most famous of the "floating palaces" of the era; the eponymous palace churned the waters of the Sound at better than 25 miles per hour. The vessel's speed and visibility inevitably elicited challenges, with one resulting in a spectacular 1847 race between the *Cornelius Vanderbilt* and the *Oregon*, which the latter won only because the captain pushed his boilers far beyond the danger point and, having run out of coal, stoked his fires with furniture and fittings on which he had just spent $30,000.

Vanderbilt was settling into the life of the millionaire he had by now become when an event three thousand miles away upset any notions he might have entertained of resting on his paddle wheels. The discovery of gold in California in 1848 triggered the mad rush of 1849 and efforts by assorted purveyors of transport to shorten the rushers' travel time and capture their travel dollars. A favorite route ran via steamship down the Caribbean to Panama, across the isthmus by mule, then up the West Coast via another steamship. Vanderbilt hit on the idea of building a canal across Nicaragua. It was a bold but not utterly impossible plan; while he sought the necessary financing he patched together a hybrid sea–land–river–lake system across Nicaragua that shortened the passage to San Francisco by two days and allowed him to seize a sizable and profitable part of the traffic.

His canal plans, however, ran afoul of the British government, which refused to sanction a Central American waterway it didn't control; they also collided with the machinations of some former associates who, during the first vacation of his life, attempted to swindle him out of control of his own company. Vanderbilt responded with a letter that became legendary in the annals of American business:

> Gentlemen:
> You have undertaken to cheat me. I won't sue you, for the law is too slow. I'll ruin you.
>
> > Yours truly,
> > Cornelius Vanderbilt

He proved as good as his word. He dumped his shares of the company on the market, driving its price down, even as he entered an alliance with one of his former Panama competitors. With customary verve he slashed fares and thereby stole customers from the objects of his vengeance, driving the share price down even further. As it bottomed out he quietly began buying; by the time his former partners were aware of what was happening he had regained control.

The next foe who stepped into his path was one of the strangest characters in the history of the Western Hemisphere. William Walker—a Tennessee-born megalomaniac whose own press releases habitually referred to him as "the grey-eyed man of destiny"—would have been a Crusader had he lived in France seven hundred years earlier, or a conquistador had he been Spanish in the sixteenth century. In the mid-nineteenth century he had to content himself trying to carve an empire out of Central America. With a band of fellow filibusters (the term was derived from and still es-

sentially meant "free-booter" before evolving into an instrument of legislative legerdemain), Walker toppled the shaky government of Nicaragua and
made himself dictator. He proceeded to cancel the concession under
which Vanderbilt operated his transit service. Adding insult to injury,
Walker granted a new concession to the double-crossing corporate faction
Vanderbilt had just defeated.

Recognizing that Walker could stand only as long as he continued to
receive supplies from abroad, Vanderbilt determined to cut off those supplies. Again he routed traffic through Panama; meanwhile he pressured persons with whom he did business to have nothing to do with Walker. Finally,
he threw support to Walker's enemies within Nicaragua. The result was
that Walker was toppled and driven out of the country. (He took his grey
eyes to Honduras, where his destiny became a date with a firing squad.)

But Central America had lost its appeal for Vanderbilt, and once more
he accepted payment—$56,000 per month this time—for retiring from a
business. He briefly entered the transatlantic trade. His second eponymous steam vessel, the *Vanderbilt*, set records for the ocean crossing, but
the outbreak of the Civil War in 1861, combined with disappointing profits, prompted him to sell out. He offered the *Vanderbilt* to the federal government for use as a warship against the Confederacy; President Lincoln
accepted and Congress voted a resolution of thanks for the generous gift.
Vanderbilt, who had intended a loan rather than a gift, was flabbergasted.
"Congress be damned!," he declared. "I never gave that ship to Congress."
On reflection, however, he decided that if he didn't want to appear unpatriotic there was nothing to be done. "Mr. Lincoln and Mr. Welles [the
navy secretary] think it was a gift, and I suppose I shall have to let her go."

Beyond appearances Vanderbilt had another reason for not fighting to
get his ship back. He had discovered a new mode of transport and a new
way of making money. For years he had been contemptuous of "them
things that go on land," as he called railroad trains; his aversion escalated
in 1833 when, on what was probably the first train ride he ever took, the
axle of one of the cars failed and he was hurled out of the train and down
a slope, nearly to his death. But the evidence of the following decades was
as undeniable as the advance of the rails, and during the early 1860s Vanderbilt decided to buy in. A friend and part-time protegé, Ward McAllister
(who later became czar of New York high society), asked for a tip: "Commodore, you will be as great a railroad king as you were once an ocean
king; and as you call me your boy, why don't you make my fortune?" Vanderbilt considered the question, then said, "Mac, sell everything you have

and put it in Harlem stock. It is now twenty-four; you will make more money than you will know how to take care of."

It is unclear if McAllister followed the advice; if he had he would indeed have made a pile of money. When Vanderbilt began buying shares in the New York & Harlem Railroad it was a miserable excuse for a road, but it had prospects that Vanderbilt saw more clearly than others. Chief among these prospects was the possibility of extending the Harlem's urban tracks south of Union Square past Wall Street to the Battery. By means that doubtless included bribery (usually deemed a normal cost of business in those days, especially in the New York of Tammany Hall), Vanderbilt persuaded the city council to grant the required permission. At once the share price of Harlem stock shot upward, passing 100 and still climbing.

Not surprisingly this performance attracted the attention of market pros, who wondered whether the high prices could be sustained. Daniel Drew doubted it. Despite being a director of the Harlem and one who had profited from the quadrupling of the share price, Drew guessed that it would fall and sold way short. To encourage the fall he resorted to some bribery of his own, paying the council to rescind the Harlem's franchise. The tactic worked; at once the price began to plummet.

But Vanderbilt was ready and, reaching deep, caught the shares on the fall. When, in addition, it became apparent that Drew and the bears had promised delivery of more shares of stock than were in existence, their scheme collapsed. Drew took a drubbing and was forced to make a private settlement with Vanderbilt, to the latter's great profit. At this time or some other, Drew reportedly uttered the words that became—or should have become—a motto to all short traders:

He that sells what isn't his'n
Must buy it back or go to prison.

Vanderbilt applied his profit from the transaction to improving the rolling stock, tracks and service of the Harlem. Before long the old derelict carried commuters with dispatch and reliability. Horace Greeley, the editor of the *New York Tribune* and a regular on the line, remarked in 1867: "We lived on this road when it was poor and feebly managed—with rotten cars and wheezy old engines that could not make schedule time; and the improvement since realized is gratifying."

Vanderbilt soon moved to expand his railroad holdings. He purchased control of the Hudson River Railroad and set his sights on the New York Central, which ran from Albany west to Buffalo. Directors of the latter countered by forming an alliance with Daniel Drew, who once again was operating a steamboat line on the Hudson. Passengers and freight from the Central were transferred to Drew's boats for the journey down the Hudson. At least they were during the warm months when the boats ran; in winter, when ice blocked the channel, they were shifted to Vanderbilt's Hudson River line under a previous agreement. In January 1867, in the dead of winter, Vanderbilt canceled the agreement. This threatened to freeze—literally—the Central out of the critical New York City market, and its directors quickly came to terms. Before the year was over Vanderbilt had taken effective control of the road. As he had with the Harlem, he invested heavily in infrastructure and service, and by the time he united it with the Hudson in 1869 (as the New York Central & Hudson River Railway) it afforded customers efficient service across the breadth and most of the length of the state.

Vanderbilt's son William would later become notorious for responding to a reporter's question whether the public should be consulted about a certain issue of corporate governance, by snorting: "The public be damned!" The father took a different view, at least before a legislative committee investigating his takeover of the Central. "I have always served the public to the best of my ability," he declared. "Why? Because, like every other man, it is my interest to do so, and to put them to as little inconvenience as possible."

Doubtless the old man—he turned seventy-five the year of the amalgamation of the Central and the Hudson—was sincere; doubtless also he didn't intend to let the public interest interfere with private interest. In 1868 Vanderbilt attempted to extend his reach still farther, launching a takeover attempt of the Erie, one of the main lines from Buffalo to Chicago. Here again he encountered Dan Drew, whose reputation as a market manipulator had survived his previous defeat at Vanderbilt's hands. One version of the conventional wisdom explained:

Daniel says up: Erie goes up.
Daniel says down: Erie goes down.
Daniel says wiggle-waggle: it bobs both ways.

Drew had formidable friends, including Jim Fisk and Jay Gould; their battle with Vanderbilt for control of the Erie became one of the business epics of the age. As Vanderbilt purchased shares, toward the goal of controlling a majority, the opposing trio finagled the issuance of tens of thousands of new shares. As the new issue was pouring out the door onto Wall

Street, Fisk gloated against Vanderbilt: "If this printing-press don't break down, I'll be damned if I don't give the old hog all he wants of Erie."

Even by the lax standards of that day such blatant shenanigans were illegal, and when Vanderbilt threatened to have his rivals arrested they grabbed corporate records and cash—reportedly $7 million—from the Erie offices and decamped across the Hudson to the friendlier environs of New Jersey. With some of that cash they persuaded the New Jersey legislature to allow them to reincorporate the Erie in the Garden State, a move that afforded a certain protection against Vanderbilt's wrath. Seeking more assurance they sent Gould to Albany to seek the blessing of the New York legislature on their coup. They had reason for hope; one journalist on the Albany beat remarked of the lawmakers: "The boys were poor and hungry after the long abstinence of the session. How beautiful then, the prospect which the Erie contest opened up to them! How they gloated over the pleasures which the fight would develop!" The boys licked their chops the more when Vanderbilt appeared ready to counter the offers of the Gould group. Loud whispers told of one state senator who accepted $15,000 from one side before selling out for $20,000 to the other. At the last moment, however, Vanderbilt decided to bear the market for votes. "A rumor ran through Albany as of some great public disaster, spreading panic and terror through hotel and corridor," recounted an eyewitness. "The observer was reminded of the dark days of the war [the Civil War, that is], when tidings came of some great defeat. . . . In a moment the lobby was smitten with despair, and the cheeks of the legislators were blanched, for it was reported that Vanderbilt had withdrawn his opposition to the bill."

Indeed he had. Counting costs, the Commodore determined that it made better sense to arrange a private peace with Gould, Drew and Fisk than to try to purchase the New York legislature. He abandoned his effort to win control of the Erie and in exchange for a payment of $1 million agreed to drop the lawsuits he had filed against the absconders.

The Erie fight did credit neither to Vanderbilt's balance sheet—he lost perhaps one to two million dollars in the takeover attempt—nor to his public reputation. He salvaged some of the latter when, in the wake of the panic of 1873, which evaporated the finances of railroads all across the country, he announced that the New York Central would continue to pay dividends as usual. He also kept thousands of men off the unemployment rolls by pushing through improvements to the recently opened Grand Central Station at Forty-second Street.

Doubtless it was partly by comparison to the likes of Drew and

Gould, but at Vanderbilt's death in 1877 he was considered something of a model of the businessman-citizen. An era that tamed the frontier by throwing aside the Indians and preserved the Union at the cost of 600,000 lives found little to fault in Vanderbilt's two-fisted approach, and much to credit in what those fists—and the spirit and intelligence to which they were attached—accomplished. "Roads which had been the playthings of gamblers and the preserves of politicians prospered under his hard, cold, daring management," asserted the *New York Herald*. "The lesson to be learned from the life of Vanderbilt is simple and impressive. Courage in the performance of duty enabled this man to become one of the kings of the earth. The hard, strong-limbed boy who guided his vessel from ferry to ferry nearly seventy years ago lived to be a ruler of men. He had no advantages in his battle, no political, social, educational aid. It was one honest, sturdy, fearless man against the world, and in the end the man won."

3

GOLDEN GRAIN

Cyrus McCormick

· · ·

O VER THE COURSE OF MORE THAN TWO CENTURIES, THE UNITED States would lead the world in any number of industries, from the fundamental (railroads, steel) to the sophisticated (microelectronics, pharmaceuticals). But in no industry was American preeminence more persistent than in the most fundamental industry of all: agriculture. From the middle of the nineteenth century to the end of the twentieth, America's farms proved a cornucopia of food and fiber that fed and clothed the American people and millions in other countries as well. This bounty, which made possible the modernization of American society, was the work of ten million hands—and might have been the work of ninety million more if not for the cussedness of Cyrus McCormick.

McCormick wasn't a brawler like Cornelius Vanderbilt, but he was combative in his own way. "The exhibition of his powerful will was at times actually terrible," his own lawyer remarked. "If any other man on this earth ever had such a will, certainly I have not heard of it." Even after he was worth millions, McCormick would refuse to pay the smallest charge if he thought a principle was involved. Once the Pennsylvania Railroad wanted $8.70 for excess baggage; McCormick contended that the baggage fee should have been included in the price of the six tickets he had purchased for himself and his family. When the railroad insisted, he canceled his trip; when the railroad proceeded to lose the bags, he initiated a lawsuit that lasted twenty-three years, generated tens of thousands of dollars in legal fees, and didn't end until after he died. (If the Penn was slow to learn, other railroads weren't. When the New York Central misplaced a trunk belonging to a McCormick relative, the road's lawyer sent a check at once. "We don't want to have a lawsuit with the McCormicks," he explained.)

McCormick came by his orneriness honestly. His ancestors were Scotch-Irish, of those clans that had fought the English in Scotland, the Irish in Ireland, and the Indians on the American frontier. Cyrus' grandfather Robert, finding life into the Pennsylvania hinterland too confining, had moved southwest into the Valley of Virginia, as the Shenandoah Valley was then called. There he sired a son, also called Robert, who in turn produced a son, Cyrus, in 1809. (Three days before Cyrus was born, across the mountains in Kentucky another Illinoisan-to-be, Abraham Lincoln, first saw the light of day; the two would collaborate to save the Union half a century later.) Committed Calvinists, McCormick's people adhered to the doctrine that God helps those who help themselves; molded by generations of borderland conflict, they helped themselves to whatever they could lay hold of and defend. By 1830, when Cyrus turned twenty-one, his father had secured twelve hundred acres, which produced a profitable diversity of grain, fruit, timber and stone. Five children, including Cyrus, amplified Robert's own labor power; nine slaves magnified it still more.

But not enough. Robert, and now Cyrus, ran up against the fundamental problem of American economic life during the eighteenth and nineteenth centuries: Although blessed with abundant natural resources, the American colonies and then the American states were chronically short of labor. Native-born Americans did their best to alleviate the shortage by reproducing at a breathtaking pace; meanwhile immigrants poured in from overseas. But so immense were the resources available for development—the land area within American borders doubled in 1783 at the end of the American Revolutionary War, and again in 1803 with the Louisiana Purchase—that labor remained the critical constraint on the growth of the economy.

In such circumstances, a single invention could have an enormous effect. Eli Whitney's cotton gin, which in the 1790s mechanized the separation of cotton fibers from cotton seeds, opened up vast new reaches of the American South to cotton culture (a culture that included slavery, which thereby gained a new lease on life).

What the cotton gin was to the South, a mechanical reaper would be to the North. The principal impediment to the spread of commercial agriculture across the Ohio Valley and beyond was the inability of farm workers to cut more than about half an acre of wheat per laborer per day.

Because wheat had the inconvenient habit of ripening all at once, and of falling to the ground and being lost within ten days or two weeks of coming ripe, wheat growers faced an annual harvest-time problem. In Europe, where hands were plentiful and labor correspondingly cheap, the problem could be solved by hiring more workers for the harvest. In America, where hands were few, the expense of hiring more workers drove costs to such levels as to prohibit large-scale cultivation. A person who could devise a method to multiply the labor power of the harvest workers would become a national hero, and wealthy besides.

Cyrus McCormick wasn't the only person to reach this conclusion, nor the first. Tinkerers in sheds and blacksmith shops all across the wheat-growing regions from New York to Illinois, and abroad as well, tried to improve on the sickle and the scythe, tools only marginally modified since the days when the Egyptians built their pyramids. Various inventors approximated success, but until the 1830s none had overcome the combined obstacles of bumpy, sloping and rock-strewn fields; horses and mules that took fright at the clattering contraptions chasing their tails; and skeptical customers—that is, farmers unwilling to bet the farm, in many cases literally, on expensive and as-yet-unproven machinery.

Cyrus McCormick had haunted the blacksmith shop on his father's farm from youth, both out of innate curiosity and as a way of avoiding field work; now he hammered together a working reaper. In 1831 he tested it on a neighbor's farm. Those who saw it accounted it "a right smart curious sort of thing"; McCormick, with the hindsight that comes from having several million dollars in one's pocket, later declared that he knew at once that this device would make his fortune.

If he really did know that, he kept it a secret while he parked his invention in a barn and went off to Kentucky to try to sell another machine, one that seemed to have more immediate promise. During the second quarter of the nineteenth century, Kentucky's perennial presidential aspirant, Henry Clay, was promoting a program of economic nationalism that he dubbed the "American system." This combination of federally financed infrastructure development and tariff-enforced import substitution would, Clay promised, enhance American prosperity by providing jobs and freeing the United States from dependence on imports. At that time, hemp was a strategic material, vital to the ropes and lines of sailing ships, as well as to the more mundane burlap sacks and twine used in every household and most businesses. Clay hoped to encourage the domestic production of hemp, which—as luck would have it—grew well in his home state. What was needed to make the American industry competitive with foreign suppliers was a cheap method of "breaking" hemp: separating the usable fibers from the rest of the plant. Robert McCormick had devised a machine to accomplish this task, and Cyrus was determined that it would do for hemp what the cotton gin had done for cotton. Unfortunately for father and son (and for Henry Clay), the McCormicks' machine never lived up to its promise, and neither did the hemp industry. (Many decades later a variety of hemp bred for other purposes would enable the plant to make a comeback, as domestic marijuana dealers applied Clay's buy-American philosophy to the illicit drug trade.)

Realizing he wasn't going to become the Eli Whitney of hemp, McCormick turned to becoming the Cyrus McCormick of wheat. He tinkered further with his reaper, then sought a patent, which he received in 1834. New demonstrations went even better than the first; after one successful show, a U.S. senator from South Carolina and a future governor of Virginia jointly declared: "The cutting was rapid and extremely clean, scarcely a stalk of grain being left, and little, if any, being lost by shattering from the work of the machine." Other observers predicted that McCormick's reaper would be "an acquisition of value and importance to the general husbandry."

Curiously, the inventor's vision clouded once more. Part of the fog followed from bad harvests in the Shenandoah Valley, which for the next few years left farmers struggling to carry the debt load they already bore; new capital purchases were out of the question. Part of the problem was McCormick's quick mind, which spun off other novelties and schemes for making money. A plow designed especially for hillside work performed to favorable reviews and promising sales. An iron mine and smelter seemed a natural for a young man who grew up beating iron at his father's forge. But the plows never caught on outside McCormick's neighborhood, and, in the wake of the Panic of 1837, the iron mine turned out to be a hole in the ground down which his money disappeared.

Only in 1839 did McCormick go back to his reaper, and then chiefly under the pressure of a rival. Obed Hussey wore a patch over his left eye and a stern look on his face; whether one or both were the consequence of his earlier career whaling out of Nantucket, this Ahab-looking Maine native didn't say. In time, Cyrus McCormick would become his Moby Dick; for now he honed his land-harpoon, a competing reaper. While McCormick was wasting time and money in iron, Hussey was winning customers in grain.

When McCormick learned of Hussey's success, he dusted off his reaper and bought advertising in the Richmond *Enquirer*. He declared that he was back in business and would be able to fill all orders in time for the 1840 harvest. The initial response was disappointing; in 1840 he sold just two machines. By his later admission—albeit not his contemporary claims—these models really weren't worth much, and he retired to his shop to craft improvements. When he reentered the market in 1842 he had a better product. He sold six reapers that year, twenty-nine the next.

In 1844 he took a trip that changed his life—and altered the course of American history. Until then his horizons had been limited, quite literally, by the ridges that enclosed the Valley of Virginia and framed the Allegheny–Appalachian uplift. In his thirty-sixth year he crossed the mountains onto the prairies that stretched to the Missouri River, and traversed that stream onto the plains that extended from there to the Rocky Mountains. As he gazed out across this vast open territory, the scales fell from his eyes. A reaper could be a convenience in the tight, enclosed fields of Virginia; on the ocean-like tracts of the West, it would be a necessity.

If McCormick had suffered from bad timing before, now he benefited from the opposite. Subsistence farmers had been living in the trans-Appalachian region since colonial times, but only with the opening of the Erie Canal in 1825 had market-minded farmers begun moving into the area. The arrival of the railroads in the 1830s and 1840s augmented the farmers' ability to get crops to market and encouraged additional settlement. Before the canals and especially the railroads, the most profitable way to market grain was often in a jug: Farmers distilled it into whiskey, which commanded a much higher price per pound. (Cyrus McCormick's father, a good temperance man but also a canny businessman, reconciled his conscience with his bottom line by refusing his workers their customary liquor ration even as he processed his grain into whiskey and sold it for twenty-five cents a gallon.) Americans in the nineteenth century consumed prodigious quantities of alcohol, not least because water supplies were frequently unhealthy; but even they could not live by booze alone. The arrival of mechanized transport held out the possibility of shipping raw grain, or grain ground into flour, to the burgeoning cities of the East.

Events outside the grain-growing districts also conspired in McCormick's favor. The failure of the Irish potato crop drove up European demand for food imports from the United States. Partly as a result, the British government in 1846 repealed the Corn Laws, the protectionist measures that heretofore had kept out American grain ("corn," in the generic British sense). The discovery of gold in California in 1848 sent a flood of bullion back East, swelling the money supply and raising farm prices, even as it siphoned labor West, thereby making mechanization all the more imperative.

Cyrus McCormick couldn't appreciate every factor that was working in his favor, but he could read the farm press. Chicago's *Union Agriculturist and Western Prairie Farmer* trumpeted: "Inventors—here is a field for you to operate in; anything that you wish to have introduced into extensive use, which you know to be really valuable, you can bring here with a good prospect of success. Bring along your machines." ("Give us a chance to advertise them," the paper added.) Another Chicago editor mentioned reapers specifically: "They are just the thing for our prairies, where more grain is sown than can possibly be gathered in the ordinary way, and their comparative cheapness puts them within the reach of every tiller of the soil. So indispensable will be their use that hereafter the sickle, the scythe, and the cradle may as well hang themselves 'upon the willow.'"

To capture the rapidly growing western market, McCormick relocated to Chicago in 1848. He set up a factory in a three-story brick building of 10,000 square feet on the north bank of the Chicago River, with convenient access to both water and rail transport. In his factory he adopted the principle of interchangeable parts pioneered by Eli Whitney (to make guns rather than cotton gins), and he installed a steam engine to drive his lathes, saws and grinders. The result was one of the first examples of mass production—and one of the most impressive. A visitor described the works:

> An angry whirr, a dronish hum, a prolonged whistle, a shrill buzz and a panting breath—such is the music of the place. You enter—little wheels of steel attached to horizontal, upright and oblique shafts, are on every hand. They seem motionless. Rude pieces of wood without form or comeliness are hourly approaching them upon little railways, as if drawn thither by some mysterious attraction. They touch them, and *presto*, grooved, scalloped, rounded, on they go, with a little help from an attendant, who seems to have an easy time of it, and transferred to another railway, when down comes a guillotine-like contrivance—they are morticed, bored, and whirled away. . . .
>
> The saw and the cylinder are the genii of the establishment. They work its wonders, and accomplish its drudgery. But there is a greater than they. Below, glistening like a knight in armor, the engine of forty-horse power works as silently as the "little wheel" [i.e., the spinning wheel] of the matron; but shafts plunge, cylinders revolve, bellows heave, iron is twisted into screws like

31

wax, and saws dash off at the rate of forty rounds a second, at one movement of its mighty muscles.

But there is a greater still than this. There by the furnace fire, begrimed with coal and dust, decorated with an apron of leather, instead of a ribbon of satin, stands the one who controls—nay, who can create the whole.

McCormick's entry into mass production was a gamble, but a necessary one. His original patent was about to expire after a normal fourteen-year run; although he sought an extension, success in that endeavor could hardly be taken for granted. Indeed, his rivals, led by Hussey, did their best to block him. The case became a cat fight for editors and a growth industry for lawyers. "McCormick can be beaten in the Patent Office, and must be beaten now or never," asserted an attorney drumming up business for the opposition. "If funds are furnished us, we shall surely beat him; but if they are not furnished, he will as certainly beat us. Please, therefore, take hold and help us to beat the *common enemy*. The subscriptions have ranged from $100 to $1,000." McCormick's opponents in the press contended that he had made enough money from his monopoly, and that to extend it would, as one indignant writer put it, "impose a tax of $500,000 a year upon the starving people of the world." McCormick battled on, even as the odds against him mounted; years elapsed while the future of an emerging industry hung in the balance. Finally the commissioner of patents delivered praise and an unfavorable verdict: "He will live in the grateful recollection of mankind as long as the reaping-machine is employed in gathering the harvest. But the Reaper is of too great value to the public to be controlled by any individual, and the extension of his patent is refused."

A less determined individual than McCormick might have retreated under this blow; instead he redoubled his efforts and drove forward. To the surprise of many—although apparently not McCormick—his short-run defeat became the basis for his long-term success, even as it vindicated the wisdom of the patent system. In his fourteen years of exclusive rights, McCormick had been able to perfect his design; now he had to best the competition by superior production, distribution and service. His ability to do so was what separated him from most other inventors and made his success not merely a technological triumph but an industrial one.

Indeed, McCormick's accomplishment (and that of those who followed him) was nothing less than to industrialize agriculture. He was the first to bring the factory system to the production of farm equipment; this, in turn, by making the reaper and its successors available to millions of farmers, brought the factory system to the production of farm crops. When machines replaced humans in the fields, productivity rose, prices fell and consumers—meaning everyone who ate—benefited.

During the several years after his move to Chicago, McCormick's factory churned out ever-growing numbers of machines. In 1849 the company fabricated 1500 machines; in 1856, 4000. By the end of the latter year McCormick had produced altogether some 16,000 reapers, mowers and reaper-mowers.

Yet production was only one part of the equation. For all the macroeconomic influences on demand, selling the reapers remained a stubbornly microeconomic affair. McCormick created a marketing machine that was as efficient among its target audience as his reapers were in standing grain. The sales process began with advertising. During the 1840s McCormick bought space in papers from New York to Illinois, wherever wheat or related grains grew. An 1849 advertisement illustrated the ease of use of "McCormick's Patent Virginia Reaper" with a picture of a young boy happily cracking the whip over the two-horse team that pulled the device, while an unperspiring man in top hat and waistcoat raked the neatly severed stalks from the platform. "Last harvest 800 of these machines were sold and used with great satisfaction and advantage," the copy read. To corroborate this assertion, the ad included testimonials from satisfied customers. In time, as his cost of advertising in other people's newspapers increased, McCormick decided to publish his own paper. Before he died the *Farmers' Advance* had a circulation of 350,000, distributed to farmers all across the country. The paper flogged McCormick products, naturally and forthrightly; one of the paper's editors explained: "Trying to do business without advertising is like winking at a pretty girl through a pair of green goggles. You may know what you are doing, but no one else does."

Advertising was no substitute for personal contact, of course, especially with farmers unused to buying from faceless corporations. McCormick representatives were initially independent agents, selling reapers on commission as part of their larger lines of goods. But as business increased, and the "harvester wars" with Hussey and other manufacturers intensified, the best of the agents were brought aboard as regular salaried employees. The marketing culture of the company reflected the determined character of the founder. One memo from corporate headquarters complained that a particular agent in Minnesota was failing to meet his quotas because he had "too many churchmen" working for him as subagents. "I believe in religion and temperance," the sales manager explained, "but it ain't worth a 'cuss' to run the Reaper trade on in Minnesota: it requires cheek & muscle and I am sorry to say some 'evasions' from the truth to successfully sell McCormick harvesters with the opposition we have. . . . We have got to fight the Devil with fire and it is no use trying to fool him on sweetened water."

The company supplemented cheek and muscle with solid sales tools. McCormick's money-back guaranty was a first of its kind. For $30 a customer could have use of a machine for six months; at the end of that trial period he could, if satisfied, pay the balance of $90 or, if unsatisfied, return the machine and get his $30 back. For farmers, these terms could hardly have been easier, since the six months allowed the farmer to harvest and market his crops and be paid for them before he had to pay McCormick. McCormick justified his credit terms with a simple statement to farmers: "It is better that I should wait for the money than that you should wait for the machine that you need." Not everyone qualified for credit, to be sure; one task of the sales force was to investigate the trustworthiness of customers. Occasionally farmers objected, but most were satisfied with McCormick's justification: "Would you, a farmer, sell a horse on credit to the first stranger who came along?"

Even as his marketers pushed product at home, McCormick took his invention abroad. In 1851 he attended the world's fair in London. The reaper elicited derision from those who noted only its ungainly appearance; the London *Times* called it "a cross between an Ashley chariot, a wheelbarrow, and a flying machine" (this was half a century before the Wright brothers got off the ground). Yet once the demonstration started, opinions changed. New York editor Horace Greeley, present for the occasion, recorded:

> It came into the field to confront a tribunal already prepared for its condemnation. Before it stood John Bull [that is, the British man-in-the-street]—burly, dogged, and determined not to be humbugged—his judgment made up and his sentence ready to be recorded. There was a moment, and but a moment, of suspense; then human prejudice could hold out no longer; and burst after burst of involuntary cheers from the whole crowd proclaimed the triumph of the Yankee Reaper. In seventy seconds McCormick had become famous. He was the lion of the hour.

Four years later McCormick won the grand prize at the Universal Exposition in Paris; the following decade the French emperor Napoleon III awarded him the Cross of the Legion of Honor after observing a trial on the royal estate at Châlons.

McCormick's growing fame, together with his success in creating an organization that ran without his direct oversight, allowed him to broaden his activities. As one of the leading citizens of Chicago he was frequently mentioned as a mayoral candidate; in 1860 he agreed to throw his hat into the ring. He lost his race, but not so badly that he didn't make a run for Congress in 1864—also unsuccessfully.

The chief political issue of the early 1860s was, of course, the Civil War. As a Southerner transplanted to the North (in 1860 he still owned slaves in Virginia), not to mention a businessman with sales on both sides of the Mason-Dixon Line, McCormick found his loyalties divided. He at first opposed the forcible preservation of the Union, an attitude that caused the *Chicago Tribune* to brand him a "rebel." Expedience, if not necessarily conviction, eventually prompted him to print a public declaration of allegiance to the Union. Yet the label of Copperhead dogged him throughout the war, and evidence suggests that on a European trip in 1862 he hoped to persuade Napoleon III to intervene at least diplomatically on the side of the South.

Even as it raised questions about his politics, the Civil War worked wonders for McCormick's business. By 1868 production reached 8000 machines per year, and it continued to grow. Yet what the Civil War did for McCormick Harvester was no more—and in some ways much less—than what McCormick Harvester did for the Civil War. Ironically for a Southern sympathizer who abhorred the idea of conflict between his native region and his adopted one, McCormick contributed materially to the North's ability to crush the South. Abraham Lincoln's secretary of war, Edwin Stanton, explained: "The reaper is to the North what slavery is to the South. By taking the place of regiments of young men in the western harvest fields, it releases them to do battle for the Union at the front and at the same time keeps up the supply of bread for the Nation and the Nation's armies. Thus without McCormick's invention, I fear the North could not win and the Union would be dismembered."

McCormick's contribution to the Union effort went even further than this. At the war's outset Southern leaders had anticipated that demand for Southern cotton would force England and perhaps France to come to the aid of the Confederacy. As things happened, Southern cotton proved less critical overseas than Northern grain, and the Europeans declined to risk alienating the North. (If it was ironic that the Virginia-born McCormick contributed so significantly to the Northern war effort, it was no less ironic that the cotton gin, vital to the South, was the invention of the

Massachusetts-born Eli Whitney. In a certain sense, the Civil War pitted McCormick against Whitney, with each fighting for what he considered to be the wrong side. McCormick won.)

Besides making labor still scarcer than before, the war drove up commodity prices, putting money in farmers' pockets and enabling them to buy more of McCormick's machines. In this respect, however, the war was a mixed blessing, for under the pressure of the conflict Washington printed inflationary greenbacks, which devalued the debt owed to McCormick by his customers. William McCormick, who joined his brother in the business (along with third brother Leander), afterward described the situation: "Creditors were running away from debtors who pursued them in triumph and paid them without mercy."

Currency remained a problem through the end of the 1860s (a circumstance Jay Gould would attempt to exploit); a more immediate challenge arose in 1871 when McCormick's factory burned down, along with the rest of Chicago. Retirement tempted, but McCormick resisted. He rebuilt the factory, larger than before, and pushed production to new records. In the process he became famously rich. Company profits, which McCormick shared more grudgingly and less generously with his brothers than they thought just, rose from $65,000 in 1849 to $1.2 million in 1880. By his death in 1884 he was one of the wealthiest persons in America.

Until the end, he was as combative as always. "Nettie," he told his wife, "life *is* a battle." No victory could be complete; the struggle never ended. Yet as he rode across the prairies and plains in his private rail car, he must have allowed that he had triumphed as far as anyone could in a continually evolving economy. One measure of his success was what were aptly called "factory farms," enormous spreads where hundreds of machines worked tens of thousands of acres, producing millions of bushels of wheat that would never have been planted, let alone harvested, without the kinds of machines McCormick made.

Another measure of his accomplishment awaited him on his return to Chicago. By bringing industry to the farm, McCormick also brought the farm to industry. Cheap food fueled the growth of Chicago and other cities, where those ninety-million hands that might have been working on farms were employed in shops and factories. McCormick's machines harvested grain; in the bargain they sowed modern America.

4

THE SPECULATOR

Jay Gould

. . .

CYRUS MCCORMICK'S ENEMIES, IN THEIR OBJECTIVE MOMENTS, would have conceded that on balance he was a constructive force in American life. At times Jay Gould's *friends* had difficulty saying as much about him.

To some degree Gould had himself to blame for his bad reputation; to some extent it owed to misunderstanding of what he spent his career doing. Even in the 1990s, speculation is an art not universally appreciated. Economists have developed theories explaining how speculation serves a useful purpose by transferring risk from those who don't like it and aren't equipped to deal with it to those who do and are. But the theories haven't entirely dispelled the notion that speculators are gamblers in a zero-sum game, bettors whose winnings derive from luck and perhaps shrewdness but not from any real good produced or worthwhile service rendered.

If such is the case at the end of the twentieth century, it was truer still in the nineteenth century, when economic theory was in its infancy and gambling was relegated to the fringes of society rather than leading off the nightly news and topping off the tax coffers of most states. Consequently it wasn't surprising that Jay Gould, the greatest speculator of his era, was also one of Wall Street's—not to say America's—most distrusted and despised characters. "The example he set is a dangerous one to follow," tut-tutted the *New York Herald*, assessing Gould's career. "The methods he adopted are to be avoided." The *New York Times* was equally critical:

"Gould was a negative quantity in the development of the country, where he was not an absolutely retarding and destructive quantity." Joseph Pulitzer of the *New York World* called Gould "one of the most sinister figures that ever flitted bat-like across the vision of the American people." A business contemporary damned him as "the worst man on earth since the beginning of the Christian era." Daniel Drew, commenting while Gould still had a couple of schemes left in him, and speaking from personal experience, declared simply: "His touch is death."

Maybe that was because Gould spent most of his life feeling death's chill fingers clutching at him. He was one of those children who survive their early years by sheer willpower; scrawny from birth, he lost his mother at four, his first stepmother within the same year and his second stepmother three years after that. His father, John Gould, who was nearly as unpopular with his neighbors in Delaware County in upstate New York as Jay would become with *his* neighbors in southern Manhattan, had to beat off armed attacks; at one point an angry local threatened to drown Jay for John's sins. John turned to drink, making him more difficult than ever. As a teenager Jay contracted typhoid fever, followed by pneumonia. Each nearly killed him; together they left him, at eighteen, facing a future clouded by likely invalidism.

Yet he refused to give in. While still a boy he announced that he would have nothing to do with farming, John Gould's occupation, but must instead go to school in the nearby town. John eyed the lad, decided he was serious and carted him off to town, where he left him at the door of the school with fifty cents and a bundle of clothes.

Jay talked a blacksmith into boarding him in exchange for keeping the man's books. Jay had no experience with ledgers and accounts, but he guessed that he knew as much as the blacksmith, or soon would—and soon did. In class he proved an apt pupil, although one essay he wrote, resurrected years later, would send critics into gales of laughter. The title was "Honesty Is the Best Policy," and it explained how conscience and scripture demanded scrupulous adherence to the highest standards of integrity. Also during this early period, Jay demonstrated a preternatural perception of life's accelerating pace. "I am growing old too fast," he declared at the ripe age of sixteen.

He accelerated his own pace to keep up. He taught himself surveying and took a job preparing a map of a nearby county. An associate who knew him then saw hints of what he would become. "He was all business in those days, as he is now. Why, even at meal times he was always talking map. . . . My father used to say, 'Look at Gould; isn't he a driver?'"

Surveying, to Gould, was only partly about locating lakes and rivers and hills and streams; it was also about locating favorable opportunities for branching out into other activities. He learned the value of hemlock trees to the leather-tanning process; he promptly formed a partnership to become a tanner himself. One of his associates, Charles Leupp, had emotional problems, perhaps aggravated by some of Gould's sharp practices; after Leupp shot himself dead—and after Gould became famous enough to have enemies—those enemies had little difficulty discerning blame for Gould in his associate's self-destruction.

If Gould felt any remorse he didn't show it. But then he made a habit—an obsession even—of keeping his emotions to himself. He tipped his hand only far enough for others to see the burning intensity with which he pursued his business interests. He didn't object to the money involved, to be sure, but business held a fascination for him that transcended balance sheets. A lawyer friend remarked this quality in Gould:

> When intensely interested in any matter, he devoted his whole concentration of thought upon that one thing, and would seem to lose interest in things, often of greater pecuniary importance but of not so much commercial fascination. He loved the intricacies and perplexities of financial problems.

His patience was equally striking. Though he felt a chronic compulsion to be making something of himself, in any given operation he could bide his time till the most promising moment. "I avoid bad luck by being patient," he once explained. "Whenever I am obliged to get into a fight, I always wait and let the other fellow get tired first."

During the 1860s Gould had opportunity aplenty to demonstrate both his intensity and his patience. With many others of that era he gravitated to New York City as the epicenter of industrializing America. Boston had been America's first financial hub; Philadelphia surpassed Boston in the eighteenth century. But after the founding in 1817 of what became the New York Stock Exchange, the cockpit of the American economy shifted to Manhattan. Improvements in communication and transportation, especially the telegraph and the railroad, allowed both the select few who operated within the walls of the Exchange and the larger number who traded on the curb outside to tap the pulse, and the accounts, of investors all across the country. The discovery of gold in California in the late

1840s, followed by the boom in railroad construction, created a huge market in mining and railroad issues; the Civil War added myriad opportunities for individuals undaunted by risk. Daniel Drew recalled the war years as wonderful for speculation. "Along with ordinary happenings," Drew declared, "we fellows in Wall Street had the fortunes of war to speculate about and that always makes great doings on a stock exchange. It's good fishing in troubled waters."

Gould and Drew fished together; for a third angler they invited Jim Fisk. "Jubilee Jim," as he was often called, was as outgoing as Gould was introverted. He slapped men on the back and women on the behind (women of a certain class, that is—the class he commonly consorted with); the door of his office on Wall Street was always open, with whiskey on the counter and cigars on the desk.

Before the fight with Vanderbilt for control of the Erie, Jay Gould was the least well known of the three, although not the least successful; during that battle he gained a national reputation as one of the most audacious, and least principled, speculators in the land. The image of Gould and Fisk dashing across the Hudson with the Erie charter in one satchel and the corporate treasury in another made them infamous; Gould became even more infamous after his partners dispatched him to Albany to arrange the company's recharter. In the public mind Gould personified the epic malevolence portrayed in one journalist's lyrical description of the corruption—and corrupters—of the legislature: "On its foul edge stood all the forces of evil in our society, like the demons in Dante's Fifth Chasm, fishing out one venal legislator after another, as Graffiacane 'hooked out Ciampola's pitchy locks and haled him up to open gaze so that he seemed an otter.'"

Now notorious, Gould maintained his reserved demeanor. Questioned by a committee investigating the possibility of malfeasance in the Erie affair, he pleaded repeated failure of memory, undergoing (in the words of an unfriendly but nonetheless appreciative eyewitness) "a curious psychological metamorphosis" into "the veriest simpleton in money matters."

All about him swirled charges of bribery, larceny and worse. "Within the past few days we have seen the most gigantic swindling operations carried on in Wall Street," a New York editor cried. A great railway "has been tossed about like a football; its real stockholders have seen their property abused by men to whom they have entrusted its interests, and who, in the betrayal of that trust, have committed crimes which in parallel cases on a smaller scale would have deservedly sent them to Sing Sing."

The publicity compelled Gould to be more circumspect, but it didn't diminish his daring in the slightest. In 1869 he attempted the most breathtaking speculative operation in the history of American finance: a corner of the gold market. For much of American history there was no gold market to speak of; either gold was the only currency worth worrying about, or other currencies—paper dollars or silver—were pegged to gold. But the Civil War had elicited a flood of paper to finance the Union effort, and the greenbacks remained in circulation four years later. In keeping with the principle that bad money drives out good, paper predominated in domestic transactions (to Cyrus McCormick's regret); abroad, where American legal-tender laws didn't apply and creditors weren't required to accept the paper, gold was the coin of the international realm. Brokers and merchants with foreign business had to juggle the two kinds of money, paying paper at home, gold abroad. These were the primary customers in the money markets.

Aside from speculators, that is. When merchants sought to lock in a favorable exchange rate between greenbacks and gold, they looked to people willing to bet they could get a better rate and would profit from the difference. Gould was among those; so was Jim Fisk. Fresh from their victory over Vanderbilt in the Erie war, the two plotted how they might accomplish an even greater triumph.

Precisely how far in advance they plotted became a matter of argument. Historian and sometime journalist Henry Adams declared of this "most brilliant and most dangerous" of all financial schemes that Gould "dwelt upon it for months." Gould himself suggested that it was more happenstance. He contended that he initially hoped merely to nudge up the price of gold as a way of promoting American farm exports; this would be good both for the farmers and for those railroads, such as the Erie, that transported their crops. But one thing led to another, he said, and the nudge grew into something bigger.

Gould may have been too modest. He recognized early on the possibilities of leverage, once remarking with evident wonder how "a man with $100,000 of money and with credit can transact a business of $20,000,000." As luck had it, twenty million would just about buy the available gold supply in New York in the late 1860s. Regarding the credit, Gould took the precaution of purchasing a bank he could count on to honor his checks even if the funds to back them hadn't come in just yet.

The scene where his coup would take place was the Gold Room, which in its few years of existence had already acquired a distinctive reputation. One denizen described it as "a cavern full of dank and noisome vapors" where "the deadly carbonic acid was blended with the fumes of stale smoke and vinous breaths." A newspaperman depicted it even less flatteringly: "Imagine a rat-pit in full blast, with twenty or thirty men ranged around the rat tragedy, each with a canine under his arm, yelling and howling at once." At the center of the room, corresponding to the place where the dogs would worry the rats to death, was a marble Cupid shooting water into the air. "The artistic conception is not appropriate," the journalist continued. "Instead of a cupid throwing a pearly fountain into the air, there should have been a hungry Midas turning everything to gold and starving from sheer inability to eat."

Such allusions were largely lost on Gould, who took a practical approach to nearly every aspect of life. Included in the purview of his practicality was politics. Referring to his railroad work, he once explained:

> It was the custom when men received nominations to come to me for contributions, and I made them and considered them good, paying dividends for the company. In a Republican district I was a strong Republican, in a Democratic district I was Democratic, and in doubtful districts I was doubtful. In politics I was an Erie Railroad man every time.

Gould adopted a similarly businesslike attitude toward the politics of the gold corner. He could estimate with considerable confidence how much privately held gold would become available at any given price from 130 (where it stood in April 1869) to the 140s and beyond. What he could *not* estimate with any accuracy was whether, when, and how energetically the federal government would enter the market. The vaults of the Treasury held enough gold to kill any corner; what was required was a decision by Washington to let the markets operate without federal intervention.

To encourage such a decision Gould cultivated a casual acquaintance named Abel Corbin who happened to be married to President Grant's sister. Corbin arranged a June 15 meeting between Gould and Grant—in itself no small stroke for Gould, considering his reputation. Gould explained how a higher price for gold would stimulate the farm economy, with benefits for the country as a whole. Grant gave Gould little reason to expect support, suggesting that the economy was overheated already. "We supposed from that conversation that the president was a contractionist," Gould testified afterward.

Late summer, however, brought bumper crops to the heartland and with them the threat, followed by the reality, of falling prices. Defending the Erie against Vanderbilt had burdened Gould with debt that demanded repayment; if the crops didn't move—over the Erie—that debt would grow all the heavier. On the other hand, if gold could be pushed upward— from its current price of 136 to the 140s—the crops would get on track and so would the Erie's revenues. In the process a person like himself who had taken a long position in gold would stand to make some nice profits.

By greater or less coincidence (Gould couldn't tell just which), the office of assistant federal treasurer in New York had recently been filled with a friend of Abel Corbin. Gould decided to welcome the new man, Daniel Butterfield, with a loan of $10,000. Terms of repayment were flexible, perhaps to the point of nonexistence.

Gould also approached Butterfield's boss. During an earlier rise in the gold price, Treasury Secretary George Boutwell had announced a decision to double federal gold sales; this promptly sent the price spiraling down. Gould wanted to ascertain whether Boutwell would take similar action in response to another rise. He wrote him a letter reiterating the argument he had made personally to Grant about the relationship between gold and American exports. If Gould had hoped for a signal as to the Treasury's intentions, Boutwell didn't provide it. He replied in the most opaque of terms.

But Grant himself tipped his hand, or seemed to, at the start of September. One of the general's old army friends had died; Grant must attend the funeral and would stop at the house of his sister and Abel Corbin. Corbin informed Gould, who made a point of dropping by. This time the president appeared much more persuaded by Gould's reasoning. As the harvest continued, the crops were piling up; some fillip was needed to find markets for them overseas. The government wouldn't undertake to raise the price of gold artificially, but neither would it interfere if gold rose on its own.

Such, at any rate, was Gould's interpretation of the president's position, and he began to act on this interpretation at once. He issued buy orders with his gold brokers; he also cut Corbin in on the profits by purchasing $1.5 million in Corbin's name. Corbin determined that appearances precluded his accepting such a boon; could Gould put the gold in his wife's name instead? It was done. Evidently Gould did something similar for Daniel Butterfield, although the assistant treasurer subsequently denied any such arrangement.

As the price approached 140, many gold holders got nervous. Some took their profits and bailed out; certain others were persuaded to stay in only when Gould assumed some of their risk. Corbin decided that delicacy had its limits; he demanded his (wife's) profits at once. Gould wrote him a check for $25,000, although because the couple's gold remained technically in Gould's name, he made the check out to himself, endorsed it and handed it to Corbin. (That this kept Corbin's name, and that of his wife, off the record was lost on neither man.)

The nervousness encouraged gold bears, heretofore hiding out, to enter the market. The high price wasn't sustainable, they judged, and they did their best to beat it down. They succeeded momentarily, with the arrow on the big brass indicator in the Gold Room twisting back to 135.

Gould summoned reinforcements. Jim Fisk's confidence had flagged following Grant's initial bearishness. "The thing began to look scary to me," he explained afterward. But Gould thought his flamboyant friend might be enticed back. "Don't you think gold has got to the bottom?" he inquired at 135. Fisk decided it had and commenced buying again.

Lest other investors divine their ultimate intentions, Gould and Fisk masked their purchases. They enlisted a veritable battalion of brokers—"fifty or sixty," Gould estimated, speaking only of the ones who worked for him; Fisk had his own dozens. None knew what the others were doing—or, rather, *who* they were doing it for; though centrally directed by the co-cornerers, the scores of buyers gave the impression of a broad bullish surge for gold. Secrecy was necessary for another reason: to keep the brokers from catching on and buying on their own account, which would drive up the price prematurely.

As the gold indicator reversed its downward course and started slowly turning up, Gould again tried to neutralize the one imponderable element in the scheme: the role of Washington. He again met with Grant, again urged the president to let gold rise naturally. He buttonholed Grant's private secretary and offered to cut him in on the profits. Although the secretary declined the offer, Gould persisted, sending him an unaddressed—and therefore presumably unincriminating—letter revealing that $500,000 in gold had been purchased on his behalf. This overture too was rebuffed.

In the meantime Gould had encouraged Corbin to write to Grant and amplify the arguments he—Gould—had been making all summer. Corbin did so, warning his brother-in-law that the gold bears wanted nothing more than a hint of government support, however implicit; they would then precipitate a collapse in the price of gold, with all the calamitous consequences such a collapse would have for farm exports and the economy as a whole.

This letter, crucial to Gould's plans, was delivered by personal courier. The courier arrived while the president was playing croquet on the lawn of a house he was visiting; on completion of the game Grant accepted the letter. He read it twice, pausing to puff on one of the cigars that were never far from his mouth. (After a momentous victory in the Civil War a cigar-maker had guaranteed the general a lifetime supply; this seemed a generous idea at the time but almost certainly contributed to Grant's death from throat cancer.) The courier asked if the president had any reply to send. "None," Grant answered. The courier, who knew neither the contents of the letter nor the hoped-for response, then wired to New York that his mission had been accomplished. "Delivered all right," he said. Unluckily for Gould, the telegraph operator receiving the message parsed it differently: "Delivered. All right."

But things weren't all right—not for Gould anyway, as he discovered before long. Corbin confronted him with disastrous news. His wife had learned that her brother had seen through Corbin's dire warning about falling gold prices; far from fearing the bears the president was determined not to let the bulls capture the market. "I must get out—instantly!" cried Corbin.

Gould now realized that he had overestimated Corbin and underestimated Grant. He told Corbin to keep his mouth shut. Referring to the letter Corbin's wife had received with the news of the president's change of heart, he muttered, "I am undone if that letter gets out." To encourage Corbin's silence he offered him $100,000; this would do double duty by keeping Corbin from noisily dumping his gold (Gould was certain Corbin couldn't sell quietly); such dumping would be tantamount to publishing the ruinous letter.

Yet Gould knew that the corner was broken; the only question was whether he could get out without losing all. Stealthily he began selling. He took care to cover sell orders with smaller purchase orders; so silently did he maneuver that even most of his brokers misunderstood his game. "I was a seller of gold that day," he explained afterward. "I purchased merely enough to make believe I was a bull."

Jim Fisk, who didn't know that Gould had suddenly changed plans, still *was* a bull. Even as Gould was dumping gold Fisk was bidding it up. He pranced about the floor of the Gold Room urging his traders on, making side bets that the price would top 145. The room was in a frenzy as the bears fought for their lives against the raging bulls. "As the roar of battle and the scream of the victims resounded through the New Street," a journalist reported from the front, "it seemed as though human nature were undergoing torments worse than any that Dante ever witnessed in hell."

At day's end Fisk still thought he was on the verge of becoming a modern Midas; Gould knew that the price of gold couldn't be sustained for more than a few hours the next day. The conspirators met at the old Opera House, which had been converted to offices of the Erie. Fisk boasted of the bear hunt he would resume on the morrow, but Gould was quiet, deep in thought and getting deeper in the pile of shredded paper he habitually and unconsciously created whenever he plotted intricate maneuvers. His silence surprised none of his associates, who knew him as one who kept his own counsel. "I had my own fish to fry," he recalled later. "I listened to what was said, but it went in one ear and out of the other. I was all alone, so to speak, in what I did, and I did not let any of those people know exactly how I stood."

Friday morning, September 24, dawned gloriously clear over Manhattan, and as the sun rose above the East River the hopes of Fisk and the gold bulls rose with it. Excitement engulfed the Gold Room in anticipation of the ten o'clock bell. The $325 million that had cleared the room the day before had tripled the transactions of the day before that; today's clearings would almost certainly be another record. The brokers would make money regardless of who else did.

The bidding began ahead of the bell; by ten o'clock the price had jumped from 143-1/4 to 150. "Take all that you can get," Fisk ordered. Gould still sold, but still slowly so as not to arouse suspicion.

The price lurched upward. After sticking briefly at 150 it leaped to 155 in scarcely five minutes. The commotion spilled across the street to the stock exchange, which was thrown this way and that by all the money surging through the gold market. One stockbroker threatened one of the gold bulls with mortal harm, saying he would shoot him personally if he kept to his crazy course. The gold bull ran across the street to the lair of the stock men, pushed his way onto the platform there and bared his chest for anyone to fire upon. But he would continue to bull gold, he vowed. Fisk, delighted, issued new orders: "Take all you can get at 160."

The bears were frantic, facing imminent ruin as they reflected on all the short sales they would have to cover at these crushing prices. The price continued to climb, to 162. Gould continued to sell, quietly cashing in while awaiting the word that had to come soon.

At 11:42 the treasury secretary in Washington ordered the sale of $4 million in gold; the message arrived in New York at 12:10 (after some delay in transmission, and allowing for the twelve-minute difference between local time in Washington and that in New York in the days before standardized zones.)

"Possibly no avalanche ever swept with more terrible violence," related the *New York Herald* of what happened next. Taking some liberty with the chronological details, the paper got the essence of the story right: "As the bells of Trinity [Church] pealed forth the hour of noon the gold on the indicator stood at 160. Just a moment later, and before the echoes died away, gold fell to 138."

The echoes were drowned out by the relieved roars of the bears, ecstatic to learn that the bells weren't tolling for them this day, and by the stunned bellowing of the bulls, astonished and angry to learn that their imminent victory had turned to defeat.

Gould and Fisk ran for their lives—literally. One eyewitness declared that had the ringleaders of the corner been caught in public "the chances were that the lamp-post near by would have very soon been decorated with a breathless body." They took refuge in the Opera House, shielded by a cordon of thugs hired to place their bodies and other blunt instruments between their bosses and those who blamed Gould and Fisk for their ruin.

Gould had managed to unload most of his gold, but the stock plunge that the gold gyrations had set in motion left him illiquid in the face of heavy margin calls. At the same time, the rapid rise in gold, followed by the even more precipitate plunge, had utterly snarled accounting procedures designed for a much more sedate era. Many people were certain Gould owed them money, but at the close of business on that Black Friday, and for weeks thereafter, no one could sort out all the intricacies of who owed what to whom.

This was precisely what Gould was banking on (not least since banking on his own bank had been complicated by a run there, triggered by the unanticipated arrival of skeptical bank examiners on the morning of Black Friday). He laid down a legal smoke screen, obtaining injunctions barring his creditors from collecting until accounts had been settled across the board. As Gould well knew, this could take months or years—especially if he failed to cooperate. He indeed failed, most infuriatingly; he procrastinated, postponed, settled with some, stonewalled others, stretching out the proceedings until his dunners despaired of getting their money or, in a few cases, died. The suits weren't fully settled until eight years after Black Friday.

Scores of brokerages perished in the panic of that day; many of those that weren't discredited financially were discredited morally. Although Gould survived financially, he found his reputation—such as it had been after the Erie fight—damaged almost beyond repair. The fact that he had not been ruined angered even more those who had. Strikingly, one person who didn't hold Gould's actions against him was Jim Fisk. Perhaps because he had never expected Gould to look after anyone except himself, perhaps because he knew that he would have acted as Gould did if he had known what Gould knew, Fisk took a philosophical view of the affair. "It was each man drag out his own corpse," he explained.

The outrage in the boardrooms and on the street against Gould led to his ouster from the presidency of the Erie. A majority of the stock in the road belonged to English investors who had been willing to give Gould their proxies while the share price advanced. But between the debt incurred in the fight with Vanderbilt and the general derangement resulting from the gold panic, Erie now swooned, and the Brits pulled their proxies and threw Gould out.

Gould found other objects for his speculatory instincts. He joined forces with his erstwhile opponent, Vanderbilt, to bull the stock of the Chicago & Northwestern Railroad—against one of his own former allies from the gold days. Henry Smith was less relaxed than Jim Fisk had been about being hung out to dry by Gould. Sputtering with anger, Smith confronted Gould: "I will live to see the day, sir, when you have to earn a living by going around this street with a hand organ and a monkey." Gould declined to be provoked. "Maybe you will, Henry. Maybe you will." But he couldn't resist adding, "And when I want a monkey, Henry, I'll send for you."

Possibly he was tired of being called a wrecker; possibly he felt he had enough money to leave the really spectacular speculations to others; perhaps he felt what his father had called "the Old Gould Disease, the Consumption that they most all Die with," catching up with him; but for whatever reason Gould now entered a period of comparatively constructive activities. He invested heavily in stock of the Union Pacific, the first transcontinental line but one that suffered from poor management and flimsy financing. By virtue of his large holdings he won a seat on the board of directors in 1874; by virtue of his shrewd intelligence he soon became the prime mover on that board. His administrative economies, investments in improvements to track and rolling stock, and well-timed takeovers of feeder and competing lines pushed the price of Union Pacific shares up by one hundred percent. Those who knew Gould from the Erie and gold-ring days waited for him to betray his own company and pocket several more tainted millions, but he didn't. He did make money on the consolidation of the Kansas Pacific with the Union Pacific (how much money he made became a source of speculation in its own right), but disinterested observers judged the merger sound. Charles Francis Adams, Jr., a longtime Gould critic who became a successor of Gould in charge of the Union Pacific, conceded, "From whatever point of view you regard it, the consolidation of 1880 seems to me, judging by the light of experience, to have worked nothing but benefit." Adams added, with revealing candor: "The transaction was far more favorable than anything which I have been able to effect during more recent years."

Even while expanding his railroad interests—eventually he controlled nearly 9,000 miles of road centered on the Missouri Pacific, as well as the Manhattan Elevated Railway—Gould diversified. He purchased the *New York World* and a majority share of the Western Union Telegraph Company. These ventures into communication provoked complaints that he was using the newspaper to sway public opinion on behalf of his business interests, and the telegraph ("Gould's Dionysian ear," one rival railroader called the Western Union) to eavesdrop on his foes. There was some truth to these charges; how much is hard to know. But Gould's *World* was the soul of impartial respectability compared to what it would become under Joseph Pulitzer, to whom Gould sold the paper, and anyone communicating sensitive intelligence in unciphered form over open wires was simply asking for trouble. (Gould wasn't the only one against whom eavesdropping charges were made.)

In the early 1890s the "Gould disease" caught up with him. He died of tuberculosis in December 1892. "There was no sorrow by his bier," reported the *World*. "There was decent respect—nothing more." Pulitzer's paper exaggerated on this point as on nearly everything. But decent respect was more than Gould could have claimed twenty years earlier, in the near wake of the Erie war and the gold corner; and if Pulitzer failed to appreciate the finer points of speculation, he was hardly alone.

5

AULD LANG SYNE

Andrew Carnegie

...

ALTHOUGH JAY GOULD WAS AHEAD OF HIS TIME IN TERMS OF SPECU-
lation, he was behind the curve in focusing on gold as the most important of the metals. Even in the hour of the attempted gold corner, the
precious yellow metal was being displaced by a metal more humble, far less
costly, but ultimately more important in propelling the American economy into the modern era. Gold was the metal of the merchant; the metal
of the industrialist was steel.

Steel served as the skeleton of America's growing cities. Steel provided
the highway for the trains that knitted the vast continent together, creating
the largest market in the world. Steel was the stuff from which were fashioned the machines that moved the nation from the epoch of muscle to
the era of steam and electricity. Steel was, in short, the indispensable element of the modernizing process, the very yardstick by which modernization was most often measured: in tons of steel produced per year.

Gould tried to control America's gold, and failed; Andrew Carnegie
tried to control its steel, and succeeded. Carnegie essentially created the
American steel industry, and in doing so arguably did more than anyone
else (except perhaps Cyrus McCormick) to thrust America into the modern age. Yet, curiously, for all the cutting-edge character of his industrial
accomplishments in America, an important part of Carnegie remained
rooted in the preindustrial mind-set and mores of the land of his birth. His

parents took the boy out of Scotland, but they never quite took Scotland out of the boy.

In fact, if Carnegie's father had had his way, they never would have taken Andy out of Scotland. Will Carnegie was a proud weaver of linen, an artisan who had mastered his craft and was making a good living at it. He had every hope of retiring in his home town of Dunfermline and watching his boys take over his looms and shop.

But then the Industrial Revolution came to Scotland. Will Carnegie discovered that he couldn't compete with the steam-driven looms that beat down his prices and stole his customers; almost overnight his livelihood vanished, taking with it his self-respect. Andrew later recollected those "dreadful days" when he saw his father reduced from independent tradesman to humble supplicant. "It was burnt into my heart then that my father, though neither 'abject, mean, nor vile,' as Burns has it, had nevertheless to

Beg a brother of the earth
To give him leave to toil.

Too often those brothers of the earth had no toil to give. Day after day Andy and his mother would wait for Will to come home and report how the search had gone. Day after day it yielded nothing. Finally Will gave up. Six decades later Andrew Carnegie could still recall the defeat in his father's voice when he said, "Andra, I can get nae mair work."

Will Carnegie may have been defeated, but Margaret Carnegie refused to surrender. Andrew's mother had been reading letters from a brother and two sisters who had emigrated to America. "This country is far better for the working-man than the old one," said one letter. Will was skeptical, but Margaret determined that the family's future lay in America if it lay anywhere at all. "I'll make a spoon or spoil a horn," she vowed— meaning, in a land where porridge spoons were fashioned of cow horn, that they would succeed in America or fail trying.

On borrowed money the family managed the Atlantic crossing. The boy who would become the richest man in America reached New York in the same year—1848—that the current holder of that title, John Jacob Astor, died just blocks away. But the Carnegies were merely passing through; greeted at the dock by a family of Dunfermliners, they were helped along to Allegheny, Pennsylvania, a working-class community across the Ohio River from Pittsburgh. There they lodged in some spare rooms of a house owned by Andrew's aunt.

Andy Carnegie turned thirteen that autumn. He had four years of schooling behind him; with poverty staring the family in the face, a decision was made that he must start working at once. A fellow Scotsman who owned a textile factory liked to employ his compatriots; he hired Andy to tend the bobbins on the power looms. The hours were long—from dark to dark that winter—and the task tedious. The pay was $1.20 per week. "I have made millions since," Carnegie wrote afterward, "but none of those millions gave me such happiness as my first week's earnings. I was now a helper of the family, a breadwinner."

He soon found a better job, or at least one that paid better. Another Dunfermline refugee owned a factory that fabricated bobbins; for two dollars a week Andy would dip the new bobbins in an oil bath and keep the boiler properly fired. The smell of the oil nauseated him and the responsibility of manning the boiler gave him nightmares that he would blow up the factory. Yet he stuck with it, although even as he did he calculated his escape. His thrifty boss made do without a clerk, but because his penmanship was poor he needed help with his statements and account books. He asked Andy what sort of hand he had; the boy's script proved satisfactory, and on occasion the bobbin-bather became amanuensis. Having got one foot in the office door, Andy soon nudged it wider. With three friends he began trekking across the river to a night school in Pittsburgh that taught double-entry bookkeeping.

Andy's obvious energy impressed those who knew him; his uncle referred him to the manager of a Pittsburgh telegraph company who needed a messenger. Andy showed up in his only suit and announced that he was ready to start at once; the telegraph man told him he could. Andy didn't require long to learn that a young man on the make couldn't have found a better employer than a telegraph company. On his routes he regularly came into contact with Pittsburgh's leading businessmen, whom he impressed by memorizing their names and faces so he could greet them on the street when they passed by. Mornings he taught himself Morse code; soon he was filling in when the regular keymen failed to come in. Before many weeks elapsed he had advanced to full-time telegrapher, a position he improved still more by becoming one of the first telegraphers in the country to learn to read the incoming messages by ear (rather than translating them letter by letter). His new post paid four dollars per week; more important, it afforded him access to all kinds of valuable information. Soon he knew as much about Pittsburgh's business affairs as anyone in the city.

His expertise and energy showed, and he was lured away by one of his best customers. Thomas Scott, the Pittsburgh-based superintendent of the Pennsylania Railroad's western division, offered him a job as his personal telegrapher and assistant. The Penn was one of the two or three most powerful railroads in America in 1853; Tom Scott was its rising star. He brought the seventeen-year-old Andy Carnegie aboard at a salary of thirty-five dollars per month.

For twelve years Carnegie was a Penn man; more specifically he was Tom Scott's man. Under Scott, Carnegie learned the art and science of railroading, including the absolutely essential task of keeping track of costs. At a time when most company owners still operated by the rules of thumb that had sufficed for the face-to-face and comparatively infrequent transactions of the preindustrial era, the big railroads had to invent procedures for collecting fares from the millions of customers the front offices would never see, for ensuring that those fares found their way from conductors to comptrollers, for dispatching trains to meet the customers, for keeping the trains running over hundreds of miles of track, for supervising the work of thousands of employees scattered across dozens of counties and sometimes several states.

Carnegie thrived on the lessons; the more he learned the more he wanted to know—and the more he wanted to act on what he had learned. One morning he arrived at the office to discover that a derailment had tied up traffic all along the line. Scott was late that day, but Carnegie, having transmitted his boss's orders in similar circumstances, was almost certain what needed to be done. "Death or Westminster," he told himself. "I knew it was dismissal, disgrace, perhaps criminal punishment for me if I erred. On the other hand, I could bring in the wearied freight-train men who had lain out all night. I could set everything in motion. I knew I could." So he did. Forging Scott's signature, he sent out order after order; the wreck was circumvented and the trains resumed rolling.

Scott was stunned when he discovered what his assistant had done. "He looked in my face for a second. I scarcely dared look in his. I did not know what was going to happen. He did not say one word." But he let Carnegie's orders stand, and he bragged to his colleagues about the dash of his assistant. "Do you know what that little white-haired Scotch devil of mine did?" he asked one associate, who confessed that he did not. "I'm blamed if he didn't run every train on the division in my name without the slightest authority." "Did he do it right?" the associate inquired. "Oh, yes, all right," Scott said. Word of Carnegie's exploit quickly circulated around the company. Shortly after, J. Edgar Thomson, the president of the Penn, dropped by to see the wunderkind. "So you are Scott's Andy," he said, satisfying his curiosity.

When Scott was promoted to general superintendent in 1855 and moved to Altoona, he took Carnegie with him; when he was named vice-president in 1859 Carnegie assumed Scott's old post in Pittsburgh as superintendent of the Penn's western division. Carnegie remained in Pittsburgh through the end of the Civil War, avoiding the draft by the accepted expedient of hiring a substitute.

Meanwhile he was becoming a capitalist in his own right. In 1856 Scott had guided his protégé to a likely investment opportunity: ten shares of stock in Adams Express Company, a privately traded, highly profitable firm. A death had put the shares into play; the current owner was pressed for cash and would sell for $600. Scott offered to lend Carnegie the money. Carnegie accepted the offer and discovered the joys of dividends. "Eureka!" he cried. "Here's the goose that lays the golden eggs."

With further help from Scott, Carnegie's goose kept laying. In 1858 Scott and Edgar Thomson entered into a partnership with Theodore Woodruff, a maker of railroad sleeping cars. The understanding was that Woodruff would provide the sleeping cars and Scott and Thomson the principal customer: the Penn. In later days such a transparent conflict of interest would not have been tolerated by the board of directors of the railroad; even in 1858 it caused Scott and Thomson sufficient concern that they disguised their role in the new partnership by placing their shares in Carnegie's name. Presumably if the Penn board took issue with the arrangement they would blame Carnegie. For his exposure Carnegie received the right to purchase one-eighth of the new company. He borrowed $217.50 to pay the first monthly installment on his portion; by the time the second installment fell due he was receiving dividends that covered that installment and all subsequent ones. Within two years his shares were yielding nearly $5,000 per annum—an amount three times his salary from the Penn. "Blessed be the man who invented sleep," Carnegie commented.

The Woodruff Sleeping Car Company proved the foundation of Carnegie's fortune. In 1861 he applied his proceeds to a new industry that was springing—or spewing—up in western Pennsylvania: oil. Two years earlier Edwin Drake had drilled the first deliberately successful oil well; now a fever for crude gripped half the state. One of Pittsburgh's leading iron men, William Coleman, a personal and professional friend of Carnegie (and later a relative by marriage), invited him to join in an oil venture. Carnegie was flattered and intrigued; he arranged to visit the oil region.

He had never seen anything like it. Some of the roughest men he had ever encountered were living in the rudest accommodations imaginable; everything—men, shanties, earth, vegetation, streams—was coated with oil that varied in thickness from a sheen to a lather to a blanket. But what most impressed Carnegie was the good humor that prevailed. "Everybody was in high glee; fortunes were supposedly within reach; everything was booming." The forest of derricks sported flags bearing the hopes and determination of their crews. One crew's motto was "Hell or China."

The visit convinced Carnegie the oil boom was real, and he joined Coleman in the Columbia Oil Company, which purchased one of the principal oil properties. Carnegie devoted $11,000 of the dividends from his sleeping-car shares to the oil business; in the first year alone this investment returned nearly $18,000.

The new venture wasn't without problems. All the gushers caused the price of oil to plummet from $5 a barrel to 10 cents. Yet even amid the gooey glut Carnegie and Coleman anticipated a coming shortage when the wells petered out, as they surely must. Aiming to capitalize on the rise in prices when the crunch hit, the partners dug a large reservoir to store their oil. They intended to fill this with 100,000 barrels of crude; at $10 a barrel their reservoir would be worth a tidy million.

Things didn't work out this way. Oil seeped steadily through the unlined bottom of the reservoir, causing their bonanza to shrink before their eyes. More important, the wells in the area just kept producing. The price improved but to nothing like ten dollars; Carnegie and Coleman's dreams of an oil corner evaporated.

Even so, Carnegie never made a better investment than in Columbia oil. Concentrating now on production rather than speculation, Columbia Oil became the most efficient producer in the area, and Carnegie became a wealthy man. A friend visited his office in 1863 and asked how he was doing. "Oh, Tom, I'm rich! I'm rich!" he replied. During the Civil War the federal government imposed an income tax; Carnegie's tax return for 1863 listed an income of nearly $48,000. The largest single portion—some $17,000—came from Columbia Oil. By contrast his salary with the Pennsylvania Railroad brought him but $2,400.

It didn't require much calculation for Carnegie to decide that he ought to concentrate his energies where his investments were, and in early 1865 he resigned from the railroad. "Thenceforth I never worked for a salary," he explained. "A man must necessarily occupy a narrow field who is at the beck and call of others. Even if he becomes president of a great corporation he is hardly his own master, unless he holds control of the stock. The ablest presidents are hampered by boards of directors and shareholders, who can know but little of the business."

Although he no longer worked for the railroad, Carnegie saw no reason why railroads ought not to work for *him*. For several years he sold railroad bonds to investors in America and Europe; he also orchestrated a merger of the Woodruff company with that of sleeping-car rival George Pullman. More portentous, Carnegie entered the field of railroad construction. For years the iron horses had suffered from the circumstance that the bridges they galloped across were made of wood and hence frequently caught fire from the sparks the horses belched. One day in 1856 Carnegie visited a site where a wooden bridge had burned, and saw an iron replacement arising amid the ashes. The image stuck in his head and gradually came to appear a vision of the future. In 1862 he organized a company to build iron bridges for the Penn. Shortly after he left the railroad in 1865 the bridge company was reorganized and recapitalized as the Keystone Bridge Company.

Carnegie's timing couldn't have been better. The end of the Civil War witnessed a boom in American railroad construction as war-worn tracks were refurbished and new tracks were flung across the continent. Keystone's iron bridges spanned small streams and large; the company's landmark accomplishment was the construction of the Eads Bridge at St. Louis, begun in 1868 and completed six years later. On the strength of this feat Keystone subsequently won the contract for the superstructure of another signature project of the time, the Brooklyn Bridge.

To keep Keystone in building materials Carnegie became an iron maker. In 1864 he helped organize the Cyclops Iron Works; the following year this was folded into the Union Iron Works. From bridge parts to rails was a logical step; equally logical but technologically more difficult was the transition from iron to steel. Each year locomotives got bigger and heavier, and each year traffic increased; as a result the iron rails that had supported trains during railroading's early years failed at a dismaying and increasing rate. On some stretches of line iron rails had to be replaced every six weeks. Steel withstood the pounding far better, but was unfeasibly expensive for widespread use.

Two developments changed the situation. In 1856 an English steel maker named Henry Bessemer discovered a technique for blowing compressed air through molten iron, drastically lowering the production cost of steel. But the technique initially worked well only with iron ore that was low in phosphorus. The second development, the opening of iron fields in

Michigan where the ore was nearly phosphorus-free, made possible the application of the Bessemer process on a wide scale.

Carnegie experimented with the Bessemer process during the late 1860s, but only after an 1872 visit to Bessemer's home plant in Derby, England, did he decide to focus on making steel by the new approach. For fifteen years he had been a fairly typical entrepreneur for his era, taking opportunities as they came, investing wherever the returns appeared likely to exceed the costs. Yet though he had prospered beyond the dreams of that penniless immigrant lad of 1848, he discovered that he didn't want to be merely a typical entrepreneur. "Whatever I engage in I must push inordinately," he commented in a moment of reflection; and he wanted to feel that he was pushing toward a truly worthy goal. He was well on his way to making a fortune; now he wanted to make a mark.

So he decided to specialize. He adapted an adage to his situation: "Put all your eggs in one basket and then watch that basket." In his autobiography he elaborated:

> I believe the true road to preeminent success in any line is to make yourself master in that line. I have no faith in the policy of scattering one's resources, and in my experience I have rarely if ever met a man who achieved preeminence in money-making—certainly never one in manufacturing—who was interested in many concerns. The men who have succeeded are men who have chosen one line and stuck to it. . . . My advice to young men would be not only to concentrate their whole time and attention on the one business in life in which they engage, but to put every dollar of their capital into it.

Looking back on his own career Carnegie explained, "As for myself my decision was taken early. I would concentrate upon the manufacture of iron and steel and be master in that."

The mastery began in earnest with the construction of the Edgar Thomson Steel Works of the newly organized Carnegie, McCandless & Company. Thomson was Carnegie's former patron at the Penn and now a partner in steel; David McCandless was an old friend of the family, a pillar of the Pittsburgh business community and therefore a magnet for the capital Carnegie needed to finance his state-of-the-art steel-rail rolling mill. The mill was situated on Braddock's Field south of Pittsburgh, where British forces under that general had met the defeat that started the French and Indian War. The appeal of the location, however, was not the bullets and bayonets the excavators unearthed but the comparative cheapness of the land and its accessibility via the Monongahela River and two railroads.

(Despite his fond memories of the Penn, Carnegie wasn't going to leave himself at that line's mercy.)

The financial panic of 1873 nearly undid the new project. Several investors had trouble making payments; Carnegie's erstwhile sponsor and current partner, Tom Scott, got in so deep on another project that he had to ask Carnegie to throw him a rope. Carnegie refused. The decision, he confessed, was "one of the most trying moments of my whole life," but he wasn't going to let personal considerations endanger the basket that now held all his best eggs. In the end the panic proved something of a blessing for Carnegie in that it reduced his construction costs and, by forcing several of his partners out, left him more firmly in control of the company.

From the day the Thomson Works opened in 1875 two principles inspired Carnegie's approach to the steel business. The first was to watch costs before everything else; the second was to set prices wherever necessary to keep his mills running at full capacity. His years on the railroad served him well in controlling costs, giving him a decided edge over the rest of the industry, as he soon discovered.

> I was greatly surprised to find that the cost of each of the various processes was unknown. Inquiries made of the leading manufacturers of Pittsburgh proved this. It was a lump business, and until stock was taken and the books balanced at the end of the year, the manufacturers were in total ignorance of the results. I heard of men who thought their business at the end of the year would show a loss and had found a profit, and vice versa.

Carnegie played his informational advantage for all it was worth— and more. On one occasion he confronted a group of rivals who wanted him to accept the smallest share in a market-rigging pool. He indignantly refused, declaring that since he could roll rails at nine dollars a ton, he would undersell them all unless they allotted him the *largest* share instead of the smallest. The poolers gave way—simply confirming his conviction that they didn't have any idea what it cost to roll a ton of rails; his costs at that point were actually fifty dollars a ton.

Yet he strove constantly to bring them down. Efficiency became an obsession with Carnegie. He adapted accounting methods from the Penn to monitor every item his mills used. "There goes that damned bookkeeper," grumbled one of his foremen. "If I use a dozen more bricks than I did last month, he knows it and comes round to ask why." Carnegie found ways to use what other companies tossed out as scrap. He hired a full-time chemist who overturned received notions about ore quality and saved millions of dollars in purchasing. Appalled at the high cost of fire insurance, Carnegie ordered his wooden buildings replaced with iron and cancelled his policies. He was always on the lookout for the latest improvements in production technology, which he implemented at once almost without regard to current cost. In one case he ordered his lieutenants to tear out a three-month-old rolling mill when he found something more efficient. Encountering a British steel man who boasted that his company maintained its equipment so well that it was still using facilities that were twenty years old, Carnegie retorted that that was precisely what was wrong with Britain's industry. "It is because you keep this used-up machinery that the United States is making you a back number."

In his instructions to his subordinates Carnegie made his philosophy succinct and explicit.

> Show me your cost sheets. It is more interesting to know how well and how cheaply you have done this thing than how much money you have made, because the one is a temporary result, due possibly to special conditions of trade, but the other means a permanency that will go on with the works as long as they last.

Carnegie's success in controlling costs was what enabled him to follow his second rule, about setting prices to where his mills would run full. And in a virtuous circle, volume was what allowed him to keep costs down in an industry in which fixed costs were a large portion of the total. "Cheapness is in proportion to the scale of production," he said. "To make ten tons of steel a day would cost many times as much per ton as to make one hundred tons."

Carnegie was so confident of his cost structure and so convinced of the need to keep the mills operating at full capacity that he was willing in a pinch to let his competitors set his prices for him. He once described a transaction to a Senate committee:

> The Union Pacific had advertised for 70,000 tons of rails, the biggest order that had been given. It was to be decided at Omaha, and all my competitors, all these agents of corporations were out at Omaha, and those bids were to be opened. I walked over to Sidney Dillon [the president of the Union Pacific]. I was able to do the Union Pacific a favor once and I did it. I said, "Mr. Dillon, I want you to do this for me: your people are out there bidding on 70,000 tons of rails. I ask you to give me those rails, and I promise to take the lowest price that is bid."

Dillon agreed. He got his rails at the lowest cost; Carnegie got a big order at a price where he could still make a profit.

Carnegie's obsessive cost regimen and his insistence on running flat out soon made his company the most efficient and highest-volume producer in the country. But he refused to be satisfied. His engineers devised methods to eliminate entire stages of the production process, routing molten iron from the blast furnace directly to the Bessemer converter and thereby saving the time and expense of remelting pig iron. Ingots were poured on moving flatcars, clearing the way for more ingots to be poured while the first batch was cooling elsewhere.

To trim costs even further, Carnegie integrated his operations both vertically and horizontally. He bought coke works to guarantee his carbon supply and iron mines to secure his ore. He acquired railroads and shipping lines to ensure the steady flow of raw materials to his mills and finished products to his customers. When the owners of a state-of-the-art steel plant at Homestead, just downstream from the Edgar Thomson Works, tripped up financially, Carnegie caught their fall and won control of their plant.

These new acquisitions brought unexpected assets and liabilities. In purchasing his largest batch of coke ovens Carnegie entered into partnership with Henry Frick, a manager as gifted as Carnegie in certain respects, as driven and as intent on becoming rich. In winning control of the Homestead works Carnegie inherited a skilled labor force but also a long-standing dispute between management and representatives of the Amalgamated Association of Iron and Steel Workers.

The combination of Frick and the Amalgamated proved explosive. Carnegie, whose father had been an outspoken advocate of working men threatened by the industrial system, and who could still remember being hoisted on his father's shoulder while Will addressed reformist rallies in Dunfermline, had long prided himself on his enlightened relationship with his employees. "My experience has been that trades-unions upon the whole are beneficial both to labor and capital," he wrote in a widely noticed 1886 essay. In another article he adopted a position even more at odds with many of his fellow industrialists—a position closer to the mind-set of preindustrial Scotland than of industrial America. In this article he decried the use of strikebreakers except in railroads and a few other industries invested with a direct public interest; as he explained: "To expect that one dependent upon his daily wage for the necessaries of life will stand peaceably and see a new man employed in his stead is to expect much. . . .

There is an unwritten law among the best workmen: 'Thou shalt not take thy neighbor's job.'"

Henry Frick had no such scruples, and after Carnegie appointed him manager of the Homestead works he determined to break the Amalgamated union, through the use of strikebreakers if necessary. Carnegie was torn between his professions of support for the rights of working men and his ongoing obsession with costs. The latter won out, although he tried to dodge responsibility by absenting himself in Scotland, his regular vacation spot, as the collision between Frick and the union approached. That collision produced a lockout of the Homestead workers in the summer of 1892 and a bloody battle between the workers and Pinkerton private security agents hired by Frick to facilitate the employment of strikebreakers. Carnegie's critics taunted:

Where was Andy, the good little boss, on this dark day?
Why, he was over in Scotland and far away.

Carnegie never forgot the taunts, not least because he recognized the truth in them. The Homestead riot proved to be a turning point in his career—indeed, in his life. Many years before, on the occasion of his thirty-third birthday, he had promised himself to get out of business before it consumed him.

Thirty-three and an income of $50,000 per annum! By this time two years I can so arrange all my business as to secure at least $50,000 per annum. Beyond this never earn—make no effort to increase fortune, but spend the surplus each year for benevolent purposes. Cast aside business forever, except for others. . . . The amassing of wealth is one of the worst species of idolatry—no idol more debasing than the worship of money. . . . To continue much longer overwhelmed by business cares and with most of my thoughts wholly upon the way to make more money in the shortest time, must degrade me beyond hope of permanent recovery.

Needless to say, Carnegie had not cast aside business; instead he had gone on to amass far more wealth. By 1890 he was worth perhaps $30 million and had an income of some $2 million per year.

But the conscience he had developed during his Scottish childhood never ceased nagging him. And even while he amassed more money he developed a philosophy for putting that money to work for others. The man of wealth, he contended, ought "to set an example of modest, unostentatious living, shunning display or extravagance; to provide moderately for the legitimate wants of those dependent upon him; and, after doing so, to consider all surplus revenues which come to him simply as trust funds which he is called upon to administer." These trust funds ought to endow universities, libraries, hospitals, parks, public meeting halls, churches and the like. Carnegie's "gospel of wealth" was summarized most famously, if negatively, in his assessment of the millionaire who took his money to his grave: "The man who dies thus rich, dies disgraced."

Carnegie penned these words in 1889, and the disgrace he felt three years later at the Homestead debacle spurred him to spend less time making money and more on giving it away. Yet as at thirty-three, events conspired to distract him. The panic of 1893 triggered the worst depression in American history to that time; as he had in the 1870s Carnegie took the challenge as an opportunity. He consolidated his holdings and modernized his facilities; while his costs fell his profits soared: from $5 million in 1895 to $40 million in 1900.

At the top of his industry and sixty-five years old, Carnegie pondered retirement. A challenge by some rivals linked to J. P. Morgan briefly reenergized his competitive instincts; he directed a counterattack into territory he traditionally had left alone. "Prompt action essential," he cabled. "Crisis has arrived. Only one policy open: start at once hoop, rod, wire, nail mills." After further technical instructions he declared confidently, "Have no fear as to the result; victory certain."

Carnegie's surprisingly vigorous response caused the Morgan group to rethink their strategy. A merger, they decided, would make more sense than a steel war. Morgan sounded out Carnegie's right-hand man, Charles Schwab. Schwab was happy enough to consider a merger, but he wasn't sure his boss was. Some days Carnegie seemed more than ready to retire; other days he acted as feisty as ever. But Morgan and Schwab had an ally in the heart of the Carnegie camp: Carnegie's wife, who thought her husband had had quite enough of the rigors of the corporate world. Play golf with him, she advised Schwab—and lose. Then bring up the idea of a merger.

Schwab did precisely that, and the scenario unfolded as Louise Carnegie anticipated. Carnegie snatched a scrap of paper lying nearby and scribbled his price. It was breathtaking by the standards of the day: $480 million. Take this to Morgan, Carnegie told Schwab.

Morgan didn't hesitate. He glanced at the informal document Schwab carried and without a second thought said, "I accept."

He would have paid more, as he admitted to Carnegie a few years later. Carnegie spoke of the transaction and remarked, "I made one mistake, Pierpont, when I sold out to you."

"What was that?" inquired Morgan.

"I should have asked you for a hundred million more than I did."

"You would have got it if you had."

What Carnegie did get was wealth almost enough to make him, in Morgan's deal-closing exaggeration, "the richest man in the world." From Morgan this was a compliment; to Carnegie it was a reminder to redouble his philanthropic efforts lest he die so rich. During the eighteen years left to him he lived up to his pledge; when his will was opened in 1919 it showed that he had donated $350 million to various causes and institutions ranging from local libraries to world peace. The Carnegie Foundation would carry on his good work long after his death.

But he left another legacy, more lasting in its own way. Summarizing his life's work in language his father and Will's fellow workers in Dunfermline would have appreciated, Carnegie once wrote:

Two pounds of iron-stone purchased on
the shores of Lake Superior and
transported to Pittsburgh;

Two pounds of coal mined in Connellsville
and manufactured into coke and
brought to Pittsburgh;

One-half pound of limestone mined
east of the Alleghenies and
brought to Pittsburgh;

A little manganese ore
mined in Virginia and
brought to Pittsburgh.

And these four and one half pounds of material
manufactured into one pound of solid steel
and sold for one cent.

That's all that need be said
about the steel business.

6

BY JUPITER

J. Pierpont Morgan

. . .

MACHIAVELLI NOTORIOUSLY COUNSELED HIS PRINCE TO MAKE men fear him if he intended to retain power; love, that other primary motivator of human action, was altogether too unreliable. J. P. Morgan knew Machiavelli's work, perhaps from an early edition acquired on one of his visits to Italy. However he got the advice, it seemed to suit his temperament and explain his actions. At the apex of his career few men in America were so widely feared as the one they called Jupiter Morgan, and none wielded more power.

The very visage of the man struck terror into the hearts of many who knew him. He had the ugliest nose in New York: a "huge, more or less deformed, sick, bulbous mass in the center of his face," according to photographer Edward Steichen, who made a profession of studying faces. The deformity of Morgan's nose was the result of a severe case of acne rosacea, which left the nose chronically inflamed. Children cried when they saw Morgan in the street; adults attempted not to look but couldn't help themselves.

Nor was his nose even his most distinctive feature. His dark eyes blazed from beneath his brow with an intensity that took the breath from those who had the temerity to meet his glance. Steichen said that looking at Morgan put him in mind of standing on a railroad track at night, in the full glare of the headlight of an express train hurtling down on him. He had to blink or turn away lest the train smash and obliterate him.

Morgan obliterated many rivals during his thirty-year domination of American finance. He also scared the daylights out of his associates. "His partners did not go near him unless he sent for them, and then they looked alarmed and darted in like office boys," reported Lincoln Steffens, the top investigative journalist of his day. Morgan worked his partners to death, in some cases literally. "The House of Morgan was always known as a part-ner-killer," said an observer who watched the bodies mount. The survivors thought it worth the effort, though. One who knew from personal experi-ence declared, "He made them all wealthy beyond their dreams."

Morgan's was no rags-to-riches story, but one of riches to more riches. He was born in Hartford, Connecticut, in 1837, the year of the most har-rowing financial panic of the first century of America's national existence. But like John Jacob Astor, Morgan's grandfather bought low in the wake of the crash, confident that bad times in a booming economy like America's couldn't last. When the economy did indeed revive, the Morgans got rich. The lesson wasn't lost on the grandson, who later asserted, "The man who is a bear on the future of the United States will always go broke."

Morgan money helped make Hartford the insurance capital of Amer-ica; it also allowed Morgan's father, J. S. Morgan, to diversify into com-modities brokering. When this business took off, J. S. decided that logistics required relocating the family to Boston. Pierpont Morgan would engage in some highly controversial business ventures in the course of his career; perhaps he acquired the habit from his father, who refused to let the abolitionist sentiments of his Boston neighbors prevent him from devel-oping a lively transatlantic trade in slave-produced southern cotton. Bro-kering being a business that fattens or starves on credit, J. S. Morgan sought to guarantee his credit lines by forming a partnership with the Lon-don banking house of George Peabody. The cotton trade and the related banking business thrived until the outbreak of the Civil War, when Abra-ham Lincoln declared cotton contraband. But the British (with the help of Cyrus McCormick) had fallen into dependence on American grain, which Morgan also sold. By the end of the war he was a powerful and very wealthy man.

It was in this context of business success that Pierpont Morgan grew up. He demonstrated a head for business almost from the cradle. Where other boys played with balls and toy soldiers Pierpont amused himself with his father's account books. He ever after took pride in his acuity with figures, in his ability to scan a ledger sheet and instantly pick out errors.

To some degree Pierpont's fascination with business reflected an uncertain constitution. A series of physical afflictions kept him from the rough-and-tumble games of the other Boston boys. The worst of his maladies was a form of inflammatory rheumatism that prompted his worried father and mother to send him to the Azores for a cure. The rheumatism subsided, to his parents' relief. But to their countervailing dismay, about the time it did the boy showed the first symptoms of the rosacea that had cursed the Morgan family for generations.

The Azores sojourn was the initial installment in an international education of the kind that would gain favor in business circles a century later. When J. S. Morgan moved the family to London to be closer to his capital sources he sent Pierpont to Switzerland to boarding school. After a couple of years among the people who were already becoming the discreet bankers to the world, Pierpont crossed the Alps to Germany for college. He enrolled at the University of Gottingen, which had a reputation for the strength of its mathematics department. The young American more than held his own in that field; one of his professors asked him to stay on after his courses ended to be his assistant. Morgan was flattered but said he had to get to work.

In 1857 he joined the Wall Street house of Duncan, Sherman & Company, the American agents of the Peabody firm of which his father was a partner. Almost at once he demonstrated both an uncanny intuition for what things were worth to different people and the audacity to act on his intuition even in the face of conventional wisdom. On a trading trip to New Orleans to buy cotton he stumbled on a cargo of coffee begging for a buyer. Although he lacked authorization from New York to make the purchase he brazened out a deal; by the time his reprimand arrived from the home office he had sold the boatload of beans for a handsome profit, neutralizing the reprimand and earning himself a nice commission.

As soon as the Civil War broke out Morgan recognized the immense, if risky, opportunities that awaited businessmen of dash and daring. He bade goodbye to his colleagues at Duncan Sherman and struck out on his own. J. Pierpont Morgan & Company, which opened its doors for business in 1862, ascended like one of the rockets that were illuminating the battlefields of the war; in 1864 the twenty-seven-year-old Morgan made more than $50,000.

The wartime windfalls ended with Lee's surrender at Appomattox, but Morgan's success hardly abated. In 1871 he joined forces with the Drexel firm of Philadelphia, creating the financial house of Drexel, Morgan & Company, headquartered at the corner of Wall and Broad streets in New

York. Almost immediately Morgan became recognized as the leading light in one of the most influential financial firms in the country. His income matched his influence: During the 1870s he regularly earned more than half a million dollars per year.

Much of Morgan's income derived from his efforts on behalf of the nation's principal railroads. During the 1870s and 1880s railroads increasingly drove the American economy, both literally and figuratively. The construction of the transcontinental railroad system allowed shippers to send goods swiftly and cheaply across the length and breadth of the country. Heretofore a textile manufacturer in Massachusetts could economically ship his products only within New England; coal mined in Kentucky, having less value per unit of weight, had an even narrower range of economic viability. The extension of the railroads enormously expanded markets for production of all kinds, from raw materials to finished goods. Indeed, the network of rail lines created the largest single market in world history to that time (a market, moreover, that was sheltered from foreign competition by America's high tariffs).

Constructing the transcontinental rail network required creating an intercontinental financial network. Much of the railroad construction took place in partnership with the federal government, which provided rights-of-way, generous quantities of land adjacent to the new roads, building materials, and credits that in some cases approached $50,000 per mile. But private capital played an even greater role. The railroads regularly floated large stock and bond issues; buyers for these typically came from the investor classes of the East Coast, Britain and continental Europe.

No one was more adept at connecting the investors to the railroads than Morgan, to the benefit of those parties and to himself. His name was known and respected on both sides of the Atlantic; his imprimatur on a stock or bond offering could be worth millions to the firm doing the issue. In 1879, when he organized a successful stock offering of $18 million for William Vanderbilt's New York Central Railroad, his commission (which, like most of his commissions, he declined to disclose) constituted a sizable part of his income that year. But Morgan wasn't satisfied to take his cut in cash; he insisted on a seat on the New York Central's board of directors. This post was worth more than the money, for it afforded him both continuing influence with the road and critical inside information regarding the state of the railroad industry as a whole.

Information, transmuted through his intelligence and experience into insight, was Morgan's stock-in-trade. He became a student of every industry with which he did business; before long he usually knew more about that industry than even those who made it their life's work. By 1880 he was the recognized American expert on railroads; between his expertise and his financial power he became the acknowledged arbiter of the affairs of the nation's principal roads.

Repeatedly Morgan was called on—sometimes by himself—to intervene in the ruinous rate and construction wars that regularly wracked the industry. One of the most epic of these pitted the Pennsylvania Railroad against the New York Central. The Central had precipitated the conflict by commencing construction on a line from Pittsburgh to Philadelphia. Steel men such as Andrew Carnegie applauded the prospect of competition to the Pennsylvania on this key route, but the Penn deemed it a declaration of war. The Penn fought back with an invasion of its own: It moved into New York, where it started dynamiting a path that would crack the Central's lucrative monopoly from New York City to Buffalo.

With many other big businessmen of his day Morgan found excessive competition distressing. It entailed duplication of effort, he believed, undermined economies of scale and wasted resources that might be more profitably employed. Nowhere was this truer than in railroads, where construction costs were a very large portion of total costs. A second line from New York harbor to Lake Erie, for example, would require an enormous investment to build and would produce only modest benefits to shippers (not to mention the toll it would exact from the Central's profits). From the standpoint of the economy as a whole it made far more sense for the Central to stick to New York and the Penn to Pennsylvania. (There was another reason for Morgan's disapproval of the Penn's poaching. The route of the Penn's proposed line ran right below his summer home on the Hudson. The blasting was deafening, and the uncouth and often unsupervised immigrant construction crews were a threat to the neighborhood—a matter distinctly disturbing to a family man with small children.)

Morgan determined to put an end to this senseless and destructive warfare. He invited the principals of the Penn to meet with him and fellow Central director Chauncey Depew. George Roberts and Frank Thomson accepted Morgan's invitation and joined him aboard his yacht, the *Corsair*. The four eased into deck chairs and took an unhurried cruise up the Hudson. Roberts and Depew did most of the talking; Thomson and Morgan listened, with Morgan occasionally giving an order to the captain regarding the operation of the vessel.

It didn't take all parties long to agree that the contest they were engaged in would probably be a loser even for the winner. Depew, of the Central, suggested calling the battle off: The Central would halt construction on its Pittsburgh–Philadelphia line if the Penn would put down tools on the road to Buffalo. Roberts didn't reject the proposal out of hand, but it quickly became clear to Morgan and the others, if not to Roberts himself, that his ego had grown entangled in his business. He simply couldn't stand the thought of losing this fight to Morgan.

The Penn president remained obdurate while the *Corsair* steamed as far north as West Point, where it turned around; he refused to yield while the craft followed the current past the entire length of Manhattan and clear to Sandy Hook. He was still holding out as evening fell and the *Corsair* approached its berth at Jersey City.

Perhaps he was persuaded by some final appeals to his pecuniary self-interest by Morgan and Depew; perhaps he felt some slight obligation to his host for what otherwise was a pleasant afternoon; perhaps he had been intending to cooperate all along but merely wanted to see Morgan sweat. For whatever reason, Roberts announced at the last moment that he would consent to a truce. "I will agree to your plan and do my part," he promised as he walked down the gangplank.

The settlement of the Penn-Central contest—the "Corsair Compact," it was called—confirmed Morgan's reputation as an industrial peacemaker and led to similar initiatives. In December 1888 and January 1889 he hosted a summit conference of the leading officials of the major American railroads. In 1887 Congress had passed the Interstate Commerce Act, which prohibited the most blatant forms of price-fixing and related collusion among railroads. The law fell short of the desires of many shippers, but the owners of the lines deemed it an unwarranted and ill-conceived encroachment on the prerogatives of capital. Morgan agreed and summoned the group of railroad men to his brownstone on Murray Hill, on the east side of Madison Avenue at Thirty-sixth, to consider a collective rejoinder. (Jay Gould, hacking his way toward a tubercular death, represented the Missouri Pacific.)

"The purpose of this meeting is to cause the members of this association to no longer take the law into their own hands when they suspect they have been wronged, as has been too much the custom heretofore, " Morgan explained. "This is not elsewhere customary in civilized communities, and no good reason exists why such a practice should continue among railroads."

Morgan's guests heard him out; they ate his food, drank his liquor and smoked his cigars. But unfortunately for his peacemaking purposes, they discovered that they had little in common besides an antipathy to government regulation. They had been bitter rivals too long to suddenly make up and join hands, even against Washington. Some congratulated Morgan for his efforts on behalf of railroad unity; others berated him for arranging financing for upstart enterprises that were challenging the hegemony of the established lines. Morgan did his best to facilitate a common front. He offered to desist from financing firms that challenged the status quo and to try to persuade his fellow bankers to follow his example. In exchange the railroads would have to agree to suspend their cutthroat competition.

Morgan succeeded in winning assent to this self-denying promise from the major eastern railroaders, but the westerners resisted. Jay Gould was hardly out Morgan's door before he gathered the westerners at the Hotel Windsor "in order to separate the discussion from the banking interests," as their spokesman said. This individual continued: "We did not swallow whole the arrangement evidently prepared for us."

Even apart from the westerners, Morgan's conference might have done the railroads more harm than good. Despite the host's best efforts at discretion, the press caught wind of the gathering; indeed, the newspapermen besieged the place. It didn't take much imagination for them or their readers to conclude that the aim of the meetings was conspiracy against the interests of shippers and their customers, and of the rail-traveling public—in other words, against the interests of the vast majority of the American people. "The New York bankers triumph," blared the *New York Times*, mistakenly but nonetheless significantly. Indignant defenders of the public weal in the state and national legislatures vowed to redouble their efforts to bring the railroads into line. They also looked harder at Morgan, the instigator of the conspiracy, than ever before.

By the 1890s common people in many parts of the country couldn't speak Morgan's name without blaspheming. Especially in the West and South, where the Populists were making deep inroads with their call for "free silver"—the remonetization of silver at the highly inflationary rate of sixteen ounces of silver to one of gold—Morgan epitomized the "money power" of the Eastern seaboard and especially New York City. Politicians of all parties kept their distance; to be linked in the popular mind to Morgan could be a career-ending disaster.

Consequently, it was with excruciating reluctance that President Grover Cleveland turned to Morgan to deliver the federal government from its gravest fiscal crisis since the Civil War. In 1893 British investors, spooked by political uncertainties in various parts of the world, began pulling their funds out of the American market; the exodus of sterling provoked a panic on Wall Street. Stock prices plunged; banks collapsed; businesses of all sorts foundered. Most ominous from the perspective of the Cleveland administration were the raids on gold that began as the faith in the dollar dwindled. As in the days of Jay Gould's gold ring, the largest supply of gold in the country sat in the vaults of the U.S. treasury, where it served to assuage the fears of money men and others who lay awake nights wondering what supported the country's paper currency. Conventional wisdom indicated that $100 million in gold was a safe floor; as long as the treasury stockpile remained above this mark the government would be reliably liquid. But should the supply dip below $100 million, normally steady dollar-holders might well take fright and dump their greenbacks for the yellow hard stuff.

In January 1895 the treasury's gold supply wavered uncertainly just above $100 million. It would nose up, dip down, then edge up again. Momentarily during the third week of the month the president and his advisers persuaded themselves that the worst was past. But near the end of the month bearish speculators succeeded in driving the gold supply through the $100 million floor on a straight line down. By the morning of January 28, Treasury Secretary John Carlisle could count a mere $58 million on hand. During the course of that Monday almost $4 million more disappeared. On Tuesday $3 million vanished. On Wednesday $4 million.

Cleveland and Carlisle grew frantic. If some device weren't found to stop the hemorrhaging the treasury might bleed to death. And if the government were forced off the gold standard there was no telling what would happen to the economy. The millions already out of work would be joined by millions more; the current social turmoil might easily yield to revolution.

With every hour critical, Cleveland turned to the one man capable of restoring confidence in the dollar and order to the markets. The president sent the assistant secretary of the treasury to meet with Morgan. William Curtis asked Morgan what he thought could be done to rescue the situation.

Morgan replied that the government should make a private contract with a syndicate of investors he would organize; this syndicate would arrange for the immediate sale of $50 million in government bonds, with an option on another $50 million. The contract would be confidential, not to be divulged until the bonds had been sold.

Morgan had a habit of appearing cool and imperturbable in negotiations. He could commit $50 million with less show of concern than most men pledging $50. In his meeting with Curtis he was his calm, unflappable self.

But he felt the danger of the situation as fully as Cleveland and Carlisle did. A dollar meltdown would endanger everything he had worked decades to build. Shortly after his meeting with Curtis he sent a cable to his London office explaining the situation succinctly: "We all have large interests dependent upon maintenance of the sound currency of the United States." Yet every crisis contained an element of opportunity. In the current case: "If this negotiation can be made, it will be most creditable to all parties and pay a good profit."

The Cleveland administration gave no immediate answer to Morgan's proposal. Even at this dire hour the perils of getting too close to Morgan made the president flinch. Meanwhile word leaked of Curtis's visit to Morgan—a visit that under present circumstances could mean only one thing—and within hours Wall Street was sizzling with rumors that Morgan was arranging a bailout of the treasury. The bond and stock markets responded hearteningly to the rumors; the drain on the treasury's gold supply slowed.

For a moment Cleveland thought he could have his cake and eat it: the confidence-building effect of a Morgan bailout without the actual bailout and its attendant political liabilities. Morgan, observing the same phenomena Cleveland saw, judged that the president was deluding himself. After hopes had been raised, if no rescue operation took place the consequences would be worse than if the matter had never been bruited. "The effect of abandonment upon all interests would now be worse than if never begun," he predicted.

Morgan decided to force the issue. He took a train from New York to Washington, where he requested a meeting with Cleveland. At first the president tried to put him off. Daniel Lamont, Cleveland's closest adviser, explained that there was no way Morgan could have a personal interview with the president. Morgan replied that he would wait. "I am going to stay here until I see him," he said.

It didn't take long. Late that night, while Morgan was passing the time at his usual hotel suite with his customary routine of solitaire, a telephone call came from the White House. President Cleveland would be pleased to meet with Mr. Morgan next morning.

Just after breakfast Morgan walked the modest distance to the president's house. He was shown at once to the family's living quarters on the second floor. The atmosphere was frenzied; aides flew in and out with the latest word from the markets of New York and Europe.

Cleveland still hoped to dodge the bullet. He told Morgan he had decided against the financier's suggested syndicate. The treasury would conduct a public sale of bonds.

Morgan, perhaps wondering why Cleveland had summoned him if he truly intended to go the public route, replied candidly. A public offering would fail, he said. The run on gold had recommenced—Morgan's sources were more reliable than Cleveland's, as both men knew—and it would continue until the treasury collapsed or the markets saw undeniable evidence that the government was committed to defending the dollar. A public issue of bonds would take too long. The government would be bankrupt before it got the transfusion it needed.

Besides, Morgan continued, a public issue wouldn't reassure European investors, who were the ones that counted in the present case. Europe had no confidence in public issues, having been burned many times in America and elsewhere. On the other hand, Europe trusted the house of Morgan and the other houses that would join his in the syndicate. Morgan reminded Cleveland of the ameliorative effect the mere rumor of a Morgan rescue had had. When Morgan spoke, the markets listened; when Morgan moved, the markets responded.

As he often did during tense negotiations, Morgan at this point played a card he had heretofore kept hidden. He perceived that he had convinced Cleveland on the economics of his proposal; what the president was still stuck on was the politics. Cleveland worried that any move that could be construed as constitutionally questionable would be precisely so construed by the legions of Morganophobes across the country. He needed a way to finesse the floating of the bonds, in particular a device that would allow him to circumvent Congress, where excoriations of Morgan were a daily occurrence.

The required device was Morgan's trump. From his experience trading bonds and gold during the Civil War he remembered a law passed then and never repealed, which authorized the president to buy coin money and pay for it with bonds. Morgan suggested that the treasury buy gold coin from his syndicate and pay for it with newly issued bonds. Congress need not be involved at all.

Cleveland was intrigued. He called for the statute books. There in section 3700 of the Revised Statutes, precisely where Morgan had indicated, was the provision he described.

Cleveland was more intrigued. But he wasn't ready to yield just yet. "What guarantee have we," he asked, "that if we adopt this plan, gold will not continue to be shipped abroad, and while we are getting it in, it will go out so that we will not reach our goal? Will you guarantee that this will not happen?"

Cleveland was asking a great deal of Morgan. For months investors in North America and Europe had been registering their lack of confidence in the dollar. The U.S. government had done everything in its power to shore up confidence but to no avail. The president was asking Morgan not simply to try to accomplish what the federal government had failed to do but to guarantee that result.

Morgan didn't hesitate. "Yes, sir," he declared. "I will guarantee it during the life of the syndicate, and that means until the contract has been concluded and the goal has been reached."

Morgan's decisiveness wrought a remarkable change in Cleveland. "My doubts disappeared," he explained later. "I found I was in negotiation with a man of large business comprehension and of remarkable knowledge and prescience." Cleveland added that he was most favorably impressed by Morgan's "clear-sighted, far-seeing patriotism."

Events of the next several days confirmed Cleveland's estimate of Morgan's business comprehension even if many observers doubted the financier's patriotism. As soon as the news broke of the Morgan–Cleveland deal, pressure on the dollar diminished. Gold stopped pouring out of the treasury and began flowing back in as investors once more preferred interest-paying bonds to reliable but unremunerative gold.

Morgan received little thanks from the political classes—but the profits he and his syndicate received from the resale of their bonds assuaged whatever hurt their feelings suffered. The government had delivered the bonds to Morgan's group at an interest rate that corresponded to a price of 104.5; the bonds quickly bounced up to 120.

Populist-minded politicians like William Jennings Bryan howled at this blatant profiteering. The Senate convened an investigation into the affair. One questioner, Senator George Vest of Missouri, demanded of Morgan, "What profit did your house make on this transaction?"

Morgan refused to answer. He offered to supply "every detail of the negotiation up to the time that the bonds became my property and were paid for"; this much was legitimately public business. But what happened to the bonds after that were no one's business but his own. "What I did with my own property subsequent to that purchase I decline to state."

Despite persistent efforts by the Senate committee, Morgan kept silent on how much money he had made rescuing the treasury. Estimates ranged from $250,000 to $16 million; reality likely lay among the lower guesses. Whatever his take, Morgan judged it no more than a fair fee for defending the full faith and credit of the government. He believed that no one else could have done what he did, and doubtless he was right. Some time after the fact, Cleveland asked Morgan how he knew he could command the cooperation of the great financial interests of Europe in the rescue. "I simply told them," Morgan replied, "that this was necessary for the maintenance of the public credit and the promotion of industrial peace, and they did it."

Morgan's prestige and power continued to grow after the treasury bailout. Rarely did he have to look for business; business came looking for him. (It didn't always come quickly enough. After Morgan visited Pope Pius X in Rome, the pontiff was heard to say, "What a pity I did not think of asking Mr. Morgan to give us some advice about our finances!") It was a case of business seeking Morgan that threw the financier into his contest with Andrew Carnegie. Several of Carnegie's rivals deputed Chicago lawyer Elbert Gary to approach Morgan for financial support against the steel king. Morgan initially demurred, judging one of the principals in the anti-Carnegie scheme, John Gates, to be a shady and unreliable character ("Bet-a-Million" Gates, he was called). Yet Morgan liked Gary, and he subsequently backed a Gary-orchestrated merger that produced Federal Steel, which then became the second-largest steel company in the country behind Carnegie Steel.

After a moment to catch their breath, Morgan and Gary decided to take on Carnegie Steel. But when Carnegie launched his preemptive counteroffensive Morgan pulled back. He didn't relish a steel war any more than he had relished rail wars; the fact that Carnegie, as part of his counteroffensive, threatened to revive the fight between the Penn and the New York Central raised the really appalling specter of a combined steel and rail war. Yet although Morgan calculated that he might not win a test of industrial strength against Carnegie, the master of industry, he reckoned that he *would* win a test of financial strength. So with the help of Louise Carnegie and Charlie Schwab he bought Carnegie out. The mega-corporation that resulted, United States Steel, was the largest combine in the world, capitalized at $1.4 billion.

The steel deal won Morgan yet more attention as the grand arbiter of American industrial affairs. This proved a mixed blessing. William Jennings Bryan's paper, the *Commoner*, jumped on a casually innocuous remark by Morgan—"America is good enough for me"—to reply:

"Whenever he doesn't like it, he can give it back to us." Humorist Finley Peter Dunne's Irish philosopher Mr. Dooley described (in brogue) Morgan at work:

> Pierpont Morgan calls in wan iv his office boys, th' prisidint iv a national bank, an' says he, "James," he says, "take some change out iv th' damper an' r-run out an' buy Europe f'r me," he says. "I intind to re-organize it an' put it on a paying basis," he says. "Call up the Czar an' th' Pope an' th' Sultan an' th' Impror Willum, an' tell thim we won't need their savices afther nex' week."

Morgan's notoriety sometimes cost him badly. In 1901, in the panicked and bloody aftermath of a fight for control of the Northern Pacific Railroad, he brokered a peace accord by means of the creation of the Northern Securities Corporation, a huge firm that promised to do for the rail industry in the northwestern quadrant of the United States what the steel trust was doing for the steel industry—namely, subordinate competition to stability and profits. Had Morgan not been the moving spirit behind Northern Securities, Theodore Roosevelt might have made an antitrust example of some other combine. But Morgan's reputation was such that the new president, a hunter who always went after the biggest game available, couldn't resist. Morgan had heard reports from friends like Marcus Hanna, the businessman–politician and manager of the late President McKinley, that Roosevelt was mildly unhinged about business; the reports now appeared to be true.

As he had done with Grover Cleveland, Morgan determined to take matters into his own hands by visiting the president. Morgan came straight to the point. "If we have done anything wrong," he declared, "send your man to see my man, and they will fix it up." Roosevelt's appeal to the courts, Morgan indicated, was unsettling and unnecessary.

"We don't want to fix it up," Roosevelt rejoined. "We want to stop it."

Morgan didn't like the president's tone. "Are you going to attack my other interests, the steel corporation and the others?"

"Certainly not," Roosevelt replied. "Unless we find they have done something we regard as wrong."

Morgan realized he would be wasting his breath on the Rough Rider. Roosevelt had decided that big businessmen like Morgan needed to be reminded that America was still a democracy and that the trusts must abide by the law just like everyone else. The suit against Northern Securities went forward; the Supreme Court ultimately sided with Roosevelt against Morgan.

The outcome of the Northern Securities case delighted Roosevelt, who continued to rail against the "criminal rich" and the "malefactors of great wealth." Morgan, naturally, was less pleased, for what Roosevelt celebrated—the reaffirmation of the supremacy of politics over business—seemed to Morgan a recipe for disaster, if not at once, then in time. And with people like Roosevelt in office that time would be all too soon.

For a moment in 1907 the time appeared nigh. Another panic gripped Wall Street, conjuring up the grim specter of a depression like that of the previous decade. Ruin was ultimately averted—but only after a temporarily chastened Roosevelt did what Cleveland had done in the 1890s: turn to Morgan for relief. Another Morgan-led syndicate arranged an infusion of liquidity, and stability returned. As before, Morgan had to take his profits in cash; popular credit was as wanting as it had been after the Cleveland bailout.

Though scarcely a surprise, this reaction prompted Morgan—now seventy and slowing down—to devote less energy to business and more to such hobbies as art collecting. Yet if his personal attachment to business weakened, his convictions regarding business remained as strong as ever. Of these a primary one was that his business was nobody's but his own. Called before the congressional Pujo Committee in 1912 to testify regarding recent irregularities on Wall Street, he vowed, "I'll go to jail rather than discuss my private affairs." Through two days of interrogation he rebuffed every question that crossed what he saw as the line between public affairs and private. But the experience reinforced his feeling that the game was no longer worth the candle, at least for one of his years. He left America for a long European trip; he died in Rome in 1913 at the age of seventy-six.

Even Morgan's most impassioned critics admitted that he was a master of the money game. But they often misjudged what his mastery consisted of. He could have told them had they asked—and on one occasion he did even though they didn't. The Pujo Committee wanted to know how it was that Morgan wielded such financial power. By its own investigations the committee staff discerned that American capitalism had recently entered a third phase. The merchant capitalism of the colonial and early national periods had long since given way to the industrial capitalism of the Civil War era and after; industrial capitalism had lately yielded to financial capitalism. So large had American enterprise become that it was the rare firm that could underwrite growth from within; the rest had to look to the financial markets for funding. This had been true of railroads from the start; by the beginning of the twentieth century it was true of nearly every industry. Morgan was a brilliant student of economic organization, having taken the mind that had impressed his mathematics professors at Gottingen and applied its powers of analysis to the relations among the various factors of production in one industry after another. Like any good student he did his homework, until he knew railroads as well as William Vanderbilt, steel as well as Andrew Carnegie and government finance better than Grover Cleveland.

So much any student of contemporary American business could discover. But there was something else—something Morgan deemed absolutely essential to success. This was his ability to judge personal character. At a time when economic relations were growing ever more impersonal, he insisted on knowing those he did business with. Carefully and shrewdly he sized up their skills; even more carefully and shrewdly he sized up their character. Certain failings he could forgive. Charlie Schwab had a weakness for gaming houses; after one wild session at Monte Carlo, Schwab jokingly apologized to his comrade-in-steel: "At least I didn't do it behind closed doors." Morgan countered, "That's what closed doors are for." But otherwise Morgan ignored the lapse.

In matters of business character, however, he brooked no compromise. As much as those who saw him shuddered at his misshapen nose, he shuddered at what he deemed the misshapen character of the Jay Goulds and Daniel Drews of the Gilded Age. He had rejected Elbert Gary's proposal to join with John Gates, for the simple reason that he distrusted Gates. Morgan explained this aspect of his business philosophy to the Pujo Committee. "The first thing is character," he volunteered, regarding what he looked for in a prospective partner. "Before money or property?" his surprised inquisitor asked. "Before money or anything else," Morgan answered. "A man I do not trust could not get money from me on all the bonds in Christendom." By contrast, upright character had opened doors for individuals of negligible collateral. "I have known a man come into my office and I have given him a check for a million dollars and I knew that he had not a cent in the world." Were there many such men?, his interrogator queried. "A good many," Morgan replied.

This exchange elicited skepticism among those who would believe only the worst of one as wealthy and powerful as Morgan. But he was entirely sincere—and he had the bottom line to confirm the wisdom of his approach. Morgan didn't pretend that philanthropy moved him an inch in making such unsecured loans; he expected to profit on all his transactions. He did profit on the great majority of them.

But what those he trusted got in exchange for his trust was something they couldn't get elsewhere: financial resources sufficient for any worthy purpose, and the seal of approval that the house of Morgan, alone among American financial firms and nearly alone among financial firms of the world, could furnish. Especially in an impersonal age, this blessing could be critical to business success. Morgan's services never came cheap, but those who hired them got value for their money.

7

THE MONOPOLY ESTHETIC

John D. Rockefeller

. . .

WHEN ADAM SMITH DESCRIBED THE "INVISIBLE HAND" OF THE marketplace, he was speaking figuratively. The author of *The Wealth of Nations* contended that the uncoordinated actions of myriad producers and consumers yielded an orderly and efficient result that gave the appearance of having been accomplished by some unseen power. John D. Rockefeller believed in invisible hands, too, but he had in mind something more specific—something specifically supernatural. Asked how he had become so rich, Rockefeller replied, "God gave me my money."

Smith and Rockefeller disagreed on something else. For Smith competition was the engine of capitalist efficiency, the spur to invention by producers and the guarantor of fair prices to consumers. Smith saw no reason to credit capitalists with higher motives than informed the actions of other people, and he was constantly concerned that businessmen would seek means to subvert the competitive mechanisms that kept their shoulders to the wheel. "People of the same trade seldom meet together," he warned, "even for merriment and diversion, but the conversation ends in a conspiracy against the public, or in some contrivance to raise prices."

Smith might have been speaking of J. P. Morgan and his railroad summits; even more, he might have been speaking of Rockefeller. Rockefeller had no use for competition. "The day of individual competition in large affairs is past and gone," he declared. "You might just as well argue that we should go back to hand labour and throw away our efficient machines."

Extending the analogy, Rockefeller likened business combinations to steam power. Certainly combinations might abuse their influence. "But this fact is no more of an argument against combinations than the fact that steam may explode is an argument against steam. Steam is necessary and can be made comparatively safe. Combination is necessary and its abuses can be minimized." In a remark often mistakenly attributed to Rockefeller himself, his son put the matter more poetically: "The American Beauty Rose can be produced in its splendor and fragrance only by sacrificing the early buds which grow up around it." John D. Jr. may have learned this principle as it applied to roses from his father, who lavished time and effort on his gardens. The son definitely learned it from his father as it applied to the oil industry, which the elder man spent decades pruning until it produced the most perfect monopoly of its day: the Standard Oil trust.

Rockefeller's aversion to competition had something to do with his upbringing. "I cheat my boys every chance I get," his father said. "I want to make them sharp. I trade with the boys and skin them and I just beat them every time I can. I want to make them sharp." Young John and his brother William weren't the only ones William Sr. cheated. The elder man was a charming ne'er-do-well who promoted one shady scheme after another—"The Celebrated Cancer Specialist," read one of his placards: "All Cases of Cancer Cured (Unless Too Far Gone, and They Can be Greatly Benefited)." Bill Rockefeller's travels carried him around the region of the lower Great Lakes; on one tour he met a woman he found at least as attractive as John's mother. Without dissolving his first marriage or informing his first wife, he married again and commenced a double existence. Eventually he abandoned his first existence and first family altogether.

But before he did he pushed John D. (who by this time was insisting on his middle initial) out the door and into life. When the boy was fourteen his father drove him into Cleveland, found him a boarding house to live in, staked him to a small savings account and told him to find his way. A few years later, when John D. needed some money to start a business, his father offered to lend him the amount. "But John," he added, doubtless with that charming smile, "the interest will be ten per cent." Subsequently he called in the loan prematurely—by design. "That's the way to make him sharp," he laughed. "That's the way to make him hustle."

John D. certainly learned to hustle. He later spoke of the "desperate determination" of his first years in business. "I was after something big," he explained, while admitting, "I did not guess what it would be." He started out in commodities; following a stint as bookkeeper for a Cleveland broker he formed a brokerage partnership of his own. The firm started off well, with sales of half-a-million dollars in its first year. The outbreak of the Civil War did for Rockefeller's business what it had done for those of Morgan and Carnegie; by war's end Rockefeller, then 25, was a tolerably wealthy man.

One of the commodities Clark & Rockefeller traded during the war was oil. The same Pennsylvania petro-boom that made Carnegie's first fortune simultaneously engaged the attention of Rockefeller; while Carnegie approached Oil Creek from Pittsburgh to the south, Rockefeller arrived via Cleveland to the west. As a broker Rockefeller noted the discrepancy between the price of crude oil, typically between 30 and 35 cents per gallon during this period, and refined oil at 80 to 85 cents. Producing oil— finding, drilling and pumping it—was a volatile business (as Carnegie discovered) and too unpredictable for Rockefeller's tastes; but refining it— a simple chemical process easily scaled up to commercial size—was comparatively steady. In 1863 Rockefeller and Maurice Clark brought into their partnership Samuel Andrews, an Englishman experienced in the refiner's art, and Clark's two brothers.

The firm thrived for two years, but the ambitious Rockefeller wanted more. Haste was the watchword of the frenetic oil industry, and as is proverbially the case, haste made waste. Everywhere he looked Rockefeller saw waste—of oil, of money, of time and human energy. This waste offended his sense of the way things ought to be; it also cried out as a source of potential profit.

Rockefeller annoyed his partners with his efforts to stem the waste. James Clark chafed under the oversight of the twenty-two-year-old "Sunday-school superintendent," as he called Rockefeller, who in turn remembered of Clark, "He didn't like it when I made him account for every barrel of oil he bought, and for all his expenses."

Rockefeller's attention to detail denoted not caution with money but rather the opposite. He wanted to trim expenses in order to secure the funds to capture more of the market. "We have an opportunity now to expand, which may not last long," he asserted. When Maurice Clark complained about the debt the company had incurred already, Rockefeller defended his strategy: "We should borrow whenever we can safely extend the business by doing so."

This difference of opinion precipitated a breakup of the company. The Clark brothers proposed an auction among the partners to determine the fate of the firm. When Rockefeller agreed, Maurice Clark, speaking for himself and his brothers, commenced the bidding at $500. Rockefeller, backed by Andrews, countered at $1000. The Clarks offered $2000; Rockefeller doubled that. The bidding continued, climbing far higher than any of the bidders had anticipated. Rockefeller's bid of $70,000 caused the Clarks to reconsider the whole affair, but after a hasty consultation they offered $72,000. Immediately Rockefeller declared, "Seventy-two thousand five hundred."

The Clarks surrendered. "I'll go no higher, John," said Maurice Clark. "The business is yours."

It would be if he could pay for it. Rockefeller wasn't sure the credit line he had arranged for the auction extended as high as this. But he put on a bold front for his soon-to-be-former partners. "Shall I give you a check for it now?" he asked Clark. To Rockefeller's relief Clark responded, "No, I'm glad to trust you for it. Settle at your convenience."

Rockefeller's lenders came through, and the firm of Andrews, Clark & Co. dissolved in favor of the new partnership of Rockefeller & Andrews. Rockefeller always judged the shedding of the timid, unimaginative but profligate Clark brothers as his business emancipation. "I ever point to the day when I separated myself from them as the beginning of the success I have made in my life," he said.

The Civil War ended two months later, and if the conflict between the states had been good for Rockefeller's business, the postwar period was even better. In time the science of the petroleum industry would become as sophisticated as that of any other basic industry, benefiting from fundamental advances in organic chemistry, chemical engineering, geophysics and a dozen other disciplines. But in 1865 the industry stood on an early technical plateau. Drillers applied methods borrowed from salt-mining; refiners distilled the crude by boiling it and sequentially drawing off and condensing gasoline (for which no large market yet existed), naphtha, and kerosene (the real prize). Because refining remained so simple, barriers to entering the refining business were low. For $30,000 to $50,000 a prospective refiner could build what amounted to a state-of-the-art works and place himself in competition with established firms. As a result refineries by the dozen sprang up along the railroads leading from the oil fields to Cleveland, Pittsburgh and Philadelphia.

The competition that resulted predictably suppressed profits. It also, to Rockefeller's orderly way of thinking, generated waste. Why should there be thirty refineries in Cleveland rather than just one? He set about remedying the situation, in the interest of both efficiency and profit. In

1870 he found some additional partners, borrowed more money and reorganized Rockefeller & Andrews into the Standard Oil Company, capitalized at $1 million.

From the start Standard was the largest refiner in Cleveland, the principal refining center in the nation; under Rockefeller's direction the company quickly began to grow larger. He exploited competition among the railroads to negotiate rebates—usually-secret discounts from posted prices—on the shipment of crude oil from the oil fields to Cleveland and on refined products from Cleveland to the markets of the East. Rockefeller saw nothing at all unethical in rebates; they were simply the railroads' way of bidding for the business of large shippers like Standard. Nor, under his or his lawyers' interpretation of existing law, were they illegal. Yet there was some question on this latter point; many people—especially small shippers—considered the railroads to be common carriers that must not discriminate among shippers.

By lowering his cost of transportation the rebates improved Rockefeller's competitive position and enabled Standard to expand at the expense of its rivals. But the continued low cost of entry into the refining business allowed new firms to spring up where old ones had closed down. Soon refining capacity outstripped available supplies of crude by perhaps three to one; prices for refined products were half of what they had been five years before.

To alleviate the situation Rockefeller sponsored something that came to be called the South Improvement scheme. The idea was to create a cartel among the strongest refiners; this would apportion the market among its members, thereby eliminating competition and raising prices. The cartel would also negotiate shipping rates with the major railroads, offering them a respite from the competition from which they in turn were suffering in vying for the business of the big refiners. Precisely because the scheme would damage the interests of the many marginal refiners and raise costs to consumers, it was developed in the strictest secrecy.

And precisely because it was developed secretly it created a terrific uproar when its existence eventually leaked out. Complaining first and loudest were the oil producers, who perceived—accurately—that the refiners' cartel would force them to accept lower prices for their crude. The producers responded to this threat by declaring war on the cartel. They embargoed crude oil to the participants in the South Improvement combination, hoping to starve the cartel into dissolution. The refiners, as they did indeed start starving, bid up the price, tempting the more marginal or less militant producers to defect. But the embargo held. (One producer, F. S. Tarbell, refused an offer of $4.50 per barrel for his entire year's production. Acceptance would have made him a rich man; refusal made him a hero to his fellow producers—and to his daughter, Ida M. Tarbell, who grew up to write a scathing and widely read exposé of Rockefeller and Standard Oil.)

The South Improvement scheme collapsed under the weight of the embargo and of the almost universally bad press the plan received at a time when kerosene was fast becoming a necessity among consumers all across the country. The cartel's principal legacy was a reputation for collusion among the refiners.

But Rockefeller was unrepentant. He remained as committed as ever to the goal of rationalizing the oil industry; he reckoned he would have to go about it by different means. If he couldn't organize the other refiners he would simply have to take them over.

Between 1872 and 1879 Rockefeller did essentially that. An honest and not uncompassionate man, he preferred to buy out his competitors at prices that were not unreasonable. "He treated everybody fairly," conceded one rival who wound up absorbed. "When we sold out he gave us a fair price." Naturally there were those who sought to improve on mere fairness. "I remember one man whose refinery was worth $6000, or at most $8000," this refiner recalled. "His friends told him, 'Mr. Rockefeller ought to give you $100,000 for that.' Of course, Mr. Rockefeller refused to pay more than the refinery was worth"—which didn't stop the man from crying that he had been robbed. At this time and later Rockefeller avoided unnecessary publicity, but when pressed on the subject he declared that he had been, if anything, too generous with many individuals and firms whose assets he purchased. "Much of it was old junk, fit only for the scrap heap." Those who accepted cash found themselves suddenly liquid; those who took Standard stock fared even better as the new ownership managed their assets more adroitly than they could have. With unaccustomed eloquence Rockefeller asserted, "The Standard was an angel of mercy, reaching down from the sky, and saying 'Get into the ark. Put in your old junk. We'll take all the risks!'"

Merciful or not, the angel was implacable. Those refiners who weren't inclined to accept Rockefeller's terms discovered that they couldn't compete. Rockefeller perfected the refining process, squeezing out inefficiencies at every step. An employee described a visit by the boss to the shop floor.

He watched a machine filling the tin cans. One dozen cans stood on a wooden platform beneath a dozen pipes. A man pulled a lever, and each discharged exactly five gallons of kerosene into a can. Still on a wooden carrier, the dozen cans were pushed along to another machine, wherein twelve tops were swiftly clamped fast on the cans. Thence they were pushed to the last machine, in which just enough solder to fasten and seal the lid was dropped on each can.

Mr. Rockefeller listened in silence while an expert told all about the various machines used to save labor and time and expense in the process. At last Mr. Rockefeller asked:

"How many drops of solder do you use on each can?"

"Forty."

"Have you ever tried thirty-eight? No? Would you mind having some sealed with thirty-eight and let me know?"

Six or seven per cent of these cans leaked. Then thirty-nine drops were tried. None leaked. It was tried with one hundred, five hundred, a thousand cans. None leaked. Thereafter every can was sealed with thirty-nine drops.

To keep his subordinates in line, Rockefeller would scan the accounts for wasteful discrepancies. "Your March inventory showed 10,750 bungs on hand," he memoed his manager in charge of barrel-stoppers. "The report for April shows 20,000 new bungs bought, 24,000 bungs used, and 6,000 bungs on hand. What became of the other 750 bungs?"

At the same time, Rockefeller refused to make a habit of micromanaging. Especially as the business expanded beyond Cleveland he relied increasingly on carefully selected lieutenants. "I remained in the background, became what you might call a fifth wheel," he explained. "We had a good organization, an excellent organization." He once articulated his philosophy to a relative newcomer among his principal subordinates, the head of his laboratories.

Has anyone given you the law of these offices? No? It is this: nobody does anything if he can get anybody else to do it. You smile; but think it over. Your department is the testing of oils. You are responsible; but as soon as you can, get some one whom you can rely on, train him in the work, sit down, cock up your heels, and think out some way for the Standard Oil to make some money.

In searching for efficiencies, one thing Rockefeller did *not* do was squeeze his workers. At a time when strikes, riots and bloodshed rocked other basic industries, Rockefeller's Standard was remarkably placid. To some extent this reflected Rockefeller's success in squelching competition; a major contributor to the unrest in railroads, steel, and coal was the competition among the rival producers. Rockefeller never had to deal with the chronic price-cutting that, translated into wage-cutting, triggered the big strikes on the railroads, in the steelworks, and in the mines.

Additionally, however, the good relations between Rockefeller and his employees reflected the philosophy of the boss. "Every head of a department in the Standard Oil has explicit instructions to treat all employees with absolute fairness," he explained. "When that policy is carried out there will never be any danger of strikes." Nor, he might have added, would there be much danger of unions, which he opposed in principle. Rockefeller might not have been the most objective commentator on such matters, but a reporter for the *New York World* with no obvious ax to grind confirmed Rockefeller's account of labor relations at Standard. "It is and has been almost wholly free from strikes and lockouts," the reporter observed of the company, "and this because it has always paid good wages and had a kindly care for its men." Rockefeller encouraged employees to purchase shares in Standard; this would make the company's success their own and vice versa.

(After his retirement, Rockefeller's reputation on the labor issue would be retroactively tarnished by violence in a 1913 strike at a Rockefeller-controlled mine in Ludlow, Colorado, in which several strikers were killed, along with two women and eleven children. As an absentee owner who had delegated managerial authority to his son and on-site personnel, Rockefeller had no direct role in the tragic mishandling of the strike, although as principal stockholder he bore ultimate responsibility.)

Against the organized efficiency of Rockefeller's Standard, few rivals could hold out for long. The most determined managed to cling to particular niches, but by the end of the 1870s Standard had achieved as close to a monopoly of American refining as any firm was likely to achieve in any industry. Between 90 and 95 percent of the country's refining capacity was under his control.

Yet Rockefeller wasn't ready to rest on his accomplishments. A story that circulated at the time had him telling his executives: "Gentlemen, our figures show that 93 per cent of the American refining industry is now in our hands. But let us not think of this 93 per cent. Let us concentrate our attention upon the remaining 7 per cent!" The story is probably apocryphal, if only because Rockefeller recognized the cost-inefficiency—and political inexpediency—of trying to clean out the last of the competition, which would stir public opinion against the Standard monopoly if forced to the wall. Those marginal refiners could do him no harm; better to leave them alone.

By contrast, outside the field of refining there were those who *could* do Standard harm. The big railroads didn't like the leverage Standard was gaining over their traffic; even less did they like what that leverage appeared to portend. "We reached the conclusion that there were three great divisions in the petroleum business—the production, the carriage of it, and the preparation of it for the market," said Joseph Potts of the Empire Transportation Company, an ally of the Pennsylvania Railroad. "If any one party controlled absolutely any of these divisions, they practically would have a very fair show of controlling the others." To forestall Standard's gaining such a show, Penn president Tom Scott in 1877 arranged to underwrite the expansion of the Empire's modest refining business into a real rival to Standard.

Rockefeller hadn't worked so hard to rationalize refining simply to stand by while some railroaders undid his work. He went straight to Scott and demanded that he and Potts retreat. "The Empire has no business whatever in the field of refining," Rockefeller declared. Politely but firmly he insisted on an "immediate withdrawal." When Scott refused, the battle was joined.

By temperament Rockefeller preferred accommodation to belligerence, but he now demonstrated a real flair for battle. He canceled a major contract with the Penn, throwing his business to Penn rivals Erie and New York Central; at the same time he placed a rush order for 600 new tanker cars to be put on those roads. To pressure the Penn further he closed down his refineries in Pittsburgh, where the Penn controlled most of the traffic, and made up the difference at his Cleveland works, where it didn't. He slashed prices of kerosene in all markets where the Empire also sold that staple.

Rockefeller might well have won anyway, but the Penn suffered from two weaknesses that surfaced quickly. The first was its precarious financial situation, which grew only more precarious as the war with Standard raged. Creditors balked at lending Scott more money in the face of Standard's scorched-earth strategy; without new money he couldn't keep up the fight. The second vulnerability involved labor relations. Smoldering unrest among railworkers flared spectacularly in the summer of 1877, smack in the middle of the struggle with Standard. The Penn, which had the worst record on labor relations of any of the main lines, was paralyzed by a strike; the strike gave way to arson and murder, leaving dozens dead and millions in property destroyed. Under the circumstances Scott deemed his battle with Rockefeller unsustainable, and—to the outrage of Potts—he withdrew from the field.

The failure of the Penn–Empire assault left Rockefeller in a nearly impregnable position vis-à-vis the railroads. Such great power did Rockefeller command that he was able not simply to negotiate rebates on Standard's own shipments but to receive payments ("drawbacks") from the railroads on the shipments of its few remaining competitors. In one instance Standard nominally paid $1.20 per barrel to ship its oil over a particular route; the railroad rebated 20 cents. Standard's rivals also paid $1.20; the railroad rebated 20 cents—but to Standard rather than to them. Because this arrangement was secret the rivals weren't aware that Standard had a 40-cent advantage over them—or that the harder they worked and the more oil they shipped, the more money Standard received.

The oil producers observed Rockefeller's conquest of the railroads with dismay bordering on despair. From the day Colonel Drake's first well had come in, refiners had depended on the producers: without crude the refiners would have nothing to refine. Now this natural order of the cosmos—as it seemed to the producers—was reversed. Standard was in a position where it could largely dictate the price it would pay the producers. Even if he didn't start swimming upstream into production—an alarming possibility, given his obvious ambition—Rockefeller could ruin the producers from where he stood.

In fear and loathing the producers gathered in Titusville, Pennsylvania, in November 1877. The deliberations of this "Petroleum Parliament" were closed to outsiders; visitors to the town who weren't unmistakably producers were scrutinized severely lest they be spies. Before long a concerted anti-Rockefeller strategy developed, centering on a plan to break the Standard stranglehold by building pipelines from the producing region to the Erie Canal and the Atlantic seaboard. These pipelines presumably would attract independent refiners who would join with the producers against Rockefeller.

Rockefeller had scant respect for the producers or their parliament. They had brought their troubles on themselves, he judged, by failing to organize and discipline themselves sooner. In their individual greed they refused to curtail production, instead glutting the market with crude that Standard would have been lunatic not to take at the lowest possible price.

"Men like spoiled children," he called them. How could he think otherwise of a group that, amid the glut, actually passed a resolution to pump more: "Whereas the shortest way to $2 oil is through 25-cent oil, therefore be it resolved that we favor pushing the drill as rapidly and diligently as possible until the goal of 25-cent oil is reached."

The producers failed flatly to defeat Rockefeller in the marketplace. Their efforts to build a pipeline simply spurred him to build pipelines of his own, outflanking them and, in the bargain, increasing his leverage with the railroads. Standard's domestic sales continued to rise; its export sales rose even more. The octopus—as the company was frequently depicted in cartoons—spread its tentacles across the globe.

These cartoons were not meant to be flattering; their tone indicated that although Rockefeller was invincible in the market he was becoming vulnerable in the political arena. The complaints of the producers, of vanquished refiners and of assorted others prompted investigations into Standard's activities. The investigations elicited additional complaints against Rockefeller, leading to demands for changes in laws governing the behavior of large corporations. They also prompted lawsuits against Standard and even a Pennsylvania indictment against Rockefeller and his associates for criminal conspiracy.

This last got Rockefeller's attention; he had no desire to try to direct the company from a Pennsylvania prison. Although he judged the indictments and other attacks wholly without merit, he consented to modify his practices. Standard didn't quite abjure the use of rebates, but the company said it wouldn't object to the abolition of the entire system of rebates and drawbacks; neither would it resist the full disclosure of rates.

This agreement solved Rockefeller's immediate legal problems, but it diminished Standard's competitive advantage; to restore the latter Rockefeller sought new ways to streamline the company's operations. What went by the name of "Standard Oil" in 1880 was actually an informal organization of the original partnership—the Standard Oil Company of Ohio—and the numerous firms that had been drawn in during the company's rapid growth. Ownership and control of those other firms rested with thirty-seven stockholders, who were also major stockholders in Standard of Ohio. They acted in concert and followed Rockefeller's lead, but they were not legally bound to do so. The informality of this arrangement had certain advantages; the directors of Standard could deny responsibility for actions taken by firms affiliated with the company but not formally controlled by it. Yet the looseness of the arrangement also entailed administrative inefficiencies that had always grated on Rockefeller's sensibilities.

Rockefeller was not an original thinker in the sense of developing novel ideas unassisted. His genius lay in adapting the ideas of others to his own purposes. So it was with the creation of the Standard Oil Trust. Trusts, in the sense of trusteeships, had existed in English common law for centuries; an adult would hold property in trust for a minor, for example. Rockefeller applied the concept to the oil business by arranging for the transfer of all the shares owned by the thirty-seven stockholders to a new group of nine trustees led by himself. In exchange the stockholders received trust certificates—in effect, shares in the new umbrella corporation. The nine trustees taken together owned two-thirds of these shares and thus two-thirds of each of the original companies.

Although Rockefeller and his associates downplayed their accomplishment—at times to the point of dishonest denial—the trust idea caught on. The nation's whiskey distillers created a trust to stifle competition in booze; the sugar refiners followed suit in sucrose. By the end of the 1880s the trust was the mode du jour of American big business.

The trend toward trusts drew additional attention from those who thought Standard and the other corporate giants wielded power unconscionable in a democracy. "Antitrust" measures were introduced and approved in several states; Congress took up similar legislation. A Senate committee subpoenaed the patron saint and reigning expert of the movement, Rockefeller himself.

Rockefeller's appearance before the committee starkly contradicted the sinister image of him current among the public at large. "He seems the embodiment of sweetness and light," declared the *New York Tribune*. "His serenity could not be disturbed. With the same sweet smile he replied to Col. Bliss's sarcasms and General Pryor's scornful adjurations. In tones melodious, clear, and deliberate he gave his testimony. . . . At times his manner was mildly reproachful, at others tenderly persuasive, but never did he betray any ill temper or vexation."

Yet neither did he prevent the passage of legislation designed to curb the kind of actions in which he had been engaged for two decades. In 1890 Congress passed and President Harrison signed the mislabeled Sherman Act ("If there was any man in the world who did not have anything to do with the Sherman anti-trust law it was John Sherman," remarked the actual author of the measure, George Hoar, with understandable indignation). The act explicitly outlawed "trusts and combinations in restraint of trade."

Fortified by the popular groundswell of antitrust opinion, the attorney-general of Ohio brought suit against Standard and in 1890 won a decision mandating the dissolution of the Standard trust. Rockefeller pondered appeal but decided against, knowing that New York prosecutors were preparing an anti-Standard case and that the federal Justice Department couldn't be far behind. After some minor stalling the Standard Oil Trust was formally dissolved in 1892.

But Rockefeller wasn't without recourse. He let the storm of public indignation rage against other corporations—the railroads, to cite the conspicuous villain during the Populist Nineties—before deciding on a new model of organization. During the previous several years corporate-friendly legislators in New Jersey had passed laws reversing long-standing tradition and allowing corporations to own stock in other corporations. Rockefeller wasn't the first to see the possibilities implicit in the change, but no one made better use of it. In 1899 the Standard Oil Company of New Jersey, one of the constituent parts of the dissolved trust, was reorganized; its capital was increased from $10 million to $110 million and its shares were multiplied commensurately. These shares were offered, successfully, in exchange for outstanding certificates of the old trust and for shares of the constituent firms. Fourteen directors controlled the enlarged New Jersey Standard, which in turn now controlled the entire Standard empire. The president of this powerful holding company was John D. Rockefeller.

Although the creation of the holding company altered the internal structure of the Standard empire, outwardly the empire behaved much as before. It continued to exercise a stranglehold on the industry. In 1900 its net assets were $205 million; by 1906 they had reached $360 million. Profits rose from $56 million in 1900 to $83 million six years later.

All this was not lost on the growing ranks of antitrust regulators. Several states and the federal government brought lawsuits against the holding company; the freshly minted federal Bureau of Corporations contributed a ceaseless stream of negative publicity. The attackers landed a heavy blow in 1907 when a federal court levied a fine of $29 million; the coup de grace came in 1911 when the Supreme Court decreed that New Jersey Standard must divest itself of all its subsidiaries.

As one who had devoted his entire adult life to creating this marvelous example of corporate consolidation, Rockefeller might have been forgiven for taking the ruling hard. In fact he maintained a remarkable degree of equanimity. A reporter covering the federal case against Standard described the appearance of the star witness for the defense, then in his seventieth year.

> Mr. Rockefeller enters. An old man—not an aged man. He is under no embarrassment. He is grave, but in his rather small light-blue eyes there is humor. He sits down and throws one leg easily over the other. There is no tremor in the long hand that he lays upon the table. He has an air of polite deference. A man with a strange, phenomenal, most unusual face!

The Supreme Court's ruling hardly surprised Rockefeller, wrongheaded though he judged it to be. It dented his confidence not at all. "Have you some money?" he asked a friend. "Buy Standard Oil." Rockefeller may or may not have seen that the oil industry was about to enter a new era, one in which petroleum products not merely lighted the world but drove it. Three years after the court's order Europe erupted into a war in which the Allies, in British prime minister David Lloyd George's words, "floated to victory on a sea of oil." In the decade that followed the war Americans took to the highways in unprecedented numbers; each automobile consumed more petroleum in an hour than the lamps of most households had consumed in a month in Rockefeller's heyday. How Rockefeller would have handled the transition is an open question; in the event, the breakup facilitated the development of new approaches to the industry's new era. It also prompted Rockefeller to complete the retirement he had begun several years earlier.

As early as the 1880s Rockefeller had run into a happy problem that occasionally confronted other captains of industry: what to do with all the money he was making. For a time he diversified into iron and steel, even striking some trepidation into Andrew Carnegie. But his first love was always oil, and he never pursued ferrous metals the way he did petroleum. Instead—like Carnegie—he invested in the public welfare, endowing the University of Chicago, the Rockefeller Institute for Medical Research, and the Rockefeller Foundation.

Rockefeller also found time for his hobbies. Until health failed just prior to his 1937 death, he spent many hours nurturing the gardens on his estates. He played golf daily, acquiring a proficiency surprising in a man his age even while employing the unorthodox locomotive method of pedaling a bicycle from shot to shot. By the testimony of playing partners he was unfailingly scrupulous in his golf scoring. "If his ball goes into the woods he plays it out no matter how many strokes it takes and counts them all," said one regular linksmate. (This individual couldn't resist a comparison: "I have played with Andy Carnegie also. And I found that Andy would bear watching—he would cheat a little on the score.")

Rockefeller perceived a parallel between golf and business, at least in this matter of straight scoring. Asked the most important element in the success of Standard Oil, he replied: "To the fact that we never deceived ourselves." He didn't say he and his associates never deceived others; sometimes that came with the territory of the oil business. But—in a parallel with his other hobby—he understood that in growing a monopoly, as in growing roses, a clear eye and cool realism were necessary to distinguish what needed pruning from what ought to be cultivated.

8

THE MECHANIC OF REVOLUTION

Henry Ford

• • •

CONVENTIONAL WISDOM CASTS BUSINESS LEADERS AS CONSERVA-tives; and in political terms the convention isn't wildly inaccurate. But in economic terms the greatest business figures are frequently radicals, cutting to the root of the status quo and grafting novelties thereon. In rare cases business leaders are outright revolutionaries, shattering accepted modes of living, overturning received notions of economic and social or-ganization, and becoming—in the rarest cases of all—cult figures for the millions who find the revolutions liberating.

Henry Ford was an unlikely radical, an improbable revolutionary and an impossible cult figure. He would have been a farmer if his father's ex-postulations and subsequent bribes had taken hold—or perhaps if his mother hadn't died when he was still a boy. "The house was like a watch without a mainspring," Ford said of her loss from the homestead near Dearborn, Michigan. He added, "I never had any particular love for the farm. It was the mother on the farm I loved."

He also loved tinkering. "I had a kind of workshop with odds and ends of metal for tools before I had anything else. In those days we did not have the toys of today; what we had were home made. My toys were all tools—they still are! And every fragment of machinery was a treasure."

The two big events the year Ford turned twelve—at any rate the ones that stuck in his memory—were his acquisition of a watch and his en-counter with a road engine eight miles out of Detroit. The watch just begged to be taken apart, although not till later did he figure out how to put it back together. "By the time I was fifteen I could do almost anything in watch repairing," he boasted.

The road engine made an even greater impression. Henry and his father William were driving to town in their horse-drawn wagon when chugging and belching over the hill came the first self-propelled vehicle either had ever seen. Portable steam engines for threshing grain and driving wood saws weren't uncommon in southern Michigan; but these were typically hauled from job to job by teams of horses. The operator of this engine, however, had devised an ingenious method of connecting the engine to the wheels of the wagon on which it rested.

William was still scratching his head at this wonder when Henry bounded off the buckboard to quiz the engineer about every facet of the device's operation. "He showed me how the chain was disconnected from the propelling wheel and a belt put on to drive other machinery. He told me that the engine made two hundred revolutions a minute and that the chain pinion could be shifted to let the wagon stop while the engine was still running." Perhaps with some advantage of hindsight, the adult Henry Ford detected a direct connection between that encounter and his life's work. "From the time I saw that road engine as a boy of twelve right forward to today, my great interest has been in making a machine that would travel the roads."

At sixteen Ford moved to Detroit to apprentice in a machine shop; the following year he transferred to a shipbuilding firm that needed a hand in the engine room. His tactile experience of the big power plants inspired him in ways books never had. "It is not possible to learn from books how everything is made—and a real mechanic ought to know how everything is made. Machines are to a mechanic what books are to a writer. He gets ideas from them, and if he has any brains he will apply those ideas."

Ford had brains, and he began applying his ideas as a service representative for the Westinghouse Engine Company. He set up new engines for customers and repaired old ones. Although these devices marked a signal step forward in easing the burden on farmers, they did so far less effectively than Ford thought they ought to. "What bothered me was the weight and the cost. They weighed a couple of tons and were far too expensive to be owned by other than a farmer with a great deal of land." As a boy the tedium of field work had driven him away from the farm; as a young adult it was drawing him back—but in the capacity of one who would change the traditional ways rather than surrender to them. "I had the idea of making some kind of a light steam car that would take the place of horses—more especially, however, a tractor to attend to the excessively hard labour of ploughing. . . . To lift farm drudgery off flesh and blood and lay it on steel and motors has been my most constant ambition."

Two roadblocks impeded that ambition. The first, which had confronted the young Cyrus McCormick, was the ingrained conservatism of farmers. Born to the labor of flesh and blood, most were content to live and die by the labor of flesh and blood. To Ford's surprise he discovered that they resisted even innovations that seemed forehead-slappingly obvious to him. Ford would accomplish his rural revolution, but not from the direction he thought.

The second impediment was the unpredictability of steam. To lighten a steam engine without sacrificing power required raising the boiler pressure. In that age of unscientific quality control, boilers had an unsettling habit of exploding beneath the seats of drivers; needless to say, this habit did nothing good for either the reputation of the machines or their sales.

Deliverance came from across the Atlantic. The Germans Daimler and Benz had developed a reliable and relatively powerful internal combustion engine that ran on gasoline; soon they began building gasoline-powered vehicles. Their success inspired other tinkerers in Europe and North America; eventually Henry Ford joined the ranks of those concluding that the future of self-propulsion lay with gasoline. By now Detroit was a hotbed of backyard mechanics and would-be inventors; Ford, whose current day job was with the Edison Illuminating Company, picked the best brains in the city en route to producing an innovative and recognizably modern two-cylinder, four-cycle engine that generated nearly four horsepower on a good afternoon. Mounted on a chassis acquired from a friend, Ford's motorcar made its maiden run on June 4, 1896—but only after the somewhat absent-minded inventor, suddenly discovering that his prototype was too large to leave the building in which it had been constructed, took an ax to bricks and summarily enlarged the door.

This "quadricycle," as Ford called it, was a brilliant success. Crowds of bicyclists swarmed behind it; admirers insisted on trying their hands at the tiller (the precursor to the steering wheel) even without the owner's permission. "Finally I had to carry a chain and chain it to a lamp post whenever I left it anywhere," Ford recalled.

Ford sold this first automobile for $200 and began building a second. Bigger, more powerful and more sophisticated, the new two-passenger model was completed in 1899 and attracted the interest of investors who staked Ford to the full-time production of automobiles for sale. The Detroit Automobile Company, as he called it, was the first venture devoted to automobiles in what would become the Motor City; in its initial year of operation it built and sold a score of vehicles.

One of the cars Ford kept he reluctantly entered in a race. "I never really thought much of racing," he said. A race revealed little about the genuine merits—reliability, ease of use, performance per dollar—of an automobile. "But as the others were doing it, I too had to do it." And he did it very well. He won his first race in 1901, upholding the honor of Detroit against a challenger from Cleveland. "The people went wild," his wife related to her brother. "One man threw his hat up and when it came down he stamped on it, he was so excited." A woman in the crowd shouted, "I'd bet fifty dollars on Ford if I had it."

This was precisely the point; and shortly after the victory Ford lined up new investors and reorganized the Detroit Automobile Company as the Henry Ford Company. Having discovered the cash value of a reputation for speed, he built two more racers: the "Arrow" and the "999." He explained:

> If an automobile were going to be known for speed, then I was going to make an automobile that would be known wherever speed was known. I put in four great big cylinders giving 80 H.P.—which up to that time had been unheard of. The roar of those cylinders alone was enough to half kill a man. There was only one seat. One life to a car was enough. I tried out the cars. . . . I cannot quite describe the sensation. Going over Niagara Falls would have been but a pastime after a ride in one of them.

Declining to race this monster car himself, Ford brought in a professional bicycle racer named Barney Oldfield. Oldfield had never driven an automobile but was a quick study and fearless. "This chariot may kill me," he told Ford while the latter was hand-cranking the car for the start of the race, "but they will say afterward that I was going like hell when she took me over the bank."

In fact Oldfield won the race, setting a speed record of just under 60 miles per hour for five miles around the Grosse Point track. And once more the victory paid off. New investors again came forward and the Henry Ford Company was reincarnated as the Ford Motor Company. The principal shareholders were Alexander Malcomson, a Detroit coal man who put up the largest part of the money, and Ford, who furnished the ideas.

Ford's fundamental idea was the one that would transform the nascent automobile industry and ultimately revolutionize American life.

> I will build a motor car for the great multitude. It will be large enough for the family but small enough for the individual to run and care for. It will be constructed of the best materials, by the best men to be hired, after the simplest designs that modern engineering can devise. But it will be so low in price that no man making a good salary will be unable to own one—and enjoy with his family the blessing of hours of pleasure in God's great open spaces.

Before Ford, automobiles were customarily accounted luxury items, playthings for the wealthy. In Newport and other watering holes for the rich, automobiles came one, two, three to the household; but across vast stretches of ordinary America, especially outside the cities, they remained rarities. Price wasn't the sole hindrance; rural roads were rough on vehicles, gasoline was scarce, and mechanics were few and replacement parts fewer. But whether or not the chicken came before the egg, without automobiles none of the supporting infrastructure would develop.

Having targeted a mass market, Ford developed a method for hitting his target.

> The way to make automobiles is to make one automobile like another automobile, to make them all alike, to make them come through the factory just alike; just as one pin is like another pin when it comes from a pin factory, or one match is like another match when it comes from a match factory.

Ford's partners required some convincing that such was the optimal strategy for the company. Alexander Malcomson preferred the fatter profits that came with more expensive models; the future of the company, he argued, lay not in the direction of the $650 Oldsmobile but toward the $3200 Pope-Hartford and perhaps even the $7000 Packard.

For three years Ford fought Malcomson for control of the company; when some bad investments elsewhere left the latter strapped, Ford seized the opportunity to buy him out. Malcomson's allies emulated his exit, and by the beginning of 1908 Ford held 58 percent of Ford Motor stock.

That autumn the first Model T rolled out the door. It was not immediately obvious that this was the car that would change the face of America, but certain innovations were apparent from the start. The frame and body sat higher above the wheels than on other cars; this allowed the T to negotiate rural ruts that high-centered the competition. The motor and drive train were completely enclosed to protect the vehicle's vitals from mud, gravel and water. A magneto driven by the flywheel replaced the customary dry batteries, allowing the engine to spark itself. The suspension was sturdy enough for the most rugged road.

As yet the price wasn't revolutionary, starting at $825. But Ford knew it would soon fall. "Charlie," he would say to his assistant while designing the car, "we're on the right track here now. We're going to get a car now that we can make in great volume and get the price way down."

This was exactly what they did. With the company now in his control, Ford devoted it single-mindedly to the efficient production of this single car. For nearly twenty years Ford Motor turned out T's and only T's—although there were three slight variations on the single theme, and not until 1914 did Ford enforce his famous policy on paint: "Any customer can have a car painted any color he wants so long as it is black."

The T was a stunning success from the outset. Anticipating the car's introduction, Ford had sent out circulars to sales agents around the country; these elicited a response that was overwhelming. "This circular alone will flood your factory with orders," predicted one representative from a small town in Pennsylvania. An Illinois agent explained that he had had to stop showing the fliers to customers for fear their eagerness would get out of hand. "We have carefully hidden the sheets away and locked the drawer," he said.

Orders poured in by the thousands; nearly 11,000 cars were sold between October 1, 1908 and September 30, 1909. During the 1910 model year (already the auto industry had set its calendar three months ahead of most other people) the T did even better: 19,000 cars. And sales continued to soar: 35,000 in 1911, 78,000 in 1912, 168,000 in 1913, 248,000 in 1914. In this last year Ford claimed 48 percent of the entire American market for automobiles.

Keeping up with demand required Ford to pioneer new methods of production. On a sixty-acre parcel in Highland Park, north of Detroit, he built the biggest and most modern automobile factory in America. Within that factory he arranged work according to a few meticulous principles. Efficiency expert Frederick Taylor was then preaching the application of scientific techniques to industrial production; Ford arrived at the same conclusions by more intuitive methods. "The principles of assembly are these," he explained.

1. Place the tools and the men in the sequence of the operation so that each component part shall travel the least possible distance while in the process of finishing.

2. Use slides or some other form of carrier so that when a workman completes his operation, he drops the part always in the same place—which place must be the most convenient place to his hand—and if possible have gravity carry the part to the next workman for his operation.

3. Use sliding assembly lines by which the parts to be assembled are delivered at convenient distances.

The culmination of Ford's system was the continuously moving line for assembling the chassis. He said the basic idea came from Chicago meatpackers who hung carcasses from overhead trolleys that passed in front of the butchers. Ford applied the principle experimentally and by increments. "We try everything in a little way first—we will rip out anything once we discover a better way, but we have to know absolutely that the new way is going to be better than the old before we do anything drastic."

Minor changes made dramatic differences. Raising by eight inches the height at which magnetos were presented to workers reduced by nearly half the time spent on this part of the process. Subdividing the assembly of the motor and parceling out the work to different men increased productivity threefold. When one subassembly line moved at sixty inches per minute the workers couldn't keep up and quality fell off unacceptably; when it moved at eighteen inches per minute they found themselves waiting for the next part. Forty-four inches per minutes proved the optimal pace. "The idea is that a man must not be hurried in his work," Ford explained. "He must have every second necessary but not a single unnecessary second."

Overall the labor savings were remarkable. A chassis that formerly required more than six hours to assemble could now be put together in just over 90 minutes. In 1916 the one-millionth Model T rolled off the line; by that year the factory was churning out 2,000 cars per day.

As Ford had forecast, these efficiencies allowed him to reduce his prices: from the $800 range to the $600s to the $400s and finally to the $300s. Ford enjoyed a near monopoly of the inexpensive end of automobile production, eventually controlling as much as 96 percent of the market for cars priced below $600. With each price cut Ford reached a new segment of the American population. "Every time you reduce the price of the car without reducing the quality, you increase the possible number of purchasers," he explained in 1916, the year the price of the Model T touring car was slashed to $360. "There are many men who will pay $360 for a car who would not pay $440. We had in round numbers 500,000 buyers of cars on the $440 basis, and I figure that on the $360 basis we can increase the sales to possibly 800,000 cars for the year." His optimistic estimate was only a little high; sales for the following year were 730,000.

Ford's success with the Model T didn't come uncontested. Oddly, his most serious early foe was a man who didn't even manufacture automobiles. George Selden was a patent attorney who liked to tinker on the side; during the 1870s he conceived an idea for a horseless carriage powered by an internal combustion engine. He never got around to building such a vehicle, but in 1879 he filed a patent application anyway. Almost as soon as he did he realized that the rapid pace of technology might render his patent quickly obsolete, and so, employing his expertise of the patent process, he repeatedly postponed final consideration by appending additions and amendments to the original application. The process dragged on until 1895 when Selden finally accepted approval of a patent that would run the standard seventeen years until 1912.

In 1903 Selden and the Electric Vehicle Company, which had purchased rights to Selden's patent, sued the Ford Motor Company for infringement. Henry Ford refused to pay what he considered to be ransom money for his own invention; his determination redoubled when the Selden suit received the support of several of Ford's rivals organized as the Association of Licensed Automobile Manufacturers. The Association attempted to intimidate Ford by taking out advertisements warning dealers and potential customers that they were liable to prosecution; Ford struck back with ads of his own promising legal protection against prosecution and declaring, "We are the pioneers of the GASOLINE AUTOMOBILE." Referring to one of the leaders of the Association, the Ford ad concluded: "Mr. Ford, driving his own machine, beat Mr. Winton at Grosse Point track in 1901. We have always been winners."

The Selden suit gave Ford the opportunity to side very publicly with the common people of America. In a period of popular hostility toward trusts of all kinds—as Rockefeller and Morgan could testify—Ford cast himself as the brave independent challenging the "auto trust." Ford was putting the people on wheels; the Association—which for the most part built luxury cars for the rich—wanted to take those wheels away. Ford later acknowledged the benefits of the suit over the Selden patent. "Probably nothing so well advertised the Ford car and the Ford Motor Company as did this suit. It appeared that we were the under dog and we had the public's sympathy."

Ford also had the sympathy, or at least the final judgment, of the courts. After a worrisome loss in federal district court—a loss that, if sustained, would have cost Ford Motor many millions of dollars—the U.S. Court of

Appeals in 1911 determined that the Selden patent, while narrowly valid, excluded nearly all automobiles then in production, including Ford's.

The victory freed Ford to expand production still more—and to deal with the problems his growing production produced. Of these a chronic one involved labor. The birth and adolescence of the automobile industry attracted tens of thousands of workers to Detroit, but as Ford doubled production almost annually the pool of qualified workers frequently fell short of what his foremen desired. To some extent the simplification of the assembly process, with each task broken down into its essentials, relieved the problem, for unskilled workers could be readily trained to tighten this nut or grease that gear. But at the same time the monotony inherent in mass production aggravated turnover. It also increased the incidence of injuries as the endless repetition, combined with the ceaseless noise of the factory floor, combined to induce, in the words of one student of the situation, "a semi-hypnotic state from which the workman's mind emerges only at intervals."

Ford experimented with various methods of relieving the monotony and generally improving workers' lot. He rotated workers from station to station about the Highland Park plant. He instituted profit-sharing, paid out in year-end bonuses. He spent time on the shop floor talking to workers. At least some workers found his hands-on approach inspiring. "God! He could get anything out of the men because he just talked and would tell them stories," recalled one admirer. "He'd never say, 'I want this done!' He'd say, 'I wonder if we can do it. I wonder.' Well, the men would just break their necks to see if they could do it."

But Ford's master stroke was his initiation of the five-dollar day. At the beginning of 1914 he reflected that even as prices continued to fall, profits soared. Profits for 1913 were twice those of 1912, which were nearly twice those of 1911, which were nearly twice those of 1910. Customers were benefiting from the falling prices, the company from the rising profits. What about the workers?

At a board meeting in January 1914 Ford answered his own question. He jotted figures on a chalk slate estimating the fundamental elements of company finance for the coming year; despite numerous revisions the amount allocated to wages always seemed too small next to profits. He raised average wages to $3 per day, then $4, then $4.50, then $4.75. One skeptic on the board, evidently wondering at this solicitude for the laboring classes, chimed in sarcastically: "So it's up to $4.75. I dare you to make it $5!"

Ford accepted the dare. Soon after this meeting he handed the press an announcement outlining a major change in labor policy. Henceforth the company would observe an eight-hour day (the industry standard was nine or ten), and would pay a basic wage of $5 per day (against the industry average of $1.80 to $2.50).

Coming after his victory over the "auto trust" in the Selden case, and amid the ever-growing popular embrace of the Model T, the inauguration of the five-dollar day marked Henry Ford as the embodiment of enlightened business leadership, the boss who looked after his men on a basis of equality and day-to-day dignity—and not simply by tossing them a library after he retired. "It is the most generous stroke of policy between captain of industry and worker that the country has ever seen," summarized one Michigan editor.

Predictably Ford's competitors and other critics looked askance at his initiative. Rival auto executives worried that he would spoil the workforce with unrealistic and unsustainable expectations. Some suspected a devious plot to corner the market in mechanical talent, a maneuver to be followed by an assembly-line speedup that would drive Ford's unit costs back down but by then would have thrown the labor market as a whole into chaos. Determined distrusters of business detected an attempt to co-opt moderate labor elements as a defense against radical unions like the Industrial Workers of the World.

Ford didn't deny that the new policy was good business. But he thought it was good business in the broadest terms. Calling his new system not simply a profit-sharing plan but a "prosperity-sharing plan," Ford envisioned the benefits of higher wages rippling outward through the economy as a whole. "All other considerations aside," he explained, "our own sales depend in a measure upon the wages we pay. If we can distribute high wages, then that money is going to be spent and it will serve to make storekeepers and distributors and manufacturers and workers in other lines more prosperous and their prosperity will be reflected in our sales." Assuming continued gains in productivity, he declared: "Country-wide high wages spell country-wide prosperity."

The five-dollar day completed Ford's transformation into something approaching a cult figure for millions of Americans, including a large portion of those overwhelmingly ordinary people who had purchased the 5.4 million Ford automobiles produced by 1921. He was revered as the quintessential American success story, the backyard inventor who defied the trusts, spurned the banks (Ford rarely borrowed, instead financing expansion from profits), respected his workers and spread the blessings of industry to the common people of America.

Perhaps unavoidably the adulation went to Ford's head. After the outbreak of World War I he orchestrated a private effort to end the fighting, chartering an ocean liner to carry a delegation of pacifists and other anti-war advocates to Europe. The "Peace Ship" failed to accomplish much beyond convincing some observers that Ford was a meddlesome megalomaniac and others that he ought to run for elective office, which he did in 1918. He won the Democratic nomination for one of Michigan's U.S. Senate seats but lost the general election by a paper-thin margin. He purchased the *Dearborn Independent*, which subsequently belied its name by becoming a mouthpiece for Ford's increasingly shrill opinions on all manner of issues. Of these opinions the most notorious was summarized by the title of a 1920 cover article: "The International Jew: The World's Problem."

During the 1920s Ford opened a new factory complex, the River Rouge plant, in Dearborn. This enormous facility sprawled across 1100 acres and represented an almost hubristic effort to achieve a nearly comprehensive vertical integration of the automobile-production process. The Rouge received coal from company mines in Kentucky and West Virginia and iron ore from company tracts in Michigan's Upper Peninsula; from the coal it made coke, which was then applied to the iron ore to make the steel that went into the Model T and the trucks and tractors that formed a growing part of the manufacturing stream. The coal also fueled the world's largest foundry, the company's glass works and the generators that supplied the electricity that powered the machines that turned, milled, stamped and welded the parts that went into the vehicles that rolled off the line by the millions.

Breathtaking as it was, the Rouge hardly achieved complete success. The same stubborn self-assurance that helped make Ford such a popular hero also made it difficult for him to retain good subordinates; one insightful observer noted: "I have a great admiration for Henry Ford, but there is one thing about him that I regret and can't understand, and that is his inability to keep his executives and old time friends about him." The Rouge was a behemoth that required an army to administer; by the mid-1920s Ford stood more alone than ever at the top of the company. To his credit he recognized the failure of his attempt at hyper-integration and soon began to spin off elements of the production process to outlying facilities.

The decision didn't come uncoerced. During the 1920s Ford's share of the automotive market slipped, slowly at first, then more rapidly. It fell from a high of 56 percent in 1921 to 34 percent in 1926. The Model T, now approaching its twentieth birthday, seemed old and stodgy next to the more innovative and stylish models coming off the Chevrolet lines at General Motors and the Plymouth lines at Chrysler. Even as he was re-thinking his River Rouge strategy, Ford reluctantly decided to retire the T—but not before completing the 15-millionth one in 1927. The successor to the T, the Model A, enabled Ford Motor to regain about half of its lost market share, but the onset of the Great Depression killed any hopes that the A might approach the T in profitability.

The 1930s were an inglorious time for Henry Ford in other respects. Like an aging despot, Ford became obsessed with perceived threats to his power. The enlightened labor policy of the 1910s gave way to a campaign of espionage, intimidation and subversion against labor unionists; for years after General Motors and Chrysler made their peace with the United Automobile Workers, Ford held out, capitulating—according to inside sources—only after Ford's wife threatened to leave him if he didn't. A flirtation with Hitler rekindled memories of his earlier anti-Semitism; his outspoken isolationism after the German invasion of Poland in 1939 struck some observers as a thin cover for Nazi apologetics.

Ford died in 1947, about a generation too late for an optimal historical reputation. To a considerable degree he suffered the fate that befalls revolutionaries who live beyond their time: to be overtaken by the forces they set in motion. More than any other individual, Ford created the automobile culture that has characterized American society for most of the twentieth century. Not everything about this car culture is admirable, as any gridlocked commuter can attest; but even so, the automobile has been one of the most profoundly democratizing influences in American history. Ford built cars for the masses, and the masses fell in love with the mobility and independence those cars provided. If they—or, in most cases, their children—moved on to other cars, they were simply exercising an aspect of the independence he had done so much to foster.

9

ORGANIZATION MAN

Alfred P. Sloan

. . .

WRITING IN THE 1960S, ALFRED P. SLOAN DIVIDED THE HISTORY OF the automobile industry into three eras. The first dated from the end of the nineteenth century to 1908; this was the era of the auto as plaything of the upper classes. The second started with Henry Ford's introduction of the Model T and ran to the mid-1920s; this was the era of the auto as vehicle for the masses. The third era commenced in the mid-1920s and continued until the time of Sloan's writing; this was the era of the auto as a mass–class phenomenon.

Sloan was modest enough not to say so explicitly in this context, but the third era began with his assumption of the presidency of General Motors; and it encompassed GM's overtaking Ford Motor as the nation's top carmaker and, eventually, GM's emergence as one of the largest industrial concerns on the planet. Sloan acknowledged Henry Ford's role in creating the car culture that made the modern auto industry possible, but he had no doubt that Ford's day, like that of every revolutionary sooner or later, had passed; the lasting fruits of the revolution would fall to those who understood how to institutionalize and manage change over the long term. As temperamentally conservative as Ford was radical, Sloan was just the man for the job.

Sloan came to the auto industry with grease under his fingers, although considerably less grease than Ford. Following a boyhood that began in New Haven and continued in Brooklyn after his father relocated his wholesale coffee, tea and tobacco business to Manhattan, Alfred Jr. studied electrical engineering at the Massachusetts Institute of Technology, then went to work for the Hyatt Roller Bearing Company of Newark. Bearings weren't what he had daydreamed about during his electrical-engineering lectures, however, and before long he left for the more congenial field of electrical refrigeration. Shortly thereafter Hyatt Bearing ran into financial problems, to the point of imminent bankruptcy. Alfred Sloan, Sr., who wanted to see his son in business on his own, arranged to bail out the bearing-maker with the understanding that Alfred Jr. would run the company. Junior wasn't thrilled, but he agreed to give the enterprise a try for six months.

Perhaps to his surprise—and maybe to his father's as well—the young man proved a natural manager, and he turned the company around. He decided to stay, and soon Hyatt Bearing was making good money. This wasn't entirely Sloan's doing, for it happened that Hyatt's bearings were well suited to the automobiles that were just beginning to be marketed in large numbers. For the first decade and a half of the twentieth century, Hyatt grew up with the auto industry. Sloan got to know Henry Ford, Walter Chrysler, Charles Nash and others who would leave their marks, if not their marques, on the carmaking business.

The man he became closest to was William Durant, the creator of General Motors. In the second decade of the twentieth century, Billy Durant was the automotive world's fox to Henry Ford's hedgehog (Sloan learned a bit from both, making him perhaps a raccoon). Where Ford pursued his vision of a people's car with a single-mindedness that bordered on monomania, Durant skipped across the landscape of the auto industry, dabbling here and dilettanting there. He had been the leading manufacturer of carriages and wagons before taking over the ailing Buick Motor Company and turning it into the top producer of autos. (He used Buick as a model—literally—for subsequent endeavors. Trying to explain to his engineers at General Motors what the next Oldsmobile should look like, he ordered them to find a two-handled crosscut saw and cut a Buick—the body of which at that time was made of wood—in half lengthwise, then again fore and aft. He pulled the pieces several inches apart in both directions. "We'll make a car a little wider than this Buick," he said. "We'll have it a little longer; more leg room. Put your regular hood and radiator on it. . . . Paint it; upholster it—and there's your Oldsmobile for the coming year.") In 1908, the same year Ford brought out the Model T, Durant organized the General Motors Company, which applied the holding-company principles pioneered by John D. Rockefeller to the manufacture of automobiles. This first General Motors subsumed Buick, Olds (later Oldsmobile), Oakland (later Pontiac), Cadillac and several other companies involved in the production of autos or auto parts.

Durant proved a better creator than administrator; within two years he had lost control of General Motors to a clique of the company's creditors. Yet, ever resilient, he joined with Louis Chevrolet to produce a car similar in spirit if not yet in execution to the Ford Model T. The car did well in the market, and within a few years the Chevrolet Motor Company had a national presence. The directors of General Motors displayed an interest; Durant swapped Chevrolet stock for General Motors stock. His growing stake in General Motors was accompanied by the reburnishing at Chevrolet of his reputation as a carmaker; when in 1916 he threatened a proxy fight for the presidency, the bankers decided to go back to their banks and leave automaking to the motor men. Durant immediately reorganized the company, transferring the charter from New Jersey to Delaware, increasing the capitalization from $60 million to $100 million and tightening the lines of authority from the center to the subsidiaries.

He also cast his eye on Hyatt Roller Bearing, which was what brought Alfred Sloan to his office in the spring of 1916. "I found Mr. Durant a very persuasive man, soft-spoken and ingratiating," Sloan said. "He was short, conservatively and immaculately dressed, and had an air of being permanently calm—though he was continuously involved in big and complicated financial deals—and he inspired confidence in his character and ability. He asked me if the Hyatt Roller Bearing company was for sale."

Sloan professed surprise at the thought of selling the firm he had spent eighteen years building—but perhaps more surprise than he actually felt. In fact for some time he had been fretting about Hyatt's unhealthy dependence on a couple of large customers, of which Ford was the largest, providing over half Hyatt's sales. If Ford placed its orders elsewhere, Hyatt would be in trouble. Taking shelter with GM, Hyatt's second largest customer, made sense. Besides, the particular bearing design that carried the weight of Hyatt's sales was approaching obsolescence. It would be superseded by something else, but whether that something else would wear the Hyatt stamp, Sloan couldn't say. Sloan was an improver, not an inventor, and he recognized the difference. As a final consideration, the sale of Hyatt at any reasonable price would make Sloan far wealthier than Hyatt was currently making him, and wealthier than it would in any feasible future.

Sloan initially asked $15 million for Hyatt. "Mr. Durant never batted an eye or ceased to smile," Sloan recalled, "and his teeth were very white. 'I'm still interested, Mr. Sloan.'" Durant proceeded to explain his great plans for the partnership of the two companies. So compelling was his exposition that he soon knocked Sloan down by a million and a half. "I have always thought I could have got the $15 million, if my nerve had held out," Sloan reflected. "But it was a big transaction for me." Durant offered half cash, half stock in a new enterprise called United Motors, which would be a supplier of parts to General Motors; when some of Sloan's partners shied away from the stock, Sloan wound up with more equity in United and less money in the bank than he had anticipated. Yet this turned out not to be such a bad thing when Durant proposed that Sloan protect his new stake by operating United as its president.

Sloan's presidency was productive but brief. In 1918 such autonomy as United exercised vanished when GM absorbed the company. Sloan's responsibilities changed less than his title; he became GM's vice president for what he had just been president of at United. More important, he also became a director of GM and a member of its executive committee.

Sloan soon discovered for himself what people who knew Billy Durant had learned long before: that his backswing was better than his follow-through. "I admired his automotive genius, his imagination, his generous human qualities, and his integrity," Sloan said. "But I thought he was too casual in his ways for an administrator, and he overloaded himself. Important decisions had to wait until he was free, and were often made impulsively." As luck—Durant's bad luck, Sloan's good luck—would have it, the vice president didn't have to put up with the president's impulsiveness for very long. A sharp post–World War I slump caught Durant out speculating; as his brokers' loans came due he had to unload his GM stock. Again he lost the presidency, this time to Pierre du Pont.

But du Pont, of the chemical family, wasn't an auto man, and he took the job primarily to protect the large Du Pont stake in GM until a permanent replacement could be found. Soon he and others began to suspect that Sloan was that replacement. During the early 1920s General Motors faced two sets of challenges, one peculiar to the corporation, the other confronting the auto industry as a whole. The peculiar set of circumstances required GM's management to devise a method for minimizing the madness inherent in a holding company masquerading as a unified firm. Durant's rechartering of the company couldn't by itself solve the essential problem of decentralization: of each division being a quasi-corporation unto itself. There were no common standards of accounting, for example—a circumstance that made it impossible for the board of directors to allocate investment rationally. The company gained something from having suppliers sheltered beneath the corporate umbrella, but because pricing of goods transferred from one division to another was haphazard and confused, the benefits were nowhere near what they should have been.

The most glaring organizational weakness was the unplanned and counterproductive placement of GM autos in the car market. GM sold ten cars that ranged in price from less than $800 for a basic Chevrolet to nearly $6000 for a loaded Cadillac. But the arrangement of these models reflected historical accident rather than any carefully conceived plan. Some of the cars competed directly against each other, effectively negating much marketing effort.

The problems endemic to the industry at large could be summarized in a four-letter word (often used as such around GM headquarters): Ford. The Model T had transformed the market for automobiles, but the industry had yet to respond to that transformation. Ford, in fact, was slowest to respond, with consequences that were already coming into view. The low price of the T had enabled Ford to dominate the low end of the market; in time, however, the T's durability pushed the low end—somewhat paradoxically—both lower and higher. Used T's could be had for half the price of new ones, yet many of them had years of service left. At the same time, a buyer who traded in his T could step up to a more expensive model for no more cash outlay than he had paid for his first car. In addition, by its very success and ubiquity, the T had elevated expectations; as the novelty of mobility wore off, drivers and passengers increasingly wanted to arrive in style or at least in a modicum of comfort. More and more drivers—and especially their wives—began insisting on such amenities as closed bodies, which kept off the rain and wind. "For twenty years we protected ourselves with a variety of rubber coats, hats, lap robes, and other makeshift things," Sloan observed. "For some reason or other, it took us a long time to realize that the way to keep dry in a motorcar was to keep the weather out of the car."

Sloan's landmark contribution to the auto industry as a whole and to General Motors in particular was to formulate solutions to these interrelated problems. While working as Pierre du Pont's "left-hand man," as he called himself (not being pushy, he allowed the right hand to another man), he crafted a comprehensive design for rationalizing the structure and operation of the company. This "Organization Study" was one of the first of its kind, and in later decades it served as a business-school model. The essential issue, as Sloan saw it, was how to capture the economies of scale of a large company without losing the flexibility of smaller, semi-independent divisions. Sloan's blueprint identified five objectives:

1. To state succinctly and definitively the relations of the subsidiary units of the corporation to one another and to the corporation as a whole.
2. To delineate the functions of the corporate management to the subsidiary parts.
3. To centralize control of all executive functions of the corporation in the president as chief executive officer.
4. To limit the number of subordinates having access to the president, so that he might focus on big issues and large policy.
5. To provide executives in each sector of the corporation with information and advice from other sectors, the better to coordinate the actions of the different sectors.

Some wag once said that Shakespeare was a fine writer except for all those clichés; Sloan was no Shakespeare, but to a certain extent his organizational study falls into the same historical trap. From the distance of three-quarters of a century some of his principles—especially the first and second—appear numbingly obvious. But at the time they were novel enough—at least within General Motors—to win him a reputation as a weighty thinker. Billy Durant's creation had grown unguidedly; until Sloan came along no one made a concerted effort to bring the disparate parts of the corporation into a coherent whole.

It was largely on the strength of this study that Sloan won the GM presidency in 1923 when du Pont stepped down. The industry hadn't quite shaken the chills that had afflicted it recurrently since the war; in 1924 sales slumped more than ten percent. GM did even worse, losing nearly thirty percent from the previous year. But things improved during the next twelve months and until the stock crash of 1929, sales for the company and industry continued to rise.

The rising market allowed Sloan to implement his ideas at GM; the implementation in turn encouraged the market to continue to rise, especially for GM. The company's share of sales grew steadily; by the end of the decade it had passed Ford to claim leadership in the industry.

If the Henry Ford era in cars had been the age of production, the Sloan era was the age of marketing. Sloan didn't originate the several marketing techniques that put GM over the top, but he made better use of them than anyone else. Installment selling fell into this category. The purchase of consumer goods on credit had been a minor part of American business for decades (Cyrus McCormick's reapers fell into the producer-goods category), but not until the establishment of the General Motors Acceptance Corporation after World War I did any carmaker extend credit to customers as a matter of course. This concept greatly expanded the market for GM cars; many more people could manage the monthly payments than could summon the lump to pay cash. So popular was the idea that other car manufacturers quickly copied it. By the mid-1920s a majority of cars were being sold on the installment plan.

Complementing credit buying were regular provisions for taking trade-ins. Until after World War I most car buyers were first-timers, but as the twentieth anniversary of the introduction of the Model T approached, a substantial portion of purchasers were back for their second or even third cars. By letting those customers use the old bangers to cover the down payments on the new models, GM made buying even easier than installments alone would have.

But Sloan's greatest contribution to the modern era in auto sales was the introduction of annual model changes. Here again the contrast to Ford was striking. Ford achieved his low production costs through almost endless production runs; but in the process he removed any substantial incentive for purchasers to buy another Ford. A Model T made in 1925 was essentially the same car as the T made in 1910; a Ford owner might as well drive his car until it stopped—which, given the reliability Ford prided his cars on, could be many thousands of miles down the road. Eventually, of course, Ford recognized the need to make improvements, and the unveiling of the Model A in 1928 became a major event in the world of automobiles, with initial sales to match.

Sloan hoped to create a similar sizzle every year. To a certain extent this was an engineering decision, following from the desire of GM's design teams to incorporate improvements on a regular basis. Sloan initially resisted a commitment to a rigid timetable of updates, leaning toward the view of some of his associates who argued that improvements ought to be incorporated discreetly, thereby lending the impression that GM vehicles were perpetually state of the art. But the marketing appeal of new and improved models pushed management in the direction of making a show of each revision. And the demands of dealers to know what was coming forced Sloan and the others toward a preannounced schedule, of which an annual version made the simplest sense.

Before long the engineering motivation for annual model changes gave way to the marketing considerations. Really significant engineering innovations—four-wheel brakes, for example, introduced on Chevrolets in 1928—were harder to come by than strictly cosmetic style changes. In 1926 GM had established styling as a separate concept, in the Cadillac division; within a short time the notion was applied to the other divisions as well.

Not deliberately, but naturally, the emphasis on annual style changes downgraded durability as an element in the thinking of GM designers. Henry Ford had wanted his cars to run forever; Alfred Sloan had no such desire. GM cars should run long enough to get their owners to their first trade-in, preferably not more than a few years after purchase. Indeed, the prospect of mounting repair bills would encourage owners to buy a new car.

But buyers should not get just a newer version of the same old car. Sloan envisioned GM's customers climbing the ladder of models from the Chevrolet to the Cadillac. When Sloan took the helm at GM the Chevrolet was no match for the Ford T in either price or quality; the new boss recognized the need to meet, if not necessarily defeat, Ford at the low end of the market. At first the company sought entry-level salvation in an air-cooled engine (the "copper-cooled engine," it was called, for the copper fins that dispersed the heat). But despite the best efforts of research engineer Charles Kettering, the company could never get the coppered cars to run right; they overheated and lost power under stress. Sloan killed the project. The move angered Kettering, who thought the concept of air-cooling ought to be pursued further, but it allowed the corporation to get on with a car it could sell. "I could not, as I saw it," Sloan said, "in the face of an expanding market hold up the programs of the corporation for an uncertain development. If I had done so I do not believe there would be a General Motors today; we would have missed the boat."

What the company did produce was a Chevrolet with a conventional water-cooled engine, priced just above Ford's T. The price was close enough to bring first-time buyers in the door of dealerships, where salesmen could explain what Chevrolet owners received for their few additional dollars. "We proposed to demonstrate to the buyer that though our car cost X dollars more, it was X plus Y dollars better," Sloan said. Moreover, with the annual improvements the Chevrolet would get progressively better while Ford would keep cranking out the same old car.

Ironically, it was Ford's decision to improve his own car that gave Chevrolet its biggest boost. Chevrolet was already creeping up on the T in sales when Henry Ford shut down his plants to convert to the Model A;

the hiatus in Ford production left low-end buyers with little choice but to buy a Chevrolet. And, as an auto-industry analyst dryly observed, "There is not on record a single instance of a refusal of a Chevrolet dealer to sell a car to a Ford owner."

By the late 1920s the GM line had been fairly well rationalized. It provided "a car for every purse and purpose," as Sloan liked to say. An industry analyst was more specific: "Chevrolet for hoi polloi, Oakland (later Pontiac) for the poor but proud, Oldsmobile for the comfortable but discreet, Buick for the striving, Cadillac for the rich." America was the land of opportunity, and the 1920s were the decade of prosperity; it was hardly outrageous for even Chevy buyers to dream of Cadillacs, with GM supplying each intervening rung.

This ladder of dreams came crashing down after the stock collapse of 1929. New cars were neither necessities, the purchase of which topped people's priorities, nor strictly luxury items, appealing only to those very rich who didn't have to worry about the general condition of the economy. Now that they were, in Sloan's conceptualization, a mass–class phenomenon, they were very sensitive to the ups and downs of the business cycle. In tough times drivers could always squeeze a few more miles out of the family flivver or buy used instead of new. They did both during the Depression, by the millions. Sales nose-dived; dealers were forced to close their doors; marginal manufacturers were pushed over the edge—leaving just three that counted: Ford, General Motors and Chrysler.

GM survived the slump better than its big rival Ford, largely because of Sloan's cautious approach to long-term strategy. After the searing experience of the early 1920s Sloan sought insurance against the vagaries of a volatile market. He and his planners estimated the rate of return on investment they thought they could achieve over the course of the business cycle—"the highest return consistent with attainable volume," in the company's formula. Then the planning team established the unit volume it thought it could average over the business cycle—"the standard volume." Finally it calculated what price—"the standard price"—it needed to charge to achieve the target return at the standard volume. And it stuck with this price almost regardless of demand (some variance was allowed for variable unit costs like labor and materials). "I believe the true economic formula in the establishment of industry's prices should disregard movement in the business cycle," Sloan said.

Sloan's formula worked. Although unit sales fell by two-thirds during the Depression, the company made a profit every year and never missed a dividend. It grew stronger during the 1930s, certainly relative to the competition; in 1937 its profits accounted for nearly four-fifths of industry profits overall. It held roughly 45 percent of the market for cars and might have gone higher but for concern regarding antitrust problems. "Our bogie is 45 percent in each price class," Sloan said. "We don't want any more than that." As for the long-term return: during the dozen years that ended in 1938—which included eight years of depression—the company averaged 18 percent on its net capital investment.

Sloan's formula certainly pleased GM's stockholders (of whom Sloan himself was by now one of the largest), but it didn't make GM's workers happy. In the face of falling demand something had to give in the supply equation, and if by Sloan's policy it wasn't price, it was production—that is, jobs. GM laid off half its workforce between 1929 and 1932. Until the arrival of Franklin Roosevelt and the New Deal there was little those who were laid off could do but grumble and go hungry, but after the Democrats guaranteed workers' right to organize—and after demand and employment began to pick up a bit—the United Auto Workers took on GM. Adopting a tactic previously employed in other industries, UAW members staged a sit-down strike in GM's Fisher Body plants in Flint, Michigan. The sit-down shut down the works; more important, the occupation of the plants kept management, which had to fear for the safety of its expensive machinery, from hiring replacements. In earlier days GM might have appealed to government for assistance, but neither Washington nor the Democratic governor of Michigan showed any inclination to use force against an important component of the newly confirmed Democratic coalition. Instead the president and the governor pressured Sloan to talk to his men.

Sloan initially refused, contending that a sit-down strike amounted to illegal trespass and seizure. But Governor Frank Murphy continued to reject calls to use the National Guard to evict the squatters. "I'm not going down in history as 'Bloody Murphy'!" he insisted. "If I send those soldiers right in on the men there'd be no telling how many would be killed." Meanwhile Secretary of Labor Frances Perkins and the White House pushed hard to get GM's management to negotiate. Moreover, the assembly lines at Ford and Chrysler were running flat out as those companies happily stole customers and market share from the industry leader—the Ford men doubtless deeming it poetic payback for the march GM had stolen on Ford during the latter's shutdown in the transition to the Model A.

After five weeks Sloan consented to talk. And on the critical issue—representation of labor—he essentially accepted the union's position. For six months the United Auto Workers would be the exclusive representative of GM's workers; during that period the union could recruit freely in GM plants. The union fully expected that by the end of that period its situation at GM would be permanently assured. This indeed was how things transpired, and after breaking through at GM the union went on to win the right to represent Chrysler's workers and, after a stubborn fight, Ford's.

The bad news for Sloan extended into 1938. In that year the Justice Department brought conspiracy charges against GM, Ford and Chrysler for allegedly compelling dealers to use company subsidiaries to finance sales. Ford and Chrysler quickly signed consent decrees to stop the practice; GM held out. Sloan and several other GM executives were tried in a federal court in Indiana, where the jury returned a decidedly ambivalent verdict: The company was guilty but the executives were not. One puzzled editorialist remarked that it appeared that "there had been a conspiracy without conspirators."

Despite this partial setback GM rolled on. Measured by sales it had become the largest industrial enterprise in America (its assets were still slightly less than those of U.S. Steel). Analysts—and competitors—marveled at Sloan's continuing ability to tie the economies of enormous scale to the nimbleness of independent initiative. Some spied Sloan's secret in the corporate structure he had created. Various analogies were summoned to describe this structure. Many followed Sloan himself in pointing to the military; as he put it, "I developed a General Staff similar in name and purpose to what exists in the army." Analyst Peter Drucker, who made his name examining General Motors during the Sloan years, granted the aptness of the military analogy but identified another as well: the Catholic Church. *Fortune* magazine saw still another parallel: the government of the United States. In a serialized study of GM and Sloan, *Fortune* explained:

> His achievement may be summed up as one of intercommunication, getting all the facts before all the people concerned. In essence, it is the democratic method applied to management, with the committee taking the place of the deliberative assembly. Each division head is a boss who can be overruled by no individual, is rarely overruled by a group. To put it another way, what Mr. Sloan has done is to set up a federal system, in which each state or division has a large degree of autonomy, only certain powers being reserved to the central government.

Others credited Sloan's personal style, which in fact belied the military model he himself adduced. "I never give orders," he was quoted as saying.

He deliberately distanced himself from Henry Ford in this regard, believing—with many others—that the aging Ford's dictatorial style was behind many of Ford Motor's problems. "Dictatorship is the most effective form of administration," Sloan observed, "provided the dictator knows the complete answer to all questions. But he never does and never will." An industry observer familiar with both Ford and Sloan declared of Sloan:

> He is as different from Mr. Ford as a man could be. He makes suggestions. He does not give commands. If he cannot persuade his subordinates that a certain policy is wise, that policy does not go through. The same principle applies to them in turn. They must persuade their own associates.

Whether as general, pope or jawboner, Sloan guided GM through the end of the Depression into the years of World War II. Sloan turned sixty-five in 1940; encroaching deafness compelled him to wear an auditory aid so strong that he had to remember to turn it down when he spoke lest the feedback destroy what remained of his hearing. Now chairman of the board rather than president, but still chief executive officer, he directed the conversion of GM's auto assembly lines to the manufacture of machine guns, antiaircraft cannons, artillery shells and various other weapons and ammunition—in addition to supervising the continued production of trucks and other items the company regularly made that adapted readily to wartime purposes. Where some companies grew fat on the cost-plus pricing of the war years, GM actually grew leaner, because the 10 percent profit the government allowed was barely half what the company had been making on its own.

The war years brought changes in other areas as well. Labor shortages compelled the company to employ people who never would have made it past the plant gates previously; among these were more than 100,000 women—so many Rosie the Riveters. Less publicized were a crew of African-American former prostitutes hired by Nicholas Dreystadt of the Cadillac division to assemble airplane gyroscopes. To the surprise of many of Dreystadt's associates, the women proved to be good workers. He also hired their former madams, saying, "They know how to manage the women"—as indeed they did. To Dreystadt's dismay, union seniority rules and veterans' preferences—not to mention racial and sexual prejudice—forced the ouster of the women after the war. When some committed suicide rather than return to their prewar work, Dreystadt lamented, "God forgive me. I have failed these poor souls."

Sloan retired as CEO several months after the war ended, leaving to others the guidance of the company and the auto industry through a second postwar boom. After twenty-three years in charge of GM he was a legend—as was the monster corporation he had nurtured. Stories abounded of GM's size and complexity. One tale had two weary businessmen unwinding at a Florida resort; cursory initial conversation revealed that they both worked in the auto industry. Further query uncovered that they both worked at General Motors. Additional investigation turned up that they were both GM vice presidents.

Sloan doubtless chuckled the first time he heard this. He was proud of the organization he had put together. "There is a strong temptation for the leading officers to make decisions themselves without the sometimes onerous process of discussion, which involves selling your ideas to others," he conceded. "The group will not always make a better decision than any particular member would make; there is even the possibility of some averaging down. But in General Motors I think the record shows that we have averaged up."

Yet Sloan acknowledged that structures existed to serve people, not the other way around. "An organization does not make decisions; its function is to provide a framework. . . . Individuals make the decisions and take responsibility for them." Sloan had made his share of decisions, and he was willing to take responsibility for the creation of one of the grand edifices of modern industry.

10

THINK—AND SELL

Thomas J. Watson

...

SOME SALESMEN ARE BORN GREAT; OTHERS ACQUIRE GREATNESS; still others have greatness thrust upon them. Thomas J. Watson fell somewhere between categories two and three. An uneventful childhood and youth in upstate New York certainly yielded no evidence of the remarkable sales ability that would enable Watson to forge the company that would be called the General Motors of business machines and later of computers. Neither did a dismal stint as a schoolteacher or a partnership in a Buffalo butcher shop that started promisingly but collapsed when his partner absconded with the cash box.

Yet the faithless partner didn't steal the cash *register*—an omission that turned out to have important consequences for Watson. The register had been purchased on credit from the National Cash Register Company; Watson now returned it. While at the local NCR office he applied for a job. John Range, the district manager, didn't see much in this gullible failure and told him to go away. Watson persisted, though, until Range gave in.

Watson's initial performance made Range think he shouldn't have. In ten days the new man made not a single sale. The problem, Watson lamented, was that no one wanted to buy a cash register. Of course they didn't, Range replied. If they *wanted* to buy them they'd come in to the office and get them themselves, and the company would be spared the trouble and expense of supporting sad excuses for salesmen like Watson. What

Watson had to find out was *why* they didn't want them. When he knew that he'd be halfway to changing their minds.

Watson listened and learned. When Range took him out on a round of calls and showed him how to parry refusals with jokes and questions, he watched and learned. After Range handed him the company sales manual, *The NCR Primer*, he read and learned. Gradually he put what he learned to work, and the orders started to come. He traveled beyond Buffalo across western New York and into Pennsylvania, making calls during the day, spending nights on the train. As he grew into a familiar presence to merchants and railway conductors, he grew into a good salesman, eventually an excellent one.

Watson's performance brought him to the attention of John Patterson, the autocrat of "the Cash," as NCR was known to its employees and others in and around the company's hometown of Dayton, Ohio. Patterson was brilliant, ruthless and arbitrary; an observer once described him as "an amalgam of St. Paul, Poor Richard and Adolf Hitler." Originally a dry-goods retailer, he had been impressed by the ability of cash registers—a relatively new product then—to keep clerks honest; now he trained a staff of salesmen to preach the virtues of cash registers across the land. In time he developed the most potent sales force in the country. Despite his own Ivy League background he disdained higher education for anyone interested in business—including himself. "What I learned mostly," he said of his Dartmouth years, "was what not to do." He preferred his recruits raw. "I think that better salesmen can be made of new, green men, who are willing and energetic, than can be made of men who have some experience in this business."

Patterson insisted on good grooming in Cash men. "You must sell yourself first," he told them. Habitually he sent promising salesmen to New York to acquire a first-class wardrobe and first-class tastes. The former would inspire customers with the company's professionalism; the latter would inspire the salesmen to greater efforts. Those salesmen who bought into the Cash system were handsomely rewarded. His best salesmen made $30,000 a year—and Patterson emphasized that he would be thrilled if they made much more. "If you can sell a million dollars in a week," he told one of his outstanding performers, "we'll hire a brass band to take your commission to you."

Watson was one of those who bought into the Cash system. His good work on the road won him promotion to branch manager in Rochester, a moribund office with flagging sales. Watson redoubled his previous efforts, discovered a competitive streak in himself that hadn't been apparent before, and turned the situation around. Rochester's sales soon set records; the district became one of the company's hottest.

John Patterson observed approvingly and in 1903 invited Watson to Dayton to discuss another promotion. This one involved a special assignment—so special, in fact, that the Cash would deny any connection to it. By this time NCR held an overwhelming advantage in sales of new cash registers, but its plans to expand its market share further were frustrated by secondhand sales. Whereas Alfred P. Sloan addressed a similar problem in autos by inaugurating annual model changes, Patterson ordered Watson to wipe out the resellers by covert methods. With Cash money Watson would set up an ostensibly independent distributorship—Watson's Cash Register and Second Hand Exchange—in New York City. This dummy firm didn't have to turn a profit; all it had to do was drive its—that is, NCR's—competitors out of business.

Watson was the ideal candidate for the job. He was unknown in Manhattan, as were his connections to NCR. He was also, as Patterson had discovered, intelligent, ambitious and not especially enthusiastic about every section of the Sherman antitrust law. In fact, as his defenders later claimed, he may not have been *aware* of every section of the Sherman antitrust law—which was all the better from Patterson's perspective. Wherever the truth lay, Watson was a tough competitor and a sound company man.

Beyond its bogus identity, Watson's New York company engaged in tactics that started at sharp and ended at fraudulent. Watson and his subordinates engaged in commercial espionage, spying on their rivals and their rivals' customers. They set up shop next door to competitors and practiced predatory pricing unconstrained by any profit considerations. The most egregious form of deception was the employment of "knockout machines." These registers were secretly made by NCR but were designed to pass for competitors' models. A druggist, for example, who had recently purchased a $200 Hallwood machine would be surprised and dismayed to discover that the druggist around the corner had purchased a nearly identical model for $100. The Hallwood representative would have to spend his time explaining that it wasn't a genuine Hallwood but a cheap imitation. Even if he succeeded, when the fake Hallwood broke down, as it invariably did, the sight of the inoperable machine awaiting replacement by a reputable model—an NCR perhaps—eroded Hallwood's reputation.

Watson did his job well enough in New York that he was transferred to Philadelphia to repeat his success, which he did. Then he was moved to

Chicago, where he organized a national secondhand campaign. In 1907 he was publicly re-embraced by the Cash, which announced that he was being brought into the NCR family as head of *its* secondhand operations. He would be based in Dayton, at the right hand of John Patterson.

This proved to be a mixed blessing. The financial rewards were real, and the path up the Cash ladder appeared clear and relatively unobstructed. But Patterson was a strange man and difficult to be around. A food and health faddist, the NCR chief inflicted his notions of self-improvement on his employees. Lectures were interspersed with compulsory calisthenics and outdoor exercise. More troubling, Patterson manifested a suspicion of success in his close associates that at times verged on paranoia; repeatedly executives who did too well were summarily sacked.

One such sacking revealed the gravest disadvantage of working for Patterson: It could earn a person prison time. In 1910 a disgruntled former Cash man blew the whistle on the NCR skulduggery. Before long Patterson faced criminal charges in state and federal courts. Watson, the loyal lieutenant, was included in the indictments. That the defendants were found guilty didn't surprise many observers, given the strength of the evidence and of popular antitrust sentiment in that progressive era. That they were not merely fined but sentenced to a year behind bars added a frisson to the schadenfreude.

Watson was indignantly unrepentant, contending that he had done no wrong but simply been caught up in a politically motivated prosecution. His indignation, however, wasn't what saved him from having to swap his pin stripes for pen stripes. Not long after the sentences were handed down a horrendous spring storm hit Ohio, hurling rivers out of their banks and burying Dayton's downtown under a dozen feet of water. John Patterson, doubtless discerning opportunity in the danger, bent every personal and corporate effort to safeguarding the citizenry and relieving the suffering. Watson, too, threw himself into the rescue, organizing a mercy mission to carry food, water, clothing and medication to the city's refugees. By the time the floodwaters had receded, the Cash men were national heroes and state saints. Under the circumstances, sending them to jail didn't seem quite as smart as it had just a couple of weeks earlier, and when an appellate court tossed out the original conviction on a technicality, the attorney general didn't have the nerve to retry the case.

Watson took this for vindication but had little opportunity to savor it. Even before the appeals court rendered its verdict Patterson delivered one of his own. In April 1914 he fired Watson. As befitted a despot he didn't reveal his reasons, but given his pattern of dismissing star subordinates it doubtless reflected an inability to tolerate strength beside the throne.

Patterson's perversity in this regard was well recognized, and the abrupt dismissal didn't materially hurt Watson's chances of finding another job. Indeed, such was his reputation in his own and related industries that he had his pick of several. The one he settled on came from the Computer-Tabulating-Recording Company, a loose amalgamation of smaller firms (organized somewhat on the model of General Motors in the pre-Sloan era) engaged in the manufacture and distribution of counting, weighing, recording and timekeeping equipment for business. Certain members of the CTR board of directors had reservations about Watson, who at the time of his recruitment still faced the possibility of prison. "Who is going to run the business while he serves his term in jail?" growled one director opposed to the idea of a convicted felon in the president's chair. In fact such reservations kept Watson from being appointed president of CTR; for the time being he settled for the post of general manager. As suited a man who had spent his entire career on commission, Watson insisted on a compensation package that tied his pay to the company's performance. He received a gentleman's salary of $25,000, some stock options and a share of the profits.

Watson knew little about the manufacture of CTR products; as at NCR his strength lay in sales. He immediately began applying what he deemed the best of the Patterson system to CTR. He met with company salesmen in small groups, then en masse. He emphasized personal appearance and comportment. The sales force represented the company to customers and to the public, he said; the company and hence the company's products would be judged by the impression conveyed by the salesmen.

Considering Watson's recent brush with the law, some of the salesmen may have been surprised to hear him stress the strictest integrity in business dealings. On the other hand, maybe they weren't surprised and simply chalked his admonitions up to hard experience. In either case he warned against uncompetitive practices. "You must not do anything that's in restraint of trade," he said. In a typical statement that linked warning to praise he declared, "No man ever won except in the one, honest, fair, and square way in which you men are working."

As Watson portrayed it, everything boiled down to individual character. "A company is known by the men it keeps," he inscribed on the wall of the CTR training center. One of his favorite motivational lectures included a listing of several terms on a blackboard.

The Manufacturers
General Manager
Sales Manager
Service Manager
Sales Man
Factory Man
Office Manager
Office Man

"We have different ideas and different work," Watson would explain, "but when you come right down to it, there is just one thing we have to deal with throughout the whole organization"—here he took his chalk and highlighted appropriately—"MAN."

The CTR man (later the IBM man) was one who understood that personal success and corporate success coincided. "You have to put your heart in the business and the business in your heart," he said. "A team that can't be beat, won't be beat." "Every individual member is an important cog in the wheel which all help to turn."

As good as he had gotten at selling cash registers, Watson proved even better at selling the *idea* of selling. The CTR sales force responded to his preachments with enthusiasm. Cheerleaders at the sales meetings led the reps in songs; these included a paean to Watson's leadership:

Mr. Watson is the man we're working for;
He's the leader of the CTR.
He's the fairest, squarest man we know.
Sincere and true, he has shown us how to play the game
And how to make the dough.

Of course this last line was the bottom line for the reps and for everyone else associated with the company. During Watson's first few years at CTR he delivered the dough. Sales doubled between 1914 and 1917, although Watson had to share credit with World War I for this. And then the postwar recession that afflicted the American economy as a whole hit CTR too. Growth slackened, then slipped into reverse. Sales slumped by a third in 1921; when the board of directors insisted, against Watson's strong recommendations, on maintaining dividends, the company ran a deficit of $200,000 for the year.

Watson reacted to the downturn by downsizing the company. He slashed spending on research, laid off sales reps and cut wages and salaries across the board—including his own—by ten percent. His decisive action upset some of the directors, including chairman George Fairchild, who judged that Watson's cuts shortchanged the timekeeping side of the business in favor of tabulating devices. Watson's problem with Fairchild solved itself with the latter's death in 1924. Significantly, in that same year Watson arranged the renaming of the company: CTR became International Business Machines.

Shortly thereafter Watson celebrated his tenth anniversary with the company. In marketing IBM already bore his stamp; now its product line began to reflect his priorities. Watson saw the core of the business as machines that manipulated information. Other companies—Underwood, most notably—built better typewriters than IBM, and Watson was content to yield them most of that market, with the important exception of a new item: electric typewriters. Watson also gave ground in scales and other weighing instruments; eventually he divested the company of that division.

Watson always said that what IBM sold was service; and the service the company provided best revolved around three basic devices. The first was the card punch, which consisted of a keyboard and a mechanism for converting keystrokes to holes in thick paper cards. The operator would enter data at the keyboard—an order from a customer, a payment received, confirmation of shipment from a supplier—and this would be stored on the card. The second device was the sorter, which read the cards at high speed and automatically sorted them according to various criteria—account name, geographic region, current balance. The third device was the accounting machine, which acted on the information on the cards—tallying inventory, billing customers, printing checks. There were variations on these essential functions, customized to suit individual firms. But the idea was to automate functions common to all businesses, thereby saving labor and money.

In keeping with his philosophy of providing a service, Watson decided that IBM should lease equipment rather than sell it. To some degree this was a natural extension of NCR's philosophy of reducing customer resistance by encouraging installment buying; in this case the installments went on forever. The advantage to the customer came from not having money tied up in equipment; the advantage to IBM was the establishment of a long-term relationship with customers. Equally to the point, the equipment required certain consumable items that the customers had to purchase. Of these the most visible were the punch cards, which IBM sold by the hundreds of millions, later billions. During the late 1920s and

1930s these humble, mindlessly low-tech items were consistently responsible for more than a third of IBM's total sales.

The interwar decades were good for Watson and IBM. During the 1920s the same economic surge that carried Sloan and General Motors to automotive preeminence swelled the ranks of the white-collar sector that constituted the primary market for business machines. Watson would have been a poor salesman not to cash in on the rising demand; as he was not a poor salesman but a superlative one, he led the company to a doubling of revenues in a competitive field.

The decade of the Great Depression proved more problematic but, for that reason, more triumphant. The general stagnation of business cut seriously into IBM's revenues for a couple of years, pushing the total down by nearly $3 million between 1931 and 1933. But the New Deal made a new niche for IBM. Franklin Roosevelt's alphabet agencies—SEC, AAA, NRA, FDIC, WPA, CCC and a score more—addressed a variety of social ills and produced goods and services of diverse sorts, but one thing they all did was chew through great gobs of information.

Unlike many of his managerial confreres Watson had no philosophical problems with the New Deal. "The New Deal is going to mean better things for the majority of people in this country," he predicted. Quite obviously the economy was malfunctioning; Watson credited Roosevelt— "the greatest research engineer that the world has ever known," he said in one especially enthusiastic moment—with doing something to try to fix things. The National Recovery Administration, the most ambitious effort by the government to coordinate the economy, struck Watson as "one of the fairest and squarest propositions that has ever been presented."

Skeptics contended that Watson's support for the New Deal dovetailed with the paternalism that had always marked his attitude toward IBM employees—a paternalism he had learned from Patterson at the Cash. (Serious critics substituted "fascism" for "paternalism" in their complaints.) Others said that of course Watson liked the NRA and the other agencies because they represented that many more potential sales. This last clause of the argument was true enough. Watson bid aggressively for the new government business; his efforts were most conspicuously rewarded when he won a major contract to supply equipment to the just-created Social Security Administration.

As a result IBM thrived during the worst decade in American business history. Between 1931 and 1940 revenues more than doubled. By the latter year the company had become the leading supplier of office machines in the nation. Its earnings were almost three times as great as those of its closest competitor, NCR.

The glow IBM cast across the general gloom gave it a unique cachet. The ubiquitous "THINK" signs that adorned company offices became both an emblem of the Watson style of business leadership and a shorthand for IBM's distinctive corporate culture. A journalist investigating the IBM phenomenon wrote:

> The face of Providence is shining upon it, and clouds are parted to make way for it. Marching onward as to war, it has skirted the slough of depression and averted the quicksands of false booms. . . . Today everything and everybody in the organization, down to the lowliest sweeper, is surrounded with the aura of an immense and everlasting success.

This writer went on to excerpt the psalms sung to Watson by IBM executives and blue-collar workers alike. "You're our leader fine," declared one company song; another asserted, "By him we are all inspired." "We know you and we love you, and we know that you have our welfare at your heart," proclaimed an employee spokesman more or less extemporaneously.

The journalist, intrigued, examined the object of the veneration. His initial impression left him somewhat puzzled, but his puzzlement soon melted before the persuasiveness of the great man.

> For so eminent and persuasive a salesman, Mr. Watson is astonishingly at variance with what is regarded as the go-getting seller. He has no dental smile. He does not pump your arm or indulge in aimless jocosities to warm up the atmosphere. A moment of dead silence does not dismay him. . . .
>
> When he begins to talk he is the kind of slightly bashful, dignified gentleman who would be the last person on earth to try to sell you anything. Therefore you lose consciousness of your sales resistance. The lines of his face have accented the tenuousness of his lips, giving him a somewhat presbyterian cast. As he continues to speak, however, his whole face lights up with the vaguely wistful sincerity, the slightly imploring earnestness that can be noted even in his sternest photographs. . . .
>
> His right hand describes a simple gesture or two, and his words flow evenly, with assurance and conviction, as if each phrase had been inspected beforehand. Whether you particularly agree with them or not, you listen to them. Mr. Watson's monumental simplicity compels you to do so. What has happened is that he has buttonholed you as effectively as if he had hurdled his desk and offered you a ten-dollar gold piece for fifty cents.

Let him discourse on the manifest destiny of I.B.M., and you are ready to join the Company for life. Let him retail plain homilies on the value of Vision, and a complex and terrifying world becomes transparent and simple. Let him expound the necessity for giving religion the preference over everything else, and you could not help falling to your knees.

This reporter remarked that IBM employees neither wondered nor questioned that Watson had been paid $442,500 the previous year; by the end of the interview the reporter didn't either.

After the Depression came World War II, and things got even better. The second global conflict of the twentieth century was the war of American production, as Alfred Sloan demonstrated; it was also the war of American bureaucracy. Keeping track of all the tanks, ships, planes, C-rations, belt buckles and antibiotics required regiments of accountants and secretaries, supported by the appropriate equipment—of which none was more appropriate than IBM's. Total company revenues tripled in just five years; pretax earnings did too, although the wartime windfall profits tax took back most of the latter gain. The company lengthened its lead over its competitors, acquiring power and momentum none of them could match.

To some extent, however, IBM's momentum propelled it past a critical fork in the road. During the war a new element entered the business-machine picture—although for several years it remained unclear whether this new element was a business machine or ever would be. The War Department and related agencies sponsored the development of advanced calculating devices to assist in scientific and especially weapons research. The creation of the atomic bomb, to cite the most spectacular example, required the solution of sets of equations that would have taken mortal mathematicians years to complete—years that would have exacted a heavy toll in the lives of America's fighting men. IBM contributed to the development of these computing machines but only in an incidental way. The heavy lifting took place on college campuses and in federal research labs; IBM supplied support equipment but little expertise.

Watson turned seventy a few months before Allied forces stormed the beaches of Normandy; he was seventy-one by the time the atomic bomb ended the war against Japan. Had he been younger he might have appreciated that these new computing machines would change his business beyond recognition. Had he been a better listener he might have heeded associates who argued that computers weren't simply something for scientists to use to solve mathematical problems; they could accomplish the same sorts of tasks his card-based systems did but far faster and more efficiently. Had his passion been the hardware of machines rather than the software of sales and service, he might have appreciated the potential of these revolutionary devices. But whenever Watson sized up a new product he first asked himself whether he could sell it to customers; in the case of computers he couldn't see any sales potential for several years at the least.

For all these reasons IBM was slow to enter the computer sweepstakes. Remington Rand, by now number two in business machines, was quicker off the mark. James Rand had the prescience to purchase rights to something called the Universal Automatic Computer when the inventors ran out of development money; the UNIVAC, as it was known, established itself as the leader in the field. The Census Bureau confirmed this judgment by purchasing one to tabulate the 1950 census.

For half a century IBM and its forerunners had owned the business of the Census Bureau; this decision stung Watson. It also elevated the career trajectory of his son, Thomas Watson, Jr. Watson Junior had been groomed for the succession for years, although for several of those years he had resisted the idea. Only during World War II, when he flew with the Army Air Corps, did he become convinced that his future lay with his father's company. Perhaps it was the imminence of death that concentrated his attention, turning him away from the playboy path he had charted; perhaps it was a growing impression that the company was simply inescapable. "IBM was hard to avoid," he recalled, speaking of his service in the Pacific. "The entire military was beginning to move by IBM cards, because warfare had become so big and complicated that bookkeeping had to be done right on the battlefield. Toward the end of the war I'd land on some Pacific atoll just taken from the Japanese and find a mobile punchcard unit there, tabulating the payroll."

At first Watson Junior was no faster than his father to recognize the revolution that electronics would bring to business machines. On the advice of one of his father's aides—who *did* see the potential of computers—Junior visited the ENIAC, the first really modern computer, at the University of Pennsylvania. "I reacted to ENIAC the way some people probably reacted to the Wright brothers' airplane," he said. "It didn't move me at all. I can't imagine why I didn't think, 'Good God, that's the future of the IBM company.' But frankly I couldn't see this gigantic, costly, unreliable device as a piece of business equipment."

Enlightenment arrived soon enough, and he began to press his father to increase spending on research into electronic computing. Watson Senior humored the lad, apparently as much to keep him interested in IBM as from any dawning conviction that computers were the company's destiny. With the clarity of perception vouchsafed to the convert, Junior couldn't fathom his father's obtuseness. "IBM was still in the Dark Ages," he said. The company's research unit hardly merited the name. "All you've got up there is a bunch of monkey-wrench engineers," he told the old man. "Don't you see? The time for hacking machines out of metal is gone. Now you're getting into a field where you have to use oscilloscopes and understand the theory of electron streams and scanning beams inside the tubes."

Perhaps Junior would have persuaded Senior unassisted, but the Korean War provided a critical additional argument in favor of computers. The war broke out in June 1950 when Senior was traveling on IBM business in Europe; as one of the nation's senior business statesmen, he wired at once to President Truman that the company was at the country's disposal. The president's people should contact Watson Junior with any suggestions. Junior seized the opportunity, and he sent one of the company's best researchers to Washington. "I knew he would volunteer IBM to build a computer for the war effort," Junior said, "and I thought that was fine. It seemed to me that if we could build a couple of one-of-a-kind machines under government contracts, we'd have a way of getting our feet wet."

Junior laid plans for a major commitment to research into electronic computing. Significantly, he didn't involve the first people his father would have brought in. "I didn't want to ask the advice of our sales or market research people, because they'd howl the minute they saw what we wanted to do." What Junior wanted to do was take a three-million-dollar gamble on a machine for which the obvious market was strictly limited. To hedge his bet—if only in the eyes of his father—he told his people to line up as many orders as they could based simply on the paper promises of the project. They came back with twenty, generously including ten maybes. To blunt complaints from the sales side Junior christened the prospective machine the Defense Calculator.

This last tactic may have been the one that persuaded Watson Senior, especially after his personal promise to Truman. Besides, Senior was ready to hand the operating reins over to his son, who in 1952 was named president of the company. Junior's gamble on computers paid off; by 1956 IBM's 700 series had nosed out Remington Rand's UNIVAC in installations, and orders for the 700s were triple those for UNIVACs.

The success of the 700 compelled Watson Senior to grant that his son had known better than he on computers; on another matter, even more contentious between the two, he was less willing to concede error. Since World War II the Justice Department had been eyeing IBM for antitrust violations; in December 1952 it brought charges. Almost certainly the suit revived memories in Watson Senior of his brush with prison decades earlier, and just as he had deemed the NCR prosecution politically motivated, so he judged this IBM one. For some time he had been a public backer of Dwight Eisenhower, who in 1952 threw the Democrats out of the White House after two decades' occupancy; Watson saw the antitrust action as the Democrats' revenge. More than that, he considered the suit unjust punishment for IBM's success against its competitors. Righteously indignant, Watson took out full-page advertisements in leading newspapers defending the company's conduct and his own.

Watson Junior understood his father's emotional sensitivity on the issue. "The terrible trauma of getting sentenced to jail for antitrust violations when he was at the Cash never really passed for Dad," Junior observed. "Thirty-five years had gone by, but it was like a raw wound to his self-respect." Yet Junior also thought his father essentially misunderstood the basis for the prosecution. "The thing Dad could never accept about monopoly law is that you don't have to *do* anything wrong to *be* in the wrong. The Department of Justice was coming after us entirely because they didn't think there was enough competition in our market." To Watson Senior the prosecution was personal; to Watson Junior it was a cost of doing business.

For this reason Junior was willing to settle. He tried to point out to Senior that the Justice Department wasn't demanding a breakup of IBM, merely a loosening of its grip—for example, by licensing some of its patents to other firms and by allowing customers to purchase its machines instead of leasing them. He added that such a loosening was what the feds were offering now; if the case went to trial more severe sanctions might result—perhaps even the dismantling of the company. And he reminded his father that the Justice Department had a daunting success record in cases that went to trial: ninety percent since the 1930s.

The differences between father and son were no secret around the company, although discretion required ignoring the outbursts these sometimes occasioned. One day the two got into a shouting match that ended with the son storming off, saying he had a cross-country plane to catch. Senior summoned a limousine and beat Junior to the airport. Whether his purpose was to continue the argument or to make peace, Junior didn't wait to find out. "God damn you, old man!" he screamed on the tarmac in front of dozens of witnesses. "Can't you ever leave me alone?"

Watson Senior may have been persuaded belatedly by his son's logic, or perhaps he was moved by his son's anger. In either event he decided that the time had come to step aside. Although the younger man might have doubted it, Watson Senior recognized his limitations. "I'm no genius," he once told his wife. "I'm smart in spots—but I stay around those spots." In his eighties now, he appreciated that the industry was moving away from his spots. Salesmanship might have sufficed in an earlier day, but product was becoming increasingly important, at least in the nascent computer business. A competitor had once grumbled of his own company's failure to keep pace with IBM: "It doesn't do much good to build a better mousetrap if the other guy selling mousetraps has five times as many salesmen." Watson Senior finally saw that those days were gone. He had built the sales force; his son would have to work on the mousetraps.

11

THE FAITH THAT LAUNCHED
A THOUSAND SHIPS

Henry J. Kaiser

. . .

THE AMERICAN WEST HAS LONG BEEN THE LAND OF MYTH; AND IN-
deed many myths sprang up around it. Perceived in terms of its vast
open spaces, from the beginning of settlement it had a higher ratio of urban
to rural population than any other part of the country. Americans wept
when the director of the 1890 census announced that the era of the western
frontier had passed; in reality more land was homesteaded after 1890 than
before. Perhaps most enduringly, the West was thought of as the land of
rugged individualism, the place where people went to escape the oppressive
reach of government; in fact no part of America was so dependent on government nor so successful in marshalling government's aid.

Henry J. Kaiser wasn't a stranger to myths; at the apex of his career he
had entire teams spinning myths about him. But far from falling for the
myths about the West, he contradicted them with his own career. He did
his best to urbanize the empty spaces, building the infrastructure on which
urban living depended. He brought the accoutrements of civilization—including masses of tourists—to territories heretofore off the beaten path.
Most to the point of the enormous success he achieved in business, he happily accepted a leading role for government in important parts of the economy. Unlike many of his business contemporaries (although not unlike
Thomas Watson), Kaiser had an abiding faith in government as an agent
of development; rather than seeing government as the enemy of business
he perceived it as a partner. "I am proud of my government," he said. "I

want to do the work and service that it wants me to do." Kaiser's faith in government—combined with a faith in himself that bordered on the hubristic (and occasionally crossed the line)—carried him through the Great Depression of the 1930s, when he played a central role in some of the landmark public construction projects of the period; but it achieved its highest fulfillment, and won Kaiser international renown, during World War II, when the Allies sailed to victory on the armada of ships built in Kaiser's shipyards.

Like many another who achieved success in the West, Kaiser was born elsewhere—in his case in upstate New York in 1882, not that far from where eight-year-old Thomas Watson was playing. As the family name suggested, Kaiser's father was German; so was his mother. Franz Kaiser changed his name to Frank not long after arrival in America in the early 1870s, but otherwise he changed little of his peasant ways and never made much of a living. While he drowned his sorrows in alcohol, his wife Mary tried to hold the family together. But her health was never good, and she died when her son was seventeen. Memories of her ill health and early death would have a major influence on one of her son's most important business ventures; for the time being it encouraged the lad to get out into the world and start making an income. He was hired as a shelf-stocker and delivery boy for a local dry-goods store. At sixteen he became a traveling salesman, drumming dry goods about the county. Meanwhile he was dabbling in photography, taking pictures with a Kodak camera invented by George Eastman of nearby Rochester. This hobby led to a vocation when he took a job selling photographic supplies; the new job in turn led to an opportunity to purchase an interest in a photography studio in the resort town of Lake Placid.

Skiing and other winter sports had yet to find their way much out of Scandinavia and the Alps; Lake Placid was an exclusively warm-weather destination at the beginning of the twentieth century. When Kaiser saw all his customers heading for sunnier climes during the winter, he decided to follow them. He traveled to Florida, hoping to establish a chain of photography-supply stores. He might have succeeded had he stuck with it longer, but he fell in love and set his heart on marriage. The father of his intended insisted that the young man prove that he could care for the girl they both loved. Kaiser must establish himself in a substantial business— not this photography silliness. He must build his daughter a home, save a thousand dollars and show an income of at least $125 per month. Until he accomplished these things, marriage was out of the question. The older man, who had a lumber business with dealings in the Pacific Northwest, suggested that Kaiser test his luck in that part of the country—which, to the father's way of thinking, was conveniently far from his daughter.

Kaiser, a romantic at heart, accepted the challenge. He bought a train ticket for the West and kept riding until he got to Spokane, Washington, the capital of what the local chamber of commerce called the "Inland Empire." The town was a slightly more civilized version of the mining camps of the Coeur d'Alene, across the state line in Idaho, where radical unionists of the Western Federation of Miners and the Industrial Workers of the World regularly waged labor war against the capitalists who owned the mines. But only *slightly* more civilized: Like nearly all western towns, Spokane had its thriving red-light district, its gambling dens, its hell-on-wheels saloons where hard-earned money was spent by hard men in hardly any time at all. Precisely what motivated Kaiser to get off the train in Spokane, rather than stay on till Seattle or Portland, is lost to memory; before long it was lost to him as well. By his later recollection he called on a hundred businesses without any luck finding employment. "Prospects looked as black as possible," he said.

One particular proprietor, a hardware merchant named James McGowan, turned Kaiser down several times. But after a fire devastated McGowan's premises he agreed to let Kaiser direct the salvage of inventory. The young man hired a score of women who scraped, cleaned and polished the soot-covered merchandise until most of it could be sold. Certain that he had proved himself to McGowan, Kaiser asked what he could do next. "You've finished your job," McGowan replied. "You're fired."

Kaiser still refused to be discouraged, and eventually McGowan put him on as a clerk at seven dollars per week. The new man at once set about memorizing the price of every nail and saw and roll of wire in the place. Like many hardware stores, McGowan Brothers counted area builders as principal customers; before long Kaiser was making the rounds of construction sites, writing orders for lumber for houses, concrete for sidewalks, reinforcing bars for a bridge spanning the Spokane River, and scores of other items.

In the process he earned enough money to win his bride, who joined him in Spokane; he also learned enough about the construction business to consider trying his own hand at it. One of his first ventures took him across the international border into Canada; in 1914 he submitted the lowest bid on a contract to pave Victoria Avenue in Vancouver, British Columbia. When the city awarded him the contract he had to post a bond of

$25,000—which was about $25,000 more than he had. He walked into the Vancouver office of the Canadian Bank of Commerce and asked for a loan. The president observed him with wonder. "You mean to sit there and inform me, young man," he said, "that you want me to loan you $25,000 and you don't even have a company, you don't even have any equipment, you don't have any men?" Kaiser looked the banker in the eye and said that, yes, that was precisely what he wanted. The banker wasn't the last man to be impressed by Kaiser's brashness; he okayed the $25,000.

Kaiser remained in Canada only briefly; when the U.S. Congress passed a 1916 bill authorizing the construction of a national highway system he headed south. He stopped briefly in Seattle and then Portland before headquartering in Oakland in 1921. In the early 1920s Kaiser built sections of U.S. 99, the main north–south highway in Washington, Oregon and California. From the start he won a reputation for efficiency in construction; his crews put down pavement at the rate of a mile per week, double the industry standard. Government inspectors initially assumed he must be short-cutting on quality, but their most rigorous tests turned up nothing except solid work.

One secret of Kaiser's success was his readiness to embrace the most modern technology. Some innovations were modest: the substitution of wheelbarrows with rubber tires and ball bearings for iron-rimmed, bearingless models. Others were more ambitious and expensive: the replacement of horse teams with tractors. When Kaiser met an engineer named Robert Le Tourneau who had a gift for improvements in earth-moving equipment, he bought out Le Tourneau's patents and put him on the payroll.

Le Tourneau's equipment helped Kaiser build his first dam, on the Feather River near Chico, California; it also helped him win a contract for his first major project in the San Francisco Bay area. These ten miles of highway demanded millions of cubic yards of gravel; with typical ambition and foresight Kaiser constructed a much larger gravel plant than he needed. When the road was finished he found himself in the gravel business.

During the late 1920s Kaiser diversified into levees and pipeline work. The levees were along the Mississippi River; Kaiser came in as a subcontractor to Warren Brothers, one of America's biggest construction firms. The pipelines ran across the Great Plains from the gas fields of Texas and Oklahoma to markets in various cities; here Kaiser's partner was Warren ("Dad") Bechtel, already a power in western construction and destined to become a global player.

In 1927 Kaiser landed his largest contract to date, and also his most exotic. Warren Brothers had won the contract to build a highway down the center of Cuba, 750 miles in all. Ralph Warren asked Kaiser if he wanted 200 miles. By some accounts Kaiser accepted the offer sight unseen; other versions have him visiting Cuba, if only cursorily, before saying yes. Either way it was a gamble, but one he was willing to take. The $20 million the contract represented was too tempting to pass up; equally important, the project offered another opportunity to learn something new. As his entire career would demonstrate, a chance to learn something new often meant as much to Kaiser as a chance to make money. It was his good fortune—and a mark of his aptitude at absorbing lessons—that the first frequently led to the second.

One of the things Kaiser learned from his Cuban venture was that conceptions of honesty and corruption differed from country to country. After nearly fifteen years in the construction business he wasn't a babe in the woods when it came to the sorts of lubrication required to keep big jobs going, but he found the quantity of grease necessary to move the Cuba job along exasperating in the extreme.

More telling, he discovered the difficulty of supervising a job so far from home. Kaiser's genius was as an orchestrator of human effort, a problem solver who responded to the inevitable disruptions in construction schedules with imagination and verve. Orchestration and problem solving couldn't be done satisfactorily from a distance; yet without abandoning all his other jobs he couldn't spend his whole time in Cuba.

The difficulties of the Cuba job didn't prevent Kaiser from finishing ahead of schedule and with a profit of more than $2 million, but when an even bigger job beckoned back in the United States he was happy to leave the swamps and jungles of the island behind. The new job was definitely a change from swamps and jungles; it took Kaiser to the driest, most sparsely vegetated part of North America. Ever since John Wesley Powell had floated down the Colorado River in 1869, westerners of a developmentalist mentality had puzzled over how to tame that unruly stream and turn it to productive use. Congress made a start in 1902 with the passage of the Newlands Act, which set aside funds from the sale of public lands in southern and western states for irrigation projects. Two decades later the feds zeroed in on one project in particular: a huge dam to be built at a bend in the Colorado just west of Las Vegas, Nevada.

Although not by initial intent, the Boulder Dam project became a lifesaver for construction companies in the West during the 1930s. The Depression killed most private construction projects; it also dried up funding for many state and local projects. Just ten months before the stock crash of 1929 Congress authorized $165 million for the Boulder Dam; by the time bidding began in 1930 it was obvious that this was by far the biggest thing going west of the Mississippi.

In fact it was too big for any one company to bid on alone. Few firms could come up with the required $5 million performance bond, and few wanted to assume alone the risks such an unprecedented undertaking entailed. The most experienced engineers could only guess at many of the costs; none could foresee all the difficulties the construction crews would encounter. As a consequence most took refuge in consortiums.

Kaiser assumed a leading part in the largest of these. The Six Companies, as the Boulder consortium was called, consisted of a partnership of Kaiser and Bechtel, with a combined 30 percent stake; MacDonald & Kahn and Utah Construction with 20 percent each; and Morrison–Knudsen, J. F. Shea and Pacific Bridge with 10 percent each. Simply putting together a bid from this group was no easy task, not least because most of the principals were as strong willed as Kaiser. The group gathered in San Francisco early in 1931 to hammer out a position; after considerable discussion they decided that each party would submit an individual estimate for the job; these would be averaged and the average taken to Denver where the formal bidding would be done.

By the time Kaiser and the others got to the Brown Palace Hotel in the Colorado capital, the competition had narrowed to the Six Companies and two other consortiums. The high bid of $59 million came from a Nebraska–Oregon venture, the middle bid of $54 million from a Maryland–Califora combine. Kaiser's Six Companies won the contract with a bid of $49 million.

Kaiser had never taken on a project as large as this, nor had anyone else in America. Simply transporting tools, materials and workers to the site was a daunting task. Housing within a reasonable commute was nonexistent; a project town—Boulder City—had to be built from scratch for the thousands of men hired. The town had to be provisioned, policed and more or less protected from the pimps, gamblers and assorted other sharps determined to separate the men from their paychecks—or what remained of their paychecks after the cost of room and board was deducted.

The work itself commenced with the blasting of diversionary tunnels through the solid rock of the canyon walls. This was dirty, dangerous work; on any given shift a man might be killed by a premature explosion, an uncontrolled rockfall or carbon monoxide from the exhaust of the trucks hauling the waste to the surface. This last hazard provoked dozens of lawsuits against Six Companies for failing to protect workers' safety; most were settled out of court, often after years of litigation.

Kaiser's job as chairman of the consortium's executive committee was to ensure a steady flow of materials to the project. Much of this was what he had been doing for years, only on a larger scale. But a substantial portion was new, for ensuring a stream of supplies required ensuring the flow of federal dollars. Because the public was paying for the project—at a time when Washington was cutting back on nearly everything else—Kaiser and his colleagues came under intense political scrutiny. When labor unions alleged that Six Companies paid below prevailing wages, Congress felt obliged to investigate. When substandard living conditions in Boulder City were reported, the legislature took a look.

On more than one occasion Congress threatened to pull the plug. Initial authorization had involved a careful balancing of regional and national interests and votes. The deepening economic depression threatened the balance. The summer of 1932 was the most traumatic in living memory. Millions of workers languished without jobs; communities of the homeless ("Hoovervilles") sprang up all about the country; families roamed from county to county and state to state desperately seeking work of any kind. As desperate as any were the thousands of World War I veterans who joined the "Bonus Army" seeking prepayment of their pensions. President Hoover took fright at this pitiful show of force and sent the real army, under Chief of Staff Douglas MacArthur, to rout the rabble and disperse them.

Kaiser arrived in Washington while the Bonus Army was still bivouacked on the banks of the Anacostia River. In testimony before the Senate he explained that the work in the West was reaching a critical stage. The coming winter would bring its usual low water; this was when the river must be turned from its channel. If the construction crews missed this deadline, many months and millions of dollars would be lost. Congress must not let the funding fail. Lest the fate of a faraway dam leave certain senators cold, Kaiser alluded to the jobless veterans camped just down Capitol Hill. Three thousand hardworking men would be thrown off the payrolls, he explained, if the construction ceased; their seven thousand dependents would be cast adrift.

Kaiser's arguments convinced Congress, although the legislature continued to grumble and periodically cut back on aspects of the project it didn't deem immediately essential. He became a regular railroad commuter between Oakland and Washington, carrying his files in his briefcase and making the club car his office. He learned the ropes of the political system, figuring out which lawmakers and which of their staff were interested and knowledgeable about public works, which needed to be educated, which could be ignored. His lobbying efforts grew easier after the 1932 election sent Herbert Hoover packing and brought Franklin Roosevelt to the White House. Roosevelt talked a tough line on federal spending while campaigning for the presidency, but once he took office he embraced a pump-priming role for the federal government. Public works like the Boulder Dam would produce such long-term benefits as flood control, irrigation and hydroelectric power; in the short term they would provide jobs to workers who would spend their paychecks and stimulate the economy of the surrounding neighborhood.

Occasionally Kaiser carried his political efforts too far. In 1935, when new reports surfaced of poor living conditions at Boulder City, with the implication that Six Companies was cutting corners to pad its profits, Kaiser launched a letter- and telegram-writing campaign protesting the innocence of the consortium. Interior Secretary Harold Ickes, an ally of Kaiser in most matters, registered irritation. "Mr. Kaiser's telegraphic bombardment has not made a favorable impression upon me," Ickes told Senator Key Pittman of Nevada. "If there has been no violation of the law, there is nothing to cause apprehension in the breast of Mr. Kaiser." Ickes described the Kaiser method: "Mr. Kaiser has telegraphed to me, he has telegraphed to the President, he has telegraphed to you, and he has telegraphed to others, who have telegraphed to me. . . . Frankly he is doing himself and his company no good by his lack of composure."

Generally, however, Kaiser was more astute. When the federal government charged Six Companies with tens of thousands of violations of the federal eight-hour law, Kaiser cranked up a team of public-relations experts to explain why, under the special circumstances of the Boulder project, a strict application of the law was not in the interest of the nation or the workers involved. The group got out a pamphlet entitled "So Boulder Dam Was Built," describing the heroic efforts to date and the glories to come; Kaiser himself went on the radio (in a none-too-subtle imitation of Roosevelt's "fireside chats") to get the message across to ordinary folks at home. In this case he succeeded in knocking the federal fine down from $350,000 to $100,000; in broader terms he regained the high ground of popular approval even as the crews pouring concrete on the dam were approaching the higher reaches of the canyon walls.

When Six Companies delivered the dam to the federal government in

1936—two years ahead of schedule—most Americans were prepared to agree that the accomplishment was indeed heroic. It was certainly profitable for the consortium's participants; they split $10 million in after-tax profits.

Although some of the other participants wanted to catch their breath after Boulder (which was officially christened Hoover Dam for the president who got construction going), Kaiser was already busy on his next project. He once explained his philosophy of contracting:

> Contractors are all alike. They start out broke, with a wheelbarrow and a piece of hose. Then suddenly they find themselves in the money. Everything's fine. Ten years later many are back where they started from—with one wheelbarrow, a piece of hose, and broke. So, before you work yourself out of the last job, line up a bigger job to pull yourself out.

The new project wasn't quite so impressive as the soaring Boulder Dam, but it was technically more of a challenge. The Columbia River dwarfed the Colorado, with an average flow as large as the Colorado at flood and a flood flow ten times that. The federal government proposed to dam the Columbia at the head of tidewater, near where the "Great River of the West" breached the Cascade Mountains. Unfortunately for the dam builders the walls of the Columbia Gorge were too far apart for the kind of canyon-spanning structure Kaiser and his associates had built athwart the Colorado; nor was it feasible to divert the entire river the way the Colorado had been.

Kaiser conceded the difficulties when making his pitch to his principal underwriter.

> Government engineers are doubtful if the dam can be constructed. Bonding companies refuse to take the risk of bonding this hazardous project. The raging waters of the Columbia can rise twenty to thirty feet within a day and rip out our work. Even the native Indians have a legend that no man will ever walk across the Columbia. But we have the faith that we can build the dam.

The project bore out Kaiser's predictions. Edgar Kaiser, Henry's son and his foreman on the Columbia project, recounted a particularly memorable moment.

> One stormy spring night when the water was high and really roaring, I was afraid we were going to lose our cofferdam so I phoned a supervisor at the dam site, a short distance upstream. "Everything is okay," he reported. "I

think we're going to be all right." Just then I looked out the window and saw a dark mass approaching. It was one of our cofferdam cribs floating down the river. With it went the unlimited hours of work of hundreds of men.

But Kaiser's group persevered, completing the Bonneville Dam a year ahead of schedule. The partners earned another $3 million.

Again Kaiser was already well along on his next job—a dam that dwarfed both Boulder and Bonneville. The Grand Coulee Dam, built across the Columbia in the scabrock country west of Spokane, would be the largest piece of construction ever attempted by humans on the planet up to that time. It was a glittering prize for Kaiser and companies, and as the bids were submitted for the initial excavation and foundation work, they had every reason to anticipate another triumph and another fat payday. Harry Morrison of Morrison–Knudsen remembered the scene in Spokane's Davenport Hotel the night before the bids were opened.

> Everyone was very cheerful and hilarious. Toasts were drunk to our success on the biggest dam of all. I remember Felix Kahn promising that at the next party he was going to put a hundred dollar bill under each lady's plate, because we'd all be in the money by then. The competition, incidentally, was staying at the same hotel; when they heard all the noise and cheering, they got kind of worried.

They shouldn't have, for when the bids were opened a consortium that went by the acronym MWAK had beaten Kaiser's group. Kaiser's associates glumly took the first train out of Spokane, but he demonstrated the canny political skills that marked his entire career. That very evening he addressed the Spokane chamber of commerce, which hadn't forgotten his earlier sojourn in that fair city. He made clear that *he* hadn't forgotten. "They say we have lost," he declared. "But we haven't lost. We have won, because Spokane won."

Thereafter he demonstrated his business skills by bringing the MWAK team in on a bid for the superstructure of the dam. This time Kaiser's (enlarged) group came in first, and when the Grand Coulee Dam began rising above the Columbia, it was Kaiser's crews that led the way. And by the time Grand Coulee was finished—a year and a half ahead of schedule—Kaiser had cemented his reputation as the great builder of the West.

His progress wasn't uniformly successful. Six Companies submitted the winning bid to dig a pair of highway tunnels linking Oakland to eastern Contra Costa County; with both Kaiser and Bechtel headquartered in the

Bay Area, the job looked like easy money. But Kaiser and the others failed to do their geology, and besides discovering an earthquake fault in their path they learned that much of the rock through which they had to dig was unstable or saturated or both. Three workers died from rockfalls; machines and prospective profits were lesser casualties. Hoping to renegotiate, Kaiser met with lawyers for the local district. In a lengthy session he pleaded for more money to meet the unexpected challenges. The lawyers listened patiently for a time, then their leader got up and opened a window. "What's that for?" asked Kaiser. "To let your tears flow out so we won't all drown," the lawyer replied. Notwithstanding the improved hydrodynamics, Kaiser and associates took a bath, losing more than $2 million on the job.

Yet if the tunnels dented Kaiser's enthusiasm for new challenges, the damage wasn't detectable to most observers. Six Companies bid for the Shasta Dam in northern California; when they lost to another group Kaiser determined to become the cement supplier to the winner. "I didn't know anything about producing cement," he conceded. "Or at least not very much. Of course, I had been in the sand and gravel business, but never in cement. So I sent my boys off East to learn how it was done, how to go about building a plant, and how to get it done in a hurry." When he submitted the low bid his competitors for the cement contract complained that he didn't have a cement plant, but he managed to persuade the appropriate agencies that he would have one soon. For their part they were happy to free themselves from dependence on the existing cement cartel, and they awarded Kaiser the contract. On Christmas Day 1939 crews at Permanente Cement presented Kaiser with the first bag of cement produced by what would become the largest cement plant in the world.

This didn't end his troubles with the cement cartel and its allies. The Southern Pacific Railroad, which had close connections to the California cementers, demanded what Kaiser considered an extortionate rate to carry his group's sand and gravel from pits, around an intervening mountain, to the dam site. In addition the railroad refused to build a spur to the pits, insisting that Kaiser construct a conveyor from the pits to the existing S. P. track. Kaiser, hoping to change the railroad directors' minds, appealed to their business sense by arguing that the huge volume he was going to ship warranted lower rates and better treatment. When this argument failed he appealed to the company's civic sense, pointing out the benefits the Shasta project would deliver to the farmers, ranchers and consumers of electricity throughout California. The directors of the railroad remained obdurate.

"Then one of my boys said to me, 'Why don't we just build our own conveyor belt the whole distance across the mountain?'" recalled Kaiser. This was more than Kaiser had been planning to take on, and he dismissed the idea. "Then he had the nerve to say to me, 'Are you chicken?' Well, I sure didn't like that either, so I said, 'I'm not chicken; we'll build it.'"

And so they did. The ten-mile belt was the longest conveyor in the world. It went up ridges and down; it crossed the Sacramento River twice; it traversed four creeks, five county roads, the main state highway and—to Kaiser's distinct pleasure—the S. P. line. Where it passed near a school a special mesh was placed to catch any falling rocks; all along the route horizontal bars were placed low over the belt to discourage thrill-seeking riders. Costing a modest $1.5 million to build, it delivered more than ten million tons of aggregate at a third less than the railroad wanted to charge. Kaiser couldn't have been happier at sticking a finger in the eye of his antagonists. "Losing out on the construction of the Shasta Dam was one of the best things that ever happened to us," he chuckled.

There was better to come—and when it did it confounded Kaiser's competitors even more than his "rubber railroad," as the giant conveyor was called. Germany's invasion of Poland in 1939 was followed several months later by the Nazi conquest of France and the Battle of Britain in the skies above England. The British hung on but not by much; during the autumn of 1940 they were desperate for merchant ships to keep their Atlantic supply line open in the face of heavy losses to German submarines. London sent a special delegation to America looking for someone—anyone—to build sixty freighters as rapidly as possible.

The challenge couldn't have suited Kaiser better. Since childhood he had been fascinated by watercraft; now that Grand Coulee was well under way he was looking for that next big job. The fact that he had never built a ship before didn't bother him, and if it bothered the British they were more impressed by his record of completing contracts ahead of schedule. That Kaiser was a novice actually worked in his favor with the U.S. government. Roosevelt sympathized with the British need for ships, but he was also exquisitely sensitive to the complaints of those who feared that he might put British interests ahead of American. By allowing the British to sign up the Kaiser group the president could convincingly assert that this new construction would in no way displace ship construction for American needs.

As he had in his terrestrial construction projects, Kaiser enlisted partners—in this case chiefly the Todd Shipyards of New York. And in point of fact the initial phase of the ship project would be as terrestrial as any of his dams, for before any ships could be built the shipyards had to be constructed. They were, at top speed. The first tractor that ventured out onto the mudflats at Richmond, on the East Bay north of Oakland, sank from sight. But after Kaiser's trucks, working at a ferocious pace, dumped 300,000 cubic yards of rock on top of it, the ground was solid enough to support the largest ship. In April 1941 the first keel was laid; four months afterward the *Ocean Vanguard* slid down the ramp into the water. Meanwhile Kaiser sent a second crew north to Portland, where it accomplished similar feats. The keel of the *Star of Oregon* was laid in May 1941; the ship was launched at the end of September.

Kaiser had always been adept at climbing steep learning curves, but when Japan attacked Pearl Harbor just ten weeks later the curve went nearly vertical. In three hours on that December Sunday morning the American demand for ships expanded exponentially. Kaiser had demonstrated he could build ships (even if he couldn't get along with his partners from Todd, who withdrew from the partnership); now the federal government asked only how many and how fast. Washington placed its first big order—for troop transports—a month after Pearl Harbor; this was followed a week later by an order for sixty cargo vessels, the Liberty ships.

Kaiser-watchers had long commented that he operated as though there was a war on; now that there really *was* a war on he worked faster and better than ever. Kaiser's recruiters scoured the country for engineers, pipe fitters, welders and other skilled personnel; when skilled workers could no longer be found, unskilled workers were pushed into crash instructional courses and then thrown into service. Entire new towns sprang up around the Kaiser shipyards at Richmond and Portland; these towns functioned on the same breakneck, round-the-clock schedule as the shipyards.

The creation of the two centers of construction activity was partly dictated by logistics, but it simultaneously served Kaiser's purpose of encouraging competition between Richmond and Portland. Kaiser's original contract specified 150 days for delivery of ships; even under the pressure of the war sixty days was an industry standard. Kaiser's Portland yard determined to do what no one had done before: to build a ship in ten days. To heighten the stakes the Portlanders issued an advance invitation to Roosevelt to attend the launch. On schedule the ship splashed into the water, to the applause of the president and the wonder of the nation. Kaiser was understandably ebullient.

> Many experts shook their heads and said we could not do it. Yet here beside us is this great craft—only ten days from keel laying to launching; and in a •

few days she will be on the ocean bearing cargo to our allies and to our soldiers. It is a miracle, no less: a miracle of God and of the genius of free American workmen.

A reporter asked Kaiser how long the ten-day record would last. "I expect that record to go by the boards in the very near future," he replied.

The record fell in Richmond. Not to be outperformed by their northern counterparts, the Californians proposed to build a ship in five days. "Five days!" exclaimed one shipyard veteran on hearing of the plan. "Hell, it'll take 'em five days to even find the keel." They found it, although much of the ship was often hard to spot for all the workers swarming about it. "It was something to see," said one man who was in the thick of the race. "Just one seething mass of shipfitters, welders, chippers. Ten chippers hacking away on a transverse seam. . . . Hose and cable a foot deep. . . . I'll be blind and deaf by next week, but it's worth it, I guess." Exactly four days, fifteen hours and twenty-six minutes after the keel was laid, the ship roared down the ramp into San Francisco Bay.

To some extent the record-breaking construction was a publicity stunt—a morale booster for wartime. Kaiser and his spokesmen denied it, of course; but if the one-off techniques used on the five-day ship had been adopted throughout Kaiser's yards they would actually have slowed construction. Yet grandstanding aside, the accomplishments of the Kaiser yards during the war were breathtaking. Together Kaiser's Richmond and Portland yards built 1490 ships, including Liberty and Victory cargo vessels, assorted troop transports and landing ships, tankers and "baby flattop" escort aircraft carriers. Considering the comparatively slow start in 1941, this meant that for most of the war Kaiser was cranking out ships at a rate of better than one a day.

The war made Kaiser famous. "Without the supply columns of Liberty ships that endlessly plowed the seas between America and England," asserted Winston Churchill, "the war would have been lost." Another British official singled out Kaiser for having "in the most literal sense the faith that moves mountains. Without his ships, it appeared then, and can be seen even more certainly in retrospect, Britain would have otherwise been forced into defeat." Joseph Stalin didn't know Kaiser personally but appreciated his contribution. "To American war production," the Soviet leader toasted, "without which this war would have been lost."

Whether the war made Kaiser rich became a matter of some controversy after the excitement of victory began to wear off. By some 1946 calculations of the federal General Accounting Office, Kaiser realized a return of $129 million on an investment of but $2.5 million. Speaking of Kaiser and others similarly situated, the accounting office's chief counsel declared, "At no time in the history of American business, whether in wartime or in peacetime, have so many men made so much money with so little risk—and all at the expense of the taxpayer." Kaiser's accountants responded with figures of their own, some of which were equally ludicrous, such as those that found that the Kaiser yards actually *lost* money—$18.6 million, to be more or less precise—from war work.

Kaiser may have known where the truth lay, but he wasn't telling. On the other hand he may not have known precisely what his profit margin on ships was. By the end of the war his costing was confused by the fact that he was buying much of the material that went into his ships—steel in particular—from his own plants; and those plants had been underwritten by the federal government on terms that were as hazy as much of the rest of wartime financing. Kaiser was almost an innocent in steel when he pitched the Reconstruction Finance Corporation for $100 million to build a steel plant in Southern California; warned that a shortage of turbo-blowers would hold up construction, Kaiser blithely assured the skeptics that his people would build their own. He actually thought they could, believing that a turbo-blower was the same thing as a turbine blower, which was used in ships. It wasn't, but he got his money anyway—and scrounged up a real turbo-blower before his mistake became too obvious.

What began as an adjunct to his shipbuilding interests became a principal operation after the war. Almost overnight, demand for new ships vanished; the thousands that had been floated during the war would glut the market for years. But a basic material like steel could be used in any number of products, including consumer goods that had been in stringently short supply since Pearl Harbor. Before the war American steel production had been concentrated in the East; Kaiser's California location gave him an edge in the burgeoning Southern California market. The established steel companies recognized this, and after the war they attempted, via continued federal controls on prices and other aspects of production, to squeeze Kaiser out. He fought back with a public-relations campaign that accused his antagonists of using their leverage to commit "an outrage against the people." Kaiser Steel survived and went on to confirm its position as the leading producer in the West; by the end of the 1950s it was a mainstay of the California economy.

Kaiser had as much trouble with the entrenched powers in aluminum as he did in steel. As part of his postwar diversification he bought up some government-owned aluminum plants. This move appeared foolish to many in light of the demobilization that was already beginning, but Kaiser was betting that aluminum would find new civilian markets even as the government's demand for airplane aluminum diminished. His bet took time to pay off. The first few years were rocky, with his costs being as much as fifty percent higher than those of Alcoa, the industry leader. But the unexpected outbreak of the Korean War in 1950 boosted demand for aluminum and allowed Kaiser Aluminum time to get its costs into line with those of its competitors. Kaiser Aluminum never displaced Alcoa as number one, but by the end of the Korean War it was pushing Reynolds for number two. Production and sales continued to grow during the late 1950s and early 1960s; at the time of Kaiser's death in 1967 aluminum was the Kaiser group's biggest moneymaker.

But long before then Kaiser's personal attention had wandered off in other directions. During the war he had proposed a fleet of 5000 cargo planes to supplement his Liberty armada. Washington went along only far enough to order three prototypes; one of these turned out to be the *Spruce Goose*, built by Howard Hughes, initially in partnership with Kaiser. Hughes's plywood albatross barely got off the water— it was a seaplane— and Kaiser's airplane-building dreams got only a little farther aloft. During the Korean War a Kaiser factory at Willow Run near Detroit (built and formerly owned by Henry Ford) produced a modest number of cargo planes, but building aircraft proved considerably more difficult than building ships, and Kaiser never mastered the art.

Part of the problem was that he was simultaneously trying to master automobiles—and at the same location. He didn't have much luck here either. As one Detroit old-timer joked, "Kaiser hasn't found out yet that automobiles don't have bows, sterns, and rudders." Another thought the Kaiser car ought to be named after the factory, sort of: "Willit Run." Kaiser's problem was more in marketing than in production; he built cars the way Henry Ford had but competed for customers enamored of Alfred P. Sloan. After losing well over $100 million, Kaiser acknowledged that autos were neither ships nor (any longer) Model T's, and he got out of the domestic car business. (For some years afterward Kaiser continued to produce motor vehicles in Brazil for the South American market.)

More successful were Kaiser's efforts to develop Hawaii as a tourist destination. Kaiser's first wife had died in 1951; in 1953 he took his new wife to the islands for a vacation. Shortly thereafter he purchased a home in Honolulu, and shortly after that he purchased an old hotel on Waikiki, which he proceeded to convert into the state-of-the-resort-art Hawaiian Village. Even as Kaiser lobbied the airlines to schedule more flights to Hawaii, he continued to develop Waikiki. In 1961 he arranged to transform 6000 acres on Oahu into an entire resort village: Hawaii Kai (a name that called "Kai-ser" to mind even as it actually made sense in Hawaiian: "kai" means "sea," and the village was indeed by the sea.)

Perhaps the most unlikely diversification of Kaiser's career was the one he considered the most significant. As an adult he liked to relate how he had cradled his dying mother in his arms and vowed that he would make it his life's work to see that other ordinary people didn't suffer and die needlessly from lack of proper health care. Perhaps this account embroidered and telescoped facts a bit, but he did demonstrate a commitment to health care. He first offered prepaid coverage to workers on the Grand Coulee project in 1938; in that isolated locale, if Kaiser didn't supply the doctors the workers simply wouldn't have been treated. As the only doctors in town, the Kaiser physicians naturally tended also to the needs of workers' wives and children, and eventually to non-Kaiser support personnel as well (including the prostitutes who followed the construction gangs and whose health or lack thereof had an intimate connection to the health or disease of workers).

The idea of prepaid health care transferred naturally to the Kaiser shipyards during World War II, where the coverage served the additional purpose of acting as a recruiting device under the wartime regime of wage controls. The American Medical Association frowned on the Kaiser company doctors as delivering low-quality care (not to mention cutting into the revenues of traditional fee-for-service physicians), but overt opposition would have been seen as unpatriotic and in any event was unnecessary while doctors were in short supply.

After the war, however, the AMA declared a war of its own on the Kaiser idea; at a time of heightened sensitivity to anything smacking of socialism the AMA denounced Kaiser for promoting "socialized" medicine. Kaiser responded that nothing could be further from the truth. He denounced initiatives leading toward a publicly funded national health care system. Health care, he said, was the responsibility of the private sector, not of government. The Kaiser program was one model of private participation but not the only one. "I believe that if there could be a few more such examples there would be a rapid development of this new type of medical service which would surpass anything thus far developed in the

United States or any other country." Kaiser delivered the same message in different words to Sidney Garfield, the head of the Kaiser program. Garfield was an idealistic type who wanted to enroll the entire country, but he wondered if he was up to the job. "Doctor, don't you worry," Kaiser told him. "You won't have to do the job yourself. If you're any good, you're going to have a great deal of competition, and that will help you do your job. You're going to be copied."

The Kaiser Permanente Medical Care Program was indeed copied. Kaiser managed to beat back both the forces of genuine socialized medicine and the opposition of the AMA. At his death Kaiser Permanente ran eighteen hospitals for its 1.7 million members; in the decades that followed it became the model for the health maintenance organizations that revolutionized health care in America. Kaiser couldn't have seen all the forces that would combine to produce that revolution, but he was well ahead of his time in understanding the essential attractiveness of HMOs to members and employers, if not always to physicians.

Of course Kaiser had been ahead of his time (as well as ahead of schedule) on most of his projects. A man of supreme self-confidence, he had always believed that whatever he set his mind to, he could accomplish. One of his managers on a construction job suggested that the world wouldn't end if the crews didn't meet one of Kaiser's typically ambitious deadlines. "After all, Mr. Kaiser, Rome wasn't built in a day."

"That's because I wasn't there," Kaiser rejoined.

12

THE GAMBLER

H. L. Hunt

. . .

W HERE HENRY KAISER MADE HIS LIVING IN FULL PUBLIC VIEW
(not least because the public was underwriting much of his work),
H. L. Hunt long loathed publicity. Some said this showed a commendable
modesty; others suggested that Hunt hid because he had much to hide, including the details of the oil deal that provided the basis for one of the two
or three greatest fortunes in America, and a scandalous inability to content
himself with one wife and family at a time.

Hunt's father thought his boy—called June, for Junior, for Haroldson
Lafayette Hunt, Jr.—far more likely to cause scandal than achieve great
wealth. Yet even Hunt Senior had to admit his son's gifts. June read early;
the family tale that had him reading the livestock report from the *St. Louis
Globe-Democrat* before he was three might be hard to believe, but he definitely demystified the printed word sooner than most children. He had a
head for numbers and something of a photographic memory. He put both
to use doing card tricks for friends—including, before long, the trick of
separating the friends from their money in games like poker. At sixteen he
decided to test his skills in a larger sphere than surrounded the family's Illinois farm; like Henry Kaiser and at about the same time, he headed west.

Also like Kaiser he had no particular destination. Unlike Kaiser, who
had a bride to win, he wandered quite awhile. He washed dishes in Kansas,
topped sugar beets in Colorado, herded sheep in Utah, played semipro
baseball in Nevada, cut timber in Arizona, poured concrete in Texas, drove

a mule team in California. In San Francisco he narrowly avoided being shanghaied by a shorthanded sea captain; a few days after his escape the city collapsed and burned in the apocalyptic 1906 earthquake and fire.

Wherever his train stopped he struck up a card game. He won more than he lost—often much more. In the hobo jungles he had to watch his back and sleep with one eye open; somewhere en route he acquired the nickname "Arizona Slim." With one installment of his winnings he enrolled in college in Indiana, despite never having finished elementary school. Evidently he did well—both in class and at campus card tables—but a bad case of tonsillitis forced him to drop out, and he never returned.

After nearly six years on the road, Hunt heard that his father had died. The old man had managed to accumulate some property and other interests during the latter part of his life; June received eighty acres, a house and $5000. He took the cash and headed south to Arkansas, to the black-soiled bottomlands of the Delta country, where he bought a farm in hopes of parlaying his modest pile into a bigger one in the annual gamble called cotton. "With 960 acres of the most fertile soil in the world," he related afterward, "I was ready to make my fortune."

Fortune wasn't ready for Hunt, however, and high water flooded him out that first year. While waiting for his fields to dry, he again took to the card tables, winning money in the richest games in the region. The Delta planters liked horses even more than they liked cards; Hunt soon was joining them at the track. He also learned checkers, becoming, by his own recollection, "the checkers champion of Chicot County" and, later and much less believably, "the best in the world."

Although his initial crop never recovered, Hunt made money when World War I drove cotton prices to record levels. Yet he subsequently lost it all when he gambled wrong and went short on cotton too soon. To salvage the situation he returned to the poker table. Sure enough, he saved the family farm (he had married by now and had a daughter) and then some, winding up with 15,000 acres. This was no mean feat, although in the postwar depression in the Delta it wasn't as impressive as it sounded.

During this period of heavy betting, Hunt heard of an even grander gamble. In southern Arkansas petroleum prospectors had recently struck oil; would-be Rockefellers were flocking by the trainload to the neighborhood of the aptly named town of El Dorado. Fifty thousand newcomers arrived in the first year. Hunt initially intended to make his play in the saloons that serviced the thirst of the oilmen for entertainment and forgetfulness; he introduced himself to the highest rollers and purchased some chips. He quickly established a reputation, and although he may not have been the "best poker player in the world," as he billed himself, he beat most of the local talent drawn in by his boast. Hoping to institutionalize his success, he opened a card game of his own, hiring a room and tables and taxing the play at each table. This first house did well enough that he opened another nearby.

Precisely how Hunt got from gambling with cards to gambling with oil wells became a matter of some speculation and much yarn-spinning. Hunt's favorite version was that he won his first oil lease at the poker table. This may have been true. Doubtless the transition also reflected the desire of El Dorado's self-appointed respectables to clean up the place. One evening Hunt received a visit from a delegation of the Ku Klux Klan, whose local subwizard warned him to close down his house. Hunt didn't scare easily, as events would show, but the white hoods and the flaming torches rather unnerved his clientele, with effects that could only be bad for business.

So Hunt decided to take a flier in the oil fields. With a partner (who happened to be a brother-in-law of Texas governor Pat Neff) he bought a half-acre lease. As luck would have it—and Hunt, for public consumption, placed great store in "the Hunt luck"—he hit oil on his first try. The luck wasn't all good, however, for the Hunt–Pickering No. 1 well lost pressure almost as soon as the oil started flowing—educating Hunt as to why the leases in that area came cheap. He didn't have the money to buy the equipment to pump the oil that remained below the surface, and he wound up almost as far in the hole as he had drilled.

But the experience touched that part of the Hunt psyche that found gambling addictive, and he determined to try again. Recognizing that much of the problem with his first well was the small size of the lease, which allowed nearby neighbors to draw from the same part of the subterranean pool, he went for a bigger lease the second time around, in an area less favored by drillers. He agreed to pay $20,000 for a forty-acre lease. That he didn't have the $20,000 proved a merely minor obstacle; he sent a friend to persuade the owner of the property, a simple farmer, not to cash Hunt's note lest word get out that he—the owner—was now a wealthy man and therefore fair prey for the con men and other fast talkers who inhabited the oil regions. The farmer thought this was good advice and congratulated himself on his cleverness in defeating those city slickers. Meanwhile Hunt hustled around and raised the money to cover his note.

Again Hunt hit oil, with one well on the new tract coming in at 5000 barrels per day. As before, the flow diminished over time, although nowhere near so drastically as with his first well. This venture more than covered its costs, and hooked Hunt on oil for good. He acquired leases in an area previously unexplored and drilled "wildcat" wells there, usually on a smile and a promise. He was a persuasive fellow; more than once, when his roughnecks were wrestling in mud to their waists with ancient and un-cooperative equipment and vowing to walk off the job, he sweet-talked them into drilling just a hundred more feet. Where other "poor boys"—a term applied to such shoestring operations—frequently reneged on leases that turned up dry, Hunt won a reputation for always paying what his handshake had pledged. By a combination of the "Hunt luck," an untu-tored but keen eye for oil geology, and a willingness to hazard everything he had earned so far to sink another well, then another and another, he bootstrapped himself to a substantial measure of success. By the mid-1920s he and his wife and four children occupied one of the largest houses in the nicest area of El Dorado, a brand-new brick structure of three stories on a lot that filled an entire city block.

Actually, Lyda and the kids occupied the house far more than Hunt did. Perpetually restless, he found any number of things to get him out of the house and often out of town. The mortar had hardly set between the bricks before he was off to Florida to see about supplementing his oil in-come with some real-estate deals. His eye for oil proved better than his eye for dirt, and he lost several thousand dollars before folding his hand in this new game.

Part of the problem may have been that his eye for women was also better—or perhaps worse, considering the trouble it got him into—than his eye for land. Much of the attraction for Hunt of his absences from home was the opportunity it afforded to sample the pleasures of nondo-mestic life. A handsome, strapping man in the prime of his mid-thirties— "one of the best-looking guys you ever saw," said a woman admirer—with a flair for fashion and pocketfuls of cash, and living, moreover, during a decade given to experiment in all manner of indulgence, Hunt didn't con-spicuously deprive himself.

Yet where other married men settled for minor flings, Hunt went the whole way to wedlock—again. In Tampa he met an attractive and trusting twenty-one-year-old woman whom he romanced and married—or at least exchanged vows with. Frania knew nothing of Lyda—and vice versa—and in fact knew her husband (properly, paramour) as "Major Franklin Hunt." The two lovebirds flitted about Florida during late 1925 and early 1926;

then Hunt took Frania to New Orleans for Mardi Gras before establishing her in an apartment in Shreveport. Several months later she bore Hunt a son, still utterly unaware that the frequent trips he took to Arkansas to tend to business also took him back to his first family.

Simply siring all the children he did during this period was nearly a full-time job; by the time Frania had her third child, Lyda had delivered six. Psychologically speaking, the dangers of this double life doubtless appealed to the same risk-loving streak that made gambling and the oil business so appealing to Hunt. In any event, even while alternately neglecting—emotionally if not financially—his two families, he never neglected an opportunity to put his fortune on the line in another oil venture.

What became the most famous of Hunt's plays commenced in the late summer of 1930. Hunt heard of a man drilling wildcat wells in a part of East Texas near Tyler. The man, C. M. Joiner, was seventy years old, but he was still hoping for that one big strike that would make his heretofore undistinguished life memorable. He didn't know much formal geology, but like most of his breed he believed he had a sixth sense for oil, and he was certain this try was going to make him rich. No slouch as a womanizer himself, Joiner specialized in widows—rich ones he had read about in the obituaries of their husbands. "Every woman has a certain place on her neck," he boasted, "and when I touch it they automatically start writing me a check. I may be the only man on earth who knows just how to locate that spot." Candor compelled him to add: "Of course, the checks are not always good." Lately the checks hadn't been much good, and in drilling on the farm of Miss Daisy Bradford he had struggled from week to week, never knowing how he'd pay his crew or buy replacements for the parts that kept breaking.

In his seven decades Joiner had learned a little about conning people besides widows. So even as he threw dust in the face of spies from the major oil companies—which, he feared, would bid prices up and force out poor boys like himself—he finagled small investors for nickels and dimes to keep his drillers driving down. He spotted some agents from Sinclair Oil lurking in the pines; for their benefit he left a promising core sample in a bucket on the rig when the crew went home for the night. The Sinclair scouts naturally reported their find to their boss—who mocked them for their gullibility. It was a plant, he said: If Joiner really had anything good he wouldn't be foolish enough to leave it lying around. Meanwhile Joiner was talking up his prospects to anyone else who would listen and selling shares to those with ready cash. Through poor arithmetic or calculated carelessness, he wound up selling substantially more than 100 percent of his operation.

This was what brought Hunt into the picture. On October 5, 1930, the third hole on the Bradford lease delivered a gusher. As Joiner danced in the rain of crude that blackened the vicinity of the wellhead, his numerous investors began to gather round. Comparing notes, they added up their portions and discovered that many of them were going to come up short. Shortly they sued.

Hunt offered to rescue Joiner. In the weeks between the first gushing and the commencement of the courtroom phase of the lawsuit, the flow from Daisy Bradford No. 3 sputtered: now strong, now nearly nonexistent. Skeptics, including experts from most of the major oil companies, doubted the existence of anything significant below the Bradford farm. Hunt, however, suspected that Joiner had hit the edge of an oil field, which would explain the stop-and-go flow. Noticing some dry holes to the east of Daisy Bradford No. 3, Hunt guessed that the field must lie to the west. It so happened that Joiner held additional leases in this area.

Consequently one afternoon when Joiner was leaving the courtroom in Dallas, Hunt approached him with an offer to buy him out. Joiner was discouraged by his legal troubles and by the failure of his well to maintain pressure, but he wasn't quite discouraged enough to sell—yet. This was all right by Hunt because Hunt didn't have the money to buy him out—yet. Within a few weeks, however, Hunt found a partner willing to front the cash to make a deal work, and Joiner slipped deeper into the morass his overly exuberant promotional efforts had created. At the end of November Hunt returned to Dallas.

He offered Joiner $1 million for his 5000 acres of leases. Hunt (or his partner, rather) would pay Joiner $25,000 at once; the balance would come from production. Most important for Joiner's immediate predicament, Hunt would assume responsibility for all the claims against Joiner.

As befitted a seasoned gambler, Hunt had an ace up his sleeve during what turned out to be a marathon bargaining session with Joiner. Hunt had arranged to pay a consultation fee to a man whose drilling outfit happened to be sinking a well on a tract in the midst of the Joiner leases to the west of Daisy Bradford No. 3; this consultant apprised Hunt of the progress of the operation. Whether Hunt in turn apprised Joiner became a matter of considerable debate; suffice it to say that the discovery of oil in the well in question encouraged Hunt to accept Joiner's counteroffer of $1.335 million.

The Joiner deal would ultimately make Hunt an extremely wealthy man, for the East Texas field that Joiner discovered proved to be the largest in the world up to that time. (As father of the region's oil industry, Joiner received the East Texas honorific "Dad.") But the wealth didn't come easily, for betwixt the promise and the fulfillment lay lawyer-years of litigation, some heavy political lobbying and much old-fashioned attention to detail. Although a gambler by nature, Hunt could apply himself when necessary. He drank little, partied seldom, and except for his undiscovered bigamy, had become a model citizen. Hunt wasn't always the most reliable witness regarding his own actions, but he wasn't far wrong when he declared, "While others played, I worked."

What he worked on first was extinguishing the claims of all those to whom Joiner had sold shares of his promised profits. Hunt quickly discovered that he didn't know the half of Joiner's legal problems; the old man had acquired clear title to but two acres of the 5000 he transferred to Hunt. Before long Hunt found himself parrying more than 300 lawsuits. Luckily for him, the Great Depression was punishing this part of Texas badly, and the threat by Hunt's lawyers of a protracted fight was sufficient to get most of the plaintiffs to settle for a few hundred dollars and costs.

Next Hunt had to deal with his oil-field neighbors. The petroleum economics of East Texas reflected the state of Texas' petroleum law, which had evolved out of Texas water law. The "rule of capture" was the norm, meaning that what a producer could coax out of the ground was his, regardless of what the coaxing did to the interests of neighbors. In the case of water, a renewable resource, the rule of capture would eventually create problems in Texas; it created problems at once for nonrenewable petroleum. By now there was no doubt that multiple wells into an oil field were like several straws into a milk shake; what went up one straw was lost to the rest. The rule of capture encouraged leaseholders to drill and pump as if their lives depended on it—because their economic lives often did.

Yet it was also known by now that overly rapid depletion of a field diminished the total production of that field, so that if some self-denying compact among the producers could be negotiated, all would benefit. Beyond this consideration was the disastrous effect the hyperactive development of the East Texas field was having on oil prices. The Depression had already tipped the balance of supply and demand toward the former by diminishing the latter; now the sudden tide of Texas oil deranged the balance completely by swelling the supply beyond anyone's recent imagination. Before long oil was almost literally cheaper than water in East Texas, trading at ten cents a barrel on the posted exchange and as little as two cents a barrel on the spot market.

On grounds both of natural-resources conservation and economic self-preservation, many producers supported a scheme of "prorationing." By government fiat—because there were too many producers for a feasible voluntary system of quotas—the East Texas producers would be limited to a particular percentage of the capacity of their wells. Not surprisingly the prorationists included those interests with deep enough pockets to forgo some immediate revenues in favor of a larger long-term payoff. Equally unsurprisingly the deeper pockets tended to come attached to the bigger britches of the major oil companies, which by this time had come around to the view that Dad Joiner's find was no fluke. Against the prorationists were the poor boys and other independents who needed the revenues now to keep their creditors at arm's length. Like the Pennsylvania producers of Rockefeller's day, they cast their opposition in populist terms of the little guys against the corporations; wrapping themselves in the Texas flag and remembering the Alamo, they denounced prorationing as anti-American and socialistic.

Hunt, the largest of the independents, found himself between the two sides. As an independent he might have adopted the pump-the-wells-dry position of the small producers; as one sitting above a sizable portion of the East Texas field he could have taken the longer view characteristic of the majors. In fact he did a bit of both. He drilled as fast as he could, and as long as others were pumping he pumped too. But at the same time he sought to organize the prorationists into a political force. He stood up at a meeting of producers in early 1931 and urged them to organize instead of cutting one another's throats. He proposed petitioning the Texas Railroad Commission, the body that had inherited oil and gas regulation by virtue of its original charter pertaining to the principal means of transporting petroleum; the commission, Hunt said, should set production quotas that would end the ruinous overproduction.

Immediately his opponents screamed, "Sellout!" Hunt, once a poor boy like the rest of them, had capitulated to the majors, they said.

Hunt denied that he was capitulating to anyone. "We don't want rules that favor major companies over independents," he said. "We want long-term conservation measures that will benefit all the operators in the field." The meeting broke up inconclusively, a couple of curses shy of fisticuffs.

When the railroad commission failed to act, Hunt and the other prorationists sent a telegram to the Texas governor, Ross Sterling, urging him to declare martial law and shut down the East Texas field by main force. Sterling, an oil man by background—a founder and former chairman of Humble Oil—allowed himself to be persuaded. He ordered in the cavalry (recent rains having rendered the roads impassable to wheeled vehicles) in the form of mounted Texas Rangers; these were supported by troops of the National Guard. The occupation of the oil field had the desired effect: It boosted the price of oil back to nearly a dollar a barrel, which was about where it had been before Dad Joiner had pricked the East Texas giant into life.

As Joiner watched the worth of that giant multiply tenfold in mere weeks, he began to have second thoughts about what he had sold to Hunt. Joiner was now a millionaire, or would be if he sat tight. But sitting tight was difficult for the feisty septuagenarian, who in fact was busy cavorting with his young secretary (while his wife and seven children waited in Oklahoma for some of his new money to come their way).

Hunt sensed Joiner's dissatisfaction, and he went back to Dallas to talk to the old man. "Mr. Joiner," he said, "I think efforts are being made to get you to sue me. I hope you don't fall for that."

Tears filled Joiner's eyes as he declared with all the sincerity he could muster: "My boy, I would never do a thing like that. I love you too much."

But of course he did sue. Guessing that he would, Hunt preempted him. He called in his chief equipment supplier and asked him to accept mortgages on his—Hunt's—properties against future payments. The supplier demurred, saying that Hunt's credit was perfectly good as far as he was concerned. But Hunt insisted, and in the wee hours before the courts opened on the day Joiner filed suit, Hunt tied up all his attachable property. Consequently when Joiner's lawyer requested a lien against Hunt's wells, he found the way blocked.

Like many lawsuits, Joiner's charged Hunt with a laundry list of sins; but the chief allegation was fraud. Hunt had misrepresented his knowledge of the drilling in the adjoining lease, Joiner asserted. If he—Joiner—had known what Hunt knew, he never would have sold so cheaply. The true value of the property he sold Hunt was $15 million, not a measly $1.3 million. Joiner demanded to be compensated for a substantial portion of the difference.

People who knew Joiner wasted little sympathy on the wily old fellow; nor were they shocked that Hunt might have cashed in on something he knew that Joiner didn't. Inside information was the coin of the realm in the oil patch, and everyone hoped to luck into some someday. Although Hunt didn't do his case much good by not being able to keep his story straight as to why he had paid the $20,000 to the driller on the adjacent lease, he fared better outside the courtroom. The halls of the courthouse crackled with rumors that he was bribing the jury and intimidating witnesses; the man said to have relayed the crucial information about the oil strike mysteriously disappeared just ahead of the subpoena server.

Whether the rumors were true or whether Hunt simply planted them to pressure Joiner, no one ever discovered. Neither did they learn just what it was that suddenly caused Joiner to abandon his suit in midtrial. Some surmised that Hunt bought Joiner off; this came to appear unlikely when Joiner had to ask Hunt for money to pay his attorney. Others hinted that Hunt found some means to blackmail the old man. Whatever the reason, Joiner abruptly decided to pull back his lawyer and leave Hunt alone. "I have made a thorough investigation and have determined to my satisfaction that the allegations of fraud in my petition are not true," he told the stunned courtroom. "I was not deceived or defrauded in any manner."

Regardless of which armhold Hunt may have applied to Joiner, it didn't prevent the old man from regularly hitting up the younger for advances against the next month's production payments. Hunt accepted Joiner's excuses on some subjects—the need for a Mexican holiday so that Joiner could divorce his Oklahoma wife and marry his secretary, for example—and would peel off a couple dozen hundred-dollar bills (the monthly production payments owed Joiner ranged up to $50,000). But he drew the line when Joiner asked for $10,000 to pay his lawyer for the suit against Hunt. Hunt declared that the attorney wasn't worth a penny over $3,000. "He lost the case, didn't he?"

Ever after, Hunt defended his buyout of Joiner as a bargain for each side. "The fact is it was a sound deal for both Joiner and me, and Joiner received through the cash, notes, and production payments more funds than he would have received by trying to operate the properties in the face of his legal difficulties, and I assumed the risk of proving up his titles." There was certainly much truth in this analysis. Hunt took a gamble and won. He once said of wildcatters, "They have had the courage to risk everything on unlikely prospects where they were not supposed to succeed"; and he thought the remark applied to him in the Joiner case. Yet a comment by an oil-man who knew Hunt from the El Dorado days also applied: "He wasn't crooked, but he could outtrade you."

While Hunt was finishing outtrading Joiner, the future of East Texas oil remained uncertain. In December 1932 the U.S. Supreme Court ruled that Governor Sterling had taken unwarranted liberties in seizing the oil field; he must withdraw the troops and release the wells. This produced a renewed orgy of drilling. In the town of Kilgore the drilling crews flattened buildings to get at the oil below; in certain parts of the town the derricks were so close together their legs intertwined. The railroad commission feebly issued orders to regulate production, but in the absence of enforcement bootleggers acted as though the commissioners were issuing edicts for Timbuktu. "Hot oil," as the outlaw crude was called, flowed by the tens of thousands of barrels. In response certain prorationists adopted dynamite as a makeshift for curtailing shipments and encouraging respect for the law.

H. L. Hunt almost certainly did not push the plunger on any detonator; he may not even have paid anyone who did. Yet everyone acknowledged that the anarchy that threatened not merely the oil fields but the entire region worked to the benefit of those, like Hunt, who were insisting that the state authorities adopt stern measures to restore order to the industry. Hunt personally went to Austin to testify on behalf of a rigorous regimen of prorationing. Without it, he said, the oil bounty would be wasted and the productive capacity of the oil fields permanently impaired if not destroyed.

Hunt and the other supporters of regulation were on the verge of legislative victory when some of their number launched a premature celebration. Their hijinks included too much alcohol and too-rough treatment of one of their opponents, who appeared next day on the floor of the Texas House of Representatives in a wheelchair. Some cynics questioned whether the chair was necessary, but necessary or not it provided just the prop the antiprorationists needed to derail the bill Hunt favored.

The whole affair, however, persuaded the railroad commission to get serious about regulation. As a test the head of the commission ordered all East Texas producers to pump flat-out on March 27, 1933; to the astonishment of even the most bullish of the area's boosters, the field demonstrated the capacity to produce 100 million barrels per day. This amount wildly exceeded demand and fairly well proved the economic argument for regulation; at the same time, the fact that many wells were pumping increasing amounts of salt water supported the conservationist case. The director of the railroad commission ordered a cap on production at 750,000 barrels per day.

This order marked a start on bringing the situation under control; more significant was a directive from the newly inaugurated president, Franklin Roosevelt, to require federal licenses for oil shipments. Aimed directly at the hot-oil shippers, this order came with fifty federal agents to enforce it.

Hunt applauded the arrival of the feds, hoping Washington would succeed where Austin had so far failed. Yet until the federal muscle actually closed the valves of the hot-oil producers, he hedged his bets. He continued to drill, believing he needed to be ready to pump with the hungriest of the producers if this latest attempt at prorationing failed.

It didn't exactly fail, but neither did it quite succeed. By the autumn of 1934 shipments of hot oil had fallen from an estimated 100,000 barrels per day to 30,000. To encourage further progress Hunt returned to Austin to suggest sending the Texas Rangers back into the fields in support of the *federales*. The federal government had suffered prestige problems in Texas since Reconstruction; the Rangers, by contrast, with their not entirely undeserved reputation of shooting first and explaining later if at all, elicited a more respectful reaction. Yet the state authorities were reluctant to be seen as hauling Washington's water (even in the service of Texas's oil), and they particularly resisted paying for the privilege. Hunt answered the second objection by arranging with some of his oil-field allies to put the Rangers on a private payroll; at this the governor withdrew his first objection and let the Rangers roll (they came in cars and trucks this time).

The reappearance of the Rangers cut the flow of hot oil to a relative trickle. Briefly the Supreme Court threatened to defeat the Rangers from afar when it invalidated the provision of the National Industrial Recovery Act that authorized federal regulation of oil. This appalled the business leadership of the oil region; the journal of the East Texas Chamber of Commerce declared, "The ruthless rules of the old game have demonstrated that competition may be the death of trade and that the rule of 'survival of the fittest' is too costly in the number that cannot survive."

Hunt concurred and now turned his political attentions to Washington. He urged Texas senator Tom Connally to reinstitute federal authority in a form that would pass constitutional muster. Hunt subsequently identified himself as a "father" of the Connally Hot Oil Act; if one allows, as Hunt did in this case, for multiple paternity, the claim was fair enough. The child proved equal to its task, and between this demonstration of federal seriousness and the continued presence of the Rangers, nearly all the hot-oil pipelines cooled off.

The rising price the chill induced deposited more money in Hunt's pocket—enough to enable him to buy out the partner who had staked him to the Joiner deal. For $5 million in cash and leases (and one Buick automobile), Hunt bought back the twenty percent he had relinquished at the time.

Hunt's partner took the money and retired to the quiet life of Tyler, Texas; Hunt, ever the gambler, couldn't bear the thought. He sent his scouts to unproven regions in West Texas, Louisiana and Arkansas, betting he could find another field like the East Texas giant. His formula was simple: "The more wells you drill, the greater chance you have of finding oil."

In fact the formula wasn't quite that simple. For public consumption Hunt continued to rely on the "Hunt luck," which provided an easy answer to questions as to how he was so successful. But luck had less to do with it than a shrewd understanding of his niche in the oil industry. As the largest of the independents, Hunt had greater reserves than those smaller fish below him on the food chain. He could afford to take risks that would ruin most of them; if nine holes turned up dry he'd still be around to bring in oil on the tenth. Yet as an independent he swam faster than the corporate whales above him on the food chain. When a new area showed promise he could get there more rapidly than the majors and have his drill pipe in the ground while they were still awaiting authorization from the home office. "H.L. always seemed to be there when the wells came in," observed an oil-field associate.

Fast was never fast enough for Hunt. "Drill, drill, drill" was the watchword at Hunt Oil, as remembered by one Hunt employee. Another declared, "You moved in a hurry. I would be up all night. I got a college education in the oil industry working there." Elaborate forecasts and analysis Hunt left to the majors; he operated on instinct—and on his innate knack with numbers. "I never saw anything like it before or since," said one of his secretaries. "Mr. Hunt could figure faster with that short little pencil of his than his engineer could figure with a slide rule."

As important as speed was, Hunt recognized that size counted too. With the profits that poured out of his wells he expanded in various directions. He created his own drilling subsidiary, Penrod Drilling. He bought a refining company and began marketing Parade gasoline. (He had a weakness for six-letter names beginning with "P," a weakness his sons inherited. In time the Hunt stable would include—in addition to Penrod Drilling and Parade Gasoline—Panola Pipeline, Placid Oil, Parade Press, and Profit Investment.) He explored export options, unfortunately picking partners with a limited near-term future in American trade: Germany and Japan.

Despite his lack of schooling, Hunt appreciated the work of scientists when they discovered something he could use. He was among the first of the East Texas oilmen to recognize the significance of the scientists' finding that salt water, rather than natural gas (as had been supposed), provided the pressure that pushed the oil to the surface. Early on he began pumping the salt water that came out of the wells back into the ground; when the practice was widely adopted it mitigated the decline in overall pressure in the East Texas field, lengthening the life of the field by decades and greatly increasing total yield. (Near the end of his life, in the 1970s, Hunt took pride in pointing out that Daisy Bradford No. 3 was still pumping oil.)

World War II drove up the price of oil and made Hunt even wealthier than before. His wealth, in turn, brought him his first taste of public exposure. At the beginning of 1948 *Fortune* magazine ran a feature on Texas as "The Land of the Big Rich." Therein it introduced Hunt to its readers:

> Probably the biggest of the Big Rich, and thus also probably the richest single individual in the U.S., is an oilman named Haralson L. Hunt, whose quiet habits and abhorrence of cameras make him an unknown even to most of his fellow Texans.

Although the magazine got Hunt's first name wrong and possibly underestimated the wealth of such other superrich as Howard Hughes and J. Paul Getty, its estimates of Hunt's wealth were probably not far off. The author calculated Hunt's daily production at around 65,000 barrels; at the going price of $2.25 per barrel this yielded a weekly gross of $1 million. Altogether Hunt's properties were worth more than a quarter-billion dollars.

Hunt had reason for shunning cameras. The secret double life he had been living with Lyda and Frania had came to an abrupt end in 1934—at least the secret part of it did—when Frania attended a party also attended by Margaret Hunt, Hunt's eldest daughter by Lyda. When the identity of Margaret was pointed out to Frania, she confronted Hunt with her new knowledge; he admitted what he had done. She decided to move back to the Northeast where she had been born, and he set her up in a house on Long Island. Eventually she and Hunt worked out a financial arrangement for their children, and in 1942 she married—legally this time—another man.

Hunt had hardly extricated himself from his relationship with Frania before he took up with yet another woman. Ruth Ray was less than half Hunt's age, but she fell as hard for him as Frania had. In 1943 she bore their son, Ray, in New York. Hunt evidently couldn't bear being separated from her and the boy, so he moved them to Dallas, where she had three more children—and where Lyda and the children who were still at home with her also now lived. In fact the two families—Hunt's first and third—lived in the same neighborhood, which made it easier for Hunt to see them both than had been the case with his first and second families. Hunt's secret life was actually something of an open secret this time around. Perhaps Hunt felt that his huge wealth immunized him from additional scandal; Lyda, for her part, had learned to look the other way regarding her husband's unconventional sense of family values. ("The finest woman I ever met," was how Frania described Lyda.)

Yet until the 1950s Hunt remained shy of cameras. Some who knew him surmised that he might be afraid of paternity suits from still other women he had had liaisons with; others said he simply didn't want to be bothered by solicitations from the countless people and institutions that couldn't resist a man with a few hundred million dollars.

In time, however, his photophobia wore off, and indeed he grew fond of publicity. He discovered conservative politics and took to newsprint and radio to retail his views. "I'm a notoriety seeker now," he said at one point. "The country is so far gone that I am willing to say anything I can to dispel the apathy of the people." He wrote not one but two autobiographies and ventured into fiction as well (some critics included the autobiographies under that category). "Except that I am slow, I am the best writer I know," he declared (the critics couldn't decide whether this was simply false or a fair reflection on Hunt's acquaintances).

Age increased his eccentricities. By his own description he became a "billionaire health crank"; hoping to capitalize on his crankiness he created a subsidiary—HLH Products—that hawked assorted vitamins, curatives and food products. "I'm H. L. Hunt, and I'm the world's richest man," he would say, "and these are my products, so you know they must be good." Frugal to the point of being tightfisted, he parried questions whether he intended to take his money with him by saying, "I'm not planning to go"; and in fact he talked of setting a record for longevity. Ever since the Dad Joiner deal he had been intrigued by the possibilities of business espionage; now he extended his intelligence-gathering to assorted critics and political radicals—as well as to his own employees and children. "We had so many guys spying on each other at one time," said one of the spies, "you almost had to wear a badge."

Spying aside, Hunt's family affairs were often difficult—which was unremarkable, given the convoluted family situation Hunt had created. Sometimes he thought his children good for nothing; on other occasions he thought they showed promise. At the time of his death in 1974, two of his sons were engaged in a gamble to make the old man proud. Taking a page from Jay Gould, Bunker and Herbert Hunt were attempting to corner the silver market. The silver market was much larger than the gold market; hence the effort stretched over a much longer period than Gould's caper, and the outcome hung in the balance seemingly forever. But when the price of silver hit $50 an ounce, Bunker and Herbert had made more money—on paper—in six months than their father had made in his entire career.

Then silver crashed and with it that new Hunt fortune. "They played a dangerous game for high stakes," observed a business editorialist. "They guessed wrong, and they lost." The father would hardly have applauded the outcome, but he would have had to admit that the boys came naturally by the instinct behind the effort.

13

EMPEROR OF THE AIR

David Sarnoff

• • •

I have in mind a plan of development which would make radio a "household utility" in the same sense as the piano or the phonograph. The idea is to bring music into the home by wireless.

While this has been tried in the past by wires, it has been a failure because wires do not lend themselves to this scheme. With radio, however, it would be entirely feasible.

For example, a radio telephone transmitter having a range of say 25 to 50 miles can be installed at a fixed point where the instrumental or vocal music or both are produced. The problem of transmitting music has already been solved in principle and therefore all the receivers attuned to the transmitting wave length should be capable of receiving such music. The receiver can be designed in the form of a simple "Radio Music Box" and arranged for several different wave lengths, which should be changeable with the throwing of a single switch or pressing of a single button.

The "Radio Music Box" can be supplied with amplifying tubes and a loudspeaking telephone, all of which can be neatly mounted in one box. The box can be placed on a table in the parlor or living room, the switch set accordingly and the music received. There should be no difficulty in receiving music perfectly when transmitted within a radius of 25 to 50 miles.

Within such a radius there reside hundreds of thousands of fami-

lies; and as all can simultaneously receive from a single transmitter, there should be no question of receiving sufficiently loud signals to make the performance enjoyable. . . . The same principle can be extended to numerous other fields as, for example, receiving lectures at home which can be made perfectly audible; also, events of national importance can be simultaneously announced and received. Baseball scores can be transmitted in the air by the use of one set installed at the Polo Grounds. . . .

The manufacture of the "Radio Music Box" including antenna, in large quantities, would make possible their sale at a moderate figure of perhaps $75 per outfit. The main revenue would be derived from the sale of "Radio Music Boxes" which if manufactured in quantities of a hundred thousand or so could yield a handsome profit when sold at the price mentioned above. . . .

It is not possible to estimate the total amount of business obtainable with this plan until it has been developed and actually tried out; but there are about 15,000,000 families in the United States alone, and if only one million or seven percent of the total families thought well of the idea it would, at the figure mentioned, mean a gross business of about $75,000,000, which should yield considerable revenue.

DAVID SARNOFF WAS AHEAD OF HIS TIME WHEN HE WROTE THIS memo to his boss at the American Marconi Corporation in 1915. Radio broadcasting was in its infancy. Ten years earlier Reginald Fessenden had demonstrated the feasibility of transmitting audio signals—and not just the dots and dashes of the wireless telegraphy that Guglielmo Marconi had pioneered. A few years later Lee De Forest broadcast a performance of the Metropolitan Opera, but problems with the quality of the signal sent him back to his workshop. In 1916 he began broadcasting from a site on the outskirts of New York to a small audience of radio hobbyists and wireless operators on ships moored in New York harbor.

De Forest—who later billed himself as the "father of radio"—was an inventor, not a businessman; transforming his technical accomplishment into commercial success required the peculiar combination of vision and drive possessed by David Sarnoff. Accounting for that vision is as difficult as accounting for any expression of virtuosity: partly good genes, partly good timing, partly good luck. Accounting for Sarnoff's drive is more straightforward. His parents were Russian Jews who, with half a million of their kinsmen, fled the poverty and oppression of their homeland for

America during the last two decades of the nineteenth century. The great pogroms had yet to begin, but young David caught a glimpse of what they would entail when he saw the czar's men deal with an expression of dissatisfaction with some aspect of autocratic rule. "As we watched the surging people," he recalled from the safe distance of many years and many more miles, "a company of mounted Cossacks came charging down. They called on the crowd to disperse. No one moved. The Cossack leader barked a word of command, and the whole company rode into the wailing mob, lashing out with their long whips and trampling women and children under the hooves of their horses. The sight sickened me and I clung to my mother's skirts."

Shortly thereafter, David, his two brothers and his mother set sail for America. David liked to tell a story of the voyage, about how he and his mother had watched with sinking hearts—and tightening stomachs—as the family's food basket began to disappear down into the hold of the ship, the victim of the sort of luggage mix-up that has plagued travelers from the earliest times to the present. Almost unthinkingly David dove into the darkness to rescue the provisions—which, being kosher, wouldn't easily be replaced afloat. Luckily for him he landed on some soft bundles rather than a crate or barrel, which would have broken his neck along with his fall. One of the seaman observed the rescue and declared, "Boy, you're going to do all right in America."

David wasn't yet ten when the family was reunited with father Abraham, who had gone ahead to find work, housing and a way to pay for the others to join him. They took up residence in a tenement on New York's Lower East Side. Unluckily his father became ill and the burden of supporting the family slipped to David's skinny shoulders. "If I don't help my family, who will?" he remembered asking himself. He started selling Yiddish newspapers for a penny apiece, a markup of 100 percent over his purchase price but barely enough to let the family get by. He supplemented his street sales with a home-delivery news route and with errands for local merchants. Blessed with a pleasing voice, he sang for pay at his synagogue and at weddings and other festivities. Eventually he purchased a newsstand with capital furnished by an anonymous benefactor who admired the boy's pluck. He and his two younger brothers staffed the stand, at the corner of Tenth Avenue and Twenty-sixth Street, and made deliveries as well.

At fifteen, with elementary school behind him and no further formal education ahead, David Sarnoff left his brothers in charge of the newsstand and took a salaried job. He meant to apply at the offices of the *New*

York Herald—an obvious choice for one who had been in newspaper re-tailing—but in his nervousness he mistook another office in the *Herald*'s building, one occupied by the Commercial Cable Company, for the news-paper's headquarters. This simple error had profound consequences for both Sarnoff and the American communications industry; instead of going to work in print he found himself in telegraphy.

Commercial Cable hired him as a messenger—at five dollars a week and ten cents an hour overtime—but Sarnoff didn't intend to remain a messenger. He purchased a practice set and, like Andrew Carnegie, taught himself to send and receive messages. In telegraph days operators would chat over the wires during lulls in the traffic, striking up electrical friend-ships not far different from those a later generation of technical types would develop on the Internet. Sarnoff, borrowing time on the wire, came to know a man named Jack Irwin who took an interest in the career of this obviously clever and ambitious young kid. When Sarnoff's employer in-sisted that he work on the Jewish holy days of Rosh Hashanah and Yom Kippur, and he refused—less from religious scruples than because he didn't want to miss a good gig singing at the synagogue—he found himself calling on Jack Irwin's assistance to find a new job.

Irwin suggested a startup company involved in transatlantic messag-ing via wireless. The Marconi Wireless Telegraph Company of America was one of twin brainchildren of the Anglo-Italian inventor-entrepreneur Marconi; although it and its English sibling appeared to have a bright fu-ture, their present was clouded by various technical and financial prob-lems. These, however, didn't worry David Sarnoff when he walked in the door of the company's New York office in September 1906, not least be-cause he knew next to nothing of them. He needed work. Although he presented himself as a telegraph operator, he accepted what was available: office boy.

He hoped to become an operator, though, and to this end kept up his skills of finger and ear; in the meantime he unknowingly again followed the example of that other immigrant telegraph boy—Carnegie—and learned a great deal about his employer's business by perusing the corre-spondence and memoranda his duties required him to handle. He also at-tached himself to company executives who could further his career. One of these, Robert Marriott, remembered how "Davey," as he was known about the office, "tried to be of assistance to people he thought could help him get what he wanted. He was noticeably clever at finding ways to be help-ful." When Marconi came over from England, Sarnoff waited on him, even delivering flowers and candies to the women Marconi pursued after hours. In not much time Sarnoff's efforts were rewarded with a promotion to telegrapher. This allowed him to travel, first to Europe as a shipboard operator, then to Nantucket Island off the Massachusetts coast.

He was back in New York, operating the Marconi Company's wireless station on the top of the Wanamaker department store on April 14, 1912, when a distress signal arrived on the airwaves from the North Atlantic, sent by the wireless operator aboard the S.S. *Olympic*: "S.S. *Titanic* ran into iceberg. Sinking fast." Sarnoff immediately notified the newspapers, and for the next seventy-two hours he stuck to his post, straining for whatever snatches of information he could coax from the ether. Crowds gathered at the base of the building, begging the young man at the top to tell them whatever he could. Lest interference distort the signals, President Taft silenced all East Coast stations save that of Sarnoff, who held the attention of the entire country. The first confirmations were mostly of survivors; gradually the names of the lost outnumbered the names of the saved. Finally, when the names stopped coming in, Sarnoff collapsed where he was and slept around the clock.

The *Titanic* disaster underscored the importance of ship-to-ship and ship-to-shore communication. Within a short while Congress mandated that all vessels carrying more than fifty souls install radio equipment and have an operator on duty twenty-four hours a day. Lately a luxury, radio quickly became a necessity.

Another, more comprehensive disaster made radio appear even more necessary. On the outbreak of World War I in August 1914, the opposing belligerents sliced one another's submarine cables. Immediately the admiralties and war ministries of the opposing governments declared wireless communication a priority. Somewhat more slowly the parties at war began to appreciate the propaganda potential in radio broadcasting.

As it historically has, American belligerency—declared in this instance in April 1917—prompted a substantial intrusion of government into what in peacetime was reserved to the private sector. President Wilson ordered all radio facilities in the United States placed under the control of the government. Sarnoff—fit, vigorous and twenty-six—received a draft notice from the army, but on the eve of his induction the navy's communications division, which oversaw radio operations, ordered him to stay where he was: He could contribute far more to the war effort in radio than in the trenches.

Meanwhile Washington's big thinkers began to consider the implications of having the foremost radio company in America beholden to a foreign firm, even if that firm was headquartered in friendly England. The issue came to a head just after the cessation of hostilities when British Marconi attempted to acquire exclusive control of the Alexander high-frequency alternator, a critical piece of radio technology developed in America by General Electric. GE informed the navy of the offer; the navy prodded the Justice Department and other agencies to suspend antitrust restrictions and related impediments to the creation of a wholly American agglomeration of the diverse technologies essential to radio. Before the end of 1919 the Radio Corporation of America was conceived and hatched. GE was the majority owner of the new company, of which the heart was the old American Marconi. Among the assets of the latter subsumed in the deal was David Sarnoff.

"Within thirty days after it was launched, David was running the Radio Corporation," remembered one veteran of that era. This was not strictly true, for Sarnoff had several superiors. Yet it certainly seemed true to many of those who worked with Sarnoff. None of those above him had his energy; none possessed his vision of the future of radio. A few who came over from American Marconi recalled Sarnoff's 1915 memo on the "Radio Music Box"; others learned in the new setting that he saw possibilities most people missed. Owen D. Young, who came from GE to be chairman of the RCA board (later he would go back to be GE chairman), called Sarnoff in to go over some of the company's figures. Sarnoff, at that time RCA's commercial manager, began with the assets.

"Mr. Sarnoff," interrupted Young, "you don't have to explain the black figures. It's the red ones I'm concerned with."

"Well, Mr. Young," Sarnoff replied, "there are liabilities as well as assets in every honest accounting, but it is not always the figures that tell the story. In this case, I believe, the greatest of our assets doesn't even show up."

"What is it?"

"Our great asset is the vast ignorance about electronics."

Young cocked his eyebrow quizzically.

"I mean it literally, Mr. Young. The ignorance is what remains to be explored and conquered—because that's where we have unlimited potentials for an industry, in fact for many industries that are still in their infancy or as yet unborn."

When Young appeared intrigued, Sarnoff seized the opportunity to explain his concept of the "Radio Music Box" and other wonders that even he could only dimly envision. But he was absolutely convinced—and he half-convinced the more seasoned Young—that radio would transform modern life. He was equally convinced that he and RCA would be the ones effecting the transformation. Projections for the first year indicated that RCA's receipts would total about $1 million. At that time GE was grossing $270 million.

"Do you realize," Young asked Sarnoff, "that GE does business at the rate of one million dollars for every working day?"

"I do," answered Sarnoff. "Now tell me, how old is your company?"

Young traced the roots back to the 1880s.

"Long before RCA is that old," Sarnoff predicted, "it will match or surpass your present rate." (In 1947, when RCA's revenues reached $300 million, Sarnoff sent the retired Young a note reminding him of their conversation. Young congratulated Sarnoff on making his boast come true.)

Owen Young and most other principals in RCA—not to mention the government regulators who were largely responsible for the company's creation—assumed that its core competency would be overseas wireless communication. For some time that indeed was the case. But Sarnoff had never lost the vision that inspired his "Radio Music Box" proposal, and almost at once he began moving the company away from point-to-point private communications and in the direction of broadcast mass communications. He updated his sales forecast of five years before, predicting to GE president E. W. Rice that RCA could sell a million radios within three years. Revenues in the third year alone would come to $45 million.

Like many other technologies, radio suffered from a chicken-and-egg syndrome. Before anyone would buy radios there had to be radio programs for them to listen to; but before broadcasters would spend money on programming they had to know there was an audience. Sarnoff proposed to supply both the chickens and the eggs. RCA, in conjunction with its corporate partners, would produce the radio receivers; at the same time it would underwrite programming. Sarnoff seized on the idea of broadcasting the heavyweight boxing championship bout between Jack Dempsey and Georges Carpentier in July 1921. Heavyweight title fights always attracted large audiences; this one generated patriotic, as well as sporting, interest by pitting the American Dempsey against the French Carpentier. Over 90,000 fans were expected at ringside in Jersey City, New Jersey; at least that many again would have attended if the arena had been larger and they had lived closer. Needless to say, most members of this other audience didn't own radio receivers; Sarnoff solved this problem by arranging for receivers, connected to large amplifiers, to be located in theaters and auditoriums throughout the eastern states. The fight was a knockout success for both Dempsey and Sarnoff, the former in the fourth round, the latter when reports of a radio audience of some 200,000 came in. RCA's president Edward Nally, initially a skeptic, cabled Sarnoff: "You have made history." Andrew White, the RCA publicist who called the fight (and later the first president of CBS), remembered the euphoria he and Sarnoff shared: "We were tired and bleary-eyed, but in our minds' eyes, Sarnoff and I were seeing the crowds that were pouring out of the-aters and halls in Pittsburgh and St. Augustine, Boston and Washington, Albany, Philadelphia, and Akron, their ears full of a modern miracle. We knew then that the era of radio for the millions had begun."

White—and Sarnoff—were right. The half-decade after the Dempsey broadcast witnessed an explosion in sales of radios in America—from $12 million in 1921 to $207 million in 1926. RCA captured the largest share of this market, although several other companies participated actively.

Analysts forecast continued rapid growth, assuming RCA and the oth-ers could sort out patent problems that vexed the swiftly evolving industry. Sarnoff benefitted from access to GE's patents, but he also sought out the best ideas from independent innovators. The most important of the inde-pendents was Howard Armstrong, a brilliant eccentric who became a reg-ular morning visitor at Sarnoff's home (where Sarnoff's children called him the "coffee man" because he was always there for coffee), a fixture at Sarnoff's office (where he wooed and eventually won Sarnoff's secretary) and a worrisome presence atop the Aeolian Building on Forty-second Street near Fifth Avenue (where he had a disconcerting habit of ascending and balancing on the pinnacle of the RCA radio tower hundreds of feet above the pavement). It didn't cost Sarnoff anything except the wages of some company security men to keep Armstrong off the tower; but for Armstrong's innovative receiving circuit he had to pay substantially. Fortu-nately Armstrong was willing to accept RCA stock; the 60,000 shares (in addition to $200,000 in cash) he received made him a multimillionaire and the largest indvidual shareholder in the company.

Yet if Armstrong was the best of radio's inventors, he wasn't the only one, and for several years patent troubles continued to handicap the in-dustry. Although a single technical standard wasn't as crucial to the devel-opment of radio as it would be to television and later to computers, the welter of different approaches and the legal maze of licensing, pirating and prosecution thereof threatened to undermine the confidence of both in-vestors and consumers. Already Sarnoff saw himself as a leader not simply of RCA (although he wasn't officially leader even there) but of the radio industry as a whole. He proposed to cut the Gordian knot, and largely succeeded, by the creation of a patent pool in which RCA and the other radio companies would make their patents available to all comers on a modest royalty basis. In the short term the arrangement cost RCA, the industry leader in research and development; Sarnoff was betting that the long-term growth of the industry as a whole would more than compensate the company. He was right: By the end of the 1920s radio had become a billion-dollar industry and RCA had grown commensurately.

He was right about something else during this same period. In 1922 Sarnoff proposed to the chairman of GE the creation of an RCA subsidiary "to be known as the Public Service Broadcasting Company or National Radio Broadcasting Company or American Radio Broadcasting Company, or some similar name." This company would create a network of radio stations that could reach a truly national audience. No other medium then in existence came close to doing so. Newspapers were local; such national magazines as circulated catered to the affluent and peculiarly literate. A national radio network, by contrast, could reach tens of millions of all classes and income categories at once. "No such audience has ever before graced the effort of even the most celebrated artist or the greatest orator," Sarnoff said. The economics of a national audience would allow the network to offer the efforts of these artists and orators on a regular basis.

At first Sarnoff saw what became the National Broadcasting Company as something between a public service and a demand-generator for RCA radio receivers. Someone besides the listeners would have to pay for broadcasting, he thought. "The greatest advantages of radio—its universality and, generally speaking, its ability to reach everybody everywhere—in themselves limit, if not completely destroy, that element of control essential to any program calling for continued payment by the public." But if the public couldn't be made to pay—directly, that is—it might pay indirectly. RCA and its allies in manufacture might foot the broadcast bill, but they would pass the cost along to consumers via higher prices for their receivers.

RCA officially incorporated NBC in 1926; the company's advertisements promised "national radio broadcasting with better programs permanently assured by this important action of the Radio Corporation of America in the interest of the listening public." Although RCA took the lead, putting the network on the air required the cooperation of the major telephone carriers, notably American Telephone and Telegraph, because the signals that went out to the radio stations in the network traveled via telephone lines. Such cooperation wasn't automatic, as American Telephone itself had ambitions in the new medium, manifested in radio stations of its own. With some difficulty Sarnoff persuaded the telephone men that their future lay on land rather than in the air; a nonaggression pact signed during the summer of 1926 formalized the boundaries between the two domains. NBC commenced broadcasting with a gala affair at New York's Waldorf-Astoria hotel in January 1927; the festivities included performances by the New York Symphony Orchestra, comedian Will Rogers and assorted other musical and vaudeville acts. Although this inaugural show—priced at $50,000 by credible estimators—reached listeners only as far away as Kansas City, by the following year NBC had earned the first word in its name by airing coast to coast.

Sarnoff's success with NBC inspired imitators, including William Paley of Philadelphia, who determined to make the Columbia Broadcasting System the equal—or better—of NBC; it also attracted the attention of federal regulators. Ten years earlier Washington had encouraged the consolidation that made RCA possible; now it determined that such consolidation no longer served the public interest or even conformed to law. The resulting antitrust suit came at a particularly bad time for RCA (and the economy as a whole): in the wake of the stock market crash of 1929. RCA's shares plunged, and for a time it appeared that not even Sarnoff could save the company. Yet after two years of litigation Sarnoff surfaced successfully. Almost from the start he had wanted to emancipate RCA from the grip of its corporate parent, GE. What he had been unable to accomplish on his own he persuaded the Justice Department to do for him: A consent decree of 1932 mandated a separation of the Radio Corporation from the electric company. "The Department of Justice handed me a lemon and I made lemonade out of it," he remarked.

Sarnoff's emancipation from GE freed him to pursue new opportunities—and some he had already started after. The addition of sound to cinema in 1927 (by Warner Brothers in collaboration with Western Electric) suggested to Sarnoff that RCA had a future in Hollywood. He hooked up with Joseph Kennedy (the patriarch of the political dynasty), who in turn had ties to the Keith–Albee–Orpheum vaudeville chain; the partnership produced a new movie studio, RKO (for Radio–Keith–Orpheum). Sarnoff put RCA into the phonograph business by purchasing the Victor Talking Machine Company, to create the RCA Victor Company.

But his heart remained in the ether. Even while the NBC radio network was adding affiliates across the country—and, together with CBS and other broadcasters, enormously expanding the market for radio receivers—Sarnoff was figuring out how to add pictures to the sounds that traversed the airwaves. As early as 1923, in a memo analogous to his "Radio Music Box" memo of 1915, he had forecast the coming of television.

> I believe that television, which is the technical name for seeing instead of hearing by radio, will come to pass in due course. . . . It is not too much to expect that in the near future, when news is telegraphed by radio—say, to the United States—of important events in Europe, South America, or the Orient, a picture of the event will likewise be sent over by radio and both will arrive simultaneously. . . . I believe that transmission and reception of motion pictures by radio will be worked out within the decade.

Working out the technical problems took longer than Sarnoff expected, complicated as they were by the economic turbulence of the Great Depression. But on April 20, 1939, Sarnoff addressed viewers from the RCA exhibit at the New York World's Fair. "Now we add radio sight to sound," he told the camera and the several hundred people watching television screens elsewhere at the fair and at RCA headquarters in midtown. "It is with a feeling of humbleness that I come to this moment of announcing the birth in this country of a new art so important in its implications that it is bound to affect all society."

Some observers questioned whether Sarnoff felt as humble as he said he did; the RCA chief (president since 1930) had a reputation for qualities at the other end of the self-assurance spectrum. But few were willing to bet against Sarnoff's forecast for television.

The new medium would have arrived more quickly had World War II not intervened. Sarnoff had joined the reserves between the wars; now as a colonel he was called on by the Signal Corps to keep its signals straight. He subsequently went to Europe to set up a broadcasting station for General Eisenhower's headquarters. The success of the operation led to Sarnoff's promotion to brigadier general; for the rest of his life he preferred the title "General" to all others.

On his return from the front, Sarnoff threw himself into redeeming his promise of television as a commercial reality. "He bullwhipped his RCA organization into making good on it," reported an industry observer from the perspective of 1948. "So television is a personal (and cosmic) mission with this determined man." The chicken-and-egg problem

Sarnoff had encountered in radio returned with a vengeance in television, for although nearly any radio receiver could pick up any radio station (this blanket statement became somewhat less true with the introduction of FM broadcasting), such was not the case with television. Each television broadcaster coded the picture in a particular way (scanning so many lines per picture, refreshing the screen so many times per second); television receivers had to be constructed to decode the particular signal.

For years the battle of television standards raged, materially slowing the spread of the new medium. Not surprisingly some of those dragging their feet and throwing grit in the gears had a stake in radio and worried that television would do them in. Sarnoff warned them to stand aside lest they be run over. "Television is too powerful a force for the public good to be stopped by misleading propaganda," he declared. "No one can retard its advance any more than carriage makers could stop the automobile, the cable the wireless, or the silent pictures the talkies."

Yet on one point Sarnoff himself seemed to stand in the way of progress. Almost from the first he had insisted that television should be broadcast in color rather than merely in black and white. This was a severe technical challenge but one he was willing to back with research money, in the amount of tens of millions of dollars. As would later occur in computer software, the issue of backward compatibility posed a thorny question for the television industry. Put simply, would existing black and white sets be able to receive the new color signals? If so, they would play such signals only in black and white; but under the incompatible scheme they wouldn't play anything at all.

Sarnoff insisted on compatibility even if this delayed the widespread introduction of color broadcasting. When the Federal Communications Commission issued an interim ruling favoring the incompatible mode championed by William Paley and CBS, Sarnoff instantly denounced the decision as "scientifically unsound and against the public interest." He continued: "No incompatible system is good enough for the American public. The hundreds of millions of dollars that present set owners would have to spend and that future set owners would have to pay to obtain a degraded picture with an incompatible system reduces today's order to an absurdity."

During hearings on the standards Sarnoff had been asked what he would do if the FCC ruled against RCA. He replied that this was "like asking a prizefighter who, after nine and a half rounds, is way ahead on points and has been gaining steadily throughout the fight, what he would do after the fight is over if he is felled by an unexpected blow in the last half of the last round. The only answer he can give is that while he may be felled, he will retain a fighting heart and will do the best he can under the circumstances."

He was more succinct in private. "We may have lost the battle, but we will win the war," he vowed after the last-round knockout punch landed. To this end he redoubled research efforts at RCA into the compatible system, putting his labs on a seven-day-a-week, eighteen-hour-a-day schedule. He regularly leaked word of progress to the public in order to embarrass the FCC into reopening the standards question. He also applied for an injunction to set aside the FCC's ruling pending further investigation. The legal challenge failed in a narrow sense but bought time—time for Sarnoff's research and public-relations campaign to take effect, and time for more consumers to buy black-and-white sets, thereby increasing the constituency for compatible color broadcasting. He also cobbled together a consortium of companies opposed, for diverse reasons, to the CBS system; these went on record as favoring compatibility.

In the face of this counteroffensive it took a brave buyer to plunk down a thousand dollars for a receiver that might soon become obsolete and that in the uncertain interim could receive only CBS broadcasts. In fact few buyers were so brave, and before long CBS suspended color broadcasts, saving its face (but not the $50 million it had put into the project) by vaguely citing the patriotic necessity of the Korean war.

By the time Congress opened hearings in 1953 into the puzzling delay of color broadcasting, Sarnoff had all his ducks in a row. The technical kinks of the consortium's—in reality RCA's—process had been worked out; nothing now prevented the commencement of compatible broadcasts. "Color TV is ready for the public," agreed the chairman of the congressional committee. "There is no reason for delay." The FCC obligingly reversed its earlier decision and approved the RCA system.

Converting this technical victory into a commercial one took time. To some extent Sarnoff had done his work too well, for the public remained skittish about color television, and, in any event, compatibility ensured that their old black-and-white sets would receive the new color broadcasts. Price was still a problem, as were public expectations—or lack thereof—regarding what television ought to supply. "I know the grass is green in Ebbets Field," said one potential buyer who chose to remain potential. "It isn't worth $600 more to find out how green."

Gradually, however, the resistance began to melt. In 1960 NBC wooed Walt Disney's popular television show away from ABC and announced that it would be broadcast in color as "Walt Disney's World of Color," with RCA and Eastman Kodak (another company with a vested interest in color) as cosponsors. That same year Sarnoff was able to report that RCA had turned a profit with its sales of color televisions for the first time.

Sarnoff had anticipated a struggle with television, but he didn't expect one that took quite so long. Never a person to discount his own achievements, he asserted that probably only RCA could have managed it. "If we hadn't owned NBC, I don't know if color would ever have taken off. The other networks just sat back on their hands. Until there was set circulation out there they wouldn't touch it. Of course the only way we could get that circulation was through NBC programs. It was our chicken and our egg, nobody else's."

Both poultry products became hot items during the early 1960s. Demand for color sets soared as color programming multiplied. During the first half of the decade RCA profits grew at triple the average of American manufacturing enterprises generally. Earnings per share rose from 72 cents to $1.70; the company became one of Wall Street's favorites. In 1965 sales topped $2 billion.

Color television was Sarnoff's last big accomplishment. His health failed in the late 1960s; he died in 1971. He left no great fortune at his passing, for although he had commanded RCA for nearly half a century, he never owned as much as half a percent of the company. Instead he took his compensation in the satisfaction that comes to those who see farther into the future than their contemporaries and, acting on their vision, bring that future into being. More than any other individual, he created the radio and television industries; those were his legacies, and all who listened and watched, his heirs.

14

FANTASY INC.

Walt Disney

. . .

O NE REASON DAVID SARNOFF HAD SUCH TROUBLE BEING TAKEN seriously with his "Radio Music Box" proposal in 1915 was that the paradigm for industrial success remained rooted in the Carnegie–Rockefeller–Ford mode of producing material objects that could support a skyscraper, fill a pipeline or bend a guardrail. The evanescence of radio waves made them seem an uncertain foundation for building a business.

Walt Disney didn't know the first thing about either Sarnoff's vision for radio or the skepticism that greeted it. In Kansas City in the years before America entered World War I, Disney had no idea that his path would cross Sarnoff's half a century later. But if he *had* known about radio he wouldn't have considered it a long shot at all. Sarnoff's radio waves had scientific substance, even if they couldn't be seen or heard by the unaided human eye and ear; this was much more than could be said for the medium in which Disney was just beginning to work. Sarnoff dealt in electromagnetism; Disney dealt in dreams.

The first dream Disney dealt in was one of his own: of being an artist. He started drawing as a boy in Marceline, Missouri; after the family moved to Kansas City his parents enrolled him in art classes for promising youth. But his precociousness stalled short of genius, and his aptitude with a pencil evolved into an after-school knack for making pocket money. He drew cartoons for the corner barber and advertisements for local merchants. Upon the American entry into the war he joined the Red Cross, being too young for the army; he sketched posters for the international relief agency between shifts driving ambulances in France.

Disney survived France, but his desire for formal education didn't. He never returned to high school, nor art school, instead taking a job with a commercial shop designing stationery for office suppliers, drawing ads for small businesses and making program covers for movie houses. The experience proved educational in its own way. "When you go to art school you work for perfection," he explained afterward. "But in a commercial art shop you cut things out, and paste things over, and scratch around with a razor blade. I'd never done any of those things in art school. Those are time-saving tricks."

In the art shop Disney encountered a young man of similar aptitude and interests although somewhat less ambition. Disney talked Ubbe Iwerks into forming a partnership for commercial artwork. They called their enterprise Iwerks–Disney, after trying Disney–Iwerks but deciding it sounded too much like an optical company. Even renamed, the business folded within a month.

Disney went back to work for a wage, this time with the Kansas City Film Ad Company. The firm's principal product was animated shorts that played before the feature films at movie theaters and hawked various products. Without quite realizing it at first, Disney had found his calling. He loved to bring his drawings to life through the magic of animation, and before long he began improving on the methods of his employer. He read everything he could buy or borrow on the techniques of the best animators in the business; arriving early and staying late, he experimented with new methods of his own devising.

He also moonlighted. He remodeled a garage into a studio and, with borrowed equipment, shot several shorts of his own. Unlike the products of his day job these were purely entertainment, designed to touch theatergoers' funny bones rather than their wallets (directly). They succeeded sufficiently that Disney gave notice to the Film Ad Company and launched his second enterprise, Laugh-O-Gram Films. He found investors among his audiences and raided Film Ad for illustrators. The first of a series of seven-minute films quickly entered production.

The company stumbled after a hopeful start. Scanty revenues necessitated salary cuts; these provoked resignations from staff who insisted on eating regularly. Disney wasn't so finicky. He gave up his apartment and lived out of his office; he dined on beans straight from the can. Yet just before the company sank under its bills he too decided to abandon ship. Like

Henry Kaiser and H. L. Hunt he headed west—in his case for California, and Hollywood in particular.

In 1923 Hollywood was already the city of dreams. The movie industry had chosen that suburb of Los Angeles for its reliably sunny, warm weather; its diversity of desert, ocean, mountain, rural and urban scenery within easy driving distance; and the wondrous light that had entranced artists at least since the time of the Spanish friars. Like the automobile industry and any number of others, the movie industry had started in a hundred separate shops but gradually sifted winners from losers, leaving a handful of survivors. At the time Disney reached Hollywood, the "big eight" studios held the lion's share of the market. They filmed, produced and distributed the movies Americans watched in ever-growing numbers. By most measures the studios *were* the movie industry.

Through brashness or ignorance Disney decided, after a half-hearted effort to find a job with one of the majors, to start a studio of his own. (He later remarked that in life there were two kinds of people. "The first kind are licked if they can't get a job. The second kind feel they can always do something, even if jobs are scarce.") Wisely he sought a niche; naturally he chose animation. As before, this meant short pieces run as fillers between the features the studios produced; it was the sort of small change the big guys left lying on the sidewalk. Designing his own letterhead and signage and dragooning his brother Roy, who was drying out a pair of tubercular lungs at a veterans hospital in the Southern California desert, he boldly announced that the Disney Brothers Studio was open for business. Evidently he felt obliged to explain his sudden flight from Kansas City to California; he told a past—and, he hoped, future—distributor of his films that he had some ideas for a "new and novel series of cartoons" and that "the making of these new cartoons necessitates being located in a production center."

Obviously Disney had the chutzpah for the film game, and his pitch paid off. In reply he received his first order: for six of the innovative cartoons he spoke of. Thrilled, he hustled Roy out of the hospital, cadged $500 from his uncle Robert (who was already providing a nominally priced place for him to sleep), rented a three-room studio for ten dollars a month, hired two illustrators (including his old partner Ub Iwerks) and commenced production of a series of shorts featuring a spunky young heroine named Alice.

The Alice movies borrowed imaginative inspiration from Lewis Carroll's Wonderland character; but in technical terms they were almost as novel as Disney's promotional literature made them sound. They combined the live action of the dauntless protagonist, played by six-year-old Virginia Davis, with an animated backdrop drawn by Disney's illustrators. Early titles "Alice Cans the Cannibals" and "Alice Chops the Suey" delighted audiences, and his distributor told him to keep shooting beyond the original six. Between 1924 and 1926 Disney Brothers produced more than fifty short films that made a minor name for the small studio and a modest income for the brothers.

Budding success encouraged a move to larger quarters. In 1926 Disney Brothers took over a newly built studio on Hollywood's Hyperion Avenue. Meanwhile, however, Walt, the acknowledged idea man of the partnership, was running out of cliffs for little Alice to hang from and villains for her to foil. He also was concluding that for all the labor-intensive techniques fully animated films required, they beat working with real people (not least, children), who sometimes resisted the demands Disney placed on them and whose notions of fair compensation escalated with the success of the films they played in.

As a consequence Disney dropped Alice in favor of Oswald the Animated Rabbit. Largely on the strength of Disney's promotional abilities this new character promised to be even more popular than Alice, and as the orders rolled in—at $2250 a picture, compared to $1500 for the early Alice films—Disney geared up production. He hired more artists, brainstormed new story lines and purchased new equipment.

Then the roof caved in—much as it did in more than one of his animations. For some time Disney had been puzzled by the fact that his distributor habitually sent his brother-in-law to pick up each new release; surely a courier could have done as well. Now Disney encountered a surprise on a visit to New York to renegotiate his contract with his distributor. Disney wanted an increase to $2500 per picture; instead he was offered $1800 on a take-it-or-leave-it basis. When Disney refused the offer he discovered the real purpose behind the brother-in-law's visits: The man was covertly recruiting Disney's employees. Several of these now abandoned Disney for the distributor, who announced plans to produce films himself. The final insult came when the distributor revealed that the new films would feature none other than Oswald the Rabbit, who was defecting too. Disney had carelessly allowed the critter to be copyrighted not in Disney's name but in that of the distributor.

Disney wouldn't repeat this mistake; in subsequent years he would gain a reputation for a rigid insistence on controlling his characters and everything they touched or that touched them. This insistence—obsession, some said—extended to characters created by others but adopted by the Disney studio; one writer lampooned Disney as "the well known author of Alice in Wonderland, the Complete Works of William Shakespeare, and the Encyclopaedia Britannica."

Disney had reason to be careful—and soon, for not long after losing Oswald he created what became one of the most valuable pieces of artistic property in history. On his rabbitless return from New York he huddled with Roy and Ub Iwerks to concoct a successor to Oswald. In his days of Kansas City poverty, Disney had formed a certain attachment to some mice that colonized his studio; perceiving greater personality in that tribe of rodents than did most of his fellow humans, he now hit on the idea of making a mouse his next star. Roy and Iwerks helped him flesh out the idea, then clothe it in red-velvet pants with big pearl buttons, oversized shoes and four-fingered gloves. And that was about all. "He had to be simple," Disney explained. "We had to push out 700 feet of film every two weeks, so we couldn't have a character who was tough to draw."

The little guy initially bore the moniker Mortimer. By one account Disney's wife nixed this as too pretentious. Another version credits the veto to a distributor who couldn't see 1920s audiences responding to a Mortimer. So Mortimer became Mickey, and Disney set him on the path to fame.

At first Mickey hitchhiked with the most famous person in the world at that moment. Charles Lindbergh had just conquered the Atlantic; Disney put Mickey in an airplane with him in a short film called *Plane Crazy*. This was followed by *The Gallopin' Gaucho*, which reprised some of the exotica of the Alice adventures.

Mickey's—and Disney's—breakthrough was their third movie together, *Steamboat Willie*. Sound-recording for films had just entered the realm of available technology; while David Sarnoff was preparing RCA's move into the field, Disney planned his own response. He was mildly taken by the thought of letting Mickey speak; he was more impressed by the possibility of having his movies sing—and clang and bang and bleat and roar. The addition of music and sound effects enormously enhanced both the action and the characterization in animated films.

Audiences, at any rate, thought so, and when *Steamboat Willie* received a two-week trial in New York, Mickey became the toast of Manhattan. Distributors shouted for the steamboat picture and whatever sequels Disney might produce. A snag developed, however, regarding terms. The distributors wanted to buy the films outright; Disney, remembering his lost rabbit, refused to relinquish control. He would license use of the films but not sell them. Eventually Disney found a distributor, Pat Powers, who was trying to popularize a new sound technology and figured that Disney's cartoons would show off the system well. For ten percent of the gross Powers would distribute the films nationwide.

Once more Disney got the studio rolling. One after another the Mickey Mouse films appeared. By the end of 1929 Mickey was almost as famous as Charles Lindbergh himself. Meanwhile Disney was diversifying artistically, exploring the potential of innovative visual and sound effects. *The Skeleton Dance* marked the beginning of a series of animated interpretations of classical music collectively entitled *The Silly Symphonies.* Although less popular than the Mickey movies, these demonstrated that Disney was no one-trick—or one-mouse—pony.

But once again Disney tripped on the business end of his art. Payments from Powers arrived late and suspiciously light; when Disney went east to demand an accounting he learned that Powers had signed Ub Iwerks to a contract to draw cartoons for *him*. Not to appear ungracious, he proceeded to offer Disney himself a job—at the princely rate of $2500 per week. Perhaps Disney really was tempted, or perhaps he simply wanted to get back some of what Powers owed him; in either case he told Powers he was considering the offer. In the meantime, he intimated, he and Roy needed some cash to pay pressing bills. Powers sweetened his offer by writing Disney a check for $5000. Disney dithered just long enough for the check to clear, then told Powers what he could do with his job.

The loss of Iwerks was less immediately threatening than the loss of the outlets Powers represented; Disney scrambled to find replacements. Fortunately the favorable reception of the first three Mickey films made them a promising property, and after a false start with MGM he cut a deal with the distribution arm of Columbia Pictures. (Subsequently he switched to United Artists, then RKO.)

Like Thomas Watson's IBM, Disney's studio thrived during the 1930s. As in Watson's case, there was a direct connection between the country's distress and Disney's success, for Disney offered escape at a moment when Americans had much to escape from. Once asked whether Mickey's adventures were intended to edify, Disney said no. He admitted that "wholesome entertainment" was his aim, but the emphasis was definitely on the entertainment. "It is not our job to teach, implant morals, or improve anything except our pictures," he said.

He certainly worked at that. To a query regarding the secret of his success, Disney responded: "Invent your own job; take such an interest in it that you eat, sleep, dream, walk, talk, and live nothing but your work until you succeed." He had little choice, having picked a challenging vocation. "Everybody was conspiring against the other one," said a Disney animator from that era, speaking of the various interests crowding for screen time, credits and slices of the gross. Disney himself declared that it was an "out-and-out cutthroat business," where a rival would be "putting a knife in your back and he'll be laughing and having a drink with you." Yet he learned his lesson, as a longtime associate explained.

> Walt's conclusion, from his experience to date in the business, was that he had determined never to be at the mercy of a distributor again. His whole salvation was in making a product that so excelled that the public would recognize it and enjoy it as the best of entertainment, and they would more or less demand to see Disney pictures. It was an extremely ambitious statement to make. . . . But Walt made a simple statement that you can lick them with "product."

And the product was going to be Disney's product. An artist who didn't last long at the Disney Studio groused, "I couldn't take it. You did what Disney wanted to do. You couldn't do what you wanted to do. It had to be just Disney; you had to think like Disney, do what Disney did."

Disney countered such complaints by pointing out that his way was working. The *New York Times* lauded him as the "Horatio Alger of the cinema"; *Fortune* asserted, "Enough has been written about Disney's life and hard times already to stamp the bald, Algeresque outlines of his career as familiarly on the minds of many Americans as the career of Henry Ford or Abraham Lincoln."

Disney's bottom line was as promising as his Algeresque outlines were familiar. During the first half of the 1930s the Disney Studio made some twenty pictures per year at a cost of around $50,000 each. In two years each film grossed an average of about $120,000. When his distributor's take was deducted, Disney netted between $20,000 and $25,000 per picture. Disney early appreciated the potential of merchandising tie-ins; these, together with residuals from previous productions, padded profits from current films; in 1934 the company made, by best guesses, $660,000.

Disney was proud of his success. From his Midwest youth he had admired such Hollywood heroes as Charlie Chaplin (who served as a comic model for Mickey Mouse) and Douglas Fairbanks, and he had had a crush on Mary Pickford; this trio now controlled United Artists, and Disney was tickled to be on a first-name basis with them—"Mary, Doug and Charlie." He was gratified from a personal perspective and delighted from a business angle when Chaplin invited him over to United Artists to examine the studio's books.

And he was thrilled when the Disney Studio released a film that made even the majors envious. "Then Charlie came over to study *our* books," Disney said with obvious pleasure. The smash in question was *Snow White and the Seven Dwarfs*. Three years in the making, the movie was Hollywood's first feature-length animated film. Heretofore Disney's work had been the sideshow; now it was the main event. Critics raved at this artistic breakthrough; audiences crowded the theaters. Disney won a special Academy Award for his achievement (the trophy consisted of a single full-sized Oscar figure and seven small ones).

Snow White was followed by other animated features: *Pinocchio, Fantasia* (the culmination of the idea that motivated the *Silly Symphonies*), *Dumbo* and *Bambi*. Each became a classic; each contributed to the legend that was growing up around its creator.

Disney wasn't shy about capitalizing on that legend. The name Disney Brothers had long since given way to Walt Disney Studio, which in turn was subsumed in Walt Disney Productions. The founder made the cover of *Time* magazine; he was constantly called on to explain his popular touch. "The public likes little fellows in comedy," he said. "Everyone picks on them and sympathy is aroused. So when they finally triumph over the bigger characters, the public rejoices with them."

Culture critics, unwilling to leave the matter at this prosaic level, probed Disney's films for deeper meanings. The leftist *People's World* praised Snow White as "Walt Disney's contribution to Marxist theory"; the *New York Times*, writing from a viewpoint considerably closer to the mainstream, called *The Three Little Pigs* a "tonic for disillusion."

Disney let the pundits pontificate; he knew very well what his films were about. "There's one thing we're selling," he told Disney artist Ken Anderson. "Just one, and that's the name 'Walt Disney.'" He went on, "If you can buy that and be happy to work under the name Walt Disney, you're my man. But if you've got any ideas of selling 'Ken Anderson,' it's best for you to forget it right now."

Of course the way to sell Walt Disney was to sell Mickey Mouse and his on-screen associates—which Disney did with a vengeance. Another culture critic, obviously less than happy with the phenomenon, in 1935 remarked on the ubiquity of the golden rodent.

> Undeniably, and appallingly, it is Mickey Mouse's day. Shoppers carry Mickey Mouse satchels and briefcases bursting with Mickey Mouse soap, candy, playing-cards, bridge favors, hairbrushes, china-ware, alarm clocks and hot-water bottles, wrapped in Mickey Mouse paper, tied with Mickey Mouse ribbon and paid for out of Mickey Mouse purses with savings hoarded in Mickey Mouse banks. At the lunch counter—Mickey Mouse table covers and napkins—they consume Mickey Mouse biscuits and dairy products, while listening to Mickey Mouse music from Mickey Mouse phonographs and radios. . . . The children live in a Mickey Mouse world. They wear Mickey Mouse caps, waists, socks, shoes. . . . They play with Mickey Mouse velocipedes, footballs, baseballs. . . . They sup from Mickey Mouse cups, porringers, and baby plates and lie down to sleep in Mickey Mouse pajamas between Mickey Mouse crib sheets.

Another view of the same phenomenon came from the trade journal *Advertising and Selling*. The author contended that emergence of the Disney "publicity machine" signaled a new era in American business development.

> The usual course of events has been reversed. Ordinarily a manufacturer gives his product a name and mark and proceeds to make them known by advertising, but in these instances the trade mark is made known first, and then applied to the goods. The publicity that is swelling Walt Disney's income cost him nothing. It was a free gift from the newspapers. But it has a tangible dollars and cents value far beyond its original aim and purpose.

Disney couldn't have known when he created Mickey Mouse that the little fellow would become the marketing marvel of the age. Yet Disney's once-burned insistence on maintaining control of his creations indicated at least an intuition of what such creations were worth, and he learned as he went along. In time the marketing of Mickey products generated far more revenue than the Mickey movies themselves.

Another Disney signature was a willingness to take chances on new technology. *Steamboat Willie* brought sound to animation; *Flowers and Trees*, one of the *Silly Symphonies*, introduced Technicolor—and won an Oscar in the bargain. (Beating out another Disney production, *Mickey's*

Orphans, for Best Short Subject. The latter, however, won its creator a special achievement award for his special mouse.)

Disney was no less alert to the potential of television when it emerged on the cutting edge of entertainment technology. As early as 1938—the year before David Sarnoff's broadcast from the New York World's Fair—Disney predicted that television, "although in its infancy, opens up a vast field of entertainment." The field remained largely unexplored, however, while American scientists and engineers fought World War II. From Disney's perspective this was just as well. The company lost a bitter strike by the Screen Cartoonists Guild in 1941; combined with disappointing box-office receipts for *Fantasia* and *Pinocchio*, the shutdown put the company a total of a million dollars in the red for 1941 and 1942. The war revived Disney's fortunes, as it did those of so many other businesses. Disney's characters went off to war, with Donald Duck especially epitomizing the spirit of American GIs, grumbling—quacking, in his case—against the military bureaucracy, evading inane regulations where possible, but always doing his patriotic duty in the final reel. Wartime shortages prevented Disney from making movies that didn't contribute to the war effort, so he hit on another formula that proved to be pure profit ever after: the re-release of films for a new generation of children and parents. In 1944 Disney brought out *Snow White* again; the movie provided essentially all of the company's profits for nongovernmental work that year.

During the decade after the war, as television emerged as the next big thing in mass entertainment, Disney embraced it enthusiastically. At Christmas 1950 Disney hosted a holiday special. Entitled "One Hour in Wonderland," the show featured clips from vintage Disney movies, appearances by live child stars and a short sneak preview of Disney's long-awaited, all-animated version of *Alice in Wonderland*. The program elicited an enormous response, prompting Disney to repeat the performance the next year. (In one measure of the show's success, the $125,000 Coca-Cola paid to sponsor the first Christmas special doubled by the next year when Johnson & Johnson laid out a record quarter-million for advertising rights.) Shortly thereafter Disney began preparing a regular program, and in 1954 the company signed a seven-year contract with ABC for a weekly show called *Disneyland*. Industry analysts hailed the potential synergy between the movie industry and television; one business commentator described the pact as "the most important development to date in relations between the old and the new entertainment form." The term "Disney Revolution" circulated in the business and entertainment press.

For Disney the deal represented far more than a venture into television. The name of the show was also the name of a new theme park that was about to open in Anaheim, California. The show—which offered viewers regular glimpses at the progress of the park—consequently became an advertisement for the park, even as the park became an advertisement for the show. (Not coincidentally ABC owned a one-third interest in the park.) Meanwhile both the show and the park, which were populated by Disney characters, became advertisements for Disney's movies, which had entered a regular cycle of withdrawal and re-release.

It was the perfect package—but there was more. In 1955 Disney invaded daytime television with *The Mickey Mouse Club*. An hour-long program that appeared just before the evening news, it introduced audiences to the "Mouseketeers," a group of charming—curmudgeons said cloying—kids who became idols for a generation of American youth. Ratings for the show shocked even Nielsen; the television-tracking company described the program as "completely dominating regular daytime television." Soon it was drawing an average audience of 12 million children and 7 million adults. Neither number was lost on advertisers.

Some of those Mouseketeers went on to star in Disney films. During the 1950s and early 1960s Disney produced a string of live-action adventure, comedy and animal movies, including *The Swiss Family Robinson*, *Twenty Thousand Leagues Under the Sea*, *The Absent-Minded Professor* and *The Shaggy Dog*. These too were fitted into the Disney fantasy package, with marketing spin-offs and, in the case of *Swiss Family Robinson* and *Twenty Thousand Leagues*, substantial acreage at Disneyland.

Initially Disney had had difficulty getting financing for Disneyland from bankers who feared it would become another Coney Island; by the late 1950s the naysayers were conceding their missed opportunity to invest in what was now one of the most popular tourist destinations in America. Travel sections in newspapers all over the country wrote it up alongside the Grand Canyon and the Gettysburg battlefield, providing free publicity not only for the park but for everything else identified with Disney. When visitors reached the park nearly all were happy they had come. A 1959 survey by the company found that 98.6 percent of visitors thought they received their money's worth at the park and 83 percent planned to return.

Disney exploited the popularity of the park to offer other companies a chance to hawk their wares—for a fee, of course. Dozens of companies took up the offer, and soon the park became, in the words of one business journal, "a wonderland of brand names with a captive viewing audience of 5,000,000 a year."

If Disneyland had a drawback, it was that there was only one of it, and that one was located far from the population centers of the East Coast. During the early 1960s Disney prepared to remedy the deficiency. On more than 27,000 acres—twice the size of Manhattan Island—the company would build a new and bigger version of Disneyland, combined with a hotel–resort complex and a carefully planned city of the future. The park would be called Disney World and the futuristic city EPCOT (for Experimental Prototype Community of Tomorrow).

Disney World and EPCOT were built as announced, but before construction was completed Walt Disney died. At the time of his passing in 1966 statistics revealed the astonishing reach of his influence. In that year, by the company's best estimates, some 240 million people (or half again the population of the United States) attended a Disney feature film. One hundred million viewed a Disney television show each week. Eight hundred million read a Disney book or magazine. Fifty million listened to Disney music or records. Eighty million purchased Disney-licensed toys or similar products. One hundred fifty million read a Disney comic strip. Eighty million saw Disney educational films. Nearly seven million pushed through the turnstiles at Disneyland.

These millions and millions of satisfied customers attested to the effectiveness of the Disney formula, which the *Wall Street Journal* summarized as: "Dream, diversify—and never miss an angle." From a business standpoint this was an apt description of Disney's method of conjuring value—in the form of Mickey Mouse and his sidekicks—from his own imagination and those of his viewers, and then fashioning a self-reinforcing cycle of promotion and sales. In time the Disney formula would be emulated throughout the world of entertainment, by pop music groups, athletes and any others who thought they could pull it off.

Yet there was something more basic at the bottom of Disney's success. As elaborate as the Disney machine grew, the inventor of it all never lost sight of his customer base. Mark Twain, perhaps the only other American storyteller with a reach comparable to Disney's (and one whose stories Disney eagerly adapted) was asked to explain his approach to writing. Twain responded that the works of the giants of literature were like wine; his, by contrast, were like water. He added, patting his wallet: "Everyone drinks water."

Disney took a similar view. With Twain, Disney shrugged off critics who derided his work as middlebrow. His films, he said, "go straight out for the honest adult, not the sophisticate, not these characters who think they know everything and you can't thrill them anymore. I go to the people who retain that, no matter how old they are, that little spirit of adventure, that appreciation of the world of fantasy." The critics weren't his customers; the audience was. "To hell with the critics," Disney said. "It's the audience we're making the picture for."

15

THE REAL THING

Robert W. Woodruff

• • •

"A SIX-MAN JAPANESE PATROL ATTEMPTED TO INFILTRATE THE lines of the 383rd regiment of the 96th infantry division early today in an attempt to blow up an ammunition dump," read the Associated Press report from Okinawa in 1945. "They missed the ammunition but did destroy a large can of Coca-Cola syrup. Angry doughboys killed them all." A West Virginia paper carrying the story put it beneath the headline: "NO WONDER!"

Dwight Eisenhower understood. In 1943 the American commander wrote to Washington from North Africa requesting equipment to set up ten bottling plants. His staff had determined that Coke was crucial to the war effort. "I had them make a survey to see just what the men wanted," Ike afterward told a congressional committee, "and more of them voted for Coca-Cola than beer." Beer might quench the men's thirst, but Coke reminded them what they were fighting for. A sergeant from Kansas explained to his parents: "It's the little things, not the big things, that the individual soldier fights for or wants so badly when away." "It's the girl back home in a drug store over a Coke, or the juke box and the summer weather." Eisenhower (another Kansan) felt exactly the same way. "I wish I could be home and go down to the cafe this morning and have a Coke with the gang," Eisenhower wrote a friend. "I can't do that here."

Yet if the general couldn't get to the cafe, he *could* see that his men received their Coke. Shortly after Allied troops landed at Normandy, Eisenhower ordered that scarce space be set aside for Coca-Cola on a cargo ship coming across the English Channel. Soon special "jungle units" were dispensing Coke from the back of two-ton trucks, shooting the soft drink straight into the canteens of the thirsty GIs. (The "jungle units" were so called from their provenance in the Pacific theater, where they were, if anything, judged more vital to the war effort than in Europe. An American soldier in New Guinea basked in the arrival of his favorite beverage: "The syrup is old and the [carbonating] gas low, but it's still our greatest luxury. The syrup is dipped with a tin spoon into an aluminum canteen cup and stirred with a stick and we still love it." He concluded: "This war should be a cinch now.")

Most corporate heads can only dream of achieving such exalted status for their principal product—of elevating some ordinary item to the realm of Mom and apple pie. Walt Disney was a brilliant marketer, as the ubiquity of Mickey Mouse and his relations revealed; but not even Mickey ever became a proxy for the American way of life, an emblem of what a generation of Americans would go to war for. This latter accomplishment was left to Robert W. Woodruff, for sixty years the driving force behind Coca-Cola. Woodruff distilled six ounces of fizzy brown sugar water into the essence of America; meanwhile he made Coca-Cola the first truly global consumer item and the most valuable product name on the planet.

Ironically, Woodruff hadn't wanted to sell soft drinks. He preferred trucks—not least since his father ran Coca-Cola and Robert didn't get along with his father. "He was much harder on me than on his other sons," Robert asserted, perhaps not allowing for the fact that Robert was clearly the most talented of Ernest Woodruff's boys. Ernest headed a group of investors that in 1919 purchased the Coca-Cola Company from the family of Asa Candler, who had sampled the beverage concocted by John Pemberton—commonly called "Doc" by his Atlanta neighbors—and found that it cured, or at least alleviated, his recurrent headaches and dyspepsia. Well it might have, for like many another patent medicine, the original Coca-Cola contained some potent ingredients, most notably cocaine, derived from the leaves of the coca plant. In the late nineteenth century cocaine possessed a reputation as a wonder drug. Public figures weren't embarrassed to endorse it or the sundry cocktails in which it was marketed. A French pharmacist named Mariani mixed cocaine with wine and sold it as "Vin Mariani"; one satisfied customer was Frederic-Auguste Bartholdi, the creator some years earlier of the Statue of Liberty, who attested that had he then had the benefit of Mariani's brew, his celebrated sculpture would have been three times the height it turned out to be. Sigmund Freud, another devotee, appreciated the vigor it supplied to certain personal pursuits. "Woe to you, My Princess, when I come," he wrote to his betrothed. "I will kiss you quite red . . . and if you are forward you shall see who is the stronger, a gentle little girl . . . or a big wild man who has cocaine in his body."

Doc Pemberton was marginally more circumspect. "The use of the coca plant not only preserves the health of all who use it," he promised, "but prolongs life to a very great old age and enables the coca eaters to perform prodigies of mental and physical labor." For his own part Pemberton might have said "coca drinkers," for he made it his business to put the best of the coca plant into a bottle. Initially he mimicked Mariani's recipe, but as local prohibition dried up the market for alcoholic beverages—while leaving cocaine curiously alone—he evolved his elixir in another direction. Almost as popular as cocaine among those who liked to experiment with their health was the extract of the African kola nut (seed, actually). The active ingredient of kola was caffeine; between the cocaine and the caffeine, a coca-kola cocktail delivered a nice kick. It took Pemberton a little tinkering and a lot of sugar to mask the bitter taste of the kola extract; eventually he added caramel coloring, lime juice, vanilla, oil of cassia and various other ingredients whose identities he adamantly refused to release to the public. Fortunately the U.S. Patent Office didn't require him to do so when, in 1886, it granted him exclusive rights to produce and distribute "Coca-Cola Syrup and Extract."

Health problems—unalleviated by his new drink, and perhaps aggravated by too many tastings of the cocaine he put in it—prevented Pemberton from making money on Coca-Cola; after some confusion, threatened litigation and the exchange of a minor amount of money, proprietary control of the drink wound up with Asa Candler. During the next thirty years Candler vigorously marketed the product even as he modified the formula—by, among other changes, removing the cocaine in response to a shift in popular perceptions of what constituted wonder drugs and what illegal euphorics. Candler's efforts brought him financial security and Coca-Cola a national presence. But he had other interests, including the reform of Atlanta politics; in 1916 he ran for mayor and won. He handed ownership of the company to his wife and five sons; after she died the boys put the company on the block, and Ernest Woodruff and his partners bought it for $25 million.

Ernest Woodruff, a financier at heart, had little interest in soft drinks per se; still less did his son. Consequently, even as Ernest sought devices to squeeze the highest return from his investment, Robert attempted to avoid being pulled into the business. As a boy growing up in the toney Inman Park neighborhood of Atlanta, Robert showed little promise in the classroom. He flunked out of high school, prompting his father to send him to that standby of southern parents determined to bring out the man in their boys: a military academy. He survived, although the headmaster told Ernest he shouldn't expect much more academically from his son. "Don't send Robert to school anymore," the headmaster urged. "You'll ruin him."

Ernest refused to listen. Hoping to make a banker of the lad, he packed Robert off to Emory College, at that time a small Methodist institution located thirty-five miles east of Atlanta. The experiment proved an utter failure. Robert spent his father's money drinking, chasing girls and hiring less festive (or merely less wealthy) drudges to do his homework for him. Later, when he gained an audience for his reflections on the optimal management of time and personnel, he liked to say: "If you can get somebody to do something better than you can do it yourself, it's always a good idea." He thought it was a good idea in college. His instructors thought otherwise; halfway through Robert's freshman year Emory's president wrote Ernest regarding Robert: "I do not think it advisable for him to return to college this term."

Perhaps Ernest expected Robert to be humbled by this latest failure. "Damn it, boy!" he berated him. "It's only three generations from shirtsleeves to shirtsleeves." But Robert was defiant rather than embarrassed. "I'll take the shirtsleeves now," he threw back at the older man.

He went to work shoveling sand at a foundry for 60 cents a day. He professed to like the work, doubtless partly because it was just the opposite of what his father had been planning for him. "Good old muscle jobs aren't so bad," he declared afterward. But neither were they so good that he refused an offer from his supervisor to move up to the office of the foundry's parent company, a manufacturer of fire extinguishers. From the office to the road didn't take long either; shortly he was extolling extinguishers to customers and soon-to-be customers throughout the Atlanta area. In the arena of sales Robert found his metier. Out from under his father's control he demonstrated an energy the older man suspected but never saw and skills of persuasion that had been stifled in the conflicted filial relationship. His employer recognized Robert's aptitude, increasing his territory, responsibilities and compensation.

The following year he switched from peddling fire extinguishers to pushing trucks. Walter White thought Robert Woodruff would make money for the Ohio-based White Motors even if he only arranged introductions to the many influential Atlanta acquaintances of his father. Perhaps Robert had shared with White another of the adages he later handed out to all and sundry: "It's just as easy to make your friends among people of consequence as among people of no consequence." It came easy enough to Robert Woodruff, to the benefit of White Motors. What White hadn't anticipated was the business Woodruff collared in the Georgia countryside. He traveled the highways and low-ways (to the point of being under water in rainy weather) of the state, introducing himself to every county commissioner and other individual with authority to purchase trucks. He explained how White trucks were just the item for the rutted clay tracks of the pine forests; flattered at the attention and convinced by the spiel, Woodruff's listeners bought trucks in fleet-lots. By 1916, when he was twenty-six, he was White's sales manager for the Southeast, making $300 a month plus expenses and 25 percent commission on his sales. More important than the money was the fact that he was winning a reputation in the Atlanta business community independent of his father.

When the United States entered World War I, Robert Woodruff perceived an opportunity to serve both his country and his employer. He enlisted in the army and immediately applied for assignment to the ordnance department. There he assisted in the design of trucks for transporting troops; not coincidentally—but profitably—White Motors happened to have chassis and other parts that fit the specifications to the decimal point. The army promoted Woodruff to major; White Motors reserved an analogous promotion awaiting his mustering out. By 1921 he was a vice president of the corporation. This required relocation; leaving Atlanta, he split time between Cleveland and New York. By the end of the following year he had been promoted again, to the second slot in the corporation, behind only Walter White, who indicated every intention of anointing the thirty-three-year-old Woodruff as his successor.

Robert's rapid success persuaded Ernest Woodruff that the boy ought to be brought into the Coca-Cola Company. The obvious job—and the only one Robert might be tempted to take—was president. The leading inside candidate for the post was a man named Harrison Jones, a stem-winding motivational speaker at sales meetings and conventions of bottlers, but one who sometimes allowed his eloquence to get the better of him. Explaining the importance of sterilizing the bottles Coca-Cola came in, Jones declared:

> The bottles before returning to the owner are frequently used for every purpose where a liquid-holding receptacle is necessary, from obtaining gasoline to clean mother's skirt, to the collection of a specimen of pathological urine for examination by the local doctor. And there are bottles which have been emptied directly by the lips of tubercular persons or by lips sore with some loathsome infectious disease, and bottles salvaged from garbage cans and from the city dump—of such does the flotsam returned to the bottler consist.

Such stirring oratory certainly motivated the bottlers not to scrimp on the hot, soapy water, but Ernest Woodruff guessed that it might not sell much Coca-Cola if Jones were given a larger platform.

So Ernest went after Robert. The other members of the Coca-Cola board encouraged him, having developed a high regard for the younger Woodruff's capacities. But Robert himself was reluctant. "I didn't know any more about the soft drink business than a pig knows about Sunday," he said later. Besides, he would be taking a substantial pay cut to come home to Atlanta and Coca-Cola. In 1922 he made $85,000 at White Motors; his father was offering him $36,000.

And then there was the whole father–son issue. Robert had no reason to think his father would be any easier to get along with than before; in fact he might well be harder to get along with as a boss than he had been as merely a father. Yet the challenge of running Coca-Cola was tempting. For most of his life Robert had tried, by one means or another, to show his father he was worth something. His success at White had made an impression, obviously. But now he had a chance to make an even bigger impression: by doing better than his old man on the old man's turf.

In later years Robert downplayed this personal angle. "The only reason I took that job," he said, "was to get back the money I had invested in Coca-Cola stock. I figured that if I ever brought the price of stock back to what I had paid for it, I'd sell and get even." This was somewhat misleading. The company had indeed fallen on hard times after the war when it borrowed heavily to buy sugar at a price that promptly crashed. But by 1923, when Robert accepted the presidency, the worst was over.

Robert Woodruff, however, had great plans for the company. With the American economy riding its wave of spending into the Roaring Twenties, he determined that Coca-Cola should ride along. In one respect he was thinking literally: As Americans piled into the cars Henry Ford and Alfred

Sloan were making for them, to drive on the highways Henry Kaiser was building for them, Woodruff spent hundreds of thousands of dollars buying ad space on the billboards that were beginning to line those highways. At the same time he intensified efforts to make Coke a year-round drink rather than the hot-weather item soft drinks had traditionally been. On an early information-gathering tour Woodruff found himself in Moose Jaw, Alberta, in the dead of winter. He knew that Coca-Cola sold well in Canada, but he was surprised to see travelers in the train station guzzling the drink when the air outside was 35 below zero. Reflecting, he realized that the indoor temperature in winter in many northern climes was higher than the outdoor temperature in summer. People got thirsty twelve months out of the year; they could be sold Coca-Cola all twelve months.

Marketing any product involves shaping people's perceptions; Woodruff's insight in marketing Coca-Cola was that it involved nothing *but* shaping perceptions. Even as singular a salesman as Thomas J. Watson regularly tried to improve his product (if not perhaps as rapidly as his son thought he ought); Woodruff made a show of refusing to improve. He adopted the position that Coca-Cola was the perfect soft drink. To tamper with it would be to ruin it. With great fanfare he retrieved the single extant copy of the original formula from its bank vault in New York, where it had been deposited as symbolic surety for those disastrous sugar loans, and he personally conveyed the sealed envelope back to Atlanta, where it was placed in another bank vault (this one located in his father's bank). He instituted a policy mandating that no one could see the formula without the express approval of the board of directors and then only if accompanied by the chairman, president or corporate secretary. No more than two company officials were authorized to know the formula at any given time; their identities were never to be publicly disclosed. In later years an addendum to the policy specified that the two knowledgeable officials must never fly on the same plane.

The point of all the hocus pocus was not secrecy but mystification. Had Woodruff merely wished to keep the formula secret he shouldn't have taken the pains he did to publicize his elaborate precautions. (One imagines corporate spies studying airline manifests to see which two top executives never traveled together.) What Woodruff wanted to convey was the impression that Coca-Cola's competitors would kill (or at least kidnap and perhaps torture one of those officials favored with the company's precious secret) to acquire knowledge of what Coke's customers could purchase for a nickel. Perfection rarely came as such a bargain.

Woodruff resorted to other maneuvers to associate Coca-Cola with quality. Hoping to garner the business of luxury cruise liners, the company created a special bottle designed to look like a split of champagne. When the ship stewards still resisted, company salesmen infiltrated the farewell parties held at dockside and left empty Coca-Cola bottles lying conspicuously around. The stewards, ever desirous of catering to their passengers' tastes, began ordering Coke by the gross.

Meanwhile the company hardly neglected the masses. Woodruff was constantly on the watch for ways to make drinking Coca-Cola more convenient; his dream was a Coke within arm's reach of every man, woman and child in the country. "Around the corner from everywhere" was an early slogan. As Americans began to buy refrigerators for their homes he pushed six-packs; to serve those public spaces without convenient electrical outlets he funded research into improved coolers. The company produced and distributed films demonstrating to soda-fountain operators the optimal way to serve Coke: at 34 degrees with chipped ice—not shaved or crushed—in a thin-sided, bell-shaped glass (which the company helpfully furnished, with the Coca-Cola logo on the side).

Woodruff was a fanatic on service. To make a point he called a meeting of his sales staff and announced that they were all fired, every one. He had decided to eliminate the sales department, he said. He let the message sink in for twenty-four hours, then hired them all back to work in the company's "service" department. His unannounced visits and his legendary gruffness put the fear of God into bottlers as well. According to one account that entered company lore, he listened with growing anger to a bottler who said that cleaning the equipment was a waste of time. His crews could clean one day, he explained, and the next day the line would be dirty again. Woodruff nearly bit through his cigar before cursing and demanding: "You wipe your ass, don't you?"

Meanwhile Woodruff blanketed the country with materials bearing the Coca-Cola emblem. In one year the company distributed a million calendars, three million desk blotters, seventeen million paper napkins, one hundred thousand streetcar signs, fifty thousand serving trays, seventy-five thousand "Ice Cold" signs and countless other items all bearing the distinctive white "Coca-Cola" script on the red field.

The objective was nothing less than the identification of Coca-Cola with the American people. "We have an opportunity, if we are equal to it," said one of Woodruff's lieutenants, "to make Coca-Cola the national beverage, the great American drink." Already the phrase "as American as Coca-Cola" was appearing in print, to Woodruff's gratification.

William Allen White, the Kansas editor who became the conscience of middle America, thought the company had already succeeded. Interviewed for *Life* magazine on his seventieth birthday, in his hometown of Emporia, White insisted on being photographed sipping a Coke at the corner soda fountain. Coca-Cola, he explained, was "a sublimated essence of all that America stands for."

Coca-Cola's corporate rivals naturally disagreed. The foremost of the challengers was Pepsi-Cola, which long played runner-up to Coke's winner. In what amounted to an admission of defeat on the quality front (Woodruff charactized this as Pepsi's "fatal error"), Pepsi fought its anti-Coke battle on price. Coke sold six-and-a-half ounces for a nickel; Pepsi sold twelve ounces for the same price. This wasn't as radical a concept as it might have seemed to some, because what went inside the bottle constituted but a small portion of the cost of the product, with the majority going to marketing, distribution and the like. But especially after the fat Twenties gave way to the thin Thirties, Pepsi's price advantage afforded it an edge at the lower end of the market.

Woodruff responded by reemphasizing Coca-Cola's commitment to quality—subtly emphasizing those aspects of the company's advertising that conveyed an upwardly mobile message—and by hounding Pepsi legally. Coca-Cola lawyers had little difficulty defending the Coca-Cola name against obvious imitators like "Co-Cola" and "Coke-Ola"—brands whose sound-alike strategy was only mildly less blatant in the North than in the South, where many people swallowed the second syllable of the first half of "Coca-Cola" along with the drink itself. The company's lawyers had more difficulty, although exhibited no less energy, defending the broader proposition that any name that included the word "cola" illegally infringed on Coca-Cola's trademark.

Woodruff and company would have sued Pepsi in U.S. courts if they thought they had any chance of success, but the name Pepsi-Cola had been in use long enough in the United States to have acquired a de facto—and hence, in the field of trademarks, a de jure—legitimacy. Instead the company took up the Pepsi challenge in Canadian courts, where Pepsi had only recently begun doing business. A victory there would crimp Pepsi's expansion plans; moreover, simply forcing Pepsi to fight a long legal battle would tie down resources that might otherwise be applied to marketing back home. After extended litigation a Canadian trial court ruled in Coca-Cola's favor. But on appeal the Canadian Supreme Court overturned the decision, granting consumers sufficient credit as to be able to distinguish between "Coca-Cola" and "Pepsi-Cola." "The general impression on the mind of the ordinary person," the court declared, "would be one of contrast, rather than similarity." Coca-Cola's lawyers appealed this decision, taking the case clear to London where the Judicial Committee of the Privy Council oversaw courts throughout the British Commonwealth. The bewigged British jurists agreed with the Canadian high court (and with Pepsi), adopting the simple expedient of looking up the word "cola" in the dictionary. Finding it, they determined that Coca-Cola had no proprietary right to it. The judges employed an even more prosaic approach to the connected question of whether the physical appearance of Pepsi's logo illegally infringed on Coca-Cola's. Turning the two labels upside-down and viewing them as if they were, in the words of one of the judges, Chinese characters, they found no excessive likeness. Pepsi could keep its name and its logo—in the British Commonwealth, at any rate.

Coca-Cola's legal assault on Pepsi assumed a different form in the United States. Suspecting that soda fountains—perhaps with Pepsi's collusion—were substituting the cheaper brand for the real thing, Woodruff sent undercover investigators into drug stores to surreptitiously gather evidence. This was whisked back to company labs, where it was analyzed and identified. When substitution was discovered—as it was in many cases—stern warnings, on legal letterhead, ensued. When these failed, lawsuits followed. The strategy didn't seriously challenge Pepsi's existence, but it served to remind that company—and its distributors—that Coca-Cola would stand for no hitch-hiking on its own success.

The approach of World War II created a set of problems for Woodruff that at least for a time overshadowed his troubles with Pepsi. During the 1930s the company attempted to expand foreign operations, especially in Europe; it succeeded most conspicuously in Germany. Unfortunately Germany's descent into Hitlerian bigotry and belligerence placed Coca-Cola in an awkward position. Coca-Cola was hardly alone in having to decide whether the bad odor of the Nazi regime irretrievably tainted the returns on investment; but for a company that first and foremost sold image—and an all-American image at that—the dilemma was especially troubling. The onset of the war in 1939 added concrete logistical challenges to those involving the etherealities of image.

When the United States joined the fighting in 1941 yet another set of problems arose. A week after Pearl Harbor the federal government ordered rationing of sugar. Heavy users like Coca-Cola were limited to 80 percent of their 1940 consumption. Had the feds adopted a baseline of 1941 the pinch on Coca-Cola wouldn't have been so painful, for 1941 had been the best year in the company's history, with record sales and record usage of sugar. To go back to 80 percent of 1940's amount would not simply short-circuit anticipated growth but require cutting off many current customers.

Fortunately there was an exception to the sugar cap: It didn't apply to production bound for the American military. And with the American military growing at an exponential rate, this loophole turned out to be large and lucrative. Initially Coke colonized the military bases and training camps where the soldiers prepared to go overseas; when the soldiers and sailors and airmen actually began to ship out, Woodruff determined that Coke must go with them. "See that every man in a uniform gets a bottle of Coca-Cola for five cents, wherever he is and whatever it costs," he ordered. This was a patriotic gesture; it was also the shrewdest bit of marketing Woodruff ever organized. He understood that whatever it cost to keep GIs supplied with Coke, the money would be well spent in terms of the company's present image and the loyalty of the next generation of customers.

Predictably Pepsi demanded equal access to American soldiers. But the War Department wasn't about to get involved in quarrels between the cola makers, and Army Chief of Staff George Marshall granted his theater commanders authority to choose the brands they thought their men wanted. General Eisenhower actually polled his men; other commanders simply adopted the market leader. Coca-Cola ended up with the lion's share of the orders.

It also got the opportunity to establish production facilities in the various theaters of combat. Specially designated technical observers—the company called them T.O.s; others dubbed them the "Coca-Cola colonels"—were assigned seats on military air transports and ferried to forward locations. There they directed the construction of bottling plants. Before long American infantrymen had the relative luxury of receiving the familiar bottles in their foxholes. Logistics limited the men to two bottles per week at first, but as demand outstripped supply a lively black market developed, and those willing to pay the price slaked their thirst as often as they could afford.

The company's public-relations office might have made much of Coca-Cola's conquest of the military market, but it didn't have to bother. War correspondents, wishing to convey the human-interest side of their big story, did the job better than the Coca-Cola publicists ever could have. An early American casualty in the European theater was a pilot who crashed in training over Scotland. He survived, after much medical attention; upon regaining consciousness his first request was for a Coke, which his commander flew to London to fetch. The story made all the military papers and most civilian ones. At Christmans 1943 *Stars and Stripes*, the army news sheet, reported the glad tidings that the Coca-Cola plant at Casablanca had begun production just in time for the holidays. Photos from various sectors of the front showed unshaven, unwashed GIs taking a break from their martial endeavors; readers could fill in for themselves the company's most famous slogan: "the pause that refreshes." The enemy added to Coca-Cola's luster, if inadvertently. Hitler's top propagandist sneered that "America never contributed anything to world civilization but chewing gum and Coca-Cola." Japan's publicists told its people, "With Coca-Cola we imported the germs of a disease from American society." The infamous "Tokyo Rose" dangled an image before the troops she sought to demoralize: "Wouldn't it be nice to have an ice-cold Coca-Cola? Can't you just hear the ice tinkling in the glass?"

With enemies like that, Coke hardly needed friends—although the endorsement of such heroes as Eisenhower and Marshall ensured that it wouldn't lack friends. The war cemented Coca-Cola's position as the quintessential American beverage. *American Legion* magazine surveyed the troops and discovered that they preferred Coke over Pepsi by a margin of eight to one.

The war also gave the company a long leg up on the competition for overseas markets at war's end. In 1945 the company operated sixty-three bottling plants spread across the globe from the South Pacific to the North Atlantic, from the Americas to Europe, Africa, the Middle East and East Asia. The British used to boast that the sun never set on their empire; it might have dipped below the horizon for Coca-Cola but not for much longer than it took to quaff an ice-cold one.

Like other dominant companies, from Rockefeller's Standard Oil to Bill Gates's Microsoft, Woodruff's Coca-Cola caught its share of criticism. Cynics during the war complained at the commingling of profits and patriotism. "Step right up and get your four delicious freedoms," mocked one reporter. "It's a refreshing war." Another asked, "What do they think this war is—the cause that refreshes?" In 1950 a friendly *Time* magazine put Coca-Cola's familiar red disk on the cover and showed it, anthropomorphized, holding a bottle of Coke to the mouth of a thirsty Earth. "World & Friend" ran the caption. Pepsi executives could only gnash their teeth in silence—and reprint columnist Walter Winchell's take on the story. Noting that Coca-Cola was one of *Time*'s regular advertisers, Winchell jibed: "*Time* mag usually pummels its Front Cover subject. But Coca-Cola is given the Kid Glove Treatment. Moral: It Pays to Advertise."

It also paid to have fans in politics. Woodruff remembered what Eisenhower had done for the company during the war, and he appreciated what the general continued to do afterward. At one stop on his victory tour Ike was asked if there was anything he needed. "Could somebody get me a Coke?" he replied. He drank it almost at a swallow—in full view of the public and of the dozens of reporters who fought each other to relay every detail of the tour to the rest of the country. The general then said he had another request. "What was it?" his hosts asked. "Another Coke."

Woodruff invited Eisenhower to his hunting camp in northern Georgia, adding bridge (which Woodruff didn't like but knew Eisenhower did) to the list of card games played around the fire in the evenings. He encouraged Eisenhower to consider a political career, and when Eisenhower evinced interest Woodruff became one of his staunchest and most generous backers. After Eisenhower's 1952 election the new president reciprocated by putting Woodruff on the Secret Service's exclusive list of visitors with standing invitations to drop by the White House. Woodruff called this his "key to the back door" and made frequent use of it. He grew so intimate with the president that on at least one occasion, when after-dinner drinks lubricated a lively discussion that started in the study and continued into Eisenhower's bedroom, the dialogue didn't end until the weary Eisenhower, having changed into his pajamas and climbed under the covers, pulled rank and ordered Woodruff off his bed and out of his bedroom.

Coca-Cola continued to get good publicity from its Ike connection. The positive photo ops were usually rather mundane: Ike having a Coke after a round of golf. Sometimes they were more exotic. Woodruff picked up his newspaper one morning to see the president, then on a tour of India, sipping Coke through a straw in that far-off land. Woodruff was grateful but not above offering a suggestion. The chairman had a long-held prejudice that Coke should be drunk, not sucked. He advised the president accordingly. Eisenhower responded with a note good-humoredly headed "Top Secret." The president explicated his rationale in terms that appealed to Woodruff's bottom line: "When I tip up a bottle of Coca-Cola for a good drink it lasts only seconds. With a straw, a lot of talk and more walking, I was able to attract more photographs and newspaper correspondents than I could possibly otherwise have done!"

Woodruff had another political connection that was equally important, if in a different way. More than any other elected official in the

South, Atlanta mayor William Hartsfield was responsible for dragging Dixie, kicking and screaming, into the twentieth century. Hartsfield was acutely sensitive to the heavy handicap the South's segregationist policies put on Southern businesses. A group of Atlanta businessmen inquired when the Atlanta airport would begin receiving international flights; Hartsfield answered witheringly, "Not until Atlanta becomes an internationally minded city. What do you plan to do with the Brazilian millionaire who flies in with some money to invest but happens to be black? Send him to the Negro YMCA? Think about it, friends."

Coca-Cola was the most internationally minded of Atlanta's businesses. (Woodruff had moved the corporate headquarters from Atlanta to Wilmington, Delaware, in 1933 after the Depression-strapped Georgia legislature passed what he considered a confiscatory tax on corporations; he brought the headquarters back after the tax was repealed in 1946.) By the early 1950s a quarter of Coca-Cola's sales revenues came from abroad; by the middle of that decade the company was selling concentrate to 418 bottlers in 92 countries and territories. (Eventually Coke would be sold in some 185 countries—more than belonged to the United Nations. It was said that with the exception of "OK," "Coca-Cola" was the most universally recognized utterance on earth.)

Even without Coca-Cola's international connections, Woodruff would have shared Hartsfield's commitment to civil-rights reform. Years earlier he had taken a strong—and at the time controversial—stand against lynching, to the point of hiring private detectives to search out those responsible for killing a black tenant farmer on one of his rural properties. The search yielded no arrests but sent a message to both blacks and whites that Woodruff wouldn't stand for such activities in the area. They largely ceased.

Like H. L. Hunt, although for more ordinary reasons, Woodruff wasn't comfortable with publicity; for many years he was Georgia's best-kept secret. Nor did he think it would do Coca-Cola any good to be drawn into open controversy. Consequently his support of civil rights took the form of quiet encouragement of Hartsfield and other reformers. Woodruff frequently cited an old saying he attributed to a wise Negro elder: "I try to cooperate with the inevitable." Woodruff believed that change was inevitable for the South; as he cooperated with it he encouraged others to do so too. He supported Lyndon Johnson's efforts on behalf of civil rights; in fact he was sitting in the Oval Office in 1968, talking civil rights, when word came from Memphis that Martin Luther King, Jr., had just been shot. After leaving the White House Woodruff placed a call to Ivan Allen,

Hartsfield's successor as Atlanta mayor—and a man whom Woodruff had been instrumental in having elected over the hard-core segregationist (and subsequent Georgia governor) Lester Maddox. Woodruff told Allen to make sure Atlanta did justice to the memory of King. He—Woodruff— would cover the cost. "Ivan," he said, "the minute they bring King's body back tomorrow—between then and the time of the funeral—Atlanta, Georgia, is going to be the center of the universe. I want you to do whatever is right and necessary, and whatever the city can't pay for will be taken care of. Just do it right."

By this time Woodruff's health was failing. He joked about it, telling of visiting his doctor, who prescribed a particular medication for one of his chronic conditions. "How long do I have to keep taking this stuff?" asked Woodruff. "How old are you?" countered the doctor. "Eighty," he said (in 1970). "Not long," said the doctor.

Yet he clung to the helm for almost another decade-and-a-half. In 1980 he arranged the elevation of Roberto Goizueta to chairman. Subsequently Woodruff—who for decades had been known around Atlanta simply as "the Boss"—told Goizueta how pleased he was that the younger man was now the boss.

"I'm not the boss," Goizueta replied.

"You're the chairman, aren't you?" said Woodruff.

"Yes."

"Then who's the boss?"

"The one who decides who's going to be chairman."

Woodruff continued to decide until 1984, when he resigned from the board of directors. He died several months later at the age of ninety-five.

During his last years he resisted changes that probably should have been made; but one change that occurred just months after his passing confirmed the essential shrewdness of his fundamental insight. In April 1985 Woodruff's successors launched the "New Coke"—a much ballyhooed update of the famous formula. Reactions varied. Pepsi declared victory in the cola wars. "They're admitting defeat!" gloated Pepsi's director of public relations. "The most famous product in the world is coming off the shelves." Pepsi chief Roger Enrico said, "After 87 years of going at it eyeball to eyeball, the other guy just blinked."

Consumers were as dismayed as Pepsi was pleased. New Coke bombed in the marketplace as generations of Coke-drinkers demanded what they had grown up with. "Next week they'll be chiseling Teddy Roosevelt off the side of Mount Rushmore," predicted a columnist for the *Washington Post*.

A New York paper declared, "The new drink will be smoother, sweeter, and a threat to a way of life." An irate correspondent wrote Coca-Cola head-quarters: "Changing Coke is like God making the grass purple or putting toes on our ears or teeth on our knees." Said another: "I don't think I would be more upset if you were to burn the flag in our front yard."

Goizueta claimed that Woodruff, on his deathbed, had given his blessing to the New Coke. Skeptics noted the absence of witnesses to this meeting and said that, in any event, Woodruff might well not have under-stood just what Goizueta was proposing. A reporter asked Pepsi's Enrico if he believed Goizueta's version. Enrico hemmed: "Well, the *New York Times* reported that Woodruff went into the hospital ten days before he died. And Roberto claims he told him in—"

"No, no, you're not getting my drift," the reporter interrupted. "Did Mr. Woodruff tell Goizueta to go ahead as a final blessing—or did he ex-pire *because* Goizueta told him he was changing the formula of Coke?"

In further defense of his action, Goizueta pointed out that in taste tests consumers preferred the New Coke to the old; Woodruff, had he lived, would have been unmoved. Woodruff understood, in a way Goizueta had to learn, that the appeal of Coca-Cola had never rested on taste alone but on a perceived connection to those ineffable, unquantifi-able memories and aspirations Coke-drinkers imbibed with their bubbly stuff. Don Keough, the company president, started to understand when he overheard a conversation at the bar in an Atlanta club:

"Have you tried it?"

"Yes."

"Did you like it?"

"Yes, but I'll be damned if I'll let Coca-Cola know that."

Keough was the one who offered the company's explanation of why it was bringing the old Coke back. If Robert Woodruff was listening, he must have nodded in agreement at Keogh's words:

> The simple fact is that all the time and money and skill poured into con-sumer research on the new Coca-Cola could not measure or reveal the deep and abiding emotional attachment to original Coca-Cola felt by so many people. . . . The passion for original Coca-Cola—and that is the word for it: passion—was something that caught us by surprise. . . . It is a wonderful American mystery, a lovely American enigma, and you cannot measure it any more than you can measure love, pride, or patriotism.

16

SWEATING BURGERS

Ray Kroc

...

CONSIDER THE HAMBURGER. RAY KROC DID AT LENGTH, STARTING with the bun.

It requires a certain kind of mind to see beauty in a hamburger bun. Yet, is it any more unusual to find grace in the texture and softly curved silhouette of a bun than to reflect lovingly on the hackles of a favorite fishing fly? Or the arrangement of textures and colors in a butterfly's wing? Not if you are a McDonald's man. Not if you view the bun as an essential element in the art of serving a great many meals fast. Then this plump yeasty mass becomes an object worthy of sober study.

Beyond the bun was the entrée of which the bun was merely the receptacle.

Now a hamburger patty is a piece of meat. But a McDonald's hamburger patty is a piece of meat with character. The first thing that distinguishes it from the patties that many other places pass off as hamburgers is that it is all beef. There are no hearts or other alien goodies ground into our patties. The fat content of our patty is a prescribed nineteen percent and it is rigidly controlled. There is much that could be written on the technical history of the McDonald's hamburger patty, the experiments with the different grinding methods, freezing techniques, and surface conformations in order to arrive at the juiciest and most flavorful piece of meat we could produce for our system. But, fascinating as that is, that's another story.

Ray Kroc left that other story to the professors at Hamburger University, who treated the eponymous morsel with as much seriousness and almost as much loving care as he did. Meanwhile he made sure America's millions would never be more than minutes away from the object of his delight.

Kroc came to burgers via milk shakes and to milk shakes via paper cups. If he had been a better piano player he might have missed fast food entirely. A Chicago boy, he played speakeasies and the odd bordello during the era of Prohibition and Al Capone. (This after a World War I stint driving ambulances in the same Red Cross company as Walt Disney. Kroc later reflected on Disney and the difference in their personalities: "He was always drawing pictures while the rest of us were chasing girls. Therein lies a lesson, because his drawings have gone on forever—and most of those girls are dead now.") During a gig with a Windy City radio station he doubled as a talent scout, signing, among others, a struggling comedy duo called Sam and Henry who didn't take off until they changed their names to Amos 'n' Andy.

But Kroc's musical talent didn't equal his ambition, and to improve his chances of striking something big he took various day jobs. Like H. L. Hunt at about the same time, he went to Florida to sell real estate; in Kroc's case the property in question was under water—a circumstance, he ever afterward explained, that wasn't as fishy as it sounded, because the submerged lots were slated to surface as prime waterfront (somewhat after the manner of John Jacob Astor's Manhattan "water lots") once the Corps of Engineers and other destiny-shapers finished their dredging, draining and lobbying. A subsequent job had less upside than wet land did but less downside as well; this appealed to Kroc's anxious young wife, who thought the Lily Tulip Cup Company a safer bet than either real estate or nightclubs.

"The ten years between 1927 and 1937 were a decade of destiny for the paper cup industry," Kroc recalled with characteristic but not entirely uncalled-for melodrama. Innovations in cup design—making them sturdier and hence more versatile—combined with changes in lifestyle to trigger an explosion in uses for the lowly throwaway containers. Playing on his ethnic (specifically Bohemian) background, Kroc haunted the neighborhoods of Chicago, selling paper beer steins to the Germans, paper spumoni dishes to the Italians and paper Povidla—prune butter—platters to the Poles ("Those folks ate an awful lot of prune butter," he noted with wonder).

Equity-light Kroc weathered the stock-market swoon of 1929, although he was convinced the crash killed his father. "He died of a cerebral hemorrhage in 1932. He had worried himself to death. On his desk the day he died were two pieces of paper—his last paycheck from the telegraph company and a garnishment notice for the entire amount of his wages." An examination of his father's effects revealed another document: a phrenologist's assessment of the boy Raymond Kroc, done in 1906 when the child was four years old. According to the report the topography of the boy's head foretold a promising career in the food industry.

Only later would the adult Ray Kroc come to appreciate the full prescience of this prediction (by then a receding hairline would make the bumpy basis of the report more obvious); for the time being he had to be satisfied with a secondhand acquaintance via paper cups. He moved a bit closer to the action when he encountered Earl Prince, an ice cream man who invented the Multimixer to spin up the milk shakes his customers slurped down by the five-gallon bucket. Prince proposed a partnership: He would manufacture the Multimixers—and whatever other brainstorms hit him while serving sundaes and shakes—and Kroc would market them. Kroc accepted.

World War II broke out before Kroc had a chance to make a splash in shakes; the war effort put Multimixers on the shelf by claiming the copper that wound their coils. But the postwar consumer boom launched Kroc on a path that quickly made him a mover among the shakers. He sold machines to Dairy Queen, Tastee-Freez and A&W Root Beer stands—these last started by a man named Willard Marriott who would continue to find the restaurant and hotel business highly hospitable.

One of Kroc's most intriguing accounts was a single store in San Bernardino, California, that required not just one Multimixer, with its five spindles, nor two nor three nor four, but eight Multimixers, for a potential total of forty simultaneous shakes. He had never heard of anyone needing that much shaking power, and he decided to have a look. What he saw that day in 1954 convinced him that the McDonald brothers, Dick and Mac, were onto something special. Like Henry Ford in autos they had stripped away everything unnecessary to efficient production—in their case, production of food. And to judge by the smiles on the faces of the customers Kroc surreptitiously sampled—he was taking a traffic survey, he said— they did so without sacrificing quality. Kroc's interest quickened. Describing a sweet young blonde he met in the parking lot, he revealed what manner of man he really was: "It was not her sex appeal but the obvious relish with which she devoured the hamburger that made my pulse begin to hammer with excitement."

Events beyond Kroc's control had placed the Multimixer business in peril, and he was open to new opportunities. The McDonald brothers' system promised just the thing. And it was quite clear they had a system. Forty shakes at a throw was only the start. The griddlemen had mastered the art of peeling the patties from their wrappers, slapping the pink disks on the hot metal, flipping them as they turned just the right hue of reddish brown, lifting them off as the sizzling subsided—and meanwhile keeping the cooktop scraped and clean of the last generation's grease and detritus.

The french fries reflected similar forethought and attention to detail. "To most people, a french-fried potato is a pretty uninspiring object," Kroc owned, speaking in the voice of the unredeemed Saul. "It's fodder, something to kill time chewing between your bites of hamburger and swallows of milk shake. That's your ordinary french fry." The Paul who'd been to Damascus—in this case, San Bernardino—knew better.

> The McDonald's french fry was in an entirely different league. They lavished attention on it. . . . The McDonald brothers kept their potatoes—top quality Idaho spuds, about eight ounces apiece—piled in bins in their back warehouse building. Since rats and mice and other varmints like to eat potatoes, the walls of the bins were of two layers of small-mesh chicken wire. This kept the critters out and allowed fresh air to circulate among the potatoes.
>
> I watched the spuds being bagged up and followed their trip by four-wheeled cart to the octagonal drive-in building. There they were carefully peeled, leaving a tiny proportion of skin on, and then they were cut into long sections and dumped into large sinks of cold water. The french-fry man, with his sleeves rolled up to the shoulders, would plunge his arms into the floating schools of potatoes and gently stir them. I could see the water turning white with starch. This was drained off and the residual starch was rinsed from the glistening morsels with a flexible spray hose. Then the potatoes went into wire baskets, stacked in production-line fashion next to the deep-fry vats.

Here the enlightened, latter-day expert revealed one of the dirty secrets of inferior fast-fooders: recycled cooking oil.

> A common problem with french fries is that they're fried in oil that has been used for chicken or for some other cooking. Any restaurant will deny it, but almost all of them do it. A very small scandal, perhaps, but a scandal nonetheless, and it's just one of the little crimes that have given the french fry a bad name while ruining the appetites of countless Americans.

The McDonald brothers weren't even tempted to such sin. They fried no chicken, no fish—only potatoes. And such potatoes, in such amounts.

Their potatoes sold at ten cents for a three-ounce bag, and let me tell you, that was a rare bargain. The customers knew it, too. They bought prodigious quantities of those potatoes. A big aluminum salt shaker was attached to a long chain by the french-fry window, and it was kept going like a Salvation Army girl's tambourine.

Kroc discerned no reason why the McDonald brothers' system should be confined to one sleepy town in the desert of southern California. They should share the good news with the rest of the country. And he volunteered to be their apostle to the Gentiles. He would reproduce their system across the land, propagating those burgers, fries and service wherever people were hungry and in a hurry.

Kroc wasn't the first to think of franchising the McDonalds' system; in fact the brothers had done some desultory disseminating of their ideas already. But they lacked Kroc's vision of a nationwide chain—largely because they lacked Kroc's drive. "We couldn't spend all the money we were making," one of the brothers remarked, speaking for both. They had no desire for a pile more. "We'd be leaving it to a church or something, and we didn't go to church."

Kroc wished he were in a position to worry about whom to leave his money to; franchising the McDonalds' system seemed a promising way to get there. Within days of his eye-opening visit to San Bernardino he proposed to the brothers that he become their national franchising agent. They agreed but set strict terms. The fees must be low: a $950 per franchise startup charge, which Kroc would get to keep, and a continuing commission of 1.9 percent of sales, of which they would get .4 percent, he 1.5 percent.

"It was a godawful contract," recalled one of Kroc's early lawyers. Kroc thought so too but saw little alternative. "I went along with it because the Multimixer business was so bad, and I had to get into something that had a future."

In fact Kroc's bad deal turned out to be a secret of his success. The typical franchising company made its money either by levying steep startup fees (a practice known as "Minnie Pearling" after the Minnie Pearl Chicken chain that made it notorious) or by selling supplies to its franchises. In the first instance the franchising company lacked much incentive to ensure the franchises' continuing success; in the second its profits came, to some degree, at the expense of its franchises.

Kroc's arrangement with the McDonald brothers forbade the first method of making money, and the fact that he had nothing to sell to franchisees except milk shake machines effectively precluded the second. In consequence he was reduced to getting his money the hard way: doing whatever he could to guarantee that the individual stores made money. As one student of McDonald's success put it: "While other franchisers were figuring out ways to pad their bottom line, McDonald's was concentrating on ways to pad its top line—the total revenues of all franchised restaurants in the McDonald's System."

Padding the top line required perfecting the system. This proved harder than Kroc thought. He had seen more than his share of hamburger stands over the years, and he fancied he had a pretty good eye for what went into what came out of them. He had scrutinized the McDonalds' system and taken careful notes. But when he opened his first store—in Des Plaines, Illinois—he couldn't get the french fries right. He did everything just as the McDonalds did it. "The result was a perfectly fine looking, golden brown potato that snuggled up against the palate with a taste like . . . well, like mush. I was aghast. What the hell could I have done wrong?" He called the brothers and went over the process step by step; nothing amiss there. He tried again—and again got mush. "This was a tremendously frustrating situation. My whole idea depended on carrying out the McDonalds' standard of taste and quality in hundreds of stores, and here I couldn't even do it in the first one!"

In his puzzlement he contacted the Potato and Onion Association and consulted their experts. They were mystified too until one of them had Kroc detail absolutely every step in the french-fry process from the ground up (actually from below the ground: in Idaho where the spuds were dug). Finally this potato maven identified the desert wind that blew through the McDonald's storage bin as the critical curing agent that converted the potatoes' sugars to starch and prevented them from browning prematurely in the fry vat. At unanticipated expense Kroc installed a ventilation system that mimicked the San Bernardino breeze and allowed him to make fries like the McDonalds'.

Although it took some effort to unravel this aspect of the McDonalds' formula, on the whole there was little secret about the brothers' approach to fast food. That little was diminished further by the big windows on their octagonal building—windows that brought the kitchen into full view of both the eating public and anyone interested in copying for free the system Kroc was selling. What distinguished Kroc from the hundreds of other fast-food entrepreneurs was his fanaticism about quality. No detail was too small to escape his notice. McDonald's hamburger patties were ten to the pound—not nine, not eleven. Where the U.S. Department of Agriculture allowed hamburger to contain up to 30 percent fat, McDonald's stipulated between 17 and 22.5 percent. There must be no additives, no hearts or other organs commonly ground into hamburger to reduce costs. Kroc supplied a fifty-point checklist to operators to enable them to detect substandard meat; he also ordered his lieutenants to police suppliers by making midnight visits to packing plants. He obsessed about cleanliness, insisting that operators keep not only their own stores and parking lots tidy but also the surrounding streets. Visiting stores, he frequently grabbed a mop himself and started swabbing; on one occasion he took a toothbrush to the holes in the strainer in the mop bucket, which had been clogged with crud that escaped the scrutiny of the manager. (It didn't escape after that.)

Kroc's insistence on stringent standards inspired the establishment of Hamburger University, as the company's training facility on the outskirts of Chicago was called. Skeptical observers found it easy to deride an institution that offered a master's in hamburgerology and whose instructors had pat answers to life's most pressing questions: "Why do we center the pickle? Because no matter where the customer bites, he'll taste a portion of pickle." But the three-week course provided a highly effective way to introduce new franchise holders to the McDonald's system; like much else about the McDonald's model it eventually was copied throughout the fast-food industry.

Under Kroc's keen eye the company got off to a fast start, at least in terms of numbers of stores. By 1961 some 250 McDonald'ses dotted suburbs across the country, with scores more in the works and hundreds more in Kroc's head. Increasingly, however, he felt constrained by the terms of his original agreement with Dick and Mac McDonald. He begrudged the money he had to pay them for all the work he was doing; more critically he felt that they simply lacked the ambition to make McDonald's all it could be.

He offered to buy them out; they responded with a price that struck him as extortionate. "I dropped the phone, my teeth, and everything else," Kroc recalled of his talk with Dick McDonald. "He asked me what the noise was, and I told him that was me jumping out of the 20th floor of the LaSalle-Wacker Building." Kroc initially understood the brothers' $2.7 million asking price to include the San Bernardino store, and on that basis he grumblingly agreed. When Dick McDonald corrected him—San Bernardino was *not* included—Kroc's anger got the better of him. "The deal is off," he shouted into the phone before hanging up to shout some more. "I closed the door to my office and paced up and down the floor calling them every kind of son of a bitch there was. I was so mad I wanted to throw a vase through the window. I hated their guts."

Yet after regaining his composure he decided that his freedom was worth the McDonald brothers' price. "It was a lot of money to pay for a name. I suppose I could have called it 'McDougall's' and started over. But I was getting old—too old to fart around [he was pushing sixty]. I decided to take their deal anyway." (Although the McDonald brothers kept their hamburger stand they relinquished the right to call it "McDonald's." With grim pleasure Kroc opened a new McDonald's across the street from the compulsorily renamed original and forced its new owners—the brothers having retired on the buyout—to fold.)

The job of financing the purchase fell to Kroc's number two, company president Harry Sonneborn. Sonneborn was a money man who hardly knew or cared what all those McDonald's customers were buying; in fact he assuaged the worries of leery lenders, who recognized what a spotty record of repayment the food-service industry had, by asserting that they misunderstood what McDonald's did. "We are not basically in the food business," he explained. "We are in the real estate business. The only reason we sell fifteen-cent hamburgers is because they are the greatest producer of revenue from which our tenants can pay us rent."

Kroc inwardly groaned whenever he heard this explanation, which essentially denied the importance of everything he was doing in his campaign for quality. But he had to concede the germ of truth in it, and in any event if it got the company the money it required he was willing to keep his groans to himself. The fact of the matter was that Sonneborn had discovered a method to make the rapid expansion pay without skewing the parallelism between the company's interests and those of the franchisees. McDonald's formed a separate company—the Franchise Realty Corporation—that located and leased store sites from property owners and then subleased them to the franchisees. Rents were keyed to store sales; as business grew at each store so did the revenues to the company. Security deposits provided additional revenue up front, partly compensating the company for the smallness of the franchise fees.

Kroc valued Sonneborn's innovation, which tided the company over some cash-short early days and set it on a sound financial footing. "Harry alone put in the policy that salvaged this company and made it a big-leaguer," Kroc said. "His idea is what really made McDonald's rich." But eventually the different approaches of the two men proved irreconcilable, and in 1967 Sonneborn, who was suffering various physical ailments, was persuaded to resign. "I had outlived my usefulness at McDonald's," he said. "I had accomplished everything I ever wanted to do there, and I wanted to live my remaining years in peace." Sonneborn had also directed a very successful public offering of McDonald's stock in 1965 (shares doubled in value nearly overnight); now he cashed in by selling his large block of the company—angering Kroc, who judged the divestiture a vote of no confidence. As in his dealings with the McDonald brothers, Kroc claimed the last laugh. Noting that what Sonneborn sold for about $12 million was worth ten times that amount scarcely a decade later, Kroc gloated: "His lack of faith in us was very costly for him."

Sonneborn's successor was a man more after Kroc's heart. Fred Turner was something of a surrogate son to Kroc, who had no children of his own, and while Turner understood the real-estate side of the McDonald's formula he also recognized which side of the bun the company's core business was buttered on. Turner may or may not have been the unnamed company executive quoted on Sonneborn's departure as saying, "Hooray, we're back in the hamburger business"; but although he subsequently commissioned a portrait of Sonneborn for the McDonald's hall of fame, he discreetly waited until Kroc died to hang it.

Turner more than justified Kroc's faith in him. Together he and Kroc oversaw an explosive expansion of the company. By the early 1970s McDonald's was adding over 200 stores per year and boosting earnings by an average of 30 percent per year. Turner resisted any temptation to change the fundamental formula and cash in on the rapid growth. "Those Chinese-money guys in fast food make me nervous," he said. "We aren't in their business; we don't sell franchises to make a buck. We're a restaurant chain."

Under pressure from competitors Kroc consented to broaden the ten-item menu that had been the basis for the company's early success. Kroc himself wasn't much at product innovation; his principal effort was an ill-fated experiment called the "Hulaburger"—two slices of cheese melted over a pineapple slab on a toasted bun. "I like the hula, but where's the burger?" asked one customer, speaking for many more. "You can't win them all," answered Kroc to himself. Yet the boss was willing to learn from his franchisees. The Filet-O-Fish sandwich originated in the desire of a Cincinnati operator to woo back Catholic customers who were walking across the street to Big Boy for fish on Fridays. The Big Mac came from Pittsburgh, where Burger King's oversized sandwich was claiming space in the stomachs of hungry steelworkers. The Egg McMuffin was a Santa Barbara invention that answered the need for an item to open the stores early. By the mid-1970s Kroc even allowed that McDonald's might someday serve pizza. But he refused to soften his prohibition against one menu item common to many fast-food stores. "There's damned good reason we should never have hot dogs," he said. "There's no telling what's inside a hot dog's skin, and our standard of quality just wouldn't permit that kind of item."

The company changed in other ways. The neon golden arches that graced—or disgraced, depending on one's taste in design—the early McDonald'ses were demoted from architecture to emblem. Tables were added indoors and drive-up windows were placed outside. Company policy against hiring women—a policy that reflected not only Kroc's social conservatism but also a desire to distance McDonald's from the teenage hangouts where pretty girls were an essential part of the decor—was dropped, although not without care. "We figured that the first women we hired should be kind of flat-chested," Kroc said. "We didn't want them to be attractive to the boys. And the first woman manager we had wore glasses and had flat shoes. She swore like a trooper."

As the company expanded from the suburbs to the inner cities, it integrated racially as well. From a handful of African-American operators in 1969 the number of black franchisees grew to more than fifty just three years later, largely as a result of active recruiting on McDonald's part. (The number subsequently grew to several hundred, until more than half the black restaurant owners in America held McDonald's franchises.)

By the 1970s McDonald's had become a major presence in American life, and Kroc something of a public figure. Kroc discovered, as had H. L. Hunt, that the loss of privacy entailed certain disadvantages. In 1972 Kroc drew criticism for personally donating $250,000 to the reelection campaign of Richard Nixon—a perfectly legal contribution that nonetheless came in for the closest scrutiny after the numerous illegalities of the Watergate affair began to surface. (Yet besides embarrassing the chairman the 1972 campaign demonstrated that McDonald's was less regimented than many people thought. Kroc and Fred Turner were addressing an audience of business students when one asked whether Kroc demanded that his executives share his politics. "I can answer that," said Turner. "Kroc voted for Nixon and I voted for McGovern." Added Kroc: "That's right, and we were both wrong.")

In 1974 Kroc purchased the San Diego Padres baseball team—chiefly because chewing-gum king Phil Wrigley wouldn't sell the Chicago Cubs, Kroc's hometown team. The hapless Padres embarrassed themselves, and their new owner, on opening day in San Diego, prompting Kroc to grab the microphone and chew the players out. Even his wife wondered if he was drunk. "I wasn't drunk," Kroc declared. "I was just plain mad as hell." So was the commissioner of baseball, who summarily issued what came to be known as the Ray Kroc rule barring all but the officially designator announcer from using the public address system at a ballpark.

Yet the source of most criticism of Kroc had less to do with politics or unsportsmanlike conduct than with his very success. Walt Disney's critics had moaned at the ubiquity of Mickey Mouse; Kroc's critics complained at the proliferation of golden arches. "If cows watched horror movies, everybody knows who their favorite monster would be," wrote Tom Robbins in *Esquire*.

> Imagine, that it's Friday midnight down on the farm and the Guernseys and the Jerseys are gathered around the barnyard TV, spellbound by the rerun of that classic bovine chiller, *Teats Up*, when suddenly the lights flicker, organ music swells, and onto the screen ambles a chesty, cherubic octogenarian in a business suit, swinging a cleaver and flashing a mystic ring with symbolic golden arches on it, and, oh, a terrified moo rises up from the herd and there is much trembling of teat and tail. At that moment, a little bullock in the back is heard to ask, "Mommy, on Halloween can I go as Ray Kroc?"
>
> To cattle, Ray Kroc is the franchise Frankenstein, the Hitler behind a Hereford holocaust, a fiend who has sent about 550,000 of their relatives to the grinder, grinning all the while and encouraging his henchmen with his macabre credo, "Remember, ten patties to the pound!"

Robbins went on to assert, "McDonald's represents mediocrity at its zenith, its most sublime. . . . Columbus discovered America, Jefferson invented it, Lincoln unified it, Goldwyn mythologized it, and Kroc Big Mac'd it." Like many of the critics, Robbins got some of his facts slightly crooked. Knowing that Kroc's original partners had been Dick and Mac McDonald, but not knowing the bitter circumstances of the breakup, Robbins mistakenly assumed that the Big Mac was named for one of the brothers. He added with a snigger: "Since these are 'family' restaurants, it's easy to understand why it wasn't named for the other."

What Robbins objected to, however, was precisely what made McDonald's attractive to so many people, namely, its consistent product.

> Thanks to Kroc, the migrating masses simply aim their stomachs at the landmark arches, sinuous of form and sunny of hue, and by the first belch they're

back on the road, fast fed and very nearly serene, which is to say, no entrepreneur has overcharged them; no maitre d' has insulted them; no temperamental chef, flirtatious waitress, or intriguing flavor has delayed them; they've neither gagged on a greasy spoon nor tripped over an *x* in a *oie roti aux pruneaux*. With McDonald's, they're secure.

Kroc, like Walt Disney before him, dismissed the criticism as something between sour grapes and simple silliness; he blasted the critics as over-educated intellectuals. "There are too many baccalaureates and too few butchers," he declared. Although he gave generously to assorted worthy causes, he refused to support traditional higher education.

> My philosophy about what education should be is best expressed right in McDonald's own Hamburger U. and Hamburger High. Career education, that's what this country needs. Many young people emerge from college unprepared to hold down a steady job or to cook or do housework, and it makes them depressed. No wonder! They should train for a career, learn how to support themselves and how to enjoy work first. Then if they have a thirst for advanced learning, they can go to night school.

Perhaps not surprisingly, Kroc's philosophy won over few of his critics. As critics do, they got the last word, carping long past Kroc's death in 1984—a year in which the company opened its eight-thousandth store and reported a net income of $343 million on $8.7 billion in sales.

Yet for all their handwringing at the banality of the burger kingdom he had created, even the critics had to concede the magnitude of Kroc's accomplishment. He gave Americans what they wanted: predictable, unpretentious fare delivered in familiar surroundings. As Tom Robbins acknowledged:

> McDonald's has served forty-five billion burgers, and every single one of them has had a smile on its face. So to Ray Kroc, grant a pardon for his crimes against cows, stay his sentence for having ambushed our individuality at Standardization Gulch. True, he has changed our habits, perhaps for the worse, but a man who can say of himself, as Kroc did, that "it requires a certain kind of mind to see beauty in a hamburger bun" is a man who can cut the mustard.

17

BENTONVILLE, U.S.A.

Sam Walton

. . .

MARCHING ACROSS AMERICA IN STEP WITH MCDONALD'S WAS another phenomenon that elicited its own chorus of complaint, albeit from a different direction and another choir. The moans against McDonald's emanated from the chattering sophisticates of the cities; the wails about Wal-Mart came from self-styled defenders of traditional values and the small-town way of life. Strikingly but not coincidentally, the anti-Wal-Mart lament included the voices of many members of the middling merchant class from which Sam Walton himself emerged.

It was somewhat surprising that Walton became the lightning rod he did—but only somewhat surprising. From boyhood in Oklahoma and Missouri he displayed a friendliness that was almost irresistibly engaging. "He was optimistic all the time," remembered a high school buddy. "He had a great smile on his face and felt like everybody was his friend." But Walton's friendly demeanor, while unfeigned, was not entirely uncalculated. "I had decided I wanted to be president of the university student body," Walton said of his days at the University of Missouri.

I learned early on that one of the secrets to campus leadership was the simplest thing of all: speak to people coming down the sidewalk before they speak to you. . . . I would always look ahead and speak to the person coming toward me. If I knew them, I would call them by name, but even if I didn't I would still speak to them. Before long, I probably knew more students than anybody in the university, and they recognized me and considered me their friend.

Although Walton wasn't elected student body president, he *was* elected to nearly every other office available, and on the whole his college experience confirmed his belief in the power of friendliness. "Mr. Walton just had a personality that drew people in," said one of his early employees. "He would yell at you from a block away, you know. He would just yell at everybody he saw, and that's the reason so many liked him and did business in the store. It was like he brought in business by his being so friendly."

Walton got into retailing after being mustered out of the military in 1945. He borrowed $20,000 from his father-in-law, put in $5,000 of his and his wife Helen's own money, and purchased a Ben Franklin variety store in Newport, Arkansas. Through hard work and that outgoing Walton nature he soon tripled business and multiplied profits even more. By 1950 his was the leading Ben Franklin store in a six-state region and probably the biggest variety store of any kind in Arkansas.

The store's success wasn't lost on Walton's landlord, who decided to acquire the business for his son. Walton had neither desire nor intention to sell—until the landlord pointed out that he didn't have any choice. Walton, through inexperience, had neglected to insist on a renewal option in his lease. "I felt sick to my stomach," Walton said of learning that five years' work was now being appropriated by someone else. "I couldn't believe it was happening to me."

Yet it was, leaving Walton to start over. He did so in Bentonville, Arkansas. For reasons of personal preference Helen had nixed any town bigger than 10,000, but even she had some reservations about their new home. "Bentonville really was just a sad-looking country town," she recollected. "I couldn't believe this was where we were going to live." Bentonville's redeeming feature was a variety store for sale at a price they could afford. Like the Newport store, this would be a Ben Franklin franchise, although it would be called Walton's Five & Dime.

With the redoubled energy of the once-frustrated entrepreneur, Walton carted the stock and fixtures from his old store to the new, taking back roads in order to avoid a weighing station that would have flagged his excessive load. At about this time he read of an innovation in variety retailing that was being tested by a couple of Ben Franklins in Minnesota: self-service. He rode an overnight bus north to investigate this cost-saving concept; impressed, he incorporated the idea in the layout of his new store.

The store opened under its new management in the summer of 1950. Walton handed out balloons to the children and bargains to everyone else. The town already had two other variety stores, but neither of those offered the consistently low prices Walton did. He kept his overhead to the minimum, working out of an office that measured eight feet by eight feet, located in a loft at the back of the store and accessible only by ladder. He was constantly on the lookout for oddball, discontinued or otherwise orphaned items. "I remember one time he made a trip to New York," a clerk from that period recalled, "and he came back a few days later and said, 'Come here, I want to show you something. This is going to be the item of the year.'"

I went over and looked at a bin full of—I think they called them zori sandals—they call them thongs now. And I just laughed and said, "No way will those things sell. They'll just blister your toes." Well, he took them and tied them together in pairs and dumped them all on a table at the end of an aisle for nineteen cents a pair. And they just sold like you wouldn't believe. I have never seen an item sell as fast, one after another, just piles of them. Everybody in town had a pair.

Almost at once the new enterprise began repeating the success story of Walton's previous venture; as it did he began looking for another such opportunity. "Maybe it was just my itch to do more business," he mused later. "And maybe, too, I didn't want all my eggs in one basket." Like many other business successes, Walton was a perpetual improver, forever eager to better his prospects. "He gets up every day bound and determined to improve something," said a longtime friend and associate. Walton was not a perfectionist; in fact he was just the opposite. Perfectionism would have slowed him down. His technique was to try something—now. If it didn't work he'd try something else. "He is less afraid of being wrong than anyone I've ever known," said this same friend. "And once he sees he's wrong, he just shakes it off and heads in another direction."

He was also a showman. "There's no question that I have the personality of a promoter," Walton once admitted. He loved nothing more than the grand opening of a new store, with its ribbons and balloons and ice cream and pony rides. Walton openings were always events, often spectacles—and occasionally disasters. A competitor who became an employee recalled one opening that fell in the last category.

In those days word was starting to get around that a guy named Sam Walton had some interesting retailing ideas, so I drove down from Springfield, where

I was with Crank Drugs at the time, to see a Wal-Mart opening. It was the worst retail store I had ever seen. Sam had brought a couple of trucks of watermelons in and stacked them on the sidewalk. He had a donkey ride out in the parking lot. It was about 115 degrees, and the watermelons began to pop, and the donkey began to do what donkeys do, and it all mixed together and ran all over the parking lot. And when you went inside the store, the mess just continued, having been tracked in all over the floor. He was a nice fellow, but I wrote him off. It was just terrible.

Needless to say, Walton's openings weren't all such fiascoes. During the 1950s he acquired one variety store after another, using borrowed money and the profits from the stores he already owned to finance the purchase of new ones. By 1960 he was the proud owner of fifteen stores.

But the returns weren't what he had hoped. Most of the stores were small; in total they did only $1.4 million in business. At the age of forty-two Walton had been in retail for fifteen years, and he thought he ought to be making more money for the kind of effort he had been putting in.

Two tactics occurred to him; together with something he was already doing they supplied the strategy that made him rich. The first was to build bigger stores. Walton had seen some bigger stores in his Arkansas–Missouri region, and he was impressed with the kind of business they did. The second idea was to discount. Discounting wasn't new in the early 1960s; since World War II various merchants had nibbled at the fair-trade laws by which Depression-era retailers had tried to curtail price competition. But discount stores tended to be small, specialized and located in cities and their near suburbs.

Walton's strategy was to build big stores that discounted everything they stocked, and to place them in small towns. He initially approached the directors of the company that franchised the Ben Franklin stores, but when he asked them to cut their standard wholesale margin in half to accommodate the low prices he intended to charge, they refused—loudly. "They blew up!" recalled Walton. "They just couldn't see the philosophy."

Walton next approached Herbert Gibson, a former barber from Berryville, Arkansas, who had gotten into discounting with the motto, "Buy it low, stack it high, sell it cheap." But Gibson had business enough of his own.

"Nobody wanted to gamble on that first Wal-Mart," Walton said; so he took the gamble himself. His brother Bud put in 3 percent; the man he hired to manage the store put in 2 percent; and he and Helen furnished the rest. "We pledged houses and property, everything we had." But this wasn't anything new. "In those days we were always borrowed to the hilt."

Financing was the easy part. With the Ben Franklin people, Walton had a ready-made supply network for his existing stores; he now had to create such a network for his new stores. And the Ben Franklin people weren't going to make the creation easy. Walton located his first Wal-Mart in Rogers, Arkansas, a town not far from Bentonville. Ben Franklin already had a store in Rogers, which heightened the suspicion the company felt for this apostate—who was now an interloper as well. "We really stirred up a hornet's nest when we opened that first store," one of the employees there recollected.

> I vividly remember opening day. Along with the crowds of shoppers, a group of officials from Ben Franklin in Chicago—all dressed in pin-striped suits—showed up. They marched in like a military delegation, and in the front of the store asked me, just as cold as they could be, "Where is Mr. Walton?" They marched on back to Sam's office without a word.
>
> They were back there about a half hour, and then they marched out without so much as a good-bye. A few minutes later, Sam came down and told Whitaker and me that they had issued an ultimatum: Don't build any more of these Wal-Mart stores.

Walton didn't take kindly to threats. Nor had he ever been overly respectful of the status quo. "In many of my core values, things like church and family and civic leadership and even politics, I'm a pretty conservative guy," he said.

> But for some reason in business, I have always been driven to buck the system, to innovate, to take things beyond where they've been. On the one hand, in the community, I really am an establishment kind of guy; on the other hand, in the marketplace, I have always been a maverick who enjoys shaking things up and creating a little anarchy.

Walton wasn't alone in shaking up the world of retailing. The year he opened his first Wal-Mart—1962—was the same year the S. S. Kresge Company opened its first K-mart (in suburban Detroit). It was also the year Woolworth opened its first Woolco discount store (in Columbus, Ohio). And it was the year the Dayton Corporation opened its first Target stores (in suburban Minneapolis–St. Paul and Duluth). In fact in 1962 nearly 550 new discount stores opened across the country; between 1960 and 1966 the number nearly tripled, to some 3,500. At the same time, the average size of stores nearly doubled and average sales per store tripled.

So if Walton was a rebel, he wasn't exactly a lonely rebel. K-mart alone threatened to crowd Wal-Mart out of existence. Before Walton had twenty stores, K-mart had 250; its total sales were as much as 100 times his.

But Walton was convinced he had a formula that would work. Overhead would be kept to a minimum, even if this meant putting stores in some rather unprepossessing locations. Wal-Mart number two filled a vacant building on what had been a cattle auction yard; it had an oppressively low eight-foot ceiling and a bare concrete floor. Wal-Mart number eight occupied an old Coca-Cola bottling plant; fixtures were hung by baling wire from the ceiling, and hangers of clothes were hooked over conduit pipe. As late as 1970 Wal-Mart rents averaged less than one dollar per square foot.

Prices reflected the low overhead—as well as Walton's insistence on adhering to a strict 30 percent markup. "Sam wouldn't let us hedge on a price at all," one of his managers from that era explained. "Say the list price was $1.98, but we had only paid 50 cents. Initially I would say, 'Well, it's originally $1.98, so why don't we sell it for $1.25?' And he'd say, 'No. We paid 50 cents for it. Mark it up 30 percent, and that's it. No matter what you pay for it, if we get a great deal, pass it on to the customer.'"

Customers responded enthusiastically to the Wal-Mart approach. If a few found the ambience lacking, far more were simply thrilled that big-city discounting had come to small-town America. "They had friends and relatives in the cities," said one of Walton's early managerial hires, "and they had visited places where discounters were operating, so when they saw this happening in their town, well, shoot, they just flocked to our stores to take advantage of it." Sales at the first Wal-Mart soon hit $1 million a year; other stores did even better.

This success provided funding for the expansion of the chain; it also provided the incentive for expanding fast. Walton said of his formula, "I knew in my bones it was going to work"; when it did he was afraid other companies would catch on and adopt it themselves. Against conventional wisdom Walton was proving that the average small town—a community, say, of 5,000 to 25,000—could support a decent-sized discount store; but not even he was willing to bet that such a town could support *two* such stores. He wanted to claim the best locations before anyone else got there.

Until 1970 he continued to fund expansion from profits and borrowing, but in that year he decided to take the company public. The initial offering went well, generating nearly $5 million. Although Walton and

members of his family retained control of the company—through ownership of 61 percent of the stock—the proceeds allowed him to pay off the
company's debts and move forward with his ambitious expansion plans.

In the first year after going public Wal-Mart added six stores; it added
thirteen stores in each of the next two years; then fourteen; then twenty-
six. Between 1976 and 1980 it opened 151 new stores, so that at the end
of 1980 Walton had 276 stores.

The promoter in Walton thrilled at this exuberant expansion. He delighted in scouting new locations in an airplane he piloted himself.

> We got a lot of great ones that way. From up in the air we could check out
> traffic flows, see which way cities and towns were growing, and evaluate the
> location of the competition—if there was any. . . . I loved doing it myself. I'd
> get down low, turn my plane up on its side, and fly right over a town. Once
> we had a spot picked out, we'd land, go find out who owned the property,
> and try to negotiate the deal right then.

With stores opening at a rate of one a month, then almost one a
week, this aspect of the job could have occupied Walton full time. But
there was also the matter of keeping the stores in business once they
opened. At first this was no great problem, for Walton simply repeated the
formula that had worked so well with his first stores. Yet there were limits
to such an approach. "One of the key elements in Wal-Mart's success has
been the lack of competition in its small, rural markets," an industry analyst noted in 1977. "It is clearly easier to operate in this kind of situation
than in a competitive one: Pricing need not be so sharp, and the 'right'
merchandise is less critical, simply because customers have no alternative." At some point Wal-Mart's expansion would put it into direct competition with other discounters. "Wal-Mart could run into serious
problems," this analyst wrote. "The future of the company appears uncertain, and we think Wal-Mart is one of those threshold companies that
runs the risk of stumbling."

The showdown came with Kmart. Until this point Walton had largely
dodged the discount giant, and to the extent Kmart noticed Walton it simply concluded that he had stolen Kmart's ideas and applied them to markets Kmart had no interest in serving. But during the late 1970s the turf of
the two companies began to overlap in a substantial way. When Kmart—
"the Genghis Khan of the discounting business," in the words of another
competitor—opened stores in four of Walton's better towns, the battle was
joined.

Walton gave the order not to yield an inch. No matter how far Kmart dropped its prices, Wal-Mart would not be undersold. North Little Rock witnessed a toothpaste war which culminated in tickled—and shiny-toothed—customers getting Crest for six cents a tube. Although Walton recognized that such extreme price-cutting couldn't last forever, in general he adopted the attitude that competition was healthy. It would require Wal-Mart to hone its performance and do even better by its customers than it had done to date. He didn't fret about the result. "We were confident we could compete," he said.

One essential to Wal-Mart's ability to compete was its rapid adoption of the latest technology. From the start Walton recognized that a key to keeping costs down and profits up was control of inventory: ordering just the right items in the right amounts. Too little inventory meant lost sales; too much inventory meant undue expense. Control of inventory, in turn, required control of information. What was selling? What was in the stores? What was on order? What had been back ordered?

Walton made a habit of visiting competitors to find out how they dealt with difficulties endemic to discounting. He would corner managers and pick their brains, not always identifying himself if they didn't ask why he was writing down everything they said. He would crawl under displays to discover how much stock rival stores kept; on one occasion (after he graduated from notepad to tape recorder) he was thrown out of a competitor's store and had his tape recorder confiscated. (He eventually flattered the owner's son into returning it.) During the 1960s he heard that Abe Marks of Hartfield Zody's was an expert in computers and how they could be employed to control inventory; he visited Marks to see how things worked there. Marks was impressed. "Sam spent a lot of time reviewing these operations and he brought some of his people up to review them," Marks recalled. "He has been just a master of taking the best out of everything and adapting it to his own needs."

In the case of computers, what Walton learned was critical to his company's success. "Without the computer, Sam Walton could not have done what he's done," Marks said. "He could not have built a retailing empire the size of what he's built, the way he built it. He's done a lot of other things right, too, but he could not have done it without the computer. It would have been impossible."

Wal-Mart was one of the first major chains to install electronic scanners at cash registers linked to a central inventory-control computer; when the data from all the stores eventually overwhelmed the telephone lines coming into the Bentonville headquarters, the company installed a satellite communications system that beamed the data from the stores to space and back down to Bentonville. Walton by then was a committed technophile, but even he at first found the price tag daunting. "It blows my mind that we spent $20 million for a satellite outfit," he said afterward. This turned out to be just the down payment; by the early 1990s the company had spent more than $500 million on its communications network.

Numerical data kept the satellite channels busy most of the time, but the system also included capability for video broadcasts—of pep talks from the chairman, among other things. Walton's motivational style was more direct than that of Thomas Watson, for example, in that Walton served as his own cheerleader. An adopted son of Arkansas, he liked to rouse the executives at the regular Saturday-morning strategy sessions with an ear-splitting rendition of the University of Arkansas's famous Hog call:

Whoooooooooooooooo Pig. Sooey!
Whooooooooooooooooooooooo Pig. Sooey!
Whoooooooooooooooooooooooooooooo Pig. Sooey!
Razorbacks!!!

Those attending the meetings knew the boss well enough not to be surprised at his irrepressible style, but some new employees at various stores might have been taken aback when the head man came around and led them all in the Wal-Mart cheer:

Give me a W!
Give me an A!
Give me an L!
Give me a Squiggly!
[This punctuation acted out with a full-body wiggle]
Give me an M!
Give me an A!
Give me an R!
Give me a T!
What's that spell?
Wal-Mart!
What's that spell?
Wal-Mart!
Who's number one?
THE CUSTOMER!!!

Walton did all sorts of other stunts at various times, some that embarrassed even him, such as his hula dance on Wall Street in payment of a challenge to the company to reach what he had considered to be a very ambitious and hence unlikely target. After it became apparent that he was going to have to dance, Walton hoped to make it a relatively low-key event, but his lieutenants couldn't resist putting their boss under the spotlight for this one. They hired a group of professional hula dancers and a ukulele band. Things got complicated when cold weather provoked protests by the dancers' union, which insisted on outdoor heaters. The police became involved, and the news media couldn't resist such a photogenic break from the ordinary financial goings-on.

There was a point to all this hype and hokum, of course. As the Wal-Mart workforce grew into the thousands and then tens of thousands, instilling the kind of work ethic and customer-centered values that had underpinned the success of the first Walton stores became a real challenge. Much as Watson had done at IBM, Walton endeavored to create a corporate culture at Wal-Mart. It was more of a challenge for him than for Watson, though, in that Watson's sales force received relatively high pay, whereas Wal-Mart's workers got little more than the minimum wage, and many worked only part time.

On the other hand, Wal-Mart benefited from the sense of community that existed in most of the small towns from which the company drew nearly all its employees. Walton took pains to fit Wal-Mart into these communities. Stores sponsored charity events, such as a kiss-the-pig contest in Cedartown, Georgia, where the manager of each department set out a jar with his or her name on it, and the manager whose jar brought in the most money for that year's worthy cause had to kiss a pig. Other stores participated in parades, including one in Fairbury, Nebraska, where a Wal-Mart precision shopping-cart drill team performed intricate mass maneuvers down the main street of the town. Numerous stores sponsored scholarships to send outstanding but needy local students to college.

Yet eventually Walton recognized that if he wanted to make employees feel as though the company was their own, he'd have to *make* it their own. In 1971 he instituted a profit-sharing plan that was unremarkable except for the performance of the stock in which most of the shared profits were invested—namely, Wal-Mart. This provided a double incentive to good performance: first for the profits to be shared, second for the appreciation of the stock in response to the strong profits. Employees who stayed with the company for several years earned a tidy nest egg; those who hung on longer got considerably more. With justifiable pride Walton pointed to such workers as one company truck driver who started in 1972 and wound up with over $700,000 in profit sharing twenty years later, and another worker who had accumulated $475,000 by the age of forty.

Walton's employees weren't the only ones getting rich from Wal-Mart stock. As sales soared during the 1970s and 1980s, doubling roughly every three years to $1.2 billion in 1980 and $26 billion in 1990, and profits climbed commensurately, mounting to $1 billion in 1990, the share price went up even faster. Wal-Mart stock split nine times by the middle of 1990; 100 of the original shares, which had sold for a total of $1,650 in 1971, multiplied into 51,200 shares worth a total of $1.7 million. In 1985 *Forbes* determined that Sam Walton was the richest man in America, a distinction he held in each of the following three years.

Walton himself was considerably prouder of another distinction. After refuting the analysts who had predicted trouble when he ran up against Kmart, Walton made believers of them. Wal-Mart consistently won praise as one of the best managed companies in America. One group of analysts went so far as to call it "the finest managed company we have ever followed."

Such praise allowed Walton to shrug off criticism that his stores were destroying the very small-town values that had made his success possible. Although Wal-Mart increasingly invaded suburban America during the 1980s and early 1990s—an offensive augmented by the rapid growth of the company's Sam's Club wholesale chain—the heart of the corporation remained in the small towns of the heartland. Walton insisted on keeping corporate headquarters in Bentonville, and he took pains to defend himself against the charge that he was the ruination of traditional life. "Of all the notions I've heard about Wal-Mart," he said not long before his death in 1992, "none has ever baffled me more than this idea that we are somehow the enemy of small-town America." Nothing could be further from the truth, he declared; if anything, Wal-Mart had been the salvation of many communities that were losing customers and jobs to larger towns nearby.

What the anti-Wal-Marters were really complaining about, he continued, was modernization. "It's almost like they want their hometown to be stuck in time, an old-fashioned place filled with old-fashioned people doing business the old-fashioned way." But life in small towns was bound to move forward, just as it did in large cities. "What happened was absolutely a necessary and inevitable evolution in retailing, as inevitable as the replacement of the buggy by the car and the disappearance of the buggy whip makers."

In any event, the decision in favor of discounters like Wal-Mart wasn't the doing of Sam Walton or any other merchant. It was the doing of the inhabitants of those small towns who chose Wal-Mart over the company's competitors. Many years after being evicted from his first store in Newport, Arkansas, essentially for succeeding too well, Walton opened a Wal-Mart there. Revenge didn't taste as sweet to him as to Ray Kroc in San Bernardino, but he couldn't deny a certain satisfaction at going up against the Ben Franklin that had been pulled out from under him. Before long the son of his old landlord was forced to liquidate. Had Wal-Mart run him out of business? Sam Walton denied it. "His customers were the ones who shut him down. They voted with their feet."

18

THE HERO OF THE HIT FACTORY

Berry Gordy

. . .

BERRY GORDY MAY HAVE LEARNED SOMETHING ABOUT MASS production and quality control from McDonald's, where he ate occasionally, like nearly everyone else of his generation. Wal-Mart came along too late to have any serious impact on his thinking; besides, during the 1960s Detroit residents didn't have much contact with Sam Walton's still-small-town empire. More influential in Gordy's business education may have been his experience on the assembly line of that mother of mass production, Ford Motor Company. At any rate, when Gordy escaped the line to pursue his true love—music—he applied the principles of mass production to the field of entertainment. In the process he created what was probably the biggest black-owned business in America and what was certainly a legend in the music industry.

Like many another impetuous young man, Gordy required some time to discern the identity of his true love. At first he wanted to be a boxer. With every other black kid in the country in the 1930s he thrilled to the news that Joe Louis, America's Brown Bomber, had defeated Max Schmelling, the German champion Hitler was touting as a paragon of the Nazi "master race." Louis's victory at once boosted black pride—"All of a sudden it wasn't so bad to be black," Gordy recalled—and made boxing appear a viable professional option. Gordy was quick with his hands and almost as quick with smart-aleck replies to teachers and other authority figures; the combination convinced a trainer at a local gym to put some

235

gloves on the boy and get him in the ring. Gordy moved quickly up the youth ranks, eventually fighting on the same card as his hero Louis.

Meanwhile, however, he developed an interest in music. An uncle who was a former concert pianist taught Berry the basics; although the boy soon tired of scales and arpeggios, he loved to improvise the boogie-woogie that was tearing up the dance halls of Detroit. He entered a few competitions, did well and convinced himself that he had what it took to make people's toes tap and their hands reach for their wallets.

As a result, when his boxing trajectory began to flatten out—he could earn a living at the fight game, it appeared, but he wasn't the next Joe Louis—he considered going into music. His personal epiphany came after an especially wearying workout one August day in 1950.

> As I sat down on a bench, my eyes fell on two posters on one of the four square pillars that supported the gym's ceiling. I got up and walked closer. The top poster announced a Battle of the Bands between Stan Kenton and Duke Ellington for that same night. The one below was advertising a bout between two young fighters, scheduled for the following Friday night. . . . I stared at both posters for some time, realizing the fighters could fight once and maybe not fight again for three or four weeks, or months, or never. The bands were doing it every night, city after city, and not getting hurt. I then noticed the fighters were about twenty-three and looked fifty; the band leaders about fifty and looked twenty-three.

Gordy decided right then to hang up his gloves. A stint in the service during the Korean War delayed his assault on the musical world, but by the time he returned to Detroit in 1953 he was ready to open a record store. He talked his brother George into putting some money into the venture, which would specialize in selling jazz. At once a difference developed between the partners. The name of the store would be "3D Record Mart"; on the sign beneath that Berry wanted to put "The House That Jams Built," referring to the improvisational practice of jazz musicians. George thought this too affected; he insisted on the simpler "House of Jazz." Berry declared that because the store was his idea, because most of the money behind it was his, and because he would run it, he ought to be able to decide what went on the sign. George was adamant—"House of Jazz." Berry appealed to their father, a plastering contractor with long experience in problem solving. Berry thought the old man would set his brother straight. Instead he set Berry straight, with an admonition the son never forgot: "Whenever they pay, they have a say."

So "House of Jazz" it was—although pressure for a change came from an unexpected direction almost immediately. Curious customers pushed through the doors, but they weren't looking for recordings of Charlie Parker, Miles Davis or other jazz stars. Instead they wanted Muddy Waters, John Lee Hooker and B. B. King. Gordy, a jazz snob, barely knew the names of these blues players. He tried to show one of the customers the error of his ways. "Jazz is complex," he said. "Jazz is as different as each musician playing it. Those blues records pretty much all say the same thing—'I love my baby, but my baby don't love me.'" The customer looked at Gordy as at a lunatic and walked out the door.

Gordy's efforts to educate his clientele lasted long enough to bankrupt his business. But just before he shuttered the place he tried an experiment. He started stocking some of the blues labels his customers had been asking for. As the word got out, customers came back—not enough of them to pull Gordy out of the hole of debt he had dug with his devotion to jazz, but enough to disabuse him of most of his artistic airs and to inculcate a healthy respect for the tastes of the record-buying public.

For the next few years he tried his hand at song writing. A day job on Ford's Lincoln-Mercury line put food on the table and, while engaging his muscles, left his mind free to work out chord progressions and lyrics in his head. His break came in 1957 when Jackie Wilson, a promising young singer whom Gordy had known from the gym, recorded a song Gordy wrote with his sister Gwendolyn. "Reet Petite" became a hit, and was followed by other swift sellers, including "Lonely Teardrops," which topped the million mark, earning Jackie Wilson a gold record that reflected favorably on Gordy.

As a songwriter Gordy had an ear for what would sell—"the best ear in the business," one observer judged. Another who watched Gordy's swift rise offered a similar observation and a partial explanation. "He knows how to make hit records. If I were religious, I'd call it a God-given talent." At times Gordy regretted not having stuck with his piano lessons longer; an industry insider suggested it was just as well he hadn't. "If a kid comes to me and says he's a music major, can play nineteen different instruments, I tell him to get his ass out. Because he's never going to make it. There's so much of a veneer on that type of person they're never going to feel the true music people want—which is very earthy, sincere music."

Gordy may or may not have heard Samuel Goldwyn's reported take on sincerity: "Sincerity is everything; once you learn how to fake that, you've got it made." But he appreciated the need to communicate sincerity to the listeners of his songs. He wrote his lyrics in the present tense to involve the listener in an ongoing crisis: A singer didn't cry that he had lost his baby but that he *was losing* his baby. He kept the lyrics simple lest they get in the way of his message, which was invariably a variation on the abiding and universal theme he had derided in his jazz days. To determine whether a particular combination of melody and lyrics worked, he applied a pragmatic, opportunity–cost criterion: "Would you buy this record for a dollar or would you buy a sandwich?"

Although lots of people were buying Gordy's songs over sandwiches, for reasons he couldn't fathom at first he was making hardly enough money to buy *himself* a sandwich. At one point he claimed to be bringing in less than thirty dollars a week. He may have been lowballing at this time in order to counter his ex-wife's legal efforts to compel an increase in alimony and child-support payments; but he certainly wasn't getting rich. Part of the problem was apparent bad faith on the part of a publisher who wasn't paying what Gordy was owed. Gordy tried to talk a lawyer into helping him collect a $1000 debt; the lawyer told him to forget it because his legal fees would eat up any settlement—as the company that owed Gordy the money well knew.

Another part of the problem was what seemed an only slightly more honest scam. "Single" records in those days typically had two songs, the lead song on the "A" side and some filler on the "B" side. Legitimate talents like Gordy wrote the A songs; nobodies frequently wrote the B tunes. But royalties were split evenly—a situation incomprehensible to Gordy until he discovered that a relative of his producer was the "B"-side author on several of his best-selling records.

Gordy grew increasingly frustrated with the system. As he told an interviewer at the time, "You can go broke with hits if someone else is producing the records." The more he learned about the business, the more inclined he was to follow the advice of a friend and fellow musician who said, "Why work for the man? Why don't you *be* the man?"

In 1959 Gordy decided to be just that. Some time earlier Gordy's parents had established a savings fund into which they and their grown children contributed ten dollars per month. Individual family members might borrow from the fund but only with the approval of the contributors. Gordy went to the group to ask for $800 to start his (second) business. His mother, who worked as an insurance agent, and his father were inclined to say yes, but his sister Esther, also a businesswoman in her own right, wanted to see some proof that the money wouldn't be wasted. "You're twenty-nine years old," she demanded of Gordy, "and what have you done so far with your life?"

Gordy didn't have much of an answer besides saying that the problem with most people was that they gave up on their dreams too soon. He would never give up on his.

"That's very nice," Esther responded. But she was more interested in the $800. "How are you going to pay it back?" She relented and signed off only after Gordy formally pledged his future royalties as security against the loan.

With the $800 Gordy established Motown Records. Every new business needs a niche to get started; Motown's niche was both its location and its moment. Then, as later, the entertainment industry clustered to the coasts; the great interior was perceived as a consumer of movies, television and music, not a producer. But compared to movies and television, music was a low-tech field with minimal barriers to entry. An independent like Motown could rent recording space and on a relative shoestring produce record masters functionally indistinguishable—by the standards of popular music, at any rate—from those produced by the big companies in New York and Los Angeles. Motown would pay to have a few thousand of the records pressed into vinyl; if a tune caught on, proceeds from the first sales would pay for additional pressings.

At the same time, Detroit, with its large black population, was thick with the talent black audiences wanted to hear. More to the point of Motown's major success, that talent was what *white* audiences increasingly wanted to hear. During the 1950s Elvis Presley, Pat Boone and a handful of other white performers had struck gold performing what was generally considered to be black music; but until the end of that decade conventional wisdom in the industry asserted that white listeners—who controlled the overwhelming majority of record-buying dollars—wouldn't buy music performed by blacks.

Gordy observed the conventional wisdom in action in the abortive career of his brother Robert. Robert had considerably more talent as a singer than Berry and almost as much talent as a songwriter. A song of his called "Everyone Was There" sold extremely well—until Robert was invited to perform it on the Dick Clark television show. The problem was that the song sounded white to radio audiences who then suffered a kind of auditory dissonance on seeing that the singer-songwriter was black. The song fell off the charts and Robert fell off the stage.

Yet despite Robert's experience, Gordy had a hunch the old verities were starting to weaken. As he later explained:

> In the music business there had long been the distinction between black and white music, the assumption being that R&B [rhythm and blues] was black and Pop was white. But with Rock 'n' Roll and the explosion of Elvis those clear distinctions began to get fuzzy. Elvis was a white artist who sang black music. What was it? (a) R&B, (b) Country, (c) Pop, (d) Rock 'n' Roll or (e) none of the above.
>
> If you picked C you were right, that is, if the record sold a million copies. "Pop" means popular, and if that ain't, I don't know what is. I never gave a damn what else it was called.

Gordy determined to produce pop music, defined in that commercial sense. He was a businessman, not a social activist, but he couldn't help noticing that the breakdown in musical categories reflected a breakdown in other, larger categories of American life. The civil rights movement was gaining momentum; the walls of segregation were starting to crumble. Gordy gambled that there would be opportunities for those who were first across the rubble. As it applied to the record industry, he guessed that if whites would buy black music performed by whites, they might be persuaded to buy black music performed by blacks.

Gordy's first task was to sign the talent to make the records his crossover customers would buy. Smokey Robinson had come to Gordy with a notebook full of songs, a sweet voice and unsinkable ambition. He needed this last to survive the scores of dunkings Gordy gave him before finding one song with sufficient promise to produce. But Robinson caught on to the Gordy formula, and his group, the Miracles, became one of Motown's mainstays. Gordy found the Temptations singing in a neighborhood not far from the Motown offices; Martha and the Vandellas came from the same part of the city. Mary Wells and Little Stevie Wonder hopped aboard the Motown train during the early 1960s, as did Marvin Gaye and the Four Tops.

But it was the Supremes who epitomized the Motown formula. When Gordy first heard this girl group he was distinctly unimpressed and told them to go back and finish high school. The least impressive of the group was Diana Ross, a skinny waif with a toothy smile who had dropped out of her only vocal class because she was sure she was going to get a D. After Gordy signed them in 1961 they took a couple of years to jell, but the more Gordy listened to them the more he became convinced that Ross had real star potential. "No one wanted to get involved with a kid who sings through her nose," said one person who refused a job as Ross's manager. Yet it was precisely the distinctive quality in Ross's voice—two notes heard on a car radio identified her to listeners—that struck Gordy as the key to her and the trio's imminent success.

That and the fact that Ross had the same drive to make it that Gordy did. She watched other acts on stage and mimicked their moves—to the point where the other performers complained that she was stealing their show. For a diva she didn't act much like a prima donna. She took direction well; if Gordy or someone else showed her something that would sell, she adopted it. One of Gordy's associates at Motown suggested a spoken monologue in the middle of the Supremes' performance of "There's a Place for Us." The passage would establish a theme of social harmony at a time when such a quality was often lacking in the nation. Gordy himself was skeptical at first; it seemed too schmaltzy. But audiences loved it—a teary-eyed Lyndon Johnson approached Ross after one performance and promised, "It's going to happen. Little by little we're getting there"—and the piece became a stock part of the group's repertoire.

Gordy quickly recognized that Ross was the supreme Supreme, the one people came to see and the reason they bought the trio's records. Subtly at first, then more overtly, he highlighted her. Where she had shared lead-singing duties with Flo Ballard, now she got all the lead parts. When this caused friction with Ballard, Gordy reminded Ballard that she could be replaced—and then replaced her. The group became "Diana Ross and the Supremes," and then simply Diana Ross when the star decided to go solo. Motown spun the breakup in positive terms as a "two-for-one stock split," although no one was surprised when the Ross shares proved far more valuable than the Supremes'.

Gordy's handling of the Supremes exemplified his commitment to quality, defined as records that sold exceptionally well. An admiring writer for *Fortune*, in an article entitled "The Motown Sound of Money," explained the Gordy philosophy: "From the start Gordy has viewed the company's basic business as the production and distribution not merely of pop records but of hits." Unlike other record executives Gordy refused to agree to contracts with artists requiring that Motown release a minimum number of their records each year. This might be good for the artists, by keeping them in the public eye, but Gordy didn't think it did anything for the company.

In Motown's early days he ordered a sign put over the offices declaring the place "Hitsville U.S.A.," and he insisted on living up to that billing. If, in his opinion, a record didn't have hit potential, he refused to release it. One result was that Motown released far fewer records than the industry average: one per week compared to five. Another was that Motown's records made the charts (lists of the top 100 songs, compiled and published by *Billboard* and *Cash Box* magazines) at a far higher rate than its competitors' records did. From 1960 to 1970, 357 of the 535 singles Motown released were hits; this two-thirds ratio was better than twice the industry average. "After a while it was like Dial-a-Hit," said one Motown songwriter. "Just like dialing the fire department." During one week in the autumn of 1966, Motown records held three of the top five slots on the pop charts; the company did even better in December 1968 when it claimed five out of the top ten, including the top three.

The singles (doubles, in reality) charts were where record companies made their reputations and no little part of their money. But markups were higher in long-playing albums (the typical single cost 10 cents to manufacture and sold to distributors for 42 cents; the typical LP cost 38 cents to manufacture and sold for $2.25). Until the Motown era LPs had largely been the domain of adult listeners to Lawrence Welk, Frank Sinatra and the like. During the 1960s, however, as teenagers acquired more purchasing power, pop-oriented companies moved into the LP market. It was tricky business, driven almost entirely by the success of singles, which had a short shelf life. Speed was everything—and no one was faster than Motown in throwing together eight or ten additional tracks to go with the hit tune. If a company caught the wave, it didn't have to spend more than an insignificant amount promoting the album, whose success was almost guaranteed by the endless radio play of the hit on stations across the country. Gordy fully exploited the logic and economics of the situation; by the late 1960s some 70 percent of Motown record sales came from albums.

As the hits rolled off the assembly line, Gordy diversified into related branches of the music business. He created a separate corporation to publish and market the songs the Motown songwriting team cranked out. Another Gordy corporation owned and operated the Motown recording studios. Yet another provided various services the Motown artists required, from advice on costumes and choreography to tips on money management and public relations and assistance preparing tax returns.

The combination of these companies—what Gordy called his "conglamorate"—gave him unprecedented control of the Motown artists and unparalleled opportunities for maximizing revenues. Sometimes this came at the expense of the artists. While record companies made their money from selling records, performers didn't, relying instead on live performances. (As late as 1975 the Jackson Five—Michael Jackson's launch vehicle—were receiving a mere 16 cents per LP album sold, or a little more than 3 cents per quintet member.) By acting as manager and booking agent, Motown could apportion the artists' time between stage and studio in ways that ensured the best return for the company, if not for the artists. Gordy was often asked about this potential conflict of interest; he responded that in most cases the artists in question were unknowns when he signed them, that Motown had invested a great deal in their development, and that the company had a right to recoup its investment. Besides, by preventing overexposure of the artists, Motown was able to extend their careers.

There was much to this argument; some Motowners went on and on and on. In a business where burnout was the norm, such Gordy protégés as Smokey Robinson, Diana Ross, Marvin Gaye and Stevie Wonder were selling in the millions twenty years after inking their first Motown contracts.

Inevitably, however, other artists decided they could do better on their own. Michael and the other Jacksons took their act elsewhere, as did Martha Reeves, the Temptations, the Four Tops, and Gladys Knight and the Pips. Gordy lost valuable song-writing talent with the exit of the trio of Eddie and Brian Holland and Lamont Dozier—lead engineers, as it were, of the Motown hit factory.

The departures did undeniable damage to the company. In the late 1960s Motown ranked with the best of the independent record companies, boasting revenues in the $30-million to $50-million range (Gordy, who owned essentially all the stock in Motown and its affiliates, refused to open his books to outsiders). As such it was probably the largest black-owned company in the nation (the great majority of black-owned businesses were also privately held, making comparisons doubly difficult). During the following decade growth tailed off. Some of the slowing resulted from the artistic defections; some followed from Gordy's generally unsuccessful efforts to branch out into films and stage productions.

Another contributor to the slowdown was changing tastes in music. Few fields are as faddish as popular music; what's hot today freezes fish tomorrow. Gordy attempted to accommodate the changes. He ventured into country music, creating the "Melodyland" label for the purpose. But this venture proved premature. Country music wouldn't take off for another decade, and when a California church that operated a theater that was also called Melodyland threatened to sue—the elders were especially incensed at a record called "The Biggest Parakeets in Town," which was not about birds but about "a big-titted broad," in the frank words of a Motown executive—Gordy decided to fold the label rather than fight.

The disappointing foray into country underscored the peculiar position of Motown—and many other black businesses. Although the great majority of Motown's customers were white, the fact that the ownership was black afforded it a special place in the black community. Gordy didn't deny that he gave preference in office hiring to African-Americans—"because they don't get as many opportunities to do that kind of work," he explained to a business journalist. To some extent Motown's success was seen as the success of the black community. This doubtless helped Motown during the early days, but it may have held the company back when continued growth required extending beyond its urban base. If Motown lost its inner-city roots, how would it be any different from the other entertainment conglomerates?

The identity problem came to a head when Gordy decided to sell the company. The 1980s transformed the pop-music industry— with the digitalization of audio, the integration of video with audio as a major marketing tool, and the merger mania that reshaped the media world—even more than the rest of corporate America. After three decades in the business, Gordy didn't have the desire to take Motown into the new era. The company was ripe for purchase and reorganization. A new owner would cut the overhead that had crept up during the flush years and not been pruned back; at the same time it could dip into the Motown library of 1960s hits and sell nostalgia to aging baby boomers.

The trouble was that the new owner wouldn't be black. Not many African-Americans had access to the kind of money Gordy expected to get from the sale of Motown, and those who did weren't interested. Gordy came under pressure to reconsider. "Selling Motown," civil rights veteran Jesse Jackson told Gordy, "would be a blow to black people all over the world."

"I know," Gordy replied. "But Jesse, allow me to use a Jesse-ism of my own. I have three choices—sell out, bail out or fall out. Which do you suggest I do?"

What he did was sell Motown to MCA for $61 million. By way of explanation he issued a statement:

> It is the nature of institutions to take on their own life and to outgrow the individuals who create them. I am proud that this African-American heritage

has been embraced by the world and has become permanently woven into the fabric of popular culture.

As a black man, Gordy had reason to be proud of what he had done; as a businessman too. The businessman—and the musician—in him may have reflected on a particular part of his accomplishment. During the 1960s American pop music experienced the "British invasion": the large-scale importation of British music and British musicians. Motown was the most conspicuous counter to this trend, and by the quality of its music it even co-opted the invaders. The Beatles' second album contained three Motown tunes; the Motown song "Money" made lots of it for both the Beatles and their fellow Brits, the Rolling Stones, as well as for Motown.

Gordy may have been thinking of that song as he signed the MCA deal. "From eight hundred dollars to sixty-one million," he reflected later. "That was money."

19

EVERY WOMAN A QUEEN

Mary Kay Ash

· · ·

IT IS JULY IN DALLAS. THE TEMPERATURE ON THE STREET IS 95 degrees, even though the sun went down two hours ago. Inside the convention center the air is twenty-five degrees cooler as the golden-coifed (golden-wigged, if you must) mistress of ceremonies glides across the stage to the microphone. Three-dozen spotlights glint off the thousand sparkling facets of her evening gown as she smiles, holds her audience in hushed anticipation for what seems minutes, then asks, "Are you ready for the most exciting moment of your life?" The answer is a swelling flood of assent that rolls from the audience of 20,000 women and across the stage, then washes back over the crowd, sweeping everyone in the house into its surging emotion.

Mary Kay lets the crowd luxuriate in the enthusiasm. Beaming beatifically, she waves to the front rows, the far rows, the right, the left, offering her benediction. For another long minute she is the queen of all she surveys; then the spotlight shifts. It isolates a woman standing at the top of a sweeping flight of stairs. A handsome, tuxedoed man accompanies her, but she is clearly the star of the moment. Drums roll and cymbals ring as she descends the stairs to be greeted with roses and a kiss by Mary Kay, who guides her to a throne on the stage and places a crown on her head. Her smile reflects the light of Mary Kay's smile; tears of pride and happiness trickle down her cheeks. The audience applauds wildly, although less in rapturous admiration now than in joyous identification.

The spotlight fades on her and finds another, much like her, at the top of the stairs. She descends to receive her reward. Then another does the same, and another.

Recognition isn't all the collected royalty collects this evening. They receive more-tangible measures of Mary Kay's esteem, including diamonds, furs and luxury cars. But quite evidently it is the recognition—the approval of Mary Kay, the admiration of their peers—that moves these women as few of them have been moved in their lives.

The ability to move people is an essential element of any business endeavor; it is for this reason that organizers of sales conventions pay top dollar to speakers who may know nothing about the business at hand but have demonstrated motivational abilities. Often these speakers are not from the business world; coaches, retired generals and the odd evangelist draw large audiences and larger speaking fees. Which demonstrates that even a world based on the cash nexus nods now and then to higher—or at least different—forms of motivation.

Few business leaders have been as successful at tapping the wellsprings of nonpecuniary motivation as Mary Kay Ash. One of that handful of people better known without a last name than with, Mary Kay fashioned a business empire based on making people feel good about themselves. "Desire for recognition is a powerful motivator," she said. "As far as I am concerned, our legacy will be that we have helped hundreds of thousands of women find out how great they really are. And that they can do anything in this world they want if they want to do it bad enough." On another occasion she boiled her secret of success down to a single rule: "Pretend that every single person you meet has a sign around his or her neck that says, 'Make me feel important.'"

It was a desire to feel important herself that launched Mary Kay on her career as an entrepreneur in 1963. She was forty-five years old at the time and not feeling very important at all. As a child in Houston in the 1920s she had had to nurse her invalid father, a tuberculosis victim, while her mother supported the family by managing a restaurant, often leaving at five in the morning and not arriving home until past nine at night. The latchkey daughter mastered Houston's streetcar system, riding unaccompanied downtown at the age of seven to purchase clothes and other necessities; if some change were left over she would stop at Kress's lunch counter for a pimento-cheese sandwich and a Coke.

She was rescued—or so it seemed to her then—at the age of seventeen by a charming, handsome, locally famous fellow who played in a band called the Hawaiian Strummers. Briefly she was the center of his life, a life that contained all the glamour and excitement her mundane existence had lacked until then. But along came a baby, and another, and another. Soon she was as tied to her new home as she had been to her old one—while her husband acted as though he had no ties at all. His music took him on the road; then the Army called; then he found another woman. By the time Mary Kay realized what had happened she was on her own with three kids to care for.

She took a job with Stanley Home Products, a Dallas-based direct seller of household cleaners and related items. Agents like Mary Kay would host parties, at which guests would be invited to try various products. The proceeds weren't much during those Great Depression years; ten dollars made a good evening's sales. But the path to success was plainly marked, and Mary Kay determined to press ahead. She later recalled attending Stanley's annual sales meeting in 1937; she had to borrow twelve dollars for the train to Dallas (and endure the admonition of the lender about how she ought to be spending the money on the children and not on running off to some "wicked convention like men go to"). Lacking a suitcase, she put her only other dress in her Stanley sample case, and she packed a pound of cheese and a box of crackers to save the cost of restaurant meals. Nearly a half-century later she recalled the impression the gathering made on her.

> Those three days changed my life. I watched them crown the top salesperson Queen of Sales, and with every fiber of my being *I wanted to be where she was.* I sat in the back row of seats in the room, because that's where I belonged. I was so far down the ladder. . . . The Queen and I were opposite in every way. She was tall, thin, brunette—and successful. I was neither tall nor thin, and I was probably the most unsuccessful person in the room. But I was so impressed with that Queen's crown and the alligator bag they presented to her that I decided on the spot that next year *I would be Queen!*

As general advice to agents, the company laid down three admonitions. "Hitch your wagon to a star"; "Get a railroad track to run on"; and "Tell somebody what you are going to do." Mary Kay decided that her star was the Queen of the company. "I hitched to that girl so hard she must have felt it, even from the back row." The railroad track was more problematic, as the company lacked a sales manual or set of written guidelines. So Mary Kay buttonholed the Queen and talked her into running through her spiel for her. Three hours later Mary Kay had nineteen pages of notes that looked like a railroad track to her. As for telling somebody, who better than the president of the company? "I marched up to the president, Mr. Frank Stanley Beveridge, and said, 'Next year *I* am going to be the Queen.'" Mr. Beveridge's response made a deep impression on Mary Kay.

> He took my hand and held it for a moment, looked me squarely in the eye, and said, "You know, somehow I think you will." Those few words literally changed my life.

An associate in later days once remarked, "If you want to understand why Mary Kay is one of the most successful business figures in this country, then you have to understand her obsession with work. She has the ability to stay focused, no matter what comes her way." She manifested this single-mindedness early on. She scheduled product parties three times a day, six or seven days a week. Her children sometimes didn't see much of her, although the situation wasn't quite as bad as some of her neighbors led themselves to believe. Before leaving for her nighttime showings she would tuck the little ones in bed and tell them to go to sleep, but Richard, the youngest, would get up, climb out the window and down a tree to the sidewalk. He would sit on the curb under a streetlight and watch for his mother's return. Worried neighbors asked the child what he was doing outside at such an hour; they clucked their tongues on hearing that he was waiting for his mother to come home from a "party."

All the partying paid off, however, when she indeed became queen of the company. (As she liked to relate, the alligator handbag awarded to the previous year's queen was unaccountably and disappointingly replaced by something identified as a "flounder light.") She continued working as the children grew up, eventually switching to World Gifts, another Dallas-based direct sales company, which hired her to be national sales director. The job was even more grueling than her previous one; on the road three weeks out of four, recruiting and training sales people, she lived out of a suitcase and raised her youngest child, whom she placed in a boarding school (the others having left home already), by telephone.

Family aside, the most trying part of the job was the lack of respect she got from male associates. "Those men didn't believe a woman had brain matter at all," she remembered. "I learned back then that as long as men didn't believe women could do anything, women were never going to have a chance." The final insult came in 1963. She asked her boss at World Gifts for money to purchase audiovisual technology for a training program for new sales people; he responded by hiring a young man to be her assistant. Swallowing her annoyance, she taught the young man everything she had learned about sales and training, whereupon he was promoted over her at twice her salary.

She was outraged at the injustice and found the various rationalizations offered unconvincing. Even twenty years after the fact her anger was apparent. "It really irked me when I was told that these men earned more because they had families to support. *I* had a family to support, too! It seemed to me that a woman's brains were worth only fifty cents on the dollar in a male-run corporation." She appealed the matter to her boss's superiors but got no satisfaction. "It was a board with seven men on it, no women," she said. Shortly thereafter she quit.

In an era of dawning feminism Mary Kay outlined a book on her experiences, but the farther she got into the book the more she realized that what she had was a plan for a business of her own. This business would be one that would treat women right—"not ruin their self-esteem." Women would be rewarded according to what they produced, not what their male bosses thought of them.

Mary Kay sank her life savings of $5000 into the enterprise, rented a tiny Dallas storefront and purchased the recipes for some skin-care formulas that had been developed by an Arkansas man who years earlier had discovered that the creams he used to tan deer hides left his hands looking younger and smoother. These "original Beauti-Control formulas" became the basis for Mary Kay's product line.

The sudden death of her current husband, who dropped dead at the kitchen table a month before launch, increased the stakes of the fledgling enterprise for its owner. But it began well, grossing nearly $200,000 in its first full year of operation. Much of the operation was modeled on Stanley Home Products, including the annual meeting—"seminar"—at which star salespeople were recognized. The first Mary Kay seminar consisted of a chicken-and-Jell-o dinner she prepared herself for 200 saleswomen, served on paper plates in her warehouse.

The Mary Kay method, as it was perfected in subsequent years, was similar to that of many direct-sales companies. For a small initial investment (rising to $100 in the 1990s) a woman received a Mary Kay makeup kit and a lesson in its use. She then would call her friends and organize a Mary Kay party, at which she would sell the cosmetics (typically for twice what she had paid) and recruit new saleswomen ("consultants"). It was in the recruiting that the real money lay for the consultants, for the first consultant earned a commission on each sale made by her recruits. The company developed a well-defined hierarchy and clearly delineated criteria for advancement. By the 1990s a consultant who brought in thirty recruits, who among them sold $16,000 worth of products in four months, became a "director." There were several thousand of these; they earned in the mid-five figures. A consultant who succeeded beyond the level of ordinary directors received one of the company's signature pink Cadillacs, modeled after one Mary Kay customized for herself. The pick of the pink-Caddie crew became "national sales directors"; this select group averaged incomes comfortably in six figures; the best of the best topped $1 million in annual income. With reason, Mary Kay boasted of making more women rich than any other company in the world.

Perhaps needless to say, this formula for success wasn't unique to Mary Kay Cosmetics—and neither, it turned out, was the formula for the company's leading product. Within a few years of the founding, Mary Kay fell out with one of her sales directors; this woman, Jackie Brown, enlisted another Mary Kay alumna to establish a rival in direct-sales cosmetics. The two approached the granddaughter of the Arkansas tanner; she sold them an interest in the company that held the rights to the creams for which Mary Kay had only the recipes. The BeautiControl Company began marketing their version as the original; within a short time the company lured away more than a dozen of Mary Kay's consultants.

This breach "broke Mary Kay's heart," according to a longtime friend and business associate. "She had loved those women and felt totally betrayed." But if her heart was broken, her resolve was only reinforced. She had refused to let men trample her; she wasn't going to let women do it either. "I'll never forget her marching down the hallways with her shoes off, determined not to let this new company do us in," this friend said. Mary Kay sued BeautiControl for trying to pirate away her customers and consultants; besides draining the BeautiControl treasury, the suit scared off some of the company's consultants and directors, most of whom weren't familiar with the nature of business lawsuits and didn't want to be familiarized. BeautiControl sued back but much less effectively; although it negotiated a 1969 settlement giving it the exclusive right to use the actual name of the Arkansas tanner in its advertisements, it ran out of money and was sold to a New Jersey direct-sales firm that couldn't revive it either. "I think it's fair to say that no one was a match for Mary Kay's charisma," offered one of the defeated BeautiControl partners; perhaps equally true was the judgment of CBS investigative reporter Morley Safer, who in a feature on Mary Kay called her a "pink panther . . . whose instinct for doing business and making money is as finely tuned as a jungle cat going for the kill."

During the 1970s the pink panther had the run of the rain forest. Sales and connections soared; by 1979 the company had passed $100 million in sales, and the number of consultants and directors reached 50,000. Mary Kay's pink Cadillacs became an unoffical trademark; the annual seminar experience dazzled the tens of thousands of consultants and directors who paid their own way and their own registration fees to attend. In a manner that was almost certainly partly calculated (or at least consciously understood) but was nonetheless sincere, Mary Kay embodied a peculiar kind of postfeminist yet extremely pro–women's-rights philosophy. Her mantra for women was God first, then family, then career—but she assured women they could have all three. God made Eve from Adam's rib, but He didn't make her to be beaten down or intimidated—and He didn't make her to earn 75 cents to Adam's dollar, Mary Kay declared. "This is why women are fed up with corporate America." (God made man, she told her consultants and directors, and then He said, "That's pretty good, but I think I could do better—*and so He created woman*.") Men shouldn't feel threatened by working wives; instead they should feel liberated. "A woman who has her husband *with her* is a woman and a half. A woman who doesn't have her husband with her is half a woman." (Mary Kay took care to explain that a different yardstick applied to unmarried women.)

This appeal to husbands was a critical part of the pitch. Understanding her audience, she recognized that husbandly vetoes could stifle many a budding Mary Kay career ("God first, family second . . ."). So she took pains to increase the comfort level of male spouses. The beauty-pageant style of the seminars was as nonthreatening as could be; the seminars also offered tips to husbands in dealing with their wives' careers. ("A car phone gives you a warm, fuzzy feeling when she's out on the road at night. You know she's got security.") In short, a Mary Kay career could be a wonderful experience for the whole family. "I promise you your wife will be making three times the money of her corporate job. Plus, you'll get the benefits of her living positively, putting God first, family second, and career third."

This mix of the old-fashioned and cutting edge, of Billy Graham and Gloria Steinem, accounted for much of Mary Kay's success; it also left her open to new challenges. Richard Heath was a senior vice president at the New Jersey company that bought BeautiControl; after an executive-suite falling out he left the company to go into direct sales on his own. With savings and a loan he bought BeautiControl; with his wife Jinger he relaunched the company in direct competition to Mary Kay.

Although the company was a partnership, Jinger Heath became the symbol of BeautiControl. A generation and a half younger than Mary Kay, she appealed to a younger generation of women, women with more education, with more straightforward career goals, with less need of reassurance that work wouldn't offend God or disrupt family life. BeautiControl offered an updated product line, including products for the entire body (Mary Kay concentrated on the face and hands) and cosmetics based on an analysis of those shades that complemented a particular woman's complexion.

Between the new products and the alternative approach, BeautiControl took off. Sales tripled to $8 million between 1983 and 1984; when the company went public in 1986 the stock jumped 50 percent overnight. With some of the $25 million they made from selling a quarter of their stock, Richard and Jinger Heath built a mansion that was gaudy even by Dallas standards. Dinner with the Heaths became a prize for top-sellers. "I'm dying," said one director from Nashville. "Not even Reba McEntire's house compares to this."

BeautiControl's revival cut into Mary Kay's success. Sales slipped badly, and the stock price (Mary Kay had gone public ten years earlier) nose-dived from 40 to 9. Analysts pointed out that some slippage was to be expected during a period of general economic recovery as women went back to regular jobs. But the fact that BeautiControl was growing while Mary Kay was shrinking seemed ominous.

Mary Kay, now in her late sixties, responded with the biggest gamble of her business life. In 1985 she leveraged a $450 million repurchase of all the company's publicly issued stock, hired a younger generation of executives, increased the commissions for sales consultants and directors, and revamped the product line. To BeautiControl's "Color Analysis" system, Mary Kay riposted its "ColorLogic" system. Dick and Jinger Heath considered this a conscious effort to confuse the public, as it may have been, especially in light of the fact that BeautiControl was promoting a line featuring such products as "SkinLogics" and "SunLogics." As before, lawsuits flew back and forth; eventually Mary Kay was forced to abandon the "ColorLogic" label but not the color-analysis approach. (The company substituted "ColorSelect.")

If the goal had been to intimidate BeautiControl, as the earlier version of the company had been intimidated twenty years before, the strategy failed. The principal result was an abiding bitterness between the companies and their personnel. One of the lead chemists for Mary Kay, after being enticed away by BeautiControl, threw a challenge over his shoulder on the way out the door. "You can circle this day on your calendar," he said, "because your days of dominance are over." On being told that Mary Kay's experts had scoffed at his new company's claim that its thigh cream reduced cellulite, this same scientist sneered, "I don't give a rat's ass what they say at Mary Kay." A Mary Kay staffer called BeautiControl "a company of froufrous"; Jinger Heath was damned as a "bimbo" and a "copycat." "Her company is a rip-off of everything we've done," said a longtime Mary Kay woman. BeautiControllers returned the insults, dismissing the Mary Kays as big-haired addicts of too much lipstick. The sniping became such a fixture of Dallas culture that the annual gay parade on Cedar Springs Avenue featured two drag queens, one costumed as Mary Kay in a pink dress and a blond wig, the other as Jinger Heath in a Chanel suit with spike heels; the entire length of the parade route they shouted "Bitch!" at each other.

At times Mary Kay affected to be above the fray. "I don't think that's necessary," she said of efforts by BeautiControl to hire away Mary Kay executives. "It doesn't show ingenuity." Yet on other occasions her animus toward her rival surfaced. "Anyone who gets fired at our company takes a taxi over there," she said. "She gets all she can from them, wrings them out, and fires them." Summarizing her disdain, Mary Kay called Jinger "the Leona Helmsley of the cosmetics business."

Even so, Mary Kay would have admitted that the competition spurred her to greater efforts. "When somebody is out there waiting for you to fall over, it keeps you on your toes," she said. During the early 1990s Mary Kay Cosmetics undertook a bit of a fashion makeover. Advertising in such women's magazines as *Glamour* and *Vogue*, it moved upscale, going after BeautiControl's customers—even as it denied doing so. "Our competition does not come from BeautiControl," said Mary Kay's head of marketing. "It comes from companies like Estée Lauder." Meanwhile Mary Kay made a major push overseas. After just two years in post-Cold War, proto-capitalist Russia, the company boasted 7000 consultants and directors who together did $10 million in sales. The company's rising Russian star was a textbook Mary Kay success story: a former schoolteacher who earned $300,000 in one year, quite possibly making her the best-compensated woman in the country. The Chinese market, which Mary Kay was pursuing even more eagerly, promised to be even bigger.

All the effort paid off. By the mid-1990s some 20 million customers were purchasing 135 million Mary Kay items per year; in 1994 sales to consultants—that is, at wholesale prices—topped $850 million. Mary Kay's personal worth was estimated at more than $325 million.

Although Mary Kay handed day-to-day direction of the company to her son Richard, she remained the spiritual guide of the firm and its 400,000 consultants. Testimonials to her leadership formed a staple of the annual seminars. One consultant presented her with a painting that portrayed her standing next to Jesus Christ; Jesus was smiling in obvious approval of her work. In the same vein, another consultant bore witness to a Mary Kay miracle. Her husband, she said, had been diagnosed with terminal cancer; he had only half a year to live. Yet Mary Kay refused to give up hope. She flew the man to a cancer specialist in Dallas whose work she had been funding; almost at once the patient's condition began to improve. The cancer went into remission. "Without you, Mary Kay," the grateful wife told the women at the seminar, "my husband would not be here with me." While the audience dissolved in tears, she added that she had spread Mary Kay cosmetics out on her husband's hospital bed and sold them to his nurses.

Naturally, speculation surfaced regarding the future of Mary Kay Cosmetics after Mary Kay. Executives at Mary Kay discounted contentions that the magic would disappear the minute the magician was gone. Perhaps more appropriately than was intended, a top executive said, "It's like saying the church and its teachings are invalid because Jesus died. Mary Kay's teachings are enduring."

Those teachings were the same as ever. In staving off her competitors Mary Kay underlined what was special about her company. BeautiControl—or some other competitor yet to emerge—might match her formulas and her organizational structure, neither of which had been really original anyway. But it was hard to imagine anyone else matching the feeling she gave to those hundreds of thousands of women who were crowned queens—personally or vicariously—at her seminars. She summarized what she saw as the meaning of her success in a 1995 interview. "I feel that God has led me into this position," she said, "as someone to help women to know how great they really are." Nor did she intend to stop helping women recognize their greatness until God called her home. "They'll have to carry me out of the building."

20

JUST DO IT

Phil Knight

• • •

I N RETROSPECT, A CAREER IN ATHLETIC SHOES WAS THE MOST OBVI-
ous thing in the world for Philip Knight. As a kid in Portland in the
1950s he ran track and cross-country; he did well enough to think he
could make the track team at the University of Oregon in Eugene, where
Bill Bowerman was winning a reputation as the best middle-distance
coach in America. Buck Knight wasn't the fastest in his cohort, but he was
fast enough to gain a spot on a record-breaking four-mile relay team.
After college he headed south, out of the rain, to the San Francisco Bay
Area, where he ran up and down the parched hills behind Stanford while
attending the business school there. An instructor assigned a paper on
starting a small business; write about something you know, he said. So
Knight sketched a plan for breaking the lock the German company Adidas had on the market for serious running shoes. The Germans made
shoes the way they made cameras: very well but expensively. Japanese
companies were invading the American camera market; why couldn't the
Japanese do the same in shoes? And who better for an American distributor than someone who knew what runners needed and wanted—a runner
himself, for instance?

Many years later Knight remembered that B-school assignment as the
turning point in his life. "I had determined when I wrote that paper that
what I wanted to do with my life was to be the best track and field shoe
distributor in the United States." This was a tall order for someone with

no capital to speak of, no knowledge of shoe manufacturing and only classroom exposure to business of any kind.

But Knight was a nervy young man, and just months after graduating he flew to Japan and visited the Kobe factory of the Onitsuka Company, maker of Tiger brand running shoes, an Adidas knockoff sold in Japan. Knight introduced himself as the head of Blue Ribbon Sports; he refrained from mentioning that Blue Ribbon existed only in his mind. This detail didn't prevent Knight from telling Onitsuka executives that Blue Ribbon was just the firm to import their shoes into the United States. Alluding to some nonexistent partners, he asked the executives to send some examples of their shoes; after he and his partners had examined them, they would place an order.

When Onitsuka responded positively, Knight had to conjure up his company almost out of thin air. He borrowed money from his father to pay for the samples; when they arrived he sent a couple of pairs to Bill Bowerman, his old coach, who quickly became his partner. On a hand-shake and $500 each, Blue Ribbon Sports began to materialize.

That first thousand dollars and a bit more went to purchase the company's initial stock: 300 pairs of Tigers. Knight packed as many as could fit in his car and drove to track meets around the Pacific Northwest. As a former competitor and continuing serious runner himself, he possessed a legitimacy most of his competitors lacked. He also possessed a circle of like-minded friends who became his first customers.

From the beginning Knight targeted Adidas. "We have the organization and product to beat Adidas," Knight told Onitsuka in 1964, with considerably more optimism than most objective observers would have thought warranted just then. "But Adidas will not die easily."

On the track Knight had gotten farther than many people with equal talent; friends and rivals alike attributed his extra success to a fierce competitive streak. Some of his business rivals now wondered whether he pushed competition too far—perhaps across the line into the unethical or even illegal. His connection with Bowerman fell into a gray area. Bowerman was an employee of the state of Oregon; state rules strictly limited moonlighting and using university facilities for private gain. For this reason and perhaps others, Bowerman took some care not to publicize his relationship with Knight and Blue Ribbon. Knight had his own reasons for keeping the connection quiet. Foremost among these was that Bowerman's endorsement would carry more weight if he weren't known to be a partner in the company whose product he was endorsing.

But Bowerman was more than a marketer; he was also an innovator. The coach endlessly fiddled with running shoes, cutting them apart, stitching them back together, taking a toe from this shoe, a heel from that, and fixing both to an upper from a third with duct tape and rubber cement. Runners in the Northwest constantly confronted wet, sloppy conditions; Bowerman had long looked for a sole that would grip the treacherous downslopes that sent runners spilling, often with torn muscles or wrenched ligaments. One Sunday morning while his wife was at church his eye fell on her open waffle iron. All of a sudden the gridded pattern struck him as the ideal solution. Before she got home to stop him, he grabbed a bottle of liquid urethane and made a rubber waffle—or would have if he had been able to get the hardened gunk off the griddle. The waffle sole—attached to an upper— eventually became one of Blue Ribbon's best sellers.

Before it did, Knight's company was no longer selling Tigers for Onitsuka but Nikes for itself. The breakup was bitter, involving business intrigue and even espionage, as well as the cultural differences that have often plagued U.S.–Japanese relations. Knight had never been satisfied with Onitsuka's production and delivery performance; Onitsuka hadn't liked leaning so heavily on such a small firm for its entrée to the richest market in the world. Onitsuka began looking behind Blue Ribbon's back for other distributors; Blue Ribbon began inquiring into alternative producers. At one point Knight put an Onitsuka employee on his own payroll as a spy, but the spy proved to be a double agent.

In early 1972 Blue Ribbon launched the Nike line, manufactured by Nippon Rubber and named for the Greek goddess of victory—a reference lost on the many who, glancing quickly at the script spelling, wondered who this "Mike" character was. Many also wondered at the logo, a stylized wing drawn by a Portland art student Knight knew, and whom he paid thirty-five dollars for her trouble. The wing—a customer would subsequently provide the name that stuck: "Swoosh"—looked confusingly like the logo of Puma brand, another German shoe that was way ahead of Blue Ribbon in sales.

The timing and location of the Nike launch couldn't have been better: That summer the Olympic trials in track and field were held at storied Hayward Field in Eugene. Bill Bowerman was the coach of the American Olympic team. Knight exploited that advantage to put Nikes on the feet of several of the top finishers. When they made national television, so did the shoes they were wearing.

One of the most visible runners at the 1972 trials—and at the Munich Olympics later that summer—was Steve Prefontaine. A cocky, anti-establishment type from the coastal logging town of Coos Bay, Prefontaine had crossed the mountains to Eugene to run for Bowerman. Eugene at that time was a greener, fitter version of Berkeley, and Prefontaine instantly became a local hero, growing more heroic with each record he shattered and each self-satisfied feather he ruffled. He particularly ruffled the feathers of the panjandrums of amateur athletics, who insisted that athletes maintain their pristine poverty if they wished to participate in the Olympics. Seeing the support athletes from the socialist countries received from their governments, Prefontaine wondered why the capitalist countries couldn't come up with a formula that would work for him and his fellows. Phil Knight found the formula; he put Prefontaine on Blue Ribbon's payroll. And Prefontaine put Blue Ribbon's Nikes on his feet.

Prefontaine was the first of a team of edgy athletes Knight recruited. (When Prefontaine died in a predawn car wreck after a party celebrating his latest nose-thumbing at the apparatchiks of amateurism, his iconic status as the James Dean of track and field was assured.) Branching out into tennis, Knight signed Ilie Nastase, a Romanian star whose nickname "Nasty" fit not just the headlines but his temperament, and John McEnroe, a brilliant ground-stroker who knew nothing of stroking the egos of tennis's hierarchy. McEnroe threw his racket and cursed the referees at Wimbledon; at the French Open he announced that Paris would be a wonderful place if not for all the Frenchmen who lived there. The Nike brat pack later expanded to include Andre Agassi, another spoiled tennis wunderkind, and basketball bad boy Charles Barkley. "Outlaws with morals," was how one consultant described the gang Knight was recruiting; some observers questioned how seriously the morals were really screened when Nike contributed to the legal-defense fund of figure skater Tonya Harding, who—despite the $25,000 donation—was convicted of conspiracy in an assault on her arch rival Nancy Kerrigan.

The corporate culture Knight encouraged at Nike Inc. (Blue Ribbon was officially rechristened in 1978) contributed to the outlaw image. Gatherings of company headmen were called "buttfaces"; sales conferences were irrigated by tequila fountains; at least one company golf tournament featured a sales rep distributing marijuana paraphernalia from his golf cart. Another conclave culminated in a fiery speech by the director of operations in Japan, nearly all of whose (Japanese) words were lost on the audience, except for his peroration in English: "Beat Adidas! Kill Puma! Eat

Tiger!" At this point the speaker began tearing a Tiger shoe apart with his teeth, while the crowd screamed, "Banzai! Banzai!" After it reached the requisite size the company became known as "the Saturday Night Live of the Fortune 500."

Some observers thought the ethos reflected the semirepressed alter ego of Knight—an interpretation Knight reinforced by admitting that he had always wanted to be surrounded by "magnificent bastards and wonderful goons." (When tattoos became the rage and Swooshes sprouted all over the Nike workforce, the boss had a discreet version inscribed on his left calf.)

Others perceived the motivational strategy of a genius. "There are people who would walk through walls for this company," explained one long-termer. "It's like the fraternity house in college. The first couple of years it's great, but by the time you are a senior it's not so great. I guess you could say we're like a club that hasn't gone bad." Another veteran was even more emphatic. "It was a holy mission, you know, to Swoosh the world. To get Swooshes on everybody's feet. We were Knight's crusaders. We would have died on the cross."

That crusading spirit propelled the company to nearly triple-digit growth rates from the mid-1960s through much of the 1970s. Nike benefited from the fitness boom in America (a boom Bill Bowerman did as much as anyone else to ignite); it also benefited from its canny marketing. "They managed to create a need where none had existed," said one industry expert. No longer would any old pair of shoes do for that jog around the block; people wanted to wear what the best in the world were wearing. The rebellious spirit of the 1960s gave way to the disillusionment of the 1970s and the self-absorption of the 1980s; but aging baby boomers could vote with their feet for an attitude they couldn't embrace with the rest of their persons. "We were the children of Holden Caulfield," Knight said, referring to the protagonist of J. D. Salinger's coming-of-age classic, *The Catcher in the Rye*. "Nobody liked the phoniness or the hypocrisy of the establishment, including the business establishment."

Needless to say, maintaining this attitude required more effort after Nike *became* the establishment—although its customers were becoming the establishment at the same time. Nike relied increasingly on advertising to convey its no-compromise approach. One television commercial showed a battered player of Australian football—a more brutal variant of the American version—looking into the camera and avowing with a straight, albeit bloodied, face: "I'm not willing to say I would die for my team, but I would be willing to go into an extended coma." A spot shown during the

Olympics declared, "You don't win silver, you lose gold." Another television ad, entitled "Search and Destroy," spit still more squarely in the eye of the Olympic ideal by casting the athletes as real warriors battling desperately for victory to a score of shrieking punk-rock music. At the end a runner vomits violently and a bloody mouthpiece flies across a backdrop of the Nike Swoosh. Knight explained the Nike philosophy: "It doesn't matter how many people you offend, as long as you're getting your message to your consumers. I say to those people who do not want to offend anybody: You are going to have a very, very difficult time having meaningful advertising."

During the 1980s Knight's in-your-face approach ran up against an opposite strategy and momentarily stumbled. While Knight was concentrating on the hard-edged, hard-core athletes, Paul Fireman acquired North American distribution rights to Reebok, a British company specializing in leather aerobic shoes for women. Fireman recognized the enormous potential for growth in casual shoes modeled on athletic wear, and before Knight could respond Reebok had raced past Nike to claim the top spot in American sales.

Besides beating Nike in the shoe stores, Reebok challenged the Nike way of doing business. "I think Nike is more of a cult, where people have to give up their individuality," Fireman told an interviewer. "I want people here to have a balanced life, one that works on various levels." Asked how he viewed his company's competition with Nike, Fireman answered that he thought it could benefit both sides. "Anytime you have competition like that, you spark ingenuity and creativity. You reach for something more within your organization."

Knight would have none of such sportsmanship. "I may be over the top on this," he said, "but I just don't want to like my competitors." He added, regarding Fireman: "I want my people to believe that whenever he and our other competitors succeed, we will be less able to do all the things we want to do." Fireman had commented, "At the end of a contest, I'd shake hands and walk away. I think he would throw a shovel of dirt on the grave." Knight didn't deny the charge, saying, "That's all right. I don't understand him either."

Knight's best weapon in his battle to beat Reebok was a basketball player who proved to be the greatest in history. This wasn't obvious in 1984, when Michael Jordan opted out of his final season at North Carolina. Knight himself wasn't an expert on basketball futures, but his people saw enormous potential in a young man with a winning personality and astonishing leaping ability. The latter inspired the campaign Nike built around Jordan and the shoe line they brought out to highlight the company's latest hero.

At the time, the Air Jordan line was more than just another shoe stream for Nike. The recession of the early 1980s had demonstrated that the athletic wear business was not, contrary to some overheated expectations of the previous decade, recession proof. Just months before signing Jordan, Nike had revealed its first ever decline in annual profits. Wall Street hammered the share price down to single digits, and the company had to dump millions of shoes for as little as a dollar per pair. Workers were laid off in what became known around Nike as the "St. Valentine's Day massacre." Knight, explaining that he wanted to make management more nimble to deal with Reebok and other challengers, declared, "Nike would rather have 30 PT boats worth $30 million each than a $900 million battleship."

In fact, Michael Jordan became the company's $900 million battleship—although rocket ship might have been a better analogy. One top Nike official borrowed still another metaphor during the planning stages of the Air Jordan campaign: "On this rock we will build a church." A sales rep from New York possibly put the feeling best, and provided the most accurate forecast, when he said, "This is going to have a halo over everything we do. Human nature is that when retailers start writing paper, they keep writing paper. Give us one good thing and we can make the rest of this junk sell better and smell better."

Air Jordan proved to be a very good thing for Nike. The line sold more than $100 million in its first year, the largest figure for any endorsement in history until then. As he had in other instances, Knight bent the rules in introducing the Air Jordan line. The code of the National Basketball Association mandated uniformity in the uniforms of teams in the league; a single player could not wear special shoes that didn't match those of the rest of his team. But Nike hadn't purchased the twenty-four feet of the entire Chicago Bulls squad, just those of Jordan. And anyway, the whole point was to make Jordan's feet stand out. The first Air Jordans—a gaudy red-and-black pair unlike anything seen before in the NBA—definitely did that. As one hometown sportswriter put it, "Michael Jordan is not the most incredible, the most colorful, the most amazing, the most flashy, or the most mind-boggling thing in the NBA. His shoes are."

The commissioner of the NBA announced sternly that if Jordan wore the shoes again his team would be fined $1000. A second infraction would cost the Bulls $5000. Beyond that the team would forfeit its games. Predictably the furor made the sports pages of newspapers all over the country. For Nike it was terrific publicity, reinforcing the outlaw image it had long cultivated (and which Jordan, in most things a gentleman of sport, largely lacked). And after the $2.5 million it was already paying for Jordan's services, it was cheap publicity—the company told Jordan and the Bulls it would cover any fines they incurred. At the same time it revved up the marketing machine to capitalize on the controversy. "On September 15, Nike created a revolutionary new basketball shoe," ran one thirty-second spot. "On October 18, the NBA threw them out of the game. Fortunately the NBA can't stop you from wearing them. Air Jordans from Nike."

The league gave in after Nike modified the shoe somewhat—a point the company's ad teams neglected to announce. Commissioner David Stern recognized that Jordan could be as good for the league as for Nike. In arriving at this conclusion, Stern heeded anecdotal evidence suggesting that a compromise was essential to reach the demographic group the NBA prized. "My kid thinks I'm an asshole because I didn't let Jordan wear those shoes," he told the Nike official behind the Air Jordan launch.

The Air Jordan campaign furthered the conversion of Nike from a shoe distributor to a marketing machine. In 1982 Knight had interviewed Dan Wieden, partner in the minuscule Portland-based ad agency Wieden & Kennedy. Wieden came out to Nike's Beaverton headquarters just west of the city and introduced himself to Knight. Knight introduced himself back: "Hi, I'm Phil Knight and I hate advertising." Wieden responded that he hated advertising too—most of it, anyway. His approach to advertising was to create a mood. "We don't set out to make ads," he said later. "The ultimate goal is to make a connection." Knight bought the concept and Wieden got the account.

One of its early efforts was a follow-up to the Air Jordan campaign. Despite the success of the Air Jordans, Knight was dissatisfied with the company's performance. "The sad fact is that Nike's not a very good company," he declared in the company newsletter, *Nike Times*, in 1986. A single product, even one as good as Air Jordan, couldn't carry the company. (Some observers, noting how heavily the company was relying on the Air Jordan line, thought the corporate name ought to be "Mikey.") It needed a broader, more compelling vision.

What it came up with was Nike Air. This shoe, which included an air cushion in the sole of a multiple-purpose shoe (a "cross-trainer") was Nike's answer to Reebok. A great deal of energy and money went into the product; one top Niker captured its meaning when he scrawled across a grease board in his office, "BET THE FARM." Weiden & Kennedy produced a commercial to unveil the line; scoring the spot was the Beatles' song "Revolution," the rights to which cost Nike a quarter-million dollars.

Whether or not the Nike Air represented a revolution in footwear, it did enable Nike to grab back the lead in sales from Reebok. And it reinforced the new ethos that drove Nike into the 1990s. "In the old days we thought of ourselves as a shoe company," said a vice president of marketing (who hadn't actually been around in the old days). "And it was very limiting to us. Our brand identity is really as a sports company, and sports have appeal and power." Knight himself described sports as "the culture of the U.S., the language of the world."

The latter part of that comment grew more germane with the passing years. To be sure, the American market continued to expand. One study in the mid-1990s revealed that the average American teenager bought ten pairs of athletic shoes per year; for Nike that cumulatively represented $1 billion in sales. Yet the overseas market was growing at a far faster rate. For some time Nike had been seeking to expand in Europe; by the early 1990s Europe accounted for a quarter of Nikes sales. More recently, in a coals-to-Newcastle turnaround, Nike shoes had become the rage in Japan. When the Air Max was introduced in 1995 it immediately elicited obsessive desire among Japanese teenagers; the street price of a pair reached $1000. By that same year foreign sales accounted for forty percent of revenues, a figure that was likely to increase. As Knight put it, "That's where the feet are."

That was also where the hands were. After starting out with shoes made in Japanese factories, Knight found new producers successively in Korea, Taiwan, Thailand, China, Indonesia and Vietnam. Nike's scouts looked for just the right combination of inexpensive labor and stable currency and government; one Hong Kong analyst, observing the migration of Nike factories, devised something called the "Nike indicator" of emerging economies. Invented lightheartedly but employed seriously, this measure was a leading indicator of economic development, and in fact many other multinational firms followed Nike's lead. Nike wasn't complaining. "If you buy the idea that industrialization is good for a nation's economy, yeah it's a decent indicator," said Nike's director of industrial relations. "We're the canary in a coal mine."

Considering that canaries warned of impending disaster, this image may have revealed more than the speaker intended. In the 1990s Nike had become sufficiently part of the establishment that it found itself the object of various anticorporate protests. Noting the high percentage of African Americans on its payroll as endorsers, some black spokespersons asked why there weren't more blacks in management positions. Others questioned whether shoes that sold for more than $100 per pair were quite the thing for poor inner-city kids; this line of skepticism grew with stories of violent robberies of the latest models of Air Jordans. Perhaps the most persistent complaints involved reported mistreatment of workers in the Asian factories that produced Nikes; at one point Nike's alleged sweatshopping became the focus of a running satire in the syndicated comic strip "Doonesbury."

Other criticisms involved potential conflicts of interest. Nike paid college coaches to outfit their teams in Nike shoes; with Nike supplying a large percentage of certain coaches' annual income, questions of divided loyalty naturally arose. "I think they've gone too far," complained one former president of a college that wore the Nike label. But Knight adopted the attitude that if it wasn't illegal, Nike would keep doing it. When the 1992 Olympics placed Michael Jordan, Charles Barkley and other Nike spokesmen in the position of playing in uniforms supplied by Reebok, which had won the right to outfit the U.S. basketball team, the Nike men on the Reebok team contrived to hide the latter label with appropriately draped American flags. "It was a disgrace to the Olympics and to America," fumed Reebok's Paul Fireman. Chuckled Knight, "That moment was by no means orchestrated from headquarters, but I thought it was great." Knight nudged the envelope further by negotiating a deal with the Dallas Cowboys football team that apparently circumvented league conventions regarding endorsement tie-ins; evidently connected to the deal was a fat endorsement contract for Cowboys' star Deion Sanders that allowed the Cowboys to evade the league's salary cap. Knight was unapologetic: "We didn't violate any NFL agreements or any laws of the land."

Eventually, however, he was forced to give ground on certain issues. Human-rights groups harassed him until the furor over working conditions in the Asian factories threatened to drown out the company's advertising; after years of ignoring or denying the charges, Knight suddenly switched course and pledged to require Nike's overseas manufacturers to bar underage workers and adhere to U.S. standards of health and safety. Independent monitors from human-rights and labor organizations would be allowed into the factories to interview workers and assess working conditions. Yet even as he unveiled this kinder, gentler side of Nike, Knight implicitly threw down a challenge to his competitors: "We believe that these are practices which the conscientious, good companies will follow in the twenty-first century."

This tactical retreat raised few expectations that either Knight or Nike would abandon the aggressive approach that had carried them to the top of their industry. In 1996, at a time when *Forbes* listed him as the sixth wealthiest individual in America and when Nike revenues were running at $6 billion annually, Knight predicted that the company would reach $12 billion in five years. Nike had already moved from shoes into other lines of athletic apparel; now it was branching out into sports licensing. This $10 billion business—in which sports teams sell the use of their names and logos—represented a major opportunity for Nike. "If we get our fair thirty percent market share," Knight said, with only half a twinkle in his eye, "it's going to be a lot of business."

At the Nike "campus" in Beaverton, a new generation of employees had replaced the original crew of crusaders that had helped launch Blue Ribbon Sports thirty years before. But somehow Knight had managed to instill much of the same sense of mission that had inspired the earlier group. "I think anyone would like to work here," said one woman in her twenties. "The people are just great." A recent transplant from the East Coast declared, "I have always felt that people here really get it. They know what is real, whether it's designing a product, distributing it, or mar- keting it. There's just no bullshit."

As for Knight himself, now in his late fifties, the philosophy of success seemed straightforward. A reporter asked him how he became one of the master marketers of the age; he responded with a reference to a quip by one of the heroes of the generation Nike shod: "How did John Kennedy become a war hero? They sank his boat." In other words, you do what you have to do to get where you need to go. Or, as Knight liked to quote Bill Bowerman: "Play by the rules, but be ferocious."

21

DRESS FOR SUCCESS

Liz Claiborne

. . .

When women first went to work, they had no sense of themselves. The clothes were all designed to make them look like mini-men. The designers took the man's pinstripe business suit and changed it just a bit so it would fit a woman. White blouse, floppy bow tie, sometimes even a four-in-hand tie. It was as if all the men were in the boardroom and all the women would be in the boardroom, too—as if everybody started at the top. But the women weren't in the boardroom.

BECAUSE THEY WEREN'T, LIZ CLAIBORNE WOULD BE. SHE HAD shown a flair for design early, at twenty-one winning a contest sponsored by *Harper's Bazaar* and moving to New York to make her career in the clothing business. It was her second sojourn in America. Born in Belgium to American parents—her father worked for Morgan Guaranty—she lived with them in Europe during the 1930s before crossing the Atlantic to New Orleans and then Baltimore. She and they crossed back over to Europe when she was in high school. As a result of the disruption she never finished high school—a matter of some later importance to her working-women customers—but she learned to sew from her mother and studied painting in Paris and Brussels. She also inhaled something esthetic from the European air. "Europeans have a more careful sense of the visual than Americans," she explained. "Americans might put a paper carton of milk on the table; Europeans would pour the milk into a pitcher and put the pitcher on the table."

Her parents opposed her choice of career—or at least the place it would be pursued. "It was—well, too New York, too rough," Claiborne said. Nor were they mollified when she chopped off her long hair, started modeling and took up with an art director from Bonwit Teller, whom she subsequently married. Her career coursed along Seventh Avenue until she landed at Jonathan Logan, where she became the chief designer for Youth Guild, the house's junior-dress division. At Jonathan Logan she developed a reputation for solid quality and equally solid professionalism. "Liz was a very private girl, very low key, not pushy, a hard worker," said her boss from that period. "She wasn't a playgirl."

Claiborne simultaneously developed some decided notions of where modern fashion was heading and Jonathan Logan wasn't. During the 1960s and early 1970s women entered the white-collar and professional labor force in record numbers. As long as office women had been overwhelmingly secretaries, they hadn't had a great deal of say about their dress codes, but as women moved into positions of authority things began to change. Many wore suits, but others found those knockoffs of the traditional male uniform uncomfortable, unfunctional or unfashionable. "My original concept," Claiborne told *Vogue* magazine, "was to dress the women who didn't have to wear suits: the teachers, the doctors, the women working in Southern California or Florida, the women in the fashion industry itself. They didn't need or necessarily want to wear suits."

She tried to persuade Jonathan Logan to go after this growing market, but her bosses there had other priorities. After waiting for her son to reach an age where he could fend for himself—"If we were going to lose everything we had, I wanted him to be old enough to handle it"—she and her second husband pooled $50,000 of their own savings with $200,000 from friends and opened Liz Claiborne, Inc., in January 1976.

The chairwoman knew precisely what she wanted her company to do.

> The goal was to clothe the working American woman. I was working myself, I wanted to look good, and I didn't think you should have to spend a fortune to do it. Only a couple of companies were catering to that emerging woman—both in traditional, suited ways. I felt we could do better.

Claiborne corroborated her own sense of fashion with informal market surveys.

I'm a great believer in fit, in comfort, in color. And I listened to the customer. I went on the selling floor as a saleswoman, went into the fitting room, heard what they liked and didn't like. Not that you do exactly what they want. What you do is digest the information and then give them what you think they ought to have.

Arthur Ortenberg, Claiborne's husband, had spent a career in the apparel trade himself, on the management side; he transferred that experience to Liz Claiborne Inc. "I believed that we could bring order, discipline and planning to this highly fragmented industry," he said. "We felt that if we could run a proper company, with high-quality products coherently presented to a defined customer, the rewards would follow."

The Claiborne formula was simple and efficient. Liz Claiborne directed the company's designers. Her distinctive style—grounded in the classics but executed in bold colors or with unexpected accents (a traditional blazer in bright fuchsia, for example)—directly targeted working women who wanted to be fashionable but couldn't see paying Calvin Klein or Bill Blass prices. Even after the company expanded to the point where Claiborne no longer had time to design specific products, her influence set the tone for everything that went out the door. "Liz is still the heart and soul of design at the company," said a Claiborne executive more than a dozen years after the company commenced business.

Claiborne's reputation as a designer, as well as her decision to stick close to the fashion mainstream, afforded a crucial sense of security to her customers. "Women are busy," she said. "They don't want to bother as much with clothes, and they need reassurance, they have to be told it's okay." And they wanted to be told quickly. "I realize my customers want simple, young, feminine clothes that take half-a-minute to pick out of a closet." Buying the Claiborne label was all about being told what was okay by someone whose taste they trusted.

Actual production of the Claiborne line was contracted out to shops overseas, mostly in Asia. The reason was the same one that motivated Phil Knight to adopt a similar strategy for Nike: namely, to control costs. Like Knight, Claiborne encountered criticism for offshoring production under less-than-ideal conditions. "But you can't match these developing countries," she said. "Let's face it, in the developing countries working in an apparel factory is a good job." As for the contention that foreign workers were stealing American jobs, she had a simple retort: "No American mother wants to see her daughter sitting in front of a sewing machine in a factory."

Coordinating distant production presented a continuing challenge. The company stationed dozens, then scores, then hundreds of employees abroad—far more than most comparably sized competitors. The effort paid off. Marveling at the logistical coordination of the Claiborne team, a vice president at Bloomingdale's lamented, "We can't do that with our own private label."

When the clothes reached America, Claiborne marketed them in a manner that emphasized quality. The company refused to put salespeople on the road, telling retailers if they wanted the product they had to come to New York and get it. Retailers were discouraged from including Claiborne products in advertisements of sales; unlike most other apparel firms, Claiborne rarely supplied "markdown money": credits to retailers to help clear out slow-moving merchandise.

Retailers put up with this strategy because Claiborne clothes sold. In an industry where only 40 to 50 percent of items typically rang the register at full price, 60 to 75 percent of Claiborne products did. And where the industry average for sales per year per square foot of store space was around $200, Claiborne hovered between $400 and $500.

Yet the company wasn't unsympathetic to retailers' concerns. Most houses brought out one line for each of the four seasons, requiring retailers to buy clothes in three-month blocks. Claiborne broke the year up into six seasons, inventing a "prespring" and a "prefall" and thereby allowing retailers to purchase goods in smaller batches. (This simultaneously eased strains on the production side by evening out manufacturing across the year.) Claiborne Inc. also made a habit of shipping merchandise weekly instead of monthly.

The Claiborne formula produced a minor miracle in the rag trade. Where Liz Claiborne had worried that she and Ortenberg might lose their initial investment, they instead started turning a profit within the first nine months. Sales hit $48 million in 1979, $117 million in 1981.

In the latter year Claiborne and Ortenberg decided to take the company public. The rationale behind what proved to be one of the most successful initial public offerings in Merrill Lynch history had less to do with funding continued expansion (although the $6.5 million raised didn't hurt) than with repaying the original investors and establishing corporate credibility. Claiborne explained:

> Even though we were doing very well, the investors' capital was locked in. It [the IPO] was to make those pieces of paper the stockholders held tradeable.

We also felt that it would give us exposure, which it certainly did. The company really took off after we went public. People began to realize we were a business, not just a fashion house; and that gave us a different kind of confidence. It gave us the courage—and the push—to forge ahead.

Whether or not courage was required, Claiborne made things look easy. Sales grew rapidly to more than $1.2 billion in 1988; profitability was even more impressive, topping 10 percent on sales and 40 percent on equity. In 1989 *Fortune* sifted its 500 for the ten most profitable firms of the preceding decade; Claiborne Inc. (which had entered the 500 in near-record time) came out on top. In 1990 Claiborne and Ortenberg were selected by the *Fortune* editors for induction into the National Business Hall of Fame. *Forbes* raved: "Perfectionism and control of every facet of design and production are the hallmarks of her company."

The ascent wasn't entirely without hesitation and missteps. Maintaining the company's rapid growth rate required expanding beyond the original competency. Claiborne had to be talked into entering the field of designer jeans. "Who needs another pair of designer jeans?" she remembered asking herself. Her associates answered: Your customers, women who trust the Claiborne label. More-formal wear and children's clothing posed a challenge in that Claiborne couldn't rely on her own eye as fully as in working wear. "I've had the most trouble in dresses and kids," she said, "since the taste there is not quite the same as mine." Marketing children's clothes posed a problem in itself. Kid's clothes were typically displayed by size rather than by price; thirty-five-dollar Claiborne outfits didn't sell well next to ten-dollar competitors. Designing and selling men's wear required climbing an entirely different learning curve. A foray into designer sheets foundered on troubles with quality control. A joint venture with Avon into cosmetics led to misunderstanding, missed opportunities and eventual litigation.

In fashion more than in certain other fields, success appeared at least partially self-limiting. "I worry about the label being everywhere," Claiborne explained. Her customers appreciated the confidence the Claiborne label gave them, but it was a confidence they didn't wish to share too widely. "Women don't like to see their clothes coming and going."

Perhaps overestimating customer confidence, the company briefly lost touch with its base. "We like to think of ourselves as the IBM of the garment district," said one Claiborne executive in the late 1980s, making a comparison that proved unfortunately apt. Like IBM, Claiborne Inc.

erred in designing what it determined its customers *ought* to want, in this case mini-skirts. Baby-boom women, their fashion sense sobered by a few extra years and a few extra pounds, revolted by going elsewhere. A chastened Liz Claiborne reflected, "We discovered that our customer is a bit older and a bit more conservative than we thought."

The biggest shock to the company came in 1989 when Claiborne announced her retirement. "Liz gone?" queried a typical pundit. "A jolting thought for millions of American women whose wardrobes and careers thrive on components that seem to come straight from the heart and soul of Mrs. Claiborne herself." Claiborne had never been comfortable with the publicity that came with success in the fashion world; whenever possible she had deflected interviewers to Ortenberg. But her trademark appearance—short-cropped hair, oversized tinted tortoise-shell glasses, pants, blazer—attracted crowds whenever she visited the department stores that were the company's best customers. At Macy's flagship store in New York's Herald Square some 600 women surrounded her as excitedly as if she were a rock star. Hugs and professions of profoundest gratitude were the order of the day.

This kind of personal identification had been crucial to the company's success. Other designers drew more ink in the fashion magazines, but none had the common touch of Liz Claiborne. "If you ask somebody in Milwaukee what designers they know, they always name Liz Claiborne," remarked Donna Ricco, a designer herself. "For working women there, it's a name they want and admire." A Claiborne customer who headed a market-research firm elaborated on this theme. "Her clothes stand out on their own," she said. "But part of the reason those clothes succeeded is that women related to her as a working woman. She's not a model. She's married. She works. She was somebody just like us."

Claiborne and Ortenberg (who announced his retirement at the same time) had been preparing to relinquish control for some time. Vice chairman Jerome Chaizen had been assuming increasing responsibility for day-to-day operations; he now stepped up to the chairmanship. "It's a well-oiled machine that will continue to run," opined an industry analyst.

Yet just how well it would run occasioned dispute. Bill Blass congratulated Claiborne and Ortenberg on leaving with laurels still on their brows. "There is a tendency in our business to overstay your welcome," Blass said. "I love the idea of stepping down. I like the idea that they know when to do it." A company insider asserted that simply realizing that Claiborne and Ortenberg would still be watching would ensure top performance: "It's like working for the ultimate mother and father; all you want to do is get A's so they'll be proud of you." On the other hand, an academic industry-watcher warned that in a field as fickle as fashion, experience like Claiborne's and Ortenberg's would be difficult to replace. "In a situation like this," he said, "the importance of these particular founders is much greater than in a business not subject to such fast change." One of Claiborne's design peers echoed this sentiment, saying, "They probably have some rising stars, but Liz was a genius in terms of predicting trends. You can't find that skill on every corner."

Wall Street initially agreed with the skeptics. The share price dropped a dollar (to $17.125) the day after the announcement, on very heavy trading (more than 2 percent of the stock changed hands). Reported insider selling—with the new chairman unloading 100,000 shares—during subsequent months didn't do much to bolster investor confidence.

Yet the market gradually came to appreciate that Claiborne and Ortenberg really *had* left the company in good hands. Sales and earnings continued to grow in the twelve months after Claiborne's retirement, with the company reporting a 21 percent jump in quarterly profits in August 1990 and projecting $200 million in annual earnings on sales of $1.7 billion. The share price, which at one point recently had doubled to 34, remained in the high twenties. This was good news for Claiborne and Ortenberg, who announced their resignation from the board of directors and their desire to gradually sell off their 6 percent stake in the company. What had begun as a $50,000 investment fourteen years earlier was now worth substantially more than $100 million.

"The sooner this company gets out from under our mythic infallibility, the better off it's going to be," Ortenberg said as he and Claiborne headed off to Montana, where they intended to work for various environmental causes and simply spend more time on the ranch they called Tranquillity. Liz Claiborne Inc. continued to thrive; in 1991 the company made *Fortune*'s top ten of corporations most admired by fellow executives, outside directors and industry analysts.

Yet it was Claiborne's entrepreneurial example rather than her choice of successors that had the largest lasting influence. Claiborne occasionally irritated feminists of a certain persuasion, as when she told a luncheon sponsored by *Working Woman* magazine, honoring her as a businesswoman: "I think we women should be recognized and honored as people, not as women managers." She certainly received her share of plaudits on strictly business terms. A Merrill Lynch analyst declared, "Liz Claiborne is one of the all-time greats, not just in the apparel industry but in the history of the stock market." A rival in the rag trade called her "a great pathfinder." *Fortune* couldn't say enough good things about her, characterizing her as "the industry's success story of the decade" and "the outstanding role model for fashion entrepreneurs." The most telling praise may have come from those who took her lesson most directly to heart—because they hoped to take it to the bank. A Goldman Sachs executive who worked with fashion startups remarked that during one period of just a few months at least three companies promised in all earnest: "We are the next Liz Claiborne."

'Twas a fond hope. It might come true if the wannabes could match the original's sense of style, her commitment to quality, her understanding of the apparel industry, and especially her sensitivity to the needs and desires of her customers. The Goldman Sachs man was too discreet to say so, but it was a fair bet, in light of this demanding set of criteria, that he insisted on being convinced.

22

THE WORLD IN REAL TIME

Ted Turner

• • •

IN JANUARY 1991 THE WORLD WITNESSED A NOVEL PHENOMENON: a war fought on live television, broadcast from behind the lines of a country targeted by a massive bombing offensive. The cameras of the Cable News Network showed the skies over Baghdad illuminated by the tracer rounds of Iraqi antiaircraft guns; viewers heard the concussion of the bombs as they rocked the earth and shattered buildings in the Iraqi capital. Not surprisingly, officials of the American government, which was spearheading the Gulf War against Saddam Hussein, looked askance at scenes of destruction that couldn't but call into question this battering of a small nation, regardless of the misdeeds of the tyrant running the place. Some critics went so far as to brand Peter Arnett, CNN's Baghdad correspondent, a traitor who was aiding and abetting Hussein's lawless brutality. CNN chief Ted Turner rejected the criticism. He conceded that Iraq was currently an enemy of the United States. "But CNN," he continued, "has had, as an international global network, to step a little beyond that. . . . We try to present facts not from a U.S. perspective but a human perspective." As for himself, he said: "I'm an internationalist first and a nationalist second."

Not everyone took Turner's avowal of humanitarian statesmanship at face value. In fairness to the skeptics there was historical reason for discounting the words of a man who for thirty years had been better known as "Terrible Ted," "Captain Outrageous" and "the Mouth of the South."

The son of a successful but ultimately unhappy advertising executive, Turner inherited the family billboard business when his father committed suicide in 1963. Precisely what the twenty-four-year-old Ted inherited was a matter of some dispute. Edward Turner had recently purchased three large divisions of a principal competitor but, caught in the cycle of fear that led to his self-destruction, suffered a grave case of buyer's remorse and quickly tried to unload them for whatever he could get. A sale was in the works at his death. Son Ted immediately set about voiding it. He threatened to argue in court that his father had been insane; he delayed and obfuscated and stalled. In the end he held on to the expanded Turner Advertising of his father's hopes rather than the diminished company of his father's fears. "I want everyone associated with this business to know that the Turner Advertising Companies fully intend to continue forging ahead," he declared in a trade-association newsletter.

For five years Turner stuck to his billboards, propelling Turner Advertising to number one in the South and fifth, by billboard count, in the country. In 1968 he bought a radio station in Chattanooga, seeing it as another advertising medium: billboards of the airwaves. The circumstances of the sale taught him a lesson. He didn't wish to appear overeager to buy the struggling station and consequently told the sellers he needed some time to think over their proposed deal. While he delayed, another buyer stole the station out from under his pen. Turner wanted the station and eventually got it, but for $300,000 more than he would have paid had he acted decisively in the first place. Ever after, Turner made a habit of moving immediately, closing same-day deals as a matter of course.

Turner-watchers from that period noted a distinctive style in his takeover strategy. "He could charm the pants off anybody when he wanted to," said a longtime associate. "Usually the fellow we acquired would turn around and work twice as hard for Ted as he ever had for himself." Another individual, who came aboard at about this time, likewise found his new boss compelling but in a strange way. "Ted Turner is without doubt one of the very smartest people I had ever met," he said. "But it took me just two seconds to figure out that he was also completely wacko. He is a brilliant idea man, but he's been a plunger from the beginning. A plunger with extraordinary business judgment."

Whether as a manifestation of his brilliant judgment or as something he serendipitously plunged into, Turner soon began exploiting a synergy between his old business and his new one. Even in flush times for outdoor advertising a few billboards go begging, vacated by their former tenants and awaiting those to come. Turner filled this dead space with ads for his own radio station, and Chattanooga drivers started tuning in.

During the next two years Turner multiplied his radio holdings; in 1970 he purchased a television station: WJRJ, Channel 17 in Atlanta. What would become Superstation WTBS didn't look so super just then. "We were certain Ted had gone crazy this time," said Turner's accountant. "That TV station was hemorrhaging, and we could see the whole company being pulled down with it." The headquarters of WJRJ occupied a run-down cinder-block building on West Peachtree Street and a slightly more kempt brick building next door. The only impressive part of the complex was the 1000-foot transmission tower that soared above the studio and offices. In winter employees discovered why most cities insist on situating such structures outside the populated districts: Ice bombs would separate from the steel girding at altitude and explode on the ground below. The company kept hard hats, and the staff used them. "We'd put on the helmets and sprint to our cars," explained a survivor. One night Turner, after fortifying himself with some spirited antifreeze, accepted a dare to climb the mast. Two hours later he returned to the ground, claiming victory; in the darkness no one could gainsay his achievement.

Making money with Channel 17 (which Turner initially rechristened WTCG, for Turner Communications Group or, as he preferred it, "Watch This Channel Grow") promised to be an equally singular achievement. Turner agreed that he had picked a loser. "The station was really at death's door," he conceded. Nor was proximity to that final portal the worst of the problems. "I didn't know anything about TV."

Yet he learned as he went, and he made the best of his bad situation. WTCG was a UHF station (as opposed to the VHF of its principal competitors), and being such, it required a certain skill on the part of viewers to receive a strong signal. Turner used to boast to advertisers about the intelligence of his audience. How did he know they were so smart? the advertisers asked. "Because you've got to be smart to figure out how to tune in a UHF station in the first place," he answered. "Dumb guys can't do it. Can you get Channel 17? No? Well, neither can I. We aren't smart enough. But my viewers are."

There were five television stations in Atlanta: the three network affiliates, Turner's Channel 17 and one other independent. The other independent looked more prosperous than Channel 17—not a difficult task, to be sure—yet suddenly it went out of business. Although Turner was as surprised as anyone, he didn't miss a beat. He proudly announced that Channel 17 had moved from fifth in the rankings to fourth, and he publicly thanked Atlanta for this vote of confidence.

True to his billboard roots, Turner never lost sight that his broadcast ventures were primarily vehicles for selling advertising space. Programming on Channel 17 featured whatever was cheap, typically reruns of situation comedies and old movies. The Federal Communications Commissions required television stations to run at least forty minutes of news per day; Turner hewed to the minimum—and often aired that at three o'clock in the morning, when no one would notice that Channel 17's news consisted chiefly of wire-service reports and send-ups of what the real reporters for the real television stations did for news. Before long Turner would revolutionize television news, but for now his motto was "No news is good news."

Since David Sarnoff had knitted together the NBC network in the 1920s, the foremost method of transmitting television signals to distant markets was by land lines, typically leased from AT&T. More recently microwaves had come into use; these obviated user charges to the telephone trust but required the expensive construction of microwave towers every twenty miles or so across the countryside. In the mid-1970s television entered the space age. Western Union and RCA launched satellites that could relay signals from a station in any one part of the country to other stations in the rest of the country. From the receiving stations the signals went out, usually via cable, to individual viewers.

Turner at once recognized the satellite revolution for what it was. "Sid," he told Sidney Topol, whose company sold satellite-transmission technology, "I want to buy an uplink. Send a salesman over and I'll get you a check." Topol was pleasantly surprised that Turner didn't seem to care about the price of a transmitter (around three-quarters of a million dollars); Turner's chief financial officer, Will Sanders, was neither surprised nor pleased. "He was always playing 'You Bet Your Company,'" Sanders said. "Every project he took on had the potential to sink him. No sooner did you feel like you were comfortable and able to breathe a little bit than we'd take on some other impossible task."

Whatever the cost, a satellite link would give Turner a national presence at a small fraction of the cost the networks were paying. In those days of strict federal regulation, gaining FCC approval for his satellite venture required considerable persuasion and no little time, but on December 17, 1976, WTCG began bouncing its signals off RCA's Satcom I satellite. On that same day the telephone receptionist at Channel 17 started answering calls with a boast that already was being made good: "The superstation that serves the nation."

Just *what* the superstation served the nation posed Turner's next problem. It wasn't going to be news. "We're essentially an escapist station," Turner had said, and he hadn't changed his mind. To the continuing diet of stale sitcoms Turner added an increasing mix of movies—which he bought rather than rented, so he could recycle them as often as he wanted. "I've got more movies on my shelves than I could play in a hundred years," lamented WTCG's general manager.

Turner also increased his coverage of that other great escape of American viewers: sports. Televising the Atlanta Braves baseball team made perfect sense for an Atlanta station. At least it had in 1973 when Turner paid $1.3 million for the right to broadcast three years of their games. But Brave though the players may have been, they weren't talented, and the owners were at a loss—a seven-figure loss—as to what to do. "Dial-a-Prayer was busy," reported the sports columnist for the *Atlanta Constitution*, "so Bob Hope of the Atlanta Braves called our sports department. When a sports publicity man starts counting on sportswriters for friendly words, it's obvious absolutely nothing is going right in his life. Indeed, Hope has to earn his daily bread selling the Braves to a populace so hostile it seems ready to storm the stadium to burn it down in protest—if anybody would ever go near the place."

The Braves' owners were obviously interested in selling; certain groups—notably a Toronto consortium that wanted to take the team north—were interested in buying. Turner didn't care much about baseball beyond the fact that it filled hundreds of hours of programming time—and that it wouldn't do so if the team left town.

Consequently, to protect his television investment Turner became a sports owner. Once again he saw a synergy he couldn't resist. As one of his close associates explained: "There are 162 games [in a baseball season]. They're three-and-a-half hours long. And by the time you do the pregame and the locker-room show and everything, you're talking about a four-hour show times 162. You'd have to lose a lot of money in sports to offset what it would cost to buy that amount of programming."

Although Turner took his usual buy-it-or-else strategy into negotiations for the team—"He gets to a point," Will Sanders said diplomatically, "where he doesn't negotiate very carefully or thoroughly and leaves too much on the table"—he cut what proved, after the fact, to be a good deal. The team turned out to have more cash on hand than Turner put down.

"So I bought it using its own money," he congratulated himself. And what he bought for less than $10 million appreciated perhaps twenty times over the next two decades.

If Turner was an unlikely baseball owner, he was an even more improbable impresario of all-news television. Turner may or may not have been the best witness on the subject when he later said: "I came up with the concept for Cable News Network even before the superstation was up on the satellite, because business is like a chess game and you have to look several moves ahead. . . . It was clear that after the superstation the next important service to the cable industry would be a twenty-four-hour news channel." Whether or not this was clear to Turner, it wasn't clear to most cable operators that he—the no-news-is-good-news man—was the person to pull it off.

The model for all-news television was all-news radio, which had done well in assorted markets for some time. But television news was inherently and considerably more expensive than radio news—at least if done right rather than in the lowball WTCG fashion. This was what had enabled the networks to maintain their tripoly. Turner, however, realized that satellite technology altered the equation critically. For a modest amount a broadcaster could now reach a national audience, one large enough to generate the advertising revenues necessary to support a credible news-gathering organization.

Of course the ad dollars wouldn't start flowing in until the news delivered the audience. Turner, guessing, calculated that it would cost him $15 to $20 million in start-up and maybe $2 million a month in operating expenses—a total of as much as $100 million—before ad revenues and cable subscriptions balanced outlays.

As before, Turner's boldness exceeded his expertise. He asked Reese Schonfeld, who subsequently became president of CNN, for recommendations on a news anchor for the network. Schonfeld suggested Dan Rather, the heir apparent—apparent to everyone besides Turner, that is—to Walter Cronkite at CBS. "Who's Dan Rather?" responded Turner.

Turner didn't get Rather, but he did get Daniel Schorr, formerly of CBS, and sundry other second-stringers. Getting space on RCA's satellite for the necessary relay equipment proved more challenging. As the parent of NBC, David Sarnoff's old company had a vested interest in not cooperating with Turner's brainstorm. RCA's engineers and lawyers claimed technical and legal difficulties in providing the service CNN needed; Turner perceived a preemptive effort to crush competition.

He fought back with his customary energy. "He went nuts on them," recalled Terry McGuirk, a Channel Seventeener who later became president of Turner Sports, and who accompanied his boss to a crucial meeting with representatives of RCA's satellite subsidiary. "He said, 'All you guys, get out of here! I want the chairman of the overall parent corporation down here, right now, because I'm going to break this company into so many small pieces that all of you will be looking for jobs!'"

An RCA lawyer present declined to be provoked. He told Turner that the language of the relevant contracts was clear; RCA didn't have to give CNN a satellite slot. And RCA wouldn't. Turner would just have to live with that fact.

Turner refused, almost violently. Reminding all present that he had put everything he owned into CNN, he spat out—through the celebrated gap in his front teeth—that he might go down, but he'd take RCA down with him. "I may be a small company, and you guys may put me out of business. But for every drop of blood I shed, you will shed a barrel."

Turner started the bloodletting at once. He sued RCA for breach of contract; meanwhile he took his case to the court of public opinion. Making the same sort of populist argument David Sarnoff had used on behalf of RCA's version of color TV, but now *against* Sarnoff's company, Turner contended that he was fighting for the rights of the little guy against the corporate behemoths. "I think the people of America need this in-depth news service, and I've been willing all along to risk everything I have to provide that service. And we're going to provide it." The only thing he required was a fair field; should CNN win that, the American people would benefit far into the future. "Barring satellite problems, we won't be signing off until the world ends. We'll be on, and we will *cover* the end of the world, *live*, and that will be our last event. We'll play the National Anthem only one time, on the first of June [the scheduled starting date], and when the end of the world comes we'll play 'Nearer My God to Thee' before we sign off."

Turner eventually got his satellite space, although not without fomenting considerable ill will toward CNN. At 6 PM on June 1 Turner declared:

> To act upon one's convictions while others wait;
> To create a positive force in a world where cynics abound;
> To provide information to people when it wasn't available before;
> To offer those who want it a choice . . .
> I dedicate the News Channel for America—the Cable News Network.

A military band played the National Anthem. As the "home of the brave" died away, Turner let out the same sort of whoop he had perfected at the home of the Braves, and the news began—not to end, per Turner's promise, until the world did.

The new network had to overcome its share of technical difficulties; it also had to surmount a more fundamental philosophical and economic challenge. The essence of news reporting was to summarize noteworthy events; were there really enough noteworthy events to sustain a round-the-clock summary? And if there were, did CNN have the money to pay for it? CNN had budgeted $30 million annually for news; the networks spent $100 to $150 million to fill less than one-tenth the air time.

The answer to these questions came in two parts. On the very first evening of broadcast—in the first half-hour, in fact—President Jimmy Carter gave an extemporaneous address from the hospital where civil rights leader Vernon Jordan was recuperating from a gunshot wound. The networks taped the appearance for later broadcast, but CNN interrupted a commercial and its regular program to carry the president live. Carter's visit to Jordan made for good Democratic politics; it made for even better CNN business. From the very outset the network began changing the way audiences conceived of the news. As practiced by CNN the news became less and less a summary of events that had already happened than a window on events that were still happening. To be sure, CNN broadcasts carried their share of recycled stories and nonstories ("Mount St. Helens has its first quiet Sunday . . ."), but viewers caught on that for breaking stories, CNN was the station to turn to.

There was a reason the networks hadn't been providing this coverage: It was unthinkably expensive to have crews ready for all contingencies. Turner and CNN got around the problem—and answered the question of how they were going to pay for their news coverage—by relying on the television equivalent of newspaper stringers. The evolution of television technology increasingly enabled local stations to cover local events in the same fashion as the national networks; Turner and CNN arranged reciprocal agreements with these stations whereby they would provide footage of breaking news in their regions to CNN in exchange for CNN's footage of news elsewhere. The networks already provided footage to their affiliates, but only on the networks' terms and generally after running the best segments on their own evening news shows. Because CNN used its material at once, it could turn that material around to the local stations almost immediately without preempting itself.

The formula was solid—but there remained considerable question whether Turner had enough money to hold out until all the pieces fell into place. At the end of 1980 CNN counted 663 participating cable services reaching 4.3 million homes. CNN's share of cable charges amounted to seventeen cents per subscriber per month; the rest of its revenue came from advertising. For the first seven months of broadcasting the network sold less than $4 million in commercials, meaning that Turner was losing roughly $2 million per month.

Costs grew as Turner added news-gathering capacity, but subscriptions and ad revenues looked likely to grow faster, raising company hopes that the network might break even by the end of 1981. Yet where Turner had pioneered, others appeared likely to follow. The major television networks, with their in-place programming infrastructure, could expand their news at modest cost. The satellite companies could undercut him on transmission. Moreover, any really big company could almost certainly outlast CNN in a war of attrition. Already industry scuttlebutt suggested that ABC was planning its own cable news service. At about the same time Westinghouse was said to be approaching the news business from the outer-space end. In August 1981 the two rumor streams converged when ABC and Westinghouse announced a joint venture in direct opposition to CNN.

Turner responded with characteristic audacity. Even as CNN had been draining his bank account he had been pondering putting up a second news network. He asked himself—and his CNN associates—what form the inevitable competition would take. Where was CNN most vulnerable? The consensus answered that something on the order of a CNN-Lite, a headline news service, would give the company the most trouble. The ABC/Westinghouse venture appeared to involve just such an approach, in addition to a fuller format; one or both would begin airing in the spring or summer of 1982. Turner immediately responded that he would launch a new network of his own in December 1981. "We're going to do our *own* headline service," he declared. "We're going to offer everything they say *they* are going to offer, except that ours will be on the air *first* and it will be *better*." Employing typically Turneresque logic, he explained, "They have only money to lose, but we have *everything* to lose."

Privately Turner described certain advantages he carried into what was quickly dubbed the "cable war."

> I figured, knowing they were two big companies and that they were both public corporations, and how slow those kinds of operations usually run, that if their losses were bigger than anticipated, the people in charge of this project would come under criticism. . . . And I knew that if they ran into unanticipated difficulties there would be friction between the two fifty-fifty partners.

You're much better off competing against a split command than against a single command because split commands spend a lot of time trying to figure out what to do and so it's easy for them to get into an argument. I find that partnerships work okay when things are going well, but they are put under a great deal of strain when things don't go as anticipated.

So even though we were very, very strapped financially, and they knew it, I decided that we would beat them to the market. We would split the market for that service, so they would not be as viable. I didn't know exactly how long we could last. I think the two of them had resources a hundred times greater than mine. I did know that in a war of attrition we'd lose.

For public consumption Turner vowed to fight to the bitter end. "The only way they're going to rid of me," he vowed, "is to put a bullet through me."

Again assuming the role of the underdog, Turner claimed to speak for the upstart cable industry against the entrenched networks. To a gathering of cable operators he read a quote attributed to an executive of the ABC/Westinghouse consortium: "The days of Mr. Turner's clear sailing are over." Turner shouted his scorn: "Clear sailing, my ass! I'm losing a million a month!" He damned ABC for an egregious conflict of interest, as evidenced by ABC news head Roone Arledge's own admission that the best stories would be reserved to ABC News rather than released to the joint venture. Turner concluded, "Anybody who goes with them is going with a second-rate, horseshit operation!"

The ABC/Westinghouse group declined to get in a shouting match with Turner, instead opting to compete on price. Initially they said they would distribute their news service for free (prompting a CNN executive to mutter, "I'd call them whores but even whores don't give it away for free"). As the competition grew more intense they went beyond free to paying cable operators fifty cents per subscriber to take the service.

Turner pushed more chips into the pot. The startup costs for CNN2 ran to nearly $20 million, the operating costs to $1.5 million per month. Through the first half of 1983 the industry watched to see which side would collapse first.

In the end Turner's prediction about the problems of running a war with other people's money proved out. Turner, who at this time owned eighty-seven percent of the stock of Turner Broadcasting, answered only to himself; the management of ABC and Westinghouse answered to all those shareholders who wanted to know why they were throwing $50 million away on this quixotic adventure. When Turner offered to bail them out for

$25 million, they accepted with relief. CNN2's president Ted Kavanau was equally relieved, albeit for a different reason. "My feeling was that their product was first rate, and if they had not been so afraid they probably would have succeeded." Kavanau read a moral into the story: "It just demonstrated what an entrepreneur like Turner could do against a corporate bureaucracy. They were a bunch of frightened guys. They blinked and folded." *Time* magazine summarized the outcome of the battle more succinctly: "David conquered Goliath with his checkbook."

After closing the doors on his new acquisition (whose anchor signed off on October 27, 1983, with the usual "That's it for now," then added, "In fact, that's it, period. And now, Ted buddy, it's in your hands!") David went after an even bigger target. In April 1985 Turner announced an unsolicited bid to acquire CBS. Since the late 1970s the rules regulating broadcasting had fallen substantially by the airwayside; during that same era the art of the hostile takeover had been honed by the genius of the junk bond, Michael Milken, and other heirs to the legacy of Jay Gould. In March 1985 Capital Cities acquired ABC; when the Justice Department yawned, Wall Street surmised that the federal chaperones who had once so closely guarded the virtue of the media were willing to let the markets value said virtue.

Even by the high standards of that period, Turner's bid for CBS strained credulity. The Turner Broadcasting System had revenues of less than $300 million; CBS, although struggling of late, brought in nearly $5 billion. The 31 million CBS shares were selling for about $110 each; Turner was offering $175 in stock and junk bonds. One industry analyst called Turner's offer a "joke," while another asserted that "the probability is zero that Ted Turner will end up with CBS." A different view came from, of all places, the Soviet foreign ministry. Turner had spent some time in Moscow and had impressed his hosts, one of whom had been stationed in Washington for eight years, where he gained additional perspective on this quintessential capitalist. The diplomat warned Ed Joyce of CBS: "Don't underestimate this Turner. Remember, the Bolsheviks were a small group, and they took over an entire country."

In fact Turner wasn't about to take over either a country or CBS. The big network lobbied hard in Washington and Albany to block Turner's bid; more effectively it swallowed a "poison pill" of nearly $1 billion in debt to buy back twenty percent of its stock. "This kills Turner's existing bid," declared an analyst who had been following the maneuverings. "It's dead in the water."

And so it was. Yet what many observers marked down as an extravagant display of hubris—the takeover effort cost TBS nearly $19 million—in fact proved to be money well spent. Merely by threatening to absorb William Paley's creation Turner established himself as a media force. Before long opportunities were looking for *him* rather than vice versa.

The most significant of these involved Metro-Goldwyn-Mayer, the grand old Hollywood studio. Kirk Kerkorian had bought into MGM in the 1970s, and into United Artists a few years later; now the veteran dealmaker wanted to talk about a deal with TBS. Turner may have entertained notions of becoming a movie mogul, but what he really wanted was to become a movie *librarian*—that is, to gain control of the thousands of movies in the MGM/UA library. Rising rental rates were eating into the profits of the Superstation. "Every time we signed a new movie contract," he explained, "it cost us more." Prices of alternative programming were rising as well; sitcoms could run upwards of $300,000 per half hour to produce.

Acquiring those old movies involved Turner in the most complicated transaction of his career. Michael Milken and Drexel Burnham Lambert engineered the deal with an offering of junk bonds that had to be sold to investors expensively skeptical that Turner could carry the debt his purchase entailed. Events proved the skeptics right, and Turner had to unload large parts of his purchase within months, even selling most of the physical assets of MGM back to Kerkorian for much less than he—Turner—had paid for them. "Ted Turner came to town fully clothed and left in a barrel," said one analyst. In effect Turner wound up paying $1.2 billion for the MGM film library, a figure conventional wisdom placed at perhaps twenty percent too high.

Turner realized he had paid too much, but better that, he judged, than letting the deal slip away. He once explained his fundamental philosophy in a sentence: "The game I'm in is building assets, and I've never minded overpaying if I know the values are there."

Of course, whether the values *were* there depended on what the buyer could make of them. In Turner's case the MGM library of nearly 3500 films formed the basis for a new network. Where WTBS, by now the most popular cable network, would stick to its reruns, and CNN and Headline News to their breaking stories, Turner Network Television (more explosively: TNT) would concentrate on quality entertainment: classic movies, championship sporting events, the best of made-for-TV films. Fittingly Turner launched TNT in October 1988 with a showing of *Gone with the Wind*. The new network was box-office boffo, starting with 17 million subscribers and topping 50 million within the first year. All of a sudden the MGM deal that had seemed such a loser just two years earlier now appeared a brilliant strategic move. If Turner had paid more than anyone else was willing to pay for those old movies, he also knew how to make more money from them than anyone else did.

In fact, however, those old movies had cost Turner more than their purchase price. Staggering under the burden of his movie-buy—interest on the debt absorbed more than a third of TBS revenues—Turner sought relief by relinquishing a large measure of control. A consortium of cable operators purchased a 37 percent stake in TBS for $562.5 million. This left Turner with a majority of the shares, but barely: 51 percent. In addition, one strand of the rescue rope required Turner to agree to a limit of $2 million that he could spend without receiving approval from twelve of the fifteen members of the board of directors.

Needless to say, this arrangement severely constrained Turner's swashbuckling style. Gerry Hogan, who had been with Turner from the early days, asked retrospectively, "How could we at Turner live with those guys? How could they be our customers and yet be our shareholders?" Relations at first proved difficult. "The board was clearly operating with another agenda," Hogan said. "Their agenda was, 'What's good for the cable industry.'" Yet it didn't take long for the two sides—the cable operators and Turner—to recognize the mutuality of substantial portions of their interests. Hogan explained later, "What's good for the cable industry has been good for Turner and vice versa."

The numbers certainly suggested as much. By the end of 1989 the four networks of TBS claimed nearly one-third of all cable viewers. The company was worth more than $5 billion. CNN, the jewel in the Turner crown, was watched in eighty-nine countries around the world, and had an operating profit of $85 million.

The tumultuous world events of the late 1980s and the 1990s simply added to the luster of CNN. The Tiananmen Square demonstrations and massacre of the spring of 1989 riveted viewers worldwide to CNN, which stuck with the story longer than its network rivals. "Karl Marx, meet Marshall McLuhan," said *Newsweek* of the immediacy of the coverage. The collapse of the Berlin Wall five months later brought home—literally, to CNN viewers—the manner in which real-time coverage of breaking events altered not only perceptions of those events but the events themselves. So did the U.S. invasion of Panama at the end of 1989, which provoked a sharp Soviet response delivered not by the traditional methods but via CNN. The *Wall Street Journal* was prompted to remark: "Who needs striped pants and diplomatic pouches? When world leaders want to talk to each other these days, they call CNN."

They continued to do so in subsequent crises. Saddam Hussein employed CNN to conduct much of what passed for Iraqi diplomacy during the Persian Gulf crisis and war of 1990–1991; George Bush later said that he learned more from CNN than from his own intelligence services. Rival CBS paid Ted Turner a similar grudging compliment. "What CBS did during the Gulf War," explained a CBS military analyst, "was watch CNN."

So did Boris Yeltsin, who several months later relied on CNN to stop a generals' coup in Moscow. As Russia's nascent democracy hung in the balance, Yeltsin climbed atop one of the tanks surrounding government headquarters, knowing CNN would get his image of defiance out to the rest of the world, which it did. In the glare of the international spotlight the coup melted away.

CNN's stunning success won Ted Turner applause from far beyond the business community. *Time* magazine named him "man of the year" for 1991, calling him a "visionary" and the "prince of the global village," who had redefined news "from something that has happened to something that is happening at the very moment you are hearing it." *Time* went on: "A war involving the fiercest air bombardment in history unfolded in real time—before the cameras. The motherland of communism overthrew its leaders and their doctrine—before the cameras. To a considerable degree, especially in Moscow, momentous things happened precisely because they were being seen as they happened."

Not everyone was so enamored of Ted Turner—and some of those who weren't spied cynicism, or at least self-interest, in *Time*'s gushing over him. Following the 1987 rescue of TBS (and the subsequent marriage of Time and Warner), Time Warner was a leading shareholder in TBS. The *Village Voice* wryly observed that the boost to TBS shares consequent to Turner's cover-boy treatment by *Time* netted the magazine's parent company a paper profit of $50 million.

The connection drew tighter. Still burdened by debt, yet convinced that the only way to survive in the modern media era was to grow, Turner cast about for partners. He spoke with Jack Welch of General Electric, who pitched the savings that would follow a merger between TBS and GE's NBC. Rupert Murdoch of News Corp. and Fox Television was said to have offered to let Turner write his own ticket in a merger.

But in the end Turner entered the embrace of Time Warner. In September 1995 the boards of the two companies announced that Time

Warner would purchase TBS. "Ted is clearly one of the most brilliant entrepreneurs of our time," said Time Warner chairman Gerald Levin. "We enthusiastically welcome Ted and his team to our family." The merger would leave Levin as chairman; Turner would become vice chairman. This arrangement raised eyebrows among those who wondered how well Turner would take orders. Turner, who in 1991 had married actress Jane Fonda, dismissed the doubts with a shrug and a joke. "I've been a CEO for thirty-three years and that's a long time for anyone," he said. "I'm married to Jane Fonda, so I know what it's like to be number two." To a reporter who brought up some past difficulties between TBS and Time Warner, Turner replied, "Now I'm Ted Time Warner. Hey, let's get the cash flow up, the stock price up, and live together happily ever after."

Regardless of Turner's view of the situation, observers noted that this new vice chairman wasn't an ordinary employee. "People who are billionaires are not employees," observed a former Turner associate. "They don't think like employees." This was especially true when the billionaire in question was also the largest shareholder in the corporation, which Turner was with more than 11 percent of Time Warner.

Turner soon began acting more like a billionaire and a major owner than hired help. "A lot of people expected Mr. Turner would ride off into the sunset after he sold his Turner Broadcasting System Inc. to Time Warner," remarked the *Wall Street Journal*. "Instead, he is off on a wild ride through the world's biggest media empire, crashing into top executives' personal fiefdoms, abruptly canceling deals, asking impertinent questions about lavish expenses, and generally giving Time Warner a one-man dose of culture shock."

One of the Time Warnerites Turner crossed had just completed a fat deal with CBS to sell that network a $50-million package of Time Warner movies. Turner demanded to know why CBS, rather than TNT or another Turner network, was getting those films. "We're family!" he shouted. The executive requested time to arrange a compromise with CBS and hinted that it would be imprudent to jeopardize Time Warner's relationship with that network. According to company sources who couldn't help eavesdropping on Turner's high-decibel end of the conversation, the new vice chairman hollered: "Who would you rather jeopardize your relationship with? A client or an 11 percent shareholder?"

Fortunately for Turner's new family, he found some outsiders to keep his wrath occupied. He got into a public row with Sumner Redstone, chairman of Viacom Inc., over Viacom's alleged neglect of Comedy Central, a television property it jointly owned with Time Warner. Turner claimed that Redstone was letting Comedy Central languish lest it compete with Viacom's MTV networks. "He will neither buy nor sell nor change, so it sits there where it is," Turner said. Redstone responded that Turner misremembered a crucial conversation: "Mr. Turner must have been at a different lunch or perhaps a different planet."

Turner's tiff with Redstone, however, was a love fest next to his brawl with Rupert Murdoch. Rumor-mongers rooted the Turner–Murdoch rivalry in the 1970s when the Australian tycoon was said to have fired some symbolic shots across the bow of Captain Ted's *Courageous* (which Turner guided to victory in the 1977 America's Cup). Whether true or not, those rumors contributed to the substantive quarrel that surrounded their business competition. Turner long complained that Murdoch blocked CNN's access to satellites necessary to penetrate the Asian market; Murdoch contended that the Time Warner–TBS deal would restrain competition in the United States. On this ground he sued to prevent consummation of the deal. When the suit failed, Turner responded by persuading Time Warner to keep Murdoch's Fox News channel off the Time Warner cable system that served the New York City market. As both men appreciated, this prevented the key advertising executives who lived in New York from watching Murdoch's competitor to CNN.

Murdoch struck back on several media fronts. When Turner's old, and Time Warner's new, Atlanta Braves came to Yankee Stadium, an airplane hired by Fox News hauled a banner overhead saying, "Hey Ted. Be Brave. Don't Censor the Fox News Channel." When the Braves made the World Series, Fox cameramen initially avoided shots of Turner in the grandstand, creating what sportswriters dubbed a "no-Ted zone." Murdoch's *New York Post* ran a photo from Jane Fonda's controversial 1972 trip to Hanoi alongside a reminder of an earlier exposure of the actress as *Barbarella* and called her "just another scatty-brained Hollywood nude-nik." Some years earlier Turner had been diagnosed with a form of manic-depressive disorder. This diagnosis apparently explained some of his more mercurial behavior; it also prompted him to take lithium to mitigate the mood swings. Now it provided the basis for a jibe by a News Corp. executive, who asserted, "Ted must be off his lithium again." A *Post* headline was hardly more delicate: "Is Ted Turner Nuts? You Decide."

Turner gave as good—or bad—as he got. He called Murdoch a "shlockmeister" and a "pretty slimy character." He compared Murdoch to Adolf Hitler, saying that "like the late Führer he controls the media for his own personal benefit." At one point he half-jokingly challenged Murdoch to a boxing match. "It would be like *Rocky*, only for old guys," he said. "If he wants, he can wear head gear. I won't."

In other respects Turner was mellowing, albeit after his own fashion. The Goodwill Games, a Turner brainchild conceived in the mid-1980s as a counter-Cold-War alternative to the Olympic Games, which had lately suffered from sequential superpower boycotts, continued to claim his attention and resources. Another gesture on behalf of world peace was even grander. In September 1997 he announced a gift of $1 billion to the United Nations. He explained the amount to CNN interviewer Larry King (keeping the coverage in house, as he had with the first two iterations of the Goodwill Games): "A billion is a good round number." He didn't profess any sophisticated understanding of the U.N.'s mission. "One for all, all for one," he said simply. "I kind of like that idea."

Recently Turner had criticized certain fellow billionaires—conspicuously Microsoft's Bill Gates—for not making the best use of their wealth. Now he issued a direct challenge to Gates and the others to match what he was doing: "I'm putting every rich person in the world on notice." He pointed out that generosity didn't have to hurt. His own net worth had grown from $2.2 billion to $3.2 billion since the first of that year, largely on the increase in the value of his Time Warner stock. Easy come, easy go. "I'm not poorer than I was nine months ago, and the world is a lot better off."

Skeptics on the subject of Turner interpreted this gesture as a latest bit of showboating, something to keep the spotlight shining his way. Kindlier souls detected an admirable emulation of the philanthropy of Carnegie and Rockefeller—made particularly fitting by the fact that the man who had done more than anyone else to shrink the world to the size of a television screen was accepting significant responsibility for the world's welfare. The prince of the global village was dipping into his treasury to improve life in villages around the globe.

Was this Turner's swan song? He suggested not. "I've still got two billion left," he said. "Maybe I can make some more and give some more away later."

The world would be watching—probably on CNN.

23

THE CELEBRITY AS
ENTREPRENEUR

Oprah Winfrey

. . .

TED TURNER WELL UNDERSTOOD THE VALUE OF CELEBRITY IN promoting his business endeavors; whether as Captain Outrageous, the big chief of the Atlanta Braves, Mr. Jane Fonda or the billionaire who bailed out the U.N., Turner appreciated that in the media business there is no such thing as overexposure.

But compared to Oprah Winfrey, Turner was a tyro. The foundation of Turner's success was the media product he delivered, most notably the programming of his networks; his celebrity was always incidental to that. By contrast, Winfrey's celebrity *was* her product; the media was simply the packaging. Winfrey was hardly the first person to become rich for being famous; her contribution to modern capitalism lay in neither her fame nor her wealth but in the entrepreneurial instincts she brought to the conversion of the former into the latter. She was a star; she became an industry.

As befit a star she hit the stage young. She was named "Orpah" after the biblical character, but "Oprah" was what people mistakenly started calling her and the name stuck. Raised by her grandmother when her single mother joined the postwar migration from the rural South to the industrial North, she spent her first six years in Kosciusko, Mississippi (named for the Polish freedom fighter of the American Revolution but pronounced locally as "kosy-ESS-ko). "Momma," as the little girl came to call her grandmother, swung a mean switch. "Those were the days when people whipped you because they could," she recalled later. "You got a

292

whipping because you got on somebody's nerves." That her grandmother claimed love prompted the beatings didn't cut much ice with the recipient then or later. "Our prisons are filled with older men who, as young men, had the living hell beat out of them," Winfrey explained. "Every parent who beat them said, 'I'm doing this because I love you.' When my grandmother used to whip my behind, she'd say, 'I'm doing this because I love you.' And I'd want to say, 'If you loved me, you'd get that switch off my butt.' I still don't think that was love."

This harsh treatment later became an item of some importance in Winfrey's career; yet even as she wished Momma would have spared the rod she acknowledged her debt to that tough old woman. "You know," she said, "I am what I am today because of my grandmother: my strength, my sense of reasoning, everything, all of that, was set by the time I was six years old."

Also by the time she was six years old, Oprah had been performing for years. It started in church when she was three

> They'd put me up on the program, and they would say, "And Little Mistress Winfrey will render a recitation," and I would do "Jesus rose on Easter Day; Hallelujah, Hallelujah, all the angels did proclaim."
>
> And all the sisters sitting in the front row would fan themselves and turn to my grandmother and say, "Ida Mae, this child is gifted."

Oprah started to think so too. "I didn't even know what 'gifted' meant, but I just thought it meant I was special." She continued to act special.

> By the time I was seven, I was doing "Invictus" by William Ernest Henley: "Out of the night that covers me, black as a pit from pole to pole, I thank whatever gods there be for my unconquerable soul." And at the time I was saying it, I didn't know what I was talking about, but I'd do all the motions— "O-u-t of the night that covers me"—and people would say, "Whew! That child can speak."

At eight Oprah took her talents to Nashville where she moved in with her father. She began speaking in various churches in the Tennessee capital; popular favorites included her youthful renditions of a series of sermons by James Weldon Johnson that told the story of God and man in seven parts, starting with the Creation and ending with the Last Judgment. On one occasion the congregation was so appreciative that she received $500 for her performance.

In high school she naturally found her way to the speech and drama clubs; her gift of tongue brought her into contact with an ever-widening circle. A trip to California to address church groups allowed a visit to Hollywood. "Daddy," she said on her return, "I got down on my knees there and ran my hand along all those stars on the street and I said to myself, 'One day I'm going to put my own star among those stars.'" At seventeen she received an invitation from President Richard Nixon to attend a White House-sponsored conference on youth; the gathering brought her into contact not only with other talented teens but with some 500 adult business leaders. Election as president of the student council and selection as most popular girl capped her high school career.

During her senior year, while pounding the pavement for the March of Dimes, Winfrey wandered into the office of Nashville radio station WVOL. She got the pledge she wanted; she also got a job offer. Her presence and voice impressed one of the disk jockeys, who asked if she was interested in weekend work. She was.

Winfrey soon pushed the door open further. "She was aggressive," recalled one of her coworkers. "Not at all shy. She knew where she was going." Shortly after she started at WVOL the station manager's house burned down. Although the local fire department failed to save the structure, the manager so appreciated the efforts of the fire fighters that he decided to have the station participate in the Miss Fire Prevention Contest; he tapped Winfrey as the station's nominee. Game for anything that might move her ahead, Winfrey accepted the nomination and won the contest. As was the custom at such events, the judges asked her what she intended as a career. Initially she had thought "school teacher" sounded like an appealing answer, but at the last moment she decided on "journalist." And what kind of journalist?, she was asked. Her knowledge of journalism was no greater than most teenagers', but that morning she had seen Barbara Walters on television, and so she said she wanted to be like Barbara Walters.

Walters continued to serve as a role model, or perhaps a prop. At nineteen, after enrolling at Tennessee State University in Nashville (where she found time to win the Miss Black Tennessee title), Winfrey applied for a job with WTV-TV, Nashville's CBS affiliate. The station was looking for a weekend anchor and ideally would have wanted someone with a bit more experience and maturity than Winfrey; but the news director decided to give her an audition. "I was such a nervous wreck," Winfrey said afterward.

I had no idea what to do or say. And I thought in my head that maybe I'll just pretend I'm Barbara Walters. I will sit like Barbara. I will hold my head like Barbara. So I crossed my legs at the ankles, and I put my little finger under my chin, and I leaned across the desk, and I pretended to be Barbara Walters.

She failed in her impersonation; the news director subsequently said he had no idea that she was trying to emulate Walters. But he liked Winfrey and hired her. She became both the first female co-anchor in Nashville and the first black co-anchor there. Although Winfrey recognized that demographics entered into the decision, she wasn't finicky. "I was a token," she said later. "But I was a happy, paid token." (Her boss put it slightly differently. "I hired you because you were a reporter," he told her later. "But I did need a black reporter.")

Winfrey's on-air partner had never shared the camera, and he required some winning over. It didn't take long. "She was a natural, completely at ease in front of the camera," he recollected. "She was the kind of person who, if she messed up, would laugh at herself. She had a voice that was unlike anything else in the South. Southerners, whether they be black or white, tend to have a dialect and a whole different sound from the rest of the country. With Oprah, there was nothing of that."

On the strength of her weekend performance Winfrey was soon promoted to the nightly news. Viewers found her engaging; so did the ABC affiliate in Baltimore. ABC had just hired Barbara Walters away from NBC for a million dollars a year; the Walters effect spilled down the food chain to the affiliates. WJZ-TV in Baltimore, like many other local stations, was moving from thirty minutes to an hour for the nightly news; Winfrey was offered a job as part of an expansion and diversification of the news team.

Paired with a local fixture often described as the Walter Cronkite of Baltimore, Winfrey soon discovered that she wasn't quite ready for prime time. Baltimore was a tough town and a tough television market; after a big publicity buildup (billboards asking "What's an Oprah?" invited Baltimore to tune in and find out) she didn't draw viewers the way she had in Nashville. "I needed to do a lot of growing," she conceded afterward. "I was twenty-two when I came here and sitting down with the god of local anchormen intimidated me."

The other problem was that hard news wasn't really her genre, as she discovered on the beat. She found it nearly impossible to keep the requisite distance from her stories. Assigned to cover a fire, she was supposed to interview a mother who had just lost her children. The woman, not surprisingly, didn't feel like talking to a stranger with a microphone and a camera, and Winfrey wasn't inclined to press her. But her bosses insisted and, against her better judgment, she went ahead. Predictably her ambivalence showed; afterward she apologized to the distraught woman. She never managed to get past this emotional connection to her subjects. "You're at a plane crash and you're standing right there and you're smelling the charred bodies," she said by way of explaining her situation, "and people are coming to find out if their relatives are in the crash and they're weeping, and you weep too because it's a tragic thing."

Fortunately for Winfrey a new manager at the station figured out how to make a virtue of her reportorial shortcomings. The nationally syndicated "Donahue" talk show had won a large following in Baltimore; the manager wanted to tap the same market with a local version. In 1977 "People Are Talking" went on the air with Winfrey as cohost. Precisely the same qualities of empathy that made her a weepy reporter made her an instant success as a talk-show host. "I came off the air," she said of her first show, "and I knew that was what I was supposed to be doing. It felt just like breathing. It was the most natural process for me."

"People Are Talking" raced up the rating charts; shortly it bumped "Donahue" to become the leading show in its category in the Baltimore market. A morning program, it grew so popular that WJZ began repeating the broadcasts in the evening. For a time the show was syndicated and replayed in other cities. This particular syndication failed to take—which wasn't surprising, given the show's local orientation—but for the first time it brought Winfrey to an at-least-semi-national audience.

She reveled in the spotlight. "I'm just a show-biz kid," she once said. And she did best when the spotlight singled her out. Although she and her cohost on "People Are Talking" professed nothing but respect for each other, after a time it became clear that he was crimping her style. Consequently when a station in Chicago, WLS-TV, inquired about having her host its floundering "A.M. Chicago" show, she responded positively.

She did have some reservations about Chicago, a city with a long history of racial tension. At her interview she addressed the matter directly.

"You know I'm black," she said.

"I'm aware of that," replied the station's general manager, perhaps wondering where this conversation was going.

"I'm interested in whether you big executive types sat around and had discussions about me being black."

"Oprah," the manager said, "let me tell you. I don't care what color you are. You can be green. All we want to do is win. I'm in the business of winning."

So was Winfrey—even as she recognized that color *did* matter, regardless of what station executives were required to say. "There aren't a lot of black people in the Chicago media," she told a reporter not long after her arrival. "And I'm the only one doing what I'm doing. When I came on the air here, it was like you could hear TVs clicking on all over the city." Curiosity motivated most of those clicks, at least initially. But Winfrey calculated that she could keep viewers tuned in once they saw her in action. "I had my own little game plan for Chicago," she told a *Sun-Times* correspondent in a typical moment of candor. "In one year, I'd walk down the street and people would know who I am. In two years people would watch me because they'd like me. In three years I'd gain acceptance—you know, I'd see Phil Donahue getting a pizza and I'd say, 'Oh, hi, Mr. Donahue. I watch your show sometimes.'"

Winfrey telescoped her timetable almost from the start. "A.M. Chicago" reversed a protracted slide in its ratings and audience share, gaining more than fifty percent over the previous year. Although WLS refrained from the big promotional campaign that had heralded Winfrey's arrival in Baltimore, Chicago viewers didn't have to ask "What's an Oprah?" for long. Within several months of taking over, Winfrey's show was expanded from thirty minutes to an hour.

The largest part of the program's appeal was its host; but a not insignificant portion related to the subject matter. Winfrey's early guest list ran heavy on garden-variety celebrities: Tom Selleck, Sally Field, Paul McCartney, Candice Bergen, the great Barbara Walters herself. But over time she—and her viewers—discovered that her real talent lay in getting otherwise ordinary people to tell of their traumas and tribulations. Here her own troubled background put her in good stead by giving her credibility and a connection to her guests—and vicariously to her audience. She shared with her audience that she had been raped by her cousin when she was nine years old and otherwise molested by other relatives and their friends. Her conversations with her guests were often as revealing of herself as of them—and sometimes more therapeutic. By her own testimony she had long harbored a feeling that somehow or other she had brought her childhood sexual abuse upon herself. "I was in the middle of an interview with a woman named Trudy Chase, who has multiple personalities and was severely abused as a child," she said.

> I think it was on that day that, for the first time, I recognized that I was not to blame. . . . It happened on the air, as so many things happen for me. It happened on the air in the middle of someone else's experience, and I thought I was going to have a breakdown on television.

Perhaps needless to say, that conversation and many others like it made for gripping viewing for the overwhelmingly female audience attuned to such issues.

The going wasn't quite so heavy on every program—although there was a definite commonality of theme. "Does sexual size matter?" she asked her audience. She thought it did. "If you had your choice, you'd like to have a big one if you could. Bring a big one home to Mama!" She interviewed a contingent of nudists, in full undress (theirs, not hers). Another hour featured film stars from a particular sector of the industry. "Don't you ever get sore?" she queried after they remarked that pornography was a grueling business, requiring long hours on the set in close quarters.

Aside from what critics characterized as the "nuts 'n' sluts" angle, another regular topic touched a different chord with many of those women viewers. Winfrey's weight had grown since her beauty-pageant days, and she made no secret of her efforts to reduce. It was unclear whether viewers were happier commiserating with her failures or applauding her sporadic successes, but whichever it was they stayed tuned. "I allow myself to be vulnerable," Winfrey said. "It's not something I consciously do. But I am. It just happens that way. I'm vulnerable, and people say, 'Poor thing. She has big hips, too.'" An appearance on the nationally broadcast Joan Rivers show gave Winfrey greater exposure than ever—and also a larger audience for her dieting efforts after she made a public bet with her host that she would lose fifteen pounds to her host's five.

Winfrey reached out to yet another audience when, after reading and being moved by Alice Walker's novel *The Color Purple*, she won a supporting role in the Steven Spielberg film adaptation. Her performance brought her critical acclaim and an Academy Award nomination. It gave magazines a new reason to put her on the front; even rival television stations in Chicago had to cover the story.

Winfrey knew what to do with all the publicity. "I want to be syndicated in every city known to mankind," she declared in 1985. There was one problem, however, at least regarding those cities known to mankind but also subject to the oversight of the Federal Communications Commission—meaning, of course, the entire American market. Part of David Sarnoff's legacy was a prohibition against the major television networks syndicating their own shows to nonaffiliates, on grounds that this would create a conflict of interest. Winfrey's employer and the producer of her show, WLS, was owned by ABC; under the FCC regime it was barred from distributing the show nationwide (if not mankind-wide).

So Winfrey needed a distributor. Some time before, she had begun to wonder whether her agent was getting her the best possible deals. Although she was making $230,000 per year, with annual increases pegged at $30,000, she suspected he might be too nice. Her employers liked him, which by itself seemed a bad sign. "Three separate people [at the station] stopped me to tell me what a great guy my agent was," she recalled, "and that didn't make sense to me." So she fired him in favor of someone not so nice. Jeffrey Jacobs was a Chicago lawyer with a reputation. "I'd heard Jeff is a piranha," said Winfrey. "I like that. Piranha is good."

Piranha certainly was good for Winfrey. Between them Winfrey and Jacobs selected as distributor King World Productions, a company founded in the 1960s by Charles King, a former radio syndicator, and inherited by his daughter and three sons after his death in 1973. Michael and Richard King, the siblings most involved in the company's operations, saw great potential in a national version of the Winfrey show. Twenty years after Berry Gordy had opened up the white market for black musical talent, African Americans were finding their niche in national television. NBC's "Today" show, featuring Bryant Gumbel, was the number one morning program; Bill Cosby's eponymous comedy led the prime-time ratings. Test-marketing indicated that Winfrey's appeal far transcended the Chicago market; the issues she dealt with touched female viewers all across the country.

The tests proved out. "Oprah is the hottest selling show I've ever had," Roger King declared a month before "The Oprah Winfrey Show" premiered nationally in September 1986. By opening day 138 stations—a syndication record—had signed on. The ratings quickly confirmed the preopening confidence. Nielsen noted, three months out, that the Winfrey show was running first in its time slot in each of the top ten television markets in the country.

From the beginning Winfrey targeted the Donahue show as the one to beat. "I'd love to go up against him head-to-head in all the markets at once," she told *USA Today* before it became apparent that she would be doing precisely that. "It would be so glorious to win!" The chief financial officer at King World put the issue somewhat differently: "We're not out to wipe Donahue off the face of the earth, but it's plausible we'll knock him off the air." Things started to get personal when Phil Donahue, who had been recording his show in Chicago, moved it to New York. King World's promotional video for the Winfrey show boasted that its client was "a major factor in getting Donahue to pack his bags for New York." Donahue denied it, saying he simply wanted to be closer to his New York-based wife, actress Marlo Thomas. Winfrey judiciously took him at his word. "Marlo, not Oprah, made him move," she said. Donahue took a road almost as high, wishing Winfrey luck—"only not in my time period."

Whatever the personal element, there was money enough to make the battle of the talk-show hosts interesting. Daytime television was generating some $2.5 billion annually in nonnetwork advertising revenues, an increase of about 300 percent over a decade earlier. Popular shows like Donahue could hook viewers for hours, to the marked benefit of a station's ad sales. The stations that didn't have Donahue looked to Winfrey to shake loose those viewers and the ad dollars that went with them.

It was almost no contest. After its fast start "The Oprah Winfrey Show" became a fixture at the top of the ratings. From the late 1980s through the mid-1990s Winfrey typically pulled in twice the audience of Donahue and other competitors. Equally to the point for advertisers, she delivered demographically: Among women aged 18 to 54 she ran away from the competition. Stations fought—and bid—hard to get Winfrey and the audience she commanded. The general manager of a station in Washington, D.C., which paid $90,000 per week in 1989 for rights in the nation's capital, explained, "Without Oprah, you're just scrambling."

As the magnitude of her drawing power became evident, Winfrey took increasing control of her show. She recaptured ownership from WLS and created a production company of her own, Harpo ("Oprah" backward), making her only the third woman in movie and television history (after Walt Disney's friend Mary Pickford and Lucille Ball) to own her own studio. She regularly ratcheted up her percentage of the revenues collected by King World, which quickly became a hostage to her success. "Nobody gets a deal like Oprah—nobody," observed one television analyst in 1993.

Although Winfrey had made her name airing controversial subjects, as she became more firmly entrenched in the establishment—and as a new crop of shock-talk shows sprang up each season—she gravitated toward the mainstream. She gained a reputation as the class of the field. "The rest of the talk shows are just tissue," remarked one industry observer. "'Oprah' is Kleenex." While still empathizing with people in trouble, she increasingly emphasized solutions to the problems her shows revealed. She took to sharing with viewers, who now numbered 15 to 20 million daily in more than 200 domestic and more than 130 foreign markets, inspirational or otherwise worthy books she had read. Apparently to her surprise and certainly to the amazement of the publishing industry, she became one of the most potent book marketers in history. Books she recommended flew off dealers' shelves; publishers responded by deluging her in new books to sample and, they hoped, endorse.

By the mid-1990s Winfrey had emerged as an arbiter of American culture, and Harpo as a money machine. "She's certainly one of the most influential people in the country because of her ability to reach so many people," asserted a veteran Winfrey-watcher. "Here's a woman who's done it all right, who has been able to build her own business into a one-woman empire. She's as big as Dan Rather, Tom Brokaw, Peter Jennings. She's sort of like the Barbara Walters of daytime television, only bigger."

But Winfrey wasn't content to confine herself to daytime television. She signed an agreement with ABC to produce six prime-time movies; when the first of these appeared in 1997 it received ABC's highest movie rating in four years—topping even the glittering remake of *Cinderella* by Walt Disney (now ABC's parent). "Oprah really is a special credential," said an advertising buyer. It wasn't lost on this buyer or on ABC that Winfrey enjoyed synergies similar to those of Walt Disney two generations earlier: of being able to promote her movies on her television show. "If I were ABC, I'd be very happy to have her as part of the family," this executive said.

As with Disney, each area of success drove up the price of others. In the fall of 1997, after publicly musing about hanging up her microphone to concentrate on her movies and other ventures, Winfrey agreed to a two-year package with King World that would extend her talk show through the 1999–2000 season. The deal would bring Harpo an estimated $120 million per year; in addition Winfrey would receive stock options in King World that could make her one of that company's largest shareholders. "At that point, Oprah reported to nobody but God," remarked one of her staff.

The King World deal cemented Winfrey's position as the top-earning figure in entertainment (ahead of director Steven Spielberg, in second place) and put her on a fast track to become the nation's first black billionaire. Like nearly every other extremely successful business person, Winfrey became a target for lawsuits. The one that garnered the most attention was an eight-figure complaint brought by a herd of cattlemen claiming that a Winfrey show on mad-cow disease had done multimillion-dollar damage to their industry and to them as individuals.

The trial took place in Amarillo, Texas, a venue as friendly as the cattlemen could expect. But Winfrey reversed the odds by bringing her show to town, where the locals lined up for tickets and fell under the same spell she cast over her fans—who, not surprisingly, already included a substantial number of Amarillans. Winfrey won the ratings race long before she won in court.

"Free speech not only lives," she declared after the favorable verdict. "It rocks!" It certainly had for Winfrey since she had started speaking freely—as well as for pay—nearly forty years before.

24

THE PARANOIA PRINCIPLE

Andrew Grove

...

S ATCHEL PAIGE HAD SEVERAL RULES FOR LONG LIFE. "AVOID FRIED meats, which angry up the blood." "If your stomach disputes you, lie down and pacify it with cool thoughts." "Keep the juices flowing by jangling around gently as you walk." "Go very light on the vices, such as carrying on in society. The social ramble ain't restful." "Avoid running at all times." Most important: "Don't look back. Something might be gaining on you."

Although Paige wasn't generally known as a business guru, his advice suited him and his particular line of work; the legendary pitcher was winning baseball games a generation after most of his contemporaries had abandoned the diamond for the den.

Whether Paige's formula applied to other fields was problematic. Andrew Grove didn't think the last rule held in the semiconductor industry. More precisely, Grove thought the prescription in Paige's warning didn't work, because the *description* *did* work—all too well. Grove was certain something was gaining on him, or would be if he wasn't constantly looking over his shoulder and increasing his pace. Every successful business leader frets about the competition now and then; Grove amplified fretfulness into what he himself labeled paranoia. And he turned paranoia into a prescription of his own, one that made him the king of the semiconductor industry and his company a standout of the postindustrial era.

Paranoia came naturally to Grove. If he thought others were after him, it was partly because for much of his first twenty years they *were* after him. And those on his trail weren't out for mere market share. A Hungarian Jew, Grove (at that time András Gróf) had to hide from Hitler's exterminators as a boy during World War II. The Communists who ruled Hungary after the war weren't quite so bloody-minded as the Nazis, but their views on the proper relation of individuals to the state was scarcely less harsh, and when Grove had the temerity to differ, he found himself on the wrong side of power once more. He fled his homeland for Austria in 1956; the following year he made his way to the United States.

Like such earlier immigrants as John Jacob Astor, Andrew Carnegie and David Sarnoff, Grove arrived with little money and few obvious prospects. Like them he wrung everything that was to be wrung from what opportunities fell his way. While learning English he attended the tuition-free City College of New York; he wound up graduating at the top of his chemical-engineering class. "I was a little astonished by that kind of ambition," said Grove's freshman adviser at CCNY. "There's some advantage in being hungry." Hunger—and a fellowship—propelled Grove through graduate study at the University of California at Berkeley; he received his Ph.D. just as the silicon revolution was breaking out in the Santa Clara Valley a few dozen miles to the south.

Grove took a job with Fairchild Semiconductor largely because of the caliber of its researchers. The two biggest guns at Fairchild were Gordon Moore and Robert Noyce. Long before other people Moore and Noyce saw the future in transistors, which were replacing vacuum tubes in electronic computers. Unluckily for Fairchild the company's directors couldn't see that far ahead, and their slowness to discern what appeared obvious to Moore and Noyce provoked the two to quit. They set up their own company, which they called Intel (short for "integrated electronics"). They invited Grove, who didn't know as much electronics as they did but already showed a gift for getting a lot out of his own and others' talents. "He's the world's most organized guy," Moore said, while confessing, "I'm pretty near the other end of the spectrum." Moore told Grove, "One day you'll run Intel," even before Intel was much to run.

The company's early business centered on producing integrated-circuit memory devices for computers. The particular approach Intel employed—the silicon-gate process—had been invented at Fairchild in Moore's department, and its adoption by Intel provoked understandable irritation at Fairchild. "Intel was *founded* to steal the silicon gate process from Fairchild," said one individual who worked at both companies.

Later Intel would take pains not to repeat Fairchild's mistake in letting a promising technology get away; in the meantime it had all it could do pushing its first major product out the door. The 1103 memory chip, introduced in 1970, presaged a revolution in the computer industry. Until then most computers had kept their internal accounts on magnetic-core memory devices; the silicon alternative—dynamic random access memory, or DRAM—was trickier to work with and as yet unproven, but it promised much denser storage. The 1103 could store a kilobit (1024 pieces of on/off information), and Intel's engineers estimated that they would soon have production ramped up to where the chip could sell for $10, or a penny a bit.

And this would be only the beginning. Sooner than just about anyone else Moore appreciated the economics of silicon. In 1965 he had written an article for *Electronics* magazine predicting that the power and complexity of integrated circuits would double every year. He later jiggered the doubling time to eighteen months, but "Moore's law," as the amended formula came to be known, provided a remarkably accurate assessment of the future of the semiconductor industry—and with it the computer industry.

Industrialists of an earlier era had had to deal with technological change, of course. John D. Rockefeller was constantly tinkering with the oil-refining process, and Andrew Carnegie was famous for tearing out old steel plants to install newer, more efficient models. But no previous industry had been built on the premise of such headlong and incessant change as the computer industry. All industries eat their young, but the computer industry ate its young for breakfast.

It would have swallowed Intel if not for Andy Grove. At first Intel had the market for DRAM chips essentially to itself, but inevitably others copied the company's success and began horning in. By the late 1970s perhaps a dozen companies—mostly American—were fighting over the memory market. Intel was the best of the bunch but by no means an automatic winner as each generation of chip emerged. An industry analyst liked to report the results as from ringside: "Round Two goes to Intel, Round Three goes to Mostek, Round Four to Texas Instruments. . . ."

Things changed in the early 1980s. Japanese firms, which had been niche players until then, mounted a frontal assault on the American memory industry. Japan's reputation for quality—won in such fields as automobiles and consumer electronics—put Intel and other American memory makers on notice; so did ominous vibrations from the Pacific's far side. "People who came back from visits to Japan told scary stories," Grove recalled.

At one big Japanese company, for instance, it was said that memory development activities occupied a whole huge building. Each floor housed designers working on a different memory generation, all at the same time: On one floor were the 16K people (where "K" stands for 1024 bits), on the floor above were the 64K people and on the floor above that people were working on 256K-bit memories. There were even rumors that in secret projects people were working on a million-bit memory. This was all very scary from the point of view of what we still thought of as a little company in Santa Clara, California.

Equally ominous was the quality question. "The quality levels attributed to Japanese memories were beyond what we thought were possible," Grove said.

And then there was financing. "The Japanese companies had capital advantages. They had (or were said to have) limitless access to funds—from the government? from parent companies through cross-subsidies? or through the mysterious workings of the Japanese capital markets that provided nearly infinite low-cost capital to export-oriented producers?"

As Grove looked west from his Silicon Valley office, it was impossible to know exactly what was fueling the Japanese offensive. "But the facts were incontrovertible: As the eighties went on, the Japanese producers were building large and modern factories, amassing a capacity base that was awesome from our perspective."

From that base the Japanese conquered the memory market. In 1980 Japanese firms owned less than 30 percent of worldwide sales, while American producers sold twice as much; by 1985 the Japanese had overtaken the Americans. Within a few years more the roles of the two sides were the reverse of what they had been at the start of the decade.

For Intel the Japanese invasion portended disaster. The company had created the memory market; now it was losing money on every chip it sold. By all evidence the losses would continue, for the Japanese had adopted a Carnegie-esque approach to pricing. As Hitachi told its distributors (in a memo acquired and reproduced by the *Wall Street Journal*): "Quote 10% below their price; if they requote, go 10% again. Don't quit until you win."

Grove had been promoted to Intel president in 1979, and as the Japanese onslaught gained force he struggled to counter it. He had always demanded much from his subordinates; now he demanded more. He announced a "125% solution" to the productivity problem: Intel's salaried workers would put in two extra hours per day. His managerial technique of "constructive confrontation" became more confrontational than ever. "I thought we all got yelled at enough by our parents when we were kids," reflected one Intel executive who left the company, in no small part as a response to Grove's bellicose style. "Now we're grown up, we shouldn't have to be in environments like this." In 1984 Grove received the dubious honor of being named by *Fortune* as one of America's toughest bosses.

Finally, as Intel's position continued to slip, Grove came to a drastic conclusion. He was in his office with Gordon Moore, at that time chairman and CEO. He looked out the window to the Ferris wheel of the Great American amusement park across the way, and perhaps reflected that the company was going in similarly aimless circles. He turned to Moore with a question: "If we got kicked out and the board brought in a new CEO, what do you think he would do?"

Moore answered, "He would get us out of memories."

Grove reflected a moment. Then he said, "Why shouldn't you and I walk out the door, come back and do it ourselves?"

Fortunately the company had somewhere to go if it left memories. Since the early 1970s Intel had developed a second kind of computer chip, the microprocessor, as a complement to its memory sales. Initially Intel's microprocessors appealed to an entirely different clientele than its memory chips; contrasting the latter to the former, one of Intel's marketers said the list for Intel's first microprocessor, the 4004, was "not so much *Who's Who* as *Who's That?*"

The scouting report on the 4004 put the chip in the primitive-but-promising category; the 4004's successor, the 8008, was less primitive and more promising. Yet even the 8008 had limited appeal. Programming this tiny computer-on-a-chip was enough to make grown men cry—which was why teenagers took to it at once. In Seattle a couple of kids named Paul Allen and Bill Gates pooled their resources to buy one of the microprocessors, which they tried to put to commercial use sampling and analyzing automobile traffic. The effort stalled and sputtered.

The subsequent generations of microprocessors were both more powerful and more user-friendly. The 8086 and its next of kin, the 8088, helped launch the personal-computer revolution by providing the brains for IBM's pathbreaking PC. The 80286 upped the ante by upping performance again. Moore's law, as was becoming evident, applied even more strikingly to microprocessors than to memory chips.

It was against this background of a growing market for microprocessors that Grove determined to jettison Intel's memory business. It wasn't easy—for him or for anyone else in the company.

As I started to discuss the possibility of getting out of the memory chip business with some of my associates, I had a hard time getting the words out of my mouth without equivocation. It was just too difficult a thing to say. Intel equaled memories in all of our minds. How could we give up our identity?

They did it by adopting a new identity—and clinging to that fiercely. In the early days of its microprocessor business Intel had adopted a policy of second-sourcing: of encouraging other chipmakers to fill the excess demand for its products. In particular Intel shared trade secrets with Advanced Micro Devices, another Silicon Valley startup; these enabled AMD to fabricate processors functionally identical to Intel's 8086 and 8088 chips. Not only did this policy protect Intel from the vagaries of a nascent and uncertain market, it reassured customers like IBM who didn't want to become dependent on a single supplier. In doing so it expanded the market for computers and chips.

The arrangement satisfied all parties—namely, Intel, AMD and IBM—through the first two generations of the personal computer. But the third generation brought a new twist—by bringing in a new player. Until this time makers of personal computers had been content to follow IBM's lead. IBM set the technical standard the others quickly "cloned" with microprocessors made by Intel (or AMD) and software licensed by Bill Gates's Microsoft. In late 1986 Compaq of Houston broke the mold by beating IBM in introducing a computer based on the newest Intel chip, the 80386.

This move fundamentally changed the business. As other cloners rushed to follow Compaq's lead, conceptual hegemony in personal computers slipped from the computer makers to the component makers. The hardware component common to all the PCs and clones was the Intel 80386; the primary software component was Microsoft's operating system.

For its part Intel reacted to this new situation by rescinding its policy of second-sourcing. Possessing what the *New York Times*'s business analyst described as "one of the most lucrative monopolies in America"—namely, control of the 80386 (colloquially the "386")—it determined to protect that monopoly. When AMD asserted that an earlier agreement with Intel covered the 386, Intel denied that it did. AMD then invoked an arbitration clause of the agreement; this triggered an extended legal battle between the two former allies and much bad blood.

Grove accepted both the legal combat and the bad blood as a cost of doing business in this new era of computing. Before long Intel became known as one of the most aggressive litigators in the industry. Grove made no apologies. "We have gone to court to protect our intellectual property from competitors who would have liked to help themselves to it," he said. "I understand that you don't make friends that way. But we spend tons of money on R&D. As a company with a disproportionate amount of intellectual property, we are forthright about stating that our property is valuable, and we want to prevent other people from helping themselves to it."

The value of Intel's intellectual property only increased with the introduction of successors to the 386. The 486 completed Intel's transformation into a maker of microprocessors; in the bargain it vaulted the company to the forefront of the world's semiconductor manufacturers. A competitor marveled of Grove: "He blew the doors off the 486 market."

An even bigger winner was the fifth-generation processor. By logic and tradition it should have been dubbed the 586, and in early development it was. But Grove—who took over from Moore as CEO in 1986—reckoned that the company could protect its monopoly and pad its profits by brand-naming its newest processor. Courts had determined that the labels 386 and 486 were generic; presumably 586 would be too. So Intel's 586 became Pentium, a name that *could* be protected.

At the same time the company launched a marketing campaign to reinforce the name recognition of Intel and its products. The "Intel Inside" blitz targeted end users rather than the computer-assembling intermediaries who actually bought the processors off the Intel lines; the "Intel Inside" decal on the outside of a computer assured retail customers that their machines were powered by the industry leader.

The "Intel Inside" campaign made marketing sense, but it also carried Grove and the rest of Intel into uncharted waters. They hit a large rock in 1994, with a jolt that set the company back half a billion dollars. Early reviews of the Pentium had been enthusiastic. The general-interest press had gee-whizzed at the 3 million transistors that were jammed into a thumbnail-sized sliver of silicon and at the 100 million cycles per second at which the processor ran. The industry press praised the Pentium's ability to handle graphics, sound and video clips, thereby adding multimedia capability to computers. The business press drooled over the $1000 price tag on early versions of the chip, predicting new record earnings for Intel and new heights for its share price.

But then something went wrong. One of the company's technical-support operators received a call from a mathematics professor at a small college in Virginia. Politely—more curious than upset—the professor reported that his Pentium wasn't working right. When he did a fairly complicated division problem, the processor gave him the wrong answer. Yes, he assured the Intel operator, he was pretty sure it was the processor and not the rest of his computer, nor the software; he had tried the same problem on another Pentium system and got the same wrong answer.

No processor had ever been introduced without bugs; flaws in the Pentium were inevitable, not least on account of the size and complexity of the project that produced it. "It's like designing a 747," the Pentium project manager said. "At any one point in the process, no single person can ever know everything that's going on in the project." The bug in the Pentium was hardly unusual in scope or seriousness. But no processor had ever received the popular buildup the Pentium got; with the great expectations came the possibility of great disappointment.

Further, Grove and Intel had not exactly endeared themselves to the computing community. Intel's customers suspected that the company manipulated supplies and introductory dates to maximize profits, often at the customers' expense. Even by the competitive standards of the computer industry Grove's approach stood out. "This is a scorch, burn and plunder strategy with one aim: Kill off competitors," said an industry analyst. "If you think Grove is determined to control the future of computing hardware, you're absolutely right."

Most critical, Grove failed to appreciate how marketing to consumers differed from marketing to producers. The engineers and other experts who bought chips for computer makers understood the comparative innocuousness of the Pentium bug, but their informed judgment now counted for less than the uninformed judgment of millions of amateur keyboard-bangers.

Ironically, the Virginia professor wasn't telling Intel anything it didn't already know and wasn't already in the process of fixing. Like publishers in second and subsequent printings of books, chip makers regularly incorporate corrections into the production process. If Intel had been thinking like a maker of consumer goods rather than of producer goods, it would simply have congratulated the professor on his keen observational skills, thanked him for his input and promised him a shiny new Pentium with the bug exterminated.

Instead it brushed him off, and he took his complaint to the Internet. Soon the news of the Pentium bug was everywhere. When Intel officials, responding to reporters' queries, tried to calm the rising uproar by saying that they knew about the problem, the response exploded in their faces.

They *knew* about the problem but still shipped flawed products? Wasn't this a cover-up? When Intel engineers explained that the average user would encounter errors at a rate of one every 27,000 years (an interval vastly longer than the expected lifetime of the Pentium chip, not to mention of the users), critics answered with figures of their own that made things look far more serious. Most devastating were the jokes

Why didn't Intel call the Pentium the 586?
Because they added 100 to 486 and got 585.99999.

What does Pentium stand for?
Perfect Enough for Nine out of Ten Instructors at the University of Montana.
    or,
Practically Everyone Thinks It's Useless for Math.

What do you get when you cross a mathematician with a Pentium?
A mad scientist.

An Intel engineer walks into a bar and orders a drink. The bartender brings him his drink and says, "That'll be five dollars." The engineer lays down five dollars and says, "Keep the change."

After Intel grudgingly agreed to replace the chips of users who could show that they made heavy use of the most division-sensitive part of the processor, another gag circulated:

Have you heard about Intel's new salary plan for its workers?
You can pick up your paycheck every other Friday but only if you can prove that you really *need* it.

The coup de grace came when IBM announced that it was halting shipment of Pentium computers. Cynics at Intel muttered that IBM was trying to make Intel look bad, out of jealousy at being upstaged as the brand name in personal computers. Whatever truth there was in that complaint, it was clear that IBM saw no reason to share the pain Intel was suffering.

Grove found this period the worst of his career. "I have survived some very difficult business situations," he said. "But this was different. It was much harsher than the others. In fact, it was unlike any of the others at every step. It was unfamiliar and rough territory. I worked hard during the day but when I headed home I got instantly depressed. I felt we were under siege—under unrelenting bombardment."

The salvos continued until Grove ran up the white flag. He offered to replace the processors of all users who wanted them replaced—whether the users were doing statistical analysis or playing computer solitaire.

It was a leap in the dark. "We had shipped millions of these chips by now," he said, "and none of us could even guess how many of them would come back—maybe just a few, maybe all of them." Grove ordered the creation of a consumer-complaints division, almost from scratch. "We had not been in the consumer business in any big way before, so dealing with consumer questions was not something we had ever had to do. Now, suddenly, we did from one day to another and on a fairly major scale." Ultimately the company took a $475 million write-off to cover the cost of the replacements and of materials pulled from the assembly line. In effect Intel paid for its Pentium fiasco with half a year of research and development.

It was an expensive lesson in customer relations, but in the end it merely delayed Intel's latest triumph. Some analysts suggested that the Pentium flap confirmed the adage that there is no such thing as bad publicity so long as the name is spelled right. Certainly more people knew about Intel and the Pentium after all the front-page and prime-time reports than had before. And because there was no competitor positioned to exploit Intel's stumble, the company lost no real ground, only a little time.

In the long term, more troubling for Grove was the discovery that he had prostate cancer. And more troubling still was that his doctors couldn't decide what to do. One said operate; a second suggested radiation–seed therapy; a third prescribed watchful waiting. Grove took matters into his own hands by examining the research literature and assessing the efficacy and side effects of the alternative treatments. Finally he decided on a novel therapy—a "smart bomb" of high-dose radiation—that had shown promise in a limited number of trials. It worked, at least in the sense of stabilizing his condition. Quarterly checkups monitored his condition; four times a year he faced a trying moment of truth.

"Did I mellow or something like that?" he asked himself regarding this heightened intimation of his mortality. "No, I don't think I did." He had always been driven by a desire to excel—"to build businesses and make a difference." Nothing had changed there. "I continue to be driven exactly the same way." If anything, he had learned to be less trusting of others, even experts. "Rely on yourself. That's what I learned out of it."

Rely on yourself, and watch the competition. By the mid-1990s Intel sufficiently dominated the microprocessor market that it was unclear exactly who or what the company's competition consisted of. Grove was a reflective type who spent a good deal of time pondering the evolution of the semiconductor and computer industries. To some extent his reflections provided material for the classes he taught at the Stanford Business School and for the best-selling management books he wrote, including *Only the Paranoid Survive*. At least equally they were designed to avert other such costly and wrenching experiences as the Pentium debacle and the forced abandonment of the memory market.

"A new horizontal industry model is replacing the old vertical one," he explained to an interviewer. The old industry had been characterized by companies like IBM (in particular the IBM of the Watsons, although Grove wasn't so specific). These companies built their computers basement to attic: silicon chips, disk drives, software, the works. The vertical model had allowed IBM to dominate the market for mainframes (such as the 700 series and its successors): the big, expensive machines purchased by big, wealthy corporations and their government counterparts. But as IBM had learned to its expense and dismay, the vertical model failed when applied to personal computers. These new machines were cheap, almost disposable by mainframe standards; for this reason they evolved much more rapidly than the mainframes. Speed of innovation became critical; because no company could sprint in several directions at once, specialists left the generalists in the dust. Software evolved one way, with Microsoft taking the lead. Intel won out in basic hardware—but Intel's experience demonstrated that a single company couldn't keep ahead in more than one area of the semiconductor industry, and it was forced to yield in memory in order to focus on processors.

Grove liked to describe the computer business as an "industrial democracy"—an unmanaged, apparently chaotic system that nonetheless worked.

> It resists central guidance. Nobody can tell anyone else what to do. Your PC might have a processor from Intel, a display from Sharp, a hard disk from Conner, memory from Toshiba, a modem from U.S. Robotics, an operating system from Microsoft, applications from four different vendors, and yet it all works together. If it didn't, none of these products would sell.

The arrangement was hard on those involved. "Industrial democracy is brutally competitive, and it can get very messy." But it enabled technology to advance very rapidly.

Yet precisely because the pace was so swift the players never had time to perfect their products.

The old mainframe computer companies were masters at integrating all the necessary pieces into a seamless system. In the PC world we're all on our own. Each company in each horizontal layer designs its products to work with everybody's else's products just well enough to sell. We have to have a minimum of integration to survive, but doing more is a luxury. That's why these products—chips and programs and computer—are not integrated enough to be easy for people to use. It took me forty hours to get my first laptop going.

(Speaking in 1993, Grove lampooned a recent announcement by the Clinton administration that it would create an integrated electronic-mail system for the entire federal government. "That's hilarious. We are not particularly incompetent at Intel, and we've been working on our little e-mail system for two years. Saddam Hussein will have free rein while the government tries to get its system to work.")

The situation was far from ideal. But Grove—the survivor of Nazi manhunts and Communist crackdowns, of two decades at the epicenter of a turbulent industry, and lately of cancer—left idealism to others; he was the consummate realist. "The pace of work these days isn't easy to live with, but welcome to the Nineties. Intel didn't create this world; we're just supplying the tools with which we can all work ourselves to death. Exhausting as it is, it's highly preferable to being unemployed."

Intel dominated its industry, but that dominance wouldn't last if the company slowed its pace. "You can't hesitate or hedge your bets. You can have the best product in the world, but if you fail to invest in enough plant and equipment to satisfy demand for it, all your efforts are wasted. All you've done is create an opportunity for someone else." To a certain degree industry leadership simply increased the burdens on the leader. "To meet the raised expectations of investors, we've got to go into a higher gear."

If Intel had gained anything—other than several billion dollars—by its preeminence, it was the luxury of knowing that its future lay in its own hands. Another person might have taken comfort from this situation. For Grove it simply allowed a redirection of concern. "There's no competitor around who can do as much damage to us as we can do to ourselves."

25

STANDARD OPERATING
PROCEDURE

Bill Gates

. . .

F EW FIRMS WERE CLOSER TO THE CUTTING EDGE OF TECHNOLOGY
than Intel; yet in a fundamental sense what Andy Grove did didn't differ materially from what Andy Carnegie had done a hundred years before.
Both were in manufacturing; each produced something tangible that
could be weighed, that took up space, that had to be warehoused, that required some physical form of transport to be delivered. Carnegie would
have had trouble understanding the electronics of what Grove did, but he
would have had no difficulty with the economics.

The success of the other of personal computing's gold-dust twins, Bill
Gates, would have been harder to explain to a nineteenth-century industrialist. Gates didn't *make* anything, at least not anything you could drop
on your foot. Nor did he quite provide a service, the way J. P. Morgan, for
example, had in finance. The closest nineteenth-century analogy to what
Gates did might have been Samuel Morse's creation of a standard language
for telegraphy, the hot new information technology of the early industrial
era. For what Gates *really* did was set standards.

Somebody had to do it. If personal computing had come of age before
the arrival of Ronald Reagan and his cadres of deregulators, the standard-
setter might have been the same FCC that David Sarnoff had tilted with
over color television. If the Cold War hadn't been already thawing and on
the verge of liquidation, it might have been the Pentagon's counterpart to
the procurers who told Henry Kaiser what kind of ships to build. But as

things happened, it was a kid from Seattle with a head for computer code and an eye for the main chance.

This latter was what distinguished Gates from a hundred other hackers who matured—or at least got older—while Andy Grove and Intel were working their wonders in silicon. The computer culture that inverted night and day, that thrived on cold caffeine and metamorphic mozzarella, that disdained convention as the refuge of the dim-witted—this was not a culture that took readily to commerce. Gates was initially so rare in this world as to be essentially unique. He could code with the best of the geeks, but he also had an instinct for the marketplace. The top-gun mentality that pervaded the realm of mathematics and hard science—Who's the smartest guy around? (and they were almost all *guys*)—carried over into computers; Gates was one of the few who took it the next step into business. The smartest guy of all would be the one who solved not just this problem on this computer, but everyone's problems on all the world's computers.

It helped that he started early. At six he attended the 1962 World's Fair in his hometown; among the exhibits was one by IBM that projected an information revolution based on computers—its own, naturally. The boy was impressed, although at the time more by the monorail and the carnival rides than by the computers. He first encountered computers academically in eighth grade, in the form of a teletype terminal connected via telephone to a General Electric time-sharing mainframe. The teacher was a novice; he later recalled giving Gates's class a fifteen-minute orientation. "And I remember that was the last time I knew more than those guys." Shortly thereafter a parent at the private school—to which Bill had been sent to unwrinkle some behavioral problems—with connections to a computer startup enlisted Gates's group to help shake down a new system. As pay for their assistance they would earn free computer time.

"It was manna from heaven," Gates recalled. In deliberately trying to crash the system, Gates and the others learned the weaknesses and strengths of the BASIC language in which it was programmed; the free computing time afforded opportunity for creativity on their own. Paul Allen, a schoolmate and subsequent cofounder of Microsoft, remembered Gates spending hours on a war game that grew and grew. "I'm not sure if it was ever finished or what it did," Allen said, "but he invested a lot of time trying to figure out how it worked."

Eventually the system was tweaked to the company's satisfaction, and the free time was terminated. But this didn't stop Gates and Allen from hacking their way past system security and cadging additional time—and apparently tampering with the accounting files in the process. When they were caught the school was more upset than the computer company, which chiefly wanted to know how they had done it, to prevent others from doing the same. "Our official position was one of concern," said a company representative. "But in the back room, it was 'Holy mackerel, if kids can do this, imagine what somebody who knew something could do.'"

Through most of high school Gates and Allen begged, borrowed and bootlegged computer time wherever they could. They contracted to write a payroll program, which turned out to be more than they had bargained for. "It was a bitch," Allen said. Other programming jobs included scheduling for their school, which carried the perk for the programmers of getting the classes they wanted at the choice times and with the right classmates, including the maximum number of the most attractive girls and the fewest and least attractive (to the girls) boys.

The most ambitious effort by the budding informational entrepreneurs had them trying to develop a computer system that would track traffic flow for municipalities. Traf-O-Data, as the entity that embodied this effort was called, proved more remarkable for its longevity than for its profitability. The essential hang-up was the hardware rather than the software; this experience probably contributed to Gates's eventual decision to leave the former to others.

While Traf-O-Data struggled, Gates and Allen honed their software skills writing code for the Bonneville Power Administration (the electrical offspring sired by the New Deal out of Henry Kaiser's dams). "It was like a dream come true," Gates said. As a high school senior he was working on state-of-the-art equipment with seasoned engineers—some of whom had serious suspicions of this scrawny kid who looked twelve and frequently acted fourteen. "We had contests to see who could stay in the building like three days straight, four days straight," he recounted with a certain pride. "Some of the more prudish people would say, 'Go home and take a bath.'" Gates subsisted on astronaut tea—Instant Tang—scooped from the jar in unwashed handfuls and eaten dry, which left an ethereal orange glow around the lips and fingernails. "We were just hardcore, writing code."

Gates entered Harvard in the autumn of 1972 and gravitated naturally toward applied mathematics and computer science. He impressed his instructors in a variety of ways. "He was a hell of a good programmer," said the director of Harvard's computer lab. Yet the personal side of the Gates equation left something to be desired. "In terms of being a pain in the ass, he was second in my whole career here. He's an obnoxious human being. . . . He'd put people down when it was not necessary, and just generally not be a pleasant fellow to have around the place."

Gates found college per se no more congenial than it found him. He preferred poker to books, and video games—which were just becoming popular—to classes. He got badly sick at the end of his freshman year, requiring hospitalization for ulcerative colitis. He dropped out, started again, dropped out again. Eventually he gave it up altogether.

Computers were far more fun. In late 1974 Paul Allen showed him a magazine article about a small computer called the Altair 8800, made by an Albuquerque company named MITS and powered by Intel's new 8080 processor. In those days small computers didn't come with software; Gates and Allen proposed to supply the deficiency. In particular they would write a version of the BASIC they had mastered in high school (and whose original authors had obligingly released it gratis into the public domain). Gates and Allen would sell their version to MITS or through MITS to that company's customers. They contacted the president of MITS and apparently—in what would become a Microsoft trademark—promised more than they were prepared to deliver at the moment. But that was fine with MITS, which wasn't ready to accept delivery of the software. "God, we gotta get going on this!" said Gates, in Allen's recollection of the MITS sale.

For the next several weeks the two slaved over their project, adapting the standard BASIC (which really wasn't very standard at all) to the idiosyncrasies of the Altair. Because they didn't own one of the machines, they simulated it on others—getting Gates into trouble with Harvard for unauthorized and excessive use of the university's computer system. Nor could they be certain until Allen flew out to Albuquerque with the program, which was coded on the paper tape that provided that generation's mass storage, that it would really run. The crucial test was simple enough. Allen typed

PRINT 2 + 2

Because most of their code was required to solve even this trivial problem, Allen knew that if the Altair got it right, the language worked. He held his breath.

4

printed the computer, leaving Allen to try to hide his relief.

The demonstration led to a deal whereby Gates and Allen received $3000 up front and royalties that ranged from $30 to $60 for each copy of their program that went out with an Altair machine. This agreement marked the beginning of Microsoft, although the name wasn't adopted (in the form "Micro-Soft") for some months yet, and the partnership remained unofficial.

By the time those details had been hammered out—with Gates talking Allen into accepting forty percent, against his own sixty, on grounds that Allen by now had taken a full-time job with MITS and presumably was devoting fewer hours to the partnership than Gates—Gates felt obliged to address an issue critical to the future of the company. In an open letter in the monthly *Computer Notes*, Gates griped that notwithstanding the uniformly enthusiastic response to Altair BASIC, its originators—Allen and himself—weren't making any money. "Why is this?" he demanded, before accusing his readers with the answer: "Most of you steal your software." He complained that coders like himself were left in the cold by the common view of the relationship between hardware and software: "Hardware must be paid for, but software is something to share. Who cares if the people who worked on it get paid?" Gates cared, and he warned that illicit copying of software would serve only to deter software writers from developing good programs. He asserted that he and Allen had run through more than $40,000 worth of computer time perfecting their current product, and he asked rhetorically, "Who can afford to do professional work for nothing?" In closing he urged the guilty to pay up and declared, "Nothing would please me more than being able to hire ten programmers and deluge the hobby market with good software."

Gates's letter elicited a variety of responses from the still-small world of personal computerists. A few fellow programmers applauded his hard-nosed stance against piracy, but many others assailed the author as insulting and greedy. They reminded him that BASIC was basically in the public domain; he and Allen were trying to sell something they hadn't originated and didn't own. Sources close to Cambridge leaked that Gates hadn't spent anywhere near the $40,000 cited in the letter, especially as most of the development was done—in the words of one printed version of the story—"on a Harvard University computer provided at least in part with government funds." This report added that there was "some question as to the propriety if not the legality of selling the results."

The software flap provided Gates his first notoriety; it also persuaded him to change Microsoft's approach to selling its products. When MITS needed a revision of BASIC for a new computer, Gates and Allen licensed it to the hardware maker—nonexclusively—for a flat fee of $31,200, payable in monthly installments over two years.

After leaving Harvard definitively, Gates joined Allen in Albuquerque, where Microsoft established its first real office and hired real employees. Allen had quit MITS to devote his entire energies to the partnership; nonetheless Gates—much the pushier of the two—managed to modify the earlier pact to increase his share: sixty-four percent to Allen's thirty-six.

Although Microsoft would come to be associated with Seattle, the distinctive style that characterized the company emerged during the Albuquerque days. "We would just work until we dropped," Allen remembered. "I used to joke that Albuquerque is a repeating pattern of a gas station, a 7-Eleven, and a movie theater." Gates put the matter more formally in an early memo: "Microsoft expects a level of dedication from its employees higher than most companies. Therefore, if some deadline or discussion or interesting piece of work causes you to work extra time some week, it just goes with the job."

In practice the "some week" of Gates's memo became nearly every week. His habit was to find a computer company that needed a customization of BASIC for its machines, to make a sales pitch promising impossibly fast delivery, and then to turn the Microsoft troops loose to meet his promise. The fact that he led from the front—that he worked harder than anyone else, programming even while he was managing, and that he took home the lowest salary in the place—averted what might have become crippling complaints.

But there was something else. In the strange world of computer coders Gates exerted an unusual appeal. By most standards and in many circumstances Gates was socially awkward. He had a curious habit of rocking when he sat or stood, almost like an infant trying to soothe himself. Strolling down a hallway he would spontaneously leap up and touch the ceiling like an adolescent boy testing his physical abilities. (Unstereotypically athletic for a computer nerd, he had a particular skill at jumping, which he liked to demonstrate by bounding from a standstill over armchairs or out of garbage cans.) He was as absentminded as the caricatured professor, constantly misplacing money, airplane tickets, credit cards, clothes and nearly anything else not permanently attached to his person. (Often a cause for amusement, his distraction became worrisome when he got behind the wheel of his sports car, which he drove as hard as he drove himself.)

Gates's managerial style was fully as confrontational as Andy Grove's. In a culture that prized being intelligent over everything else—including being rich—Gates was constantly screaming "That's the stupidest thing I've ever heard" to subordinates who usually considered themselves unusually intelligent. If a listener failed to understand a Gates statement, he typically repeated the same words, only louder. An early Microsoftie described the effect of the technique: "You know, like 'You stupid idiot. This is what I said. Just listen to what I say.'" Another old-timer (admittedly a relative term in the craft of computing) remembered being figuratively struck in the middle of a presentation when Gates began literally banging his head on the table and shouting, "You think I am an idiot! Don't use that logic on me!"

Those who got along best with Gates were the ones who stood their ground and shouted back. Paul Allen's nose-to-nose sessions with his partner became the stuff of company lore. One employee remembered hearing a set-to that started in an office on the eighth floor, spilled into the hallway, continued across the lobby and emptied into the elevator, which carried the screamers down the shaft and mercifully out of earshot. Thinking the peace of the place had been restored, the employee went back to work—just in time to hear Gates and Allen emerge from the entrance on the ground floor, still screaming. They deafened each other in the parking lot for another half-hour, to the amazement, although no longer the surprise, of the neighbors.

The battles eventually wore Allen down. "You'd see Paul go home after one of these marathon screaming sessions that was five hours long, and he wouldn't show up at work for three or four days," recounted one witness. "He was just physically wrung out." But it was something else—Hodgkin's disease—that caused Allen to reconsider his priorities and ultimately, in 1983, retire from Microsoft.

Gates, on the other hand, thrived on the combat, and if it wore Allen out it motivated the other employees. A journalist who for several months played fly-on-the-Microsoft-wall described the chairman in action.

Although I had attended meetings before at which Gates had exploded in anger, I was mystified now at the palpable nervousness in the room. Gates's guests were terrified. Yet his tantrums had always struck me as a kind of act, a contrivance. His is an odd sort of rage that explodes and subsides instantly, as if it were turned on and off by a toggle switch. When not expostulating, Gates sits stock-still in his chair, his gaze directed at the edge of the table in front of him, his mind wholly concentrated on what he is being told. His displays of wrath always seem more Socratic than Hitlerian, designed not to intimidate or insult, but to elicit more thorough thought. It is not uncommon, toward the end of a scream-punctuated meeting, for him to say calmly, "Okay . . . go ahead," as if his tantrum had never taken place.

Contrived or genuine, Gates's wrath worked. Those nervous employees held him in awe. "He has this laserlike ability to hone in on the absolute right question to ask," said one person who made vice president.

> You may think you have everything totally prepared, and the one area you weren't quite sure about, somehow he just finds it right away, and asks you the one right question. He'll know intricate low-level detail about a program, and you wonder, "How does he know that? He has no reason ever to get to that level!" Some piece of code, or some other technology Microsoft isn't even involved in. You just shake your head.

Another top Microsoft executive concurred.

> He's a maniac. Bill knows more about the product than any of us. And you go into the meetings and you come out sweating because, if there is any flaw, he will land on it immediately and pick it to bits. He is just unbelievable.

A third individual wondered at Gates's ability to absorb and integrate information. Gates, this person declared, occupied "the center of one of the information centers of the universe." Gates sucked up information about all sorts of things at a breathtaking speed. "If information were some kind of tribute, he'd be Kubla Khan."

Gates admitted that his managerial style sometimes accentuated the negative. "We're always trying to figure things out, look at our mistakes, give ourselves a hard time," he said. "I've always been fairly hardcore about looking at what we did wrong. We're not known for reflecting back on the things that went well." On another occasion he was more direct: "We can be pretty brutal about the parts that don't do well."

Some of his subordinates understood the strategy even as they trembled at the prospect of the next eruption of Mt. William. One described a complement to Gates's habit of venting his unhappiness so forcefully.

> For a guy who's allegedly a brainy nerd, Bill is extremely charismatic. He can really make you want to please him. That's one of the reasons the company works. And when he's not happy, it usually seems like disappointment, like he thought that maybe you understood along with him a direction towards a vision, a grand architecture of some kind, then you came back to him with something flawed.

Gates's vision took time to develop; through the early 1980s he had all he could do simply staying one step ahead of the competition. Until 1981 small computers were small potatoes: toys for hobbyists but not the sort of thing for businesses to take seriously. Only when IBM weighed in with its Personal Computer did the industry win real credibility. Microsoft, as much through Gates's aggressive marketing as through superior software, rode to credibility alongside—or rather inside—the IBM PC. Microsoft wasn't IBM's first choice for an operating system for the PC, but CP/M, the leading operating system, wasn't suited to the IBM architecture, and its owner, Digital Research, wasn't sure it wanted to make the necessary revisions at a price IBM wanted to pay. IBM had been interested in Microsoft's BASIC; now it asked Gates if he had an operating system as well.

He didn't but knew where to get one. Microsoft had moved to Seattle—carrying Gates and Allen back home—after outgrowing its Albuquerque sponsor MITS. Gates knew that Seattle Computer Products, a small firm down the road, had an operating system, a CP/M knockoff it called the Quick and Dirty Operating System. Without telling Seattle Computer what they wanted the system for, Gates and Allen bought QDOS (whose name was cleaned up to DOS: "Disk Operating System") for a total of $75,000. Then they turned around and licensed DOS to IBM. The precise terms of the licensing agreement were never disclosed, but they apparently involved an advance of several hundred thousand dollars against royalties. (The package included BASIC and other Microsoft languages, making the exact contribution of DOS to the deal even more difficult to determine.)

The money, however, was the least important part of the pact. IBM got DOS but not all of DOS: Microsoft withheld the right to license the operating system to other computer makers. As Gates explained afterward:

> Our restricting IBM's ability to compete with us in licensing MS-DOS to other computer makers was the key point of the negotiation. We wanted to make sure only we could license it. We did the deal with them at a fairly low price, hoping that would help popularize it. . . . We knew that good IBM products are usually cloned, so it didn't take a rocket scientist to figure out that eventually we could license DOS to others. We knew that if we were ever going to make a lot of money on DOS it was going to come from the compatible guys, not from IBM.

Events unfolded as Gates anticipated. In hopes of encouraging the development of software applications, IBM opted for an accessible "open architecture" for the PC; this had the side effect of allowing easy reproduction of the PC's hardware. Cloners like Compaq soon began producing IBM equivalents; more nimble than the computer giant, the cloners eventually overtook the cloned. Conceivably the cloners could have developed their own operating systems, but like IBM they decided it was cheaper to purchase Microsoft's DOS off the shelf. Microsoft held other software firms at bay by pricing its product low—an easy matter because the program was already written—and relying on volume to keep the bottom line solid. As a result DOS became the standard operating system for the industry.

The most important holdout against the ubiquitization of DOS was the Macintosh computer built by Apple. The Macintosh was more intuitive in use than the DOS machines, employing a graphical user interface (GUI, pronounced "gooey") instead of the abstruse and error-intolerant command lines of DOS. In other words—rather, in other pictures—a user with a pointing device (a "mouse," for its round body and long, tail-like wire) could simply point and click and let the computer figure out what was wanted. Especially as proselytized by Steve Jobs, Apple's cofounder and resident guru, and as advertised by a spectacular Super Bowl commercial showing a fearless woman warrior assaulting the Orwellian citadel of computer-corporate conformity (read: IBM), the Macintosh presented itself as the wave of the future.

Which, in a sense, it turned out to be—but as rendered by Bill Gates, not Steve Jobs. Even as DOS became the champion operating system, Gates rowed Microsoft downstream into applications software. To some extent this represented a return to the company's original competency: consumer products for computer users. The first computer users had employed BASIC and other languages to accomplish their esoteric tasks; the much larger and less specialized group that now embraced the PC and the Macintosh demanded spreadsheets, word processors and other real-world tools. To at least an equal extent Microsoft's move into applications was simply a matter of following the money. The VisiCalc spreadsheet and the WordStar word processor proved to be cash cows for Software Arts and MicroPro, respectively, and Gates saw no reason not to poach on the pastures where they grazed.

In 1982 Microsoft released Multiplan, its own spreadsheet, and at the beginning of 1984 an improved version of the same. Unfortunately, the state of the spreadsheet art was improving faster than Microsoft was improving Multiplan; the 1-2-3 program by Lotus leaped into first place among spreadsheets and pulled Lotus into first place among software makers overall.

Microsoft's Word initially encountered a similar reaction. Despite some novel features and a marketing blitz that included the distribution of demonstration diskettes in the 100,000 subscription copies of *PC World*, the word processor started off sluggishly. WordStar was overtaken in the backstretch, but by WordPerfect, a dark horse from Utah, rather than Word.

Yet the success of Microsoft's competitors simultaneously underwrote Microsoft's success. The rapid growth of personal computing (a term that was somewhat misleading, as most of the machines sold during the 1980s were for office, rather than strictly personal, use) depended on the development of attractive applications software. Although Microsoft's applications weren't the most attractive, the company benefited from the overall growth by selling more of its system software.

That system software was constantly being improved, but still it suffered by comparison with the Macintosh system, the gold standard for ease of use by nonspecialists. Consequently, even while he defended—somewhat defensively—the precision and power of DOS, Gates guided Microsoft into the world of GUIs.

He did so in a manner that infuriated his rivals and popularized a neologism: "vaporware." At least since Gordon Moore pronounced his law regarding the forever-falling price of computer power, would-be buyers have been sorely tempted to postpone purchases. Wait six months, goes the reasoning, and you'll get a better product for less money. Hardware and software makers alike have exploited this mind-set, repeatedly announcing new products before those products were ready, in hopes of preempting purchases of competitors' products. Gates didn't originate this strategy—IBM had been employing it with mainframes for years—but he developed it into an art form.

In November 1983, two months before the debut of the Macintosh but many months after that newest Apple's essential GUIness was evident, Microsoft announced Windows. This revolutionary new operating system, the company said, would employ a graphical interface that would make it unprecedentedly easy to work with. In other words—words Microsoft took pains to avoid—it would be much like the Macintosh system.

The only problem was that Windows didn't exist. And for all the high-performance, hypertensive atmosphere at Microsoft headquarters, there wasn't a chance in the world it would exist by its projected release date of early 1984. That date came and went with no Windows opening.

The spring of 1984 slipped by: no Windows. August was announced, and arrived productless. During that autumn the auguries indicated January 1985; in January they pointed to May. A second hopeful summer faded into autumn with no Windows. Only in November 1985 did Gates finally deliver the new system—not quite soon enough to avoid being awarded *InfoWorld*'s "Golden Vaporware Award" for a product that for so long hadn't been substantial enough even to rate the label "software."

After the prolonged delay, the response to Windows was tepid. "Windows is a slug on 8088 PCs," said one influential reviewer, "an impossibility on floppy-disk PCs." Yet this reviewer, more prescient than many, thought Gates's new product had legs, even if they weren't moving very fast at the moment. "I am a Windows fan, not because of what it is today, but what it almost certainly will become."

Apple also saw a future for the new operating system and naturally reacted differently. Now headed by John Sculley, Apple judged Windows a rip-off of the Macintosh system and sued. Gates and his lieutenants defended their actions and their product, claiming that earlier agreements allowing Microsoft to incorporate the look and feel of the Macintosh system into applications programs implicitly covered the current Microsoft operating system as well. In any event, they pointed out, Apple itself had appropriated the GUI style from Xerox's Palo Alto Research Center. If a style was proprietary, Apple was in trouble too. Apple and Microsoft carried their fight beyond the courtroom to the computer trade shows, with Sculley and Gates getting publicly and repeatedly hot and bothered, to the amusement of the conventioneers and the pecuniary interest of the stock analysts watching from the galleries.

The latter group had been monitoring Microsoft closely since the company went public in 1986. The IPO was a roaring success; overnight Gates became one of the wealthiest people in the country. As a result celebrity inevitably surrounded him. He was feted by *Forbes*, trumpeted by *Time*, profiled by *People* and contextualized by *Fortune*, whose 1987 cover story asserted that the thirty-something (thirty-one, to be precise) sultan of software had "apparently made more money than anyone else his age, ever, in any business." Analogies to business superstars of earlier eras abounded; a favorite in the columns of commentary was Henry Ford, the young tinkerer who struck it big with a design that brought a new technology to the masses and revolutionized America in the process.

Gates knew enough about Ford to know that he too had been sued for stealing other people's ideas, and the fact that Ford had beaten that suit encouraged Gates to keep fighting Apple. The suit went on and on, dragging well into the 1990s before the courts finally decided that Apple's claim—like that of Ford's foes eighty years earlier—was without substantial merit. Apple could copyright code but couldn't monopolize a general approach to computing. It won in an esthetic sense but not in a legal sense.

And not in a business sense. After the yawns that greeted the initial release of Windows, reactions improved as the product improved. Second and subsequent generations ran faster and froze less frequently. Meanwhile third-party programmers found their way around Windows' complexities, and Microsoft's own applications caught on. Although the alliance with IBM expired following the hardware giant's decision to develop its own GUI system, by that time Windows had an insurmountable lead in the operating-systems market for computers modeled on the IBM PC.

By that time as well, Gates's vision for the computer industry was coming into focus. The metaphor of a "desktop" was common currency among program designers and industry pundits, with the computer screen mimicking the appearance of the work surface executives were familiar with. Whether or not the metaphor was any more apt than the "horseless carriage" had been in the early days of cars (which didn't really enter their own until Ford and other automakers abandoned the equine analogy), it provided a vocabulary to describe software. In this idiom, Gates wanted to own the desktop. Computer users would power up with the Windows operating system, then slide seamlessly into one of Microsoft's applications, now bundled into an "office suite" of programs. Through aggressive marketing, Microsoft persuaded leading computer manufacturers to install its line of products in the hardware they sold; consumers could now take their machines out of the box, plug them in and start to work, almost unaware that any alternative to Microsoft existed.

So aggressive was Microsoft's marketing—or simply so successful—that the company's competitors cried foul. One practice that particularly galled rivals was an arrangement whereby computer makers paid Microsoft per computer shipped rather than per software package installed. Microsoft defended this practice as an accounting convenience: It was easier to verify the number of machines that went out the door than the contents of disk drives. But to historically aware observers, the effect recalled the "drawbacks" John D. Rockefeller's Standard Oil got from the railroads on its competitors' shipments. A computer maker might install a program by a Microsoft competitor, but Gates's company had to be paid—as of course did the competitor. Not surprisingly this double duty discouraged the installation of those competing programs. Like John D.'s practice, Gates's eventually provoked such controversy as to force its discontinuance.

By the 1990s Microsoft's hold on computer software matched Standard Oil's grip on petroleum products a hundred years before. "By any normal test, Microsoft is a monopoly," declared the *Economist* magazine. "This software colossus's domination of the personal computer's operating-system market is complete. Microsoft's Windows is to be found on just about every desktop and laptop PC in the world." This London-based advocate of free-market capitalism went on to describe Gates as being simultaneously "admired by consumers as a benevolent dictator who gives the people what they want, and deeply feared by competitors, who must watch him define their own stand-alone products out of existence, one by one."

The resemblance to Rockefeller surfaced otherwise as well. Like Rockefeller's Standard, Gates's Microsoft produced profits at a rate that outstripped the company's ability to reinvest them in its central business; Microsoft's cash reserves mounted into the several billions. And like Rockefeller's Standard, Gate's Microsoft absorbed or intimidated competition so effectively as to preclude any serious challenge to its predominance. Philippe Kahn of Borland International briefly gave Gates a run for his money in computer languages; during this period Kahn called the Microsoft chairman "Citizen Gates" and asserted that his aim was to control "not just the software industry but the whole world." Yet even Kahn was finally forced to quit the contest. "If I've learned anything, it's not to fight battles I can't win," he said. Referring to firms still in the field, he added, "What I don't understand are the companies that, instead of learning from the past, head straight for disaster."

Often Microsoft's massive war chest sufficed to scare off rivals. Gates was candid about this aspect of his strategy, at least behind the walls of the Microsoft campus. He told a group of key people working on a multimedia project:

> You know, you basically have to convince the other guys not to spend enough money to compete with us, to keep just making it harder and harder, move the terms up, budgeting, promotion, and quality, we just keep raising the bar, and eventually maybe one of them will try to do stuff with us. But a lot of them will just say, "Forget it."

Those who didn't forget it included only the wariest and most combative. After Netscape stole a march on Microsoft in Internet software, Gates evidently suggested an alliance that would involve some sharing of technology. Netscape chief James Barksdale declined, balking particularly at Gates's condition that Microsoft have a seat on the Netscape board of directors. Barksdale reasoned: "Why would you want a spy on your board? It's a classic Microsoft game. They learn more about you so they can hollow you out to the core. . . . They have a winner-takes-all attitude and anybody who thinks you can buddy up to them is just plain naive." (Precisely who said what between Microsoft and Netscape became a key issue in acrimonious litigation.)

Sun Microsystems wasn't exactly naive, just insufficiently suspicious. Sun promoted the Java language as an alternative to Windows; Gates, after initially dismissing Java as inconsequential, decided to license it for Microsoft. But he insisted on the right to "improve" Java in Microsoft's implementation. Whether the changes Microsoft made constituted improvements was a matter of interpretation; beyond doubt they made it different, to the point of at least partial incompatibility. Because of Microsoft's huge user base, Sun found itself facing the distinct possibility of seeing Microsoft seize the standard-setting role for Sun's own product. Outflanked, Sun sued.

Gates's parade from conquest to conquest spawned a psychological condition that sometimes seemed epidemic among his competitors. Industry pundit Esther Dyson called it "Bill Envy," and explained: "Just about all the guys in the business have it. It makes them feel inadequate and it makes them do stupid things. He's the Rorschach blot of the industry. What people think of Bill tells more about them than it does about him." Not surprisingly, almost no one owned up to the ailment. "I don't have Bill Envy," Sun's Scott McNealy said. "I have a great wife, a nice house, and I'm sure my kid is smarter than his kid." Another rival, who was forced to seek shelter with Sun, reflected rhetorically, "Is there Bill Envy in Silicon Valley?" His answer: "There's money envy in Silicon Valley, and Bill's got a lot of money."

That envy presumably grew as Gates's fortune ballooned. One Billophobic technophile created a site on the World Wide Web that constantly reported the downs and mostly ups of Gates's paper wealth. Another obsessive—blessed in this case with a sense of humor—calculated a "Too Small a Bill for Bill" index, which revealed that, in light of the $16-billion increase in his wealth during a runup of the Microsoft share price in the first half of 1997, if Gates were heading to work and saw a $10,000 bill lying on the street, he should resist the temptation to stop and pick it up. Instead he should proceed straight to the office, where he would make more than $10,000 in those four seconds saved.

Gates generally ignored the personal sniping—although a remark by Philippe Kahn that he (Gates) wasn't really a technical person but rather an image maker set him off. "God, fuck this guy!" Gates blurted. "I mean, I really hate this guy. . . . I'm so much more technical than that guy is, Jesus Christ!"

But he couldn't ignore the intense scrutiny the federal Justice Department applied to Microsoft's marketing strategy. During the 1990s the company constantly fought charges of anticompetitive practices. In the autumn of 1998 the federal government and twenty states joined forces against Gates and Microsoft in inaugurating what pundits called the most important antitrust suit since the breakup of Standard Oil in 1911. Gates, although a less appealing witness than Rockefeller had been, followed John D. in denying all wrongdoing. Microsoft, he said, played hard—and well—but by the rules.

Industry observers often remarked the seeming paradox that Gates acted as though Microsoft was still a startup company long after it had attained behemoth status. Not for Gates any such self-limiting strategy as Alfred P. Sloan had adopted in autos; Microsoft was as uncompromisingly competitive at $10 billion in sales as it had been before it sold its first million.

Gates saw nothing paradoxical in the matter at all. Microsoft might dominate software at the moment, but that was no guarantee of future dominance. "There's not a single line of code here today that will have value in, say, four or five years' time," he told his software developers. Windows was the darling du jour, but that could change overnight. "Today's operating systems will be obsolete in five years."

H. Ross Perot, another computer billionaire, understood what Gates was up against and why he did what he did. "His is an industry where the faster you run the faster you have to run," Perot said. "If he could create software and sit on it for twenty years, he'd probably be bored. But the minute it hits the market shrinkwrapped he'd better be on the next one, right? There is no halftime in his business. You don't even get to go to the locker room and rest."

Compared to Sloan's auto industry—or Andy Grove's semiconductors or Andy Carnegie's steel—Gates's software was a business marked by insubstantial products and immaterial barriers to entry. Gates liked to say that the only thing that stood between Microsoft and mediocrity was the bright ideas of his top thinkers. "Take our twenty best people away," he declared, "and I will tell you that Microsoft would become an unimportant company." It was this possibility that kept him pushing so hard.

Yet immaterial barriers weren't no barriers. Having set the standards for software, Microsoft benefited enormously from those standards. "I really shouldn't say this," he had explained way back in 1981, speaking of the existence of standards, "but in some ways it leads, in an individual product category, to a natural monopoly: where somebody properly documents, properly trains, properly promotes a particular package and through momentum, user loyalty, reputation, sales force, and prices builds a very strong position with that product." By the late 1990s Microsoft had been setting standards for nearly two decades; its position was indeed very strong.

A Microsoft-watcher during most of those two decades summarized Gates's accomplishment—and what it meant for Gates, Microsoft and the industry:

> Microsoft really isn't in the software business; it's in the standards business. Microsoft succeeds not because it writes the best code but because it sets the best standards. Microsoft Windows—the personal computer software that made Gates a septibillionaire—was nurtured and developed to be a standard, not just another operating system.

Somebody had to set the standards; without them the modern computer industry could never have matured as it did. Gates might dispute his critics' charges of megalomania and deny the allegations that Microsoft was the Standard Oil of the information age, but to a considerable degree he had to recognize that such carping came with the territory of standard-setting. He didn't appreciate the criticism, but neither did he give any sign of surrendering the territory.

THE BOTTOM LINE

I F ANDREW CARNEGIE WOULD HAVE HAD TROUBLE UNDERSTANDING
much of what Bill Gates did, John Jacob Astor would have had more
trouble still. A technological gulf separated Astor's preindustrial era from
Gate's postindustrial one; what was (literally) child's play in the latter was
beyond fantasy in the former.

Technology aside, however, the business world of Gates—and Andrew Grove and Ted Turner and the rest of their information-age cohort—would have been quite comprehensible to Astor and Cornelius
Vanderbilt and other pioneers of American capitalism. When the dying
Astor declared that if he could live again he would buy every square foot of
Manhattan, he was talking about the same kind of asset-building strategy
Turner followed in acquiring the Atlanta Braves and the MGM film library. When Vanderbilt ate, drank and slept at the helm of his sailboat, the
better to beat his rivals, he prefigured the Tang-stained Gates and his
round-the-clock coders. Jay Gould's market manipulations would grow
even more illegal in the twentieth century, landing the likes of Turner's
takeover teammate Michael Milken in jail; but though the techniques of
speculation changed, the basic principles didn't—as the sons of H. L.
Hunt discovered.

If certain fundamentals persisted from Astor's day to Gates's, what can
be said about the nature of great success in American business? What did
these giants have in common? What set them apart from lesser mortals?

First, all had good health and abundant energy. With rare exceptions,
the people profiled here had iron constitutions and energy enough for half-
a-dozen careers each. Astor tramping across the frozen wilderness of
Canada, Vanderbilt standing long watches on the water, Cyrus McCormick
endlessly tinkering with his reaper and Henry Ford with his flivver, Sam
Walton crawling under the counters of the opposition and flying over
prospective locations, Ray Kroc policing franchisees' parking lots, Oprah
Winfrey taping 200 shows a year, Gates pulling repeated all-nighters—such

illustrations could be multiplied to demonstrate the prosaic but revealing fact that as a group, these twenty-five put in more hours more energetically than almost any other group comparable in size and diversity. Sustained intense effort is hardly a sufficient condition for great accomplishment in business, but it would appear to be a necessary one.

Second, they were hungry. In some cases the hunger was physical and either actually felt or plausibly anticipated. Immigrant kids Carnegie and Sarnoff knew what it meant to miss a meal; they went to work young because it was that or not eat. Older immigrants Astor and Grove had another belt notch or two between themselves and growling stomachs, but even they could hear the wolf at the door on restless nights. Among the native born, few felt real poverty growing up, but several understood that only their own efforts would lift them above the dull or otherwise unsatisfactory circumstances in which fate had positioned them. Vanderbilt escaped the family farm in a sailboat; McCormick on his reaper; Gould by means of surveying instruments. Bill Rockefeller dumped his boy in the nearest town. Henry Kaiser went west to win a wife. H. L. Hunt got into oil after being flooded out of cotton and run out of cards. Music rescued Berry Gordy from the boxing ring and the auto assembly line. J. P. Morgan, who went from rich to richer, was the oddity here.

Third, each felt an intense identification with his or her work. Call it a different form of hunger, a gnawing ambition, but each individual profiled here perceived business success in very personal terms. Often this perception approached, even crossed, the line that separates the normal from the neurotic. It is a truism that well-adjusted, well-rounded people don't change the world. Well-rounding takes the edge off; without that edge people rarely have the sharpness to slice to the front of any field, whether politics, science, literature, the arts or business. Ordinary people don't put themselves through his trials required to become president of the United States; Michelangelo had to be at least mildly unbalanced—not to say off balance—to spend those years bent over backward painting the ceiling of the Sistine Chapel. A really well-adjusted Carnegie would have followed his own advice during his thirties to broaden himself and pursue other interests; but that hypothetical Carnegie wouldn't have made Carnegie Steel into the colossus it became. Rockefeller kept working, driving, expanding, accumulating even after he could no longer figure out what to do with all his money. Phil Knight hadn't been the fastest runner of his generation, but Nike was going to win victories that had eluded him on the track. Ted Turner's colleagues dreaded his manic moments, but these provided impetus that propelled Turner Broadcasting to the front ranks of the media world. Andy Grove's brush with death hardly deflected him from his goal of making Intel the mightiest electronics company in history. Bill Gates, like Thomas Watson before him, couldn't accommodate the antitrusters without surrendering something of himself.

Fourth, these twenty-five possessed an ability to persuade others to buy into their personalization. To some extent, of course, the buy-in was precisely that. Ford's five-dollar day bought him loyalty his competitors couldn't match; Walton's sales force praised their leader as the man who showed them how to "make the dough"; Walton's employees grew comfortable, sometimes wealthy, on their Wal-Mart shares; Microsoft brewed millionaires by the coffee-house–ful. But money was only one tool among several. At least as important was the desire of subordinates to meet the expectations of their bosses—and of themselves after they internalized the corporate culture. "They all drink the same Kool-Aid," explained one of Gates's groupies after deprogramming. Mary Kay Ash early mastered the art of nonmonetary motivation, making her consultants queen for a day at the annual seminar and queen for a year or career in their own minds. Knight's squires at Nike zealously joined his nose-thumbing crusade against the old Turks of the athletic establishment. Hunt got more from his roughnecks through sweet talk and straight dealing than cash could have purchased. Not many people possessed Sam Walton's natural (and calculated) ebullience, but the enthusiasm and down-home friendliness that characterized Wal-Mart's customer relations eased the opposition to what the whale on the bypass was doing to the minnows of Main Street. The sight of Ray Kroc sweeping the parking lot inspired, or shamed, franchisees to hygiene they didn't know they cared about.

Fifth and finally, each of the twenty-five had a creative vision. The first four elements of success were essential, but what really lifted the giants above the rest was the ability to envision where the world, or their part of it, was going, and to act on that vision in a creative way. Astor saw New York marching north across Manhattan, and built an empire in the line of the march; Vanderbilt perceived steam displacing sail, and fashioned a fleet freed from the wind; Carnegie imagined a steel works with the last inefficiency pounded out, and constructed successively closer approximations; Rockefeller dreamed of the perfect monopoly, and nearly achieved it; Morgan envisioned an industrial and financial edifice secure from the tremors of unbridled competition and government incompetence, and went far toward building it; Ford foresaw a nation on wheels, and put it there; Alfred

Sloan perceived the need for flexibility in the corporation of the future, and pioneered new principles of industrial organization to achieve it; Sarnoff saw a mass audience for news and entertainment, and created his "Radio Music Box" to deliver them; Walt Disney spied synergies in movies and television that enabled him to create a total entertainment package; Kroc tasted the future in San Bernardino, and served it to the nation; Walton brought the discounts of the city to the countryside; Liz Claiborne liberated working women from suits and designer prices; Turner delivered news to the world as it happened; Grove enforced Moore's law of increasing computer power, and added his own of increasing profits; Gates saw an industry aching for standards, and established them.

Needless to say, these creative responses to approaching trends were self-serving—but they weren't *simply* self-serving. From the days of Adam Smith, self-interest has been the acknowledged driving force of capitalism; the secret of the market system is that one person's self-interest can simultaneously serve the interests of others. Buyers and sellers, producers and consumers, investors and entrepreneurs take reciprocal advantage of each other. Success rewards those who can discover or create areas of reciprocity; the larger the area, the greater the success. The people depicted here created the largest areas of reciprocity, supplying goods and services that millions of people could find nowhere else at such a combination of quality and price. They were captains of industry; but like officers of volunteer regiments, they held their posts at the sufferance of those they led.

To be sure, the terms of the transaction weren't always equal. A single consumer of kerosene in 1898 had few alternatives to Rockefeller's Standard, just as the average computer buyer in 1998 could hardly avoid Gates's Microsoft. Perhaps in some ideal world selections would always be unconstrained. But in the real world, choices are inevitably shaped by what has gone before. Voters in general elections have to choose between survivors of the primaries, who in turn survived previous winnowing. Men and women choose spouses not from the opposite sex at large but from that subset with whom they come into contact. Likewise with kerosene and computers, reapers and running shoes, steel rails and health plans, cosmetics and cable stations, theme parks and talk shows, hamburgers and highways, oil wells and soft drinks. The winners in each round—those who best please their customers—advance to the next round. The number of players may diminish in succeeding rounds, but they get better at what they do. And should their performance flag, others stand ready for a chance to fill the deficiency.

Giants trip; masters stumble. Ask Astor about beaver hats, Carnegie about Homestead, Gould about gold, Ford about model changes, Sloan about unions, Watson about computers, Gordy about movies, Grove about memory, Gates about the Internet. Success breeds success, but doesn't guarantee it. In fact, nothing guarantees it.

This is just as well, for guarantees are the death of the entrepreneurial spirit. The masters of enterprise succeeded despite uncertainty and because of it. What they earned by their success was the opportunity to stumble more sensationally than their rivals and to pick themselves up and do it again.

BIBLIOGRAPHY

Nearly all the individuals portrayed in this book have been studied at length. The list below indicates some of the more important works on each, and those that have been helpful in the writing here. A small number of more general titles have also been included, as well as periodicals from which information has been taken.

1. John Jacob Astor

Haeger, John Denis. *John Jacob Astor*. 1991.
Hoy, C. I. *John Jacob Astor*. 1936.
Porter, Kenneth Wiggins. *John Jacob Astor*. 1931.
Smith, Arthur D. Howden. *John Jacob Astor*. 1929.

2. Cornelius Vanderbilt

Andrews, Wayne. *The Vanderbilt Legend*. 1941.
Lane, Wheaton J. *Commodore Vanderbilt*. 1942.
Smith, Arthur D. Howden. *Commodore Vanderbilt*. 1927.

3. Cyrus McCormick

Casson, Herbert N. *Cyrus Hall McCormick*. 1909.
Hutchinson, William T. *Cyrus Hall McCormick*. 1930–35.
McCormick, Cyrus. *The Century of the Reaper*. 1931.
In Memoriam: Cyrus Hall McCormick. 1884.

4. Jay Gould

Ackerman, Kenneth D. *The Gold Ring*. 1988.
Adams, Charles F., and Henry Adams. *Chapters of Erie and Other Essays*. 1871; reprint 1967.
Grodinsky, Julius. *Jay Gould*. 1957.
Klein, Maury. *The Life and Legend of Jay Gould*. 1986.
United States House of Representatives. *Gold Panic Investigation*. 1870; reprint 1974.

5. Andrew Carnegie

Carnegie, Andrew. *Autobiography*. 1920.
Carnegie, Andrew. *The Andrew Carnegie Reader*. Edited by Joseph Frazier Wall. 1992.
Hacker, Louis. *The World of Andrew Carnegie*. 1968.
Hendrick, Burton J. *The Life of Andrew Carnegie*. 1932.
Livesay, Harold C. *Andrew Carnegie and the Rise of Big Business*. 1975.
Wall, Joseph Frazier. *Andrew Carnegie*. 1970.

6. J. Pierpont Morgan

Allen, Frederick Lewis. *The Great Pierpont Morgan*. 1949.
Carosso, Vincent P. *The Morgans*. 1987.
Chernow, Ron. *The House of Morgan*. 1990.
Corey, Lewis. *The House of Morgan*. 1930.
Jackson, Stanley. *J. P. Morgan*. 1983.
Sinclair, Andrew. *Corsair*. 1981.
Winkler, John K. *Morgan the Magnificent*. 1930.

7. John D. Rockefeller

Chernow, Ron. *Titan*. 1998.
Ernst, Joseph W., ed. *"Dear Father"/"Dear Son."* 1994.
Flynn, John T. *God's Gold*. 1932.
Hawke, David Freeman. *John D*. 1980.
Nevins, Allan. *John D. Rockefeller*. 1940; updated and reissued as *Study in Power*, 1953.
Rockefeller, John D. *Random Reminiscences of Men and Events*. 1909.
Tarbell, Ida M. *The History of the Standard Oil Company*. 1904.

8. Henry Ford

Collier, Peter, and David Horowitz. *The Fords*. 1987.
Ford, Henry. *My Life and Work*. 1922.
Ford, Henry. *Today and Tomorrow*. 1926.
Graves, Ralph H. *The Triumph of an Idea*. 1935.
Jardim, Anne. *The First Henry Ford*. 1970.
Lacey, Robert. *Ford*. 1986.
Leonard, Jonathan Norton. *The Tragedy of Henry Ford*. 1932.
Nevins, Allan, and Frank Ernest Hill. *Ford*. 1954–63.
Stern, Philip Van Doren. *Tin Lizzie*. 1955.
Sward, Keith. *The Legend of Henry Ford*. 1948.

9. Alfred P. Sloan

Cray, Ed. *Chrome Colossus*. 1980.
Drucker, Peter F. *Concept of the Corporation*. 1993 rev. ed.
Keller, Maryann. *Rude Awakening*. 1989.

Sloan, Alfred P., Jr. *Adventures of a White-Collar Man*. 1941.
Sloan, Alfred P., Jr. *My Years with General Motors*. 1972 rev. ed.

10. Thomas J. Watson

Rodgers, William. *Think*. 1969.
Sobel, Robert. *IBM*. 1981.
Watson, Thomas J., Jr. *Father, Son & Co*. 1990.

11. Henry Kaiser

De Kruif, Paul. *Kaiser Wakes the Doctors*. 1943.
Foster, Mark S. *Henry J. Kaiser*. 1989.
Heiner, Albert P. *Henry J. Kaiser*. 1991.

12. H. L. Hunt

Brown, Stanley H. *H. L. Hunt*. 1976.
Burst, Ardis. *The Three Families of H. L. Hunt*. 1988.
Hunt, H. L. *H. L. Hunt, Early Days*. 1973.
Hunt, H. L. *Hunt Heritage*. 1973.
Hurt, Harry, III. *Texas Rich*. 1981.

13. David Sarnoff

Bilby, Kenneth. *The General*. 1986.
Dreher, Carl. *Sarnoff*. 1977.
Lewis, Tom. *Empire of the Air*. 1991.
Lyons, Eugene. *David Sarnoff*. 1966.
Sarnoff, David. *Looking Ahead*. 1968.
Sobel, Robert. *RCA*. 1986.

14. Walt Disney

Eliot, Marc. *Walt Disney*. 1993.
Mosley, Leonard. *Disney's World*. 1985.
Schickel, Richard. *The Disney Version*. 1985 rev. ed.
Smoodin, Eric, ed. *Disney Discourse*. 1994.
Watts, Stephen. *The Magic Kingdom*. 1997.

15. Robert Woodruff

Allen, Frederick. *Secret Formula*. 1994.
Enrico, Roger, and Jesse Kornbluth. *The Other Guy Blinked*. 1986.
Kahn. E. J. *The Big Drink*. 1960.
Martin, Milward. *Twelve Full Ounces*. 1962.

Oliver, Thomas. *The Real Coke, The Real Story*. 1986.
Pendergrast, Mark. *For God, Country and Coca-Cola*. 1993.

16. Ray Kroc

Boas, Max, and Steve Chain. *Big Mac*. 1976.
Kroc, Ray. *Grinding It Out*. 1977.
Love, John F. *McDonald's*. 1995 rev. ed.

17. Sam Walton

Trimble, Vance H. *Sam Walton*. 1990.
Vance, Sandra S., and Roy V. Scott. *Wal-Mart*. 1994.
Walton, Sam. *Sam Walton, Made in America*. 1992.

18. Berry Gordy

Benjaminson, Peter. *The Story of Motown*. 1979.
George, Nelson. *Where Did Our Love Go?* 1985.
Gordy, Berry. *To Be Loved*. 1994.
Taraborrelli, J. Randy. *Motown*. 1986.
Waller, Don. *The Motown Story*. 1985.

19. Mary Kay Ash

Ash, Mary Kay. *Mary Kay*. 1981.
Ash, Mary Kay. *Mary Kay on People Management*. 1984.
Ash, Mary Kay. *Mary Kay: You Can Have It All*. 1995.

20. Phil Knight

Katz, Donald R. *Just Do It*. 1994.
Strasser, J. B., and Laurie Becklund. *Swoosh*. 1991.

21. Liz Claiborne

Daria, Irene. *The Fashion Cycle*. 1990.

22. Ted Turner

Bibb, Porter. *It Ain't As Easy As It Looks*. 1993.
Goldberg, Robert, and Gerald Jay Goldberg. *Citizen Turner*. 1995.
Vaughan, Roger. *The Grand Gesture*. 1975.
Vaughan, Roger. *Ted Turner*. 1978.
Whittemore, Hank. *CNN*. 1990.
Williams, Christian. *Lead, Follow, or Get Out of the Way*. 1981.

23. Oprah Winfrey

King, Norman. *Everybody Loves Oprah*. 1987.
Mair, George. *Oprah Winfrey*. 1994.
Waldron, Robert. *Oprah*. 1987.

24. Andrew Grove

Grove, Andrew S. *High Output Management*. 1983.
Grove, Andrew S. *One-on-One with Andy Grove*. 1987.
Grove, Andrew S. *Only the Paranoid Survive*. 1996.
Jackson, Tim. *Inside Intel*. 1997.

25. Bill Gates

Cusumano, Michael A., and Richard W. Selby. *Microsoft Secrets*. 1995.
Dayton, Doug. *Selling Microsoft*. 1997.
Edstrom, Jennifer, and Marlin Eller. *Barbarians Led by Bill Gates*. 1998.
Ichbiah, Daniel, and Susan L. Knepper. *The Making of Microsoft*. 1991.
Manes, Stephen. *Gates*. 1993.
Moody, Fred. *I Sing the Body Electronic*. 1995.
Stross, Randall E. *The Microsoft Way*. 1996.
Wallace, James, and Jim Erickson. *Hard Drive*. 1992.
Wallace, James, and Jim Erickson. *Overdrive*. 1997.
Zachary, G. Pascal. *Showstopper*. 1994.

More general works

Brands, H. W. *The Reckless Decade*. 1995.
Bryant, Keith L., Jr., and Henry C. Dethloff, *A History of American Business*. 1990 rev. ed.
Chandler, Alfred D., Jr. *Giant Enterprise*. 1964.
Chandler, Alfred D., Jr. *The Visible Hand*. 1977.
Cochran, Thomas C., *200 Years of American Business*. 1977.
Cochran, Thomas C., and William Miller, *The Age of Enterprise*. 1942.
Flynn, John T. *Men of Wealth*. 1941.
Holbrook, Stewart H. *The Age of the Moguls*. 1953.
Josephson, Matthew. *The Robber Barons*. 1934.
Livesay, Harold C. *American Made*. 1979.
Minnigerode, Meade. *Certain Rich Men*. 1927.
Myers, Gustavus. *History of the Great American Fortunes*. 1936.

Periodicals (and news services)

American Heritage
Atlanta Constitution and Journal
Barron's

Bibliography

Black Enterprise
Business Week
Cable News Network Financial
Computer Reseller News
Drug & Cosmetic Industry
Ebony
Economist
Esquire
Executive Excellence
Forbes
Fortune
Gannett News Service
Incentive
Jet
Life
Los Angeles Times
Ms.
Nation's Business
New York Times
Newsweek
PR Newswire
Rolling Stone
Sales & Marketing Management
Texas Monthly
Time
USA Today
Vogue
Wall Street Journal
Working Woman

ACKNOWLEDGMENTS

For their special help in making this book possible, the author would like to thank Bruce Nichols of The Free Press, James D. Hornfischer of Literary Group International, and Harold C. Livesay of Texas A&M University.

INDEX

Index

Index

NBC (National Broadcasting Company),
176–178, 278, 280, 288
Neff, Pat, 154
Netscape, 328–329
New Coke, 209–210
New Deal, 116, 127, 317
Newlands Act of 1902, 138
New York Central & Hudson River Rail-
road, 23
New York Central Railroad, 22–24, 27,
67–69, 75, 88
New York & Harlem Railroad, 22
New York Stock Exchange, 39
Nicaragua, 20, 21
Nike, 258–266, 269, 334, 335
Nippon Rubber, 258
Nixon, Richard, 220, 294
Northern Pacific Railroad, 76
Northern Securities Corporation, 76–77
North West Company, 5, 6
Noyce, Robert, 304

Ogden, Aaron, 17–18
Oil, 54–55, 82–94, 153–165, 327–328
Oldfield, Barney, 98
Oldsmobile, 109, 115
Onitsuka Company, 257, 258
Only the Paranoid Survive (Grove), 313
Opium War of 1839–1842, 4
"Oprah Winfrey Show, The," 299–301
Oregon (ship), 19
Ortenberg, Arthur, 269–273
Oswald the Animated Rabbit, 185, 186

Pacific Bridge Company, 139
Paige, Satchel, 303
Paley, William, 177, 179, 286
Panic of 1837, 9–10, 29, 65
Panic of 1873, 58
Panic of 1893, 62, 70–72
Panic of 1907, 77
Parade Gasoline, 164
Patterson, John, 121–124, 127
Pearl Harbor, 146
Pemberton, John, 196, 197
Pennsylvania Railroad, 26–27, 53–56, 58,
68–69, 75, 88–89
Penrod Drilling, 164
Pentium processor, 309–312
Pepsi-Cola, 203–206, 209

Perkins, Frances, 116
Permanente Cement, 144
Perot, H. Ross, 330
"Petroleum Parliament," 89
Pickford, Mary, 189, 300
Pittman, Key, 141
Pius X, Pope, 75
Pontiac, 109, 115
Populism, 70
Potts, Joseph, 88, 89
Powell, John Wesley, 138
Powers, Pat, 187
Prefontaine, Steve, 259
Presley, Elvis, 239, 240
Prince, Earl, 213
Pujo Committee, 77, 78
Pulitzer, Joseph, 38, 49
Pullman, George, 56
Puma brand, 258, 259

Radio, 168–169, 172–179, 181, 182
Railroads, 21–25, 30, 39, 40, 48–49,
53–56, 67–68, 70, 75, 77, 87–89,
144, 145
Rand, James, 130
Range, John, 120
Rather, Dan, 280
Ray, Ruth, 165
RCA (Radio Corporation of America),
173–181, 278, 280–281
RCA Victor Company, 177
Reagan, Ronald, 315
Reaper, invention of, 27–35
Reconstruction Finance Corporation, 148
Redstone, Sumner, 289–290
Reebok, 261–265
Reeves, Martin, 243
Remington Rand, 130, 131
Retailing, 226–234
Revolutionary War, 2, 3, 27
Reynolds Aluminum, 149
Ricco, Donna, 272
Rice, E.W., 174
Rivers, Joan, 298
RKO (Radio-Keith-Orpheum), 177, 187
Robbins, Tom, 221, 222
Roberts, George, 68–69
Robinson, Smokey, 240, 243
Rockefeller, John D., 80–94, 102, 109,
291, 305, 327–328, 334–336

352